Born to Belonging

OTHER BOOKS BY MAB SEGREST

Living in a House I Do Not Own (poems)
My Mama's Dead Squirrel: Lesbian Essays on Southern Culture
Memoir of a Race Traitor

Born to Belonging

Writings on Spirit and Justice

Mab Segrest

RUTGERS UNIVERSITY PRESS

New Brunswick, New Jersey, and London

Library of Congress Cataloging-in-Publication Data

Segrest, Mab, 1949–

Born to belonging : writings on spirit and justice / Mab Segrest.

p. cm.

Includes bibliographical references and index.

ISBN 0-8135-3100-4 (alk. paper) — ISBN 0-8135-3101-2 (pbk. : alk. paper)

1. Segrest, Mab, 1949—Journeys. 2. Lesbian activists—Travel. 3. Capitalism. 4. Heterosexism.
5. Racism. I. Title.

HQ75.25 .S44 2002

305.48'9664—dc21   2002017825

British Cataloging-in-Publication information is available from the British Library.

Manufactured in the United States of America

In Memory of Audre Lorde

To Marta Benavides and
All the Bodhisattvas

CONTENTS

PREFACE

Zora Neale Hurston tells the story in *Dust Tracks on the Road* of climbing up a huge chinaberry tree at her front gate to look out over the world toward the horizon, which was there every way she turned. "It grew upon me," she realized, "that I ought to walk out to the horizon and see what the end of the world was like." She was held back for a good while by the daring of the thing. But finally she recruited her friend Carrie to accompany her. Zora had a hard time sleeping the entire night before their agreed-on departure, so excited was she by the possibility the journey presented to "find out about the end of things." She knew their beginning was in her mama's room. But the next morning, Carrie met Zora to say she could not go. "It looked so far," Carrie explained, "that maybe we wouldn't get back by sundown, and then we would get a whipping." Zora hit Carrie out of frustration and a broken heart, then went home and hid under her house. "But I did not give up on the idea of my journey," she asserts. "I was merely lonesome for someone brave enough to undertake it with me."[1]

Born to Belonging is a collection of travel narratives undertaken in the spirit of Zora Hurston, and I have been blessed in these journeys by the number of friends brave enough to take them with me for whatever while. I have not found the neat transit from the beginning to the end of things that Zora seemed to expect. These are trips from provisional beginnings to multiple destinations toward an end of clarifying for myself and, with luck, for my readers the powerful nexus between spirituality and movements for justice.

Even in periods of the (blessed) solitude that writing allows and requires, I was seldom lonesome and never alone. Conversations, stories, books, chapters, articles, narratives, e-mails, Web sites, phone calls, visits with and from friends, foes, family members, strangers, strangers-becoming-friends: these constantly informed and enriched my writing process. A remarkable array of information was available at my fingertips on the Web, from reports of the African National Congress to ways to translate Wade-Giles into Pinyin Chinese. The digital/computer revolution drives the age, making information capital and turning money into electronic impulse. It crashes national economies and rearranges the global assembly line. But computer technology also makes possible new forms of interpersonal and grassroots communication. E-mail and attached files made keeping in touch and swapping manuscripts easy and increased the strength of the word-web from which all writing swings.

My ambition to work across as many registers as I have attempted (history, philosophy, literary criticism, travel essay, geography, economics, theology) was in many ways as foolish as Zora's decision to find the end of the world. The result of my efforts is no doubt radically imperfect, as am I. Its strengths derive from all of my accompaniment, and I would like to thank all those who helped me in my journeys.

I have great gratitude for Brook Glaefke, whose generosity and trust afforded me the year of writing time to finish this book. What this time meant for me was the luxury of immersion in language, and whatever beauty is in this book I owe to Brook. Thanks as well to my buddies Suzanne Pharr, Joan Garner, and Pam McMichael, who encouraged me to seek the financial help I needed to do the writing that compelled me. My great appreciation also goes to friends who literally accompanied me on these travels then generously allowed me to write about them: Marta Benavides, Jacqui Alexander, Ku'umeaaloha Gomes, and Laura Flanders; and to my father and sister for, again, letting me have my truths.

Thanks to the U.S. Urban-Rural Mission Board (US/URM) for providing a rich and often contentious space in which to reflect on issues of spirituality and social justice. Thanks to those on US/URM who modeled for me a transformative Christian faith. My appreciation also goes to the members of the Community, Church, and Sexuality Task Force of US/URM for taking on such a formidable task of trying to understand human sexuality in all its pain and beauty from myriad cultural and spiritual perspectives. This book in no way speaks officially for URM or the World Council of Churches.

Thanks to the specific organizers and community organizations who hosted me and helped instruct me in the complexities of their particular locations: to the People's Fund (in Honolulu), Na Mamo o Hawai'i, the Nation of Hawai'i, Project South, Empty the Shelters, the Southeast Regional Economic Justice Network, South Africa's National Coalition for Gay and Lesbian Equality, Gays and Lesbians of Zimbabwe, the International Gay and Lesbian Human Rights Commission, the global Urban-Rural Mission. Thanks to Jerome Scott, Pat Hussain, and Holly Levinson in Atlanta; to Barbara Ellen Smith for hosting me in Memphis; to Colleen Kelly and Cha Smith for hosting me on my first visit; and to Ku'umeaaloha Gomes and Kalei Puha and their daughter, Keikilani, on my second Honolulu visit. Thanks to the women of MADRE for company and good dinner conversations in Beijing.

Thanks to all my friends in Tuskegee for welcoming me back in.

Born to Belonging argues for an intersubjective understanding of the self. Its text reflects an intertextuality with other writing and interbeing with friends and readers. Thanks to Bob Moser of the *North Carolina Independent Weekly* and Dave Perkins of *Brightleaf* for providing great editing of the original Atlanta and Memphis essays; to Birgit Rasmussen for skillful suggestions for an earlier version of "Of Soul and White Folks"; to readers elin O'Hara slavick, David Richardson, Jennifer Manion, Melissa Schrift, Marta Benavides, Laura Flanders, Ku'umeaaloha Gomes, Scot Nakagawa, Suzanne Pharr, tyrell haberkorn, Becky Thompson, Aime Carillo Rowe, Barbara Culbertson, and Sara Jarvis, who read drafts of different chapters at different times. Thanks to old friends Helen Langa and Eleanor Holland for helping me think about the cover art. Thanks especially to Jacqui Alexander for her careful reading and compassionate listening and for her friendship over the years.

Thanks to Martha Heller at Rutgers for originally approaching me and for helping me shape the concept of this book; and to Leslie Mitchner, editor in chief, for letting me find my way through the various ups and downs of the writing journey to this final destination that suits us both.

Thanks to the congregation at All Souls Unitarian Universalist Church in Durham for spiritual and emotional support and to the staff of Southern Dharma Retreat Center and to Linda Gooding for her Taoist retreats. Thanks to Gabriella Tal, bodyworker extraordinaire, who carried me over the hardest humps and helped me to imagine being in the arms of God.

Thanks to Riki Friedman, my walking buddy, for our daily 7 A.M. excursions, an hour's regular sharing and talking things through.

My eternal thanks to Harriet Ellenberger (formerly Harriet Desmoines, founding editor of *Sinister Wisdom*) for reentering my life at a crucial time to provide clear editing and advice in shaping the final manuscript, an act of friendship above and beyond the call of duty or the compensation I could provide.

Thanks to my Southern/Queer literature classes at the University of North Carolina (1998) and Duke University (2001) and to my Duke FOCUS class (2001) for our intergenerational conversations that gave me much hope. This book is also for you, with my conviction that your choices, your lives, and your spirits matter deeply.

Thanks finally to Annie and Barbara, to whom and with whom I belong, every day in every way. Thanks to Annie for a daughter-writer's support, for your understanding of my process, and for your graceful surrendering of the computer (instant messaging and all) the times I needed it. I am increasingly proud to read your own passionate and principled words. My gratitude to Barb for our conversations on spirituality over the years, for your constant prayers and ministrations in my sometimes stuck behalf, and for the deeper levels of love and support you gave me as I worked to finish this book, which is both mine and ours.

The following essays were printed in different versions and are used with permission: "Of Soul and White Folks" appeared as "The Souls of White Folks," in *The Making and Unmaking of Whiteness*, ed. Birgit Brander Rasmussen, Eric Klineberg, Irene J. Nexica, and Matt Wray (Durham, N.C.: Duke University Press, 2001). "Atlanta: The 1996 Olympics, Co'Cola, and the Wealth of Nations" appeared in "The

Real Thing? A Look at the Underside of Olympic Development," in the *North Carolina Independent Weekly*, July 28, 1996. "Memphis: Received in Graceland" appeared as "Received in Graceland," in *Brightleaf: A Southern Review of Books* (September 1997). The text of the speech in "Honolulu: Hawai'i Nei" appeared as "Hawaiian Sovereignty/Gay Marriage, *Ka Huliau*," in *This Is What Lesbian Looks Like: Dyke Activists Take on the Twenty-first Century*, ed. Kris Kleindienst (Ithaca, N.Y.: Firebrand Books, 1999). Part of "Beijing: Mao, the Tao, and the Fourth World Conference on Women" appeared as "Waiting for Hillary," in the September 1995 *North Carolina Independent Weekly*.

BORN TO
BELONGING

Our whole and only aim consists in putting religious and political questions in a self-conscious, human form.

—KARL MARX

Let me say it this way. I believe every creative act, every poem, every painting, every honest question or honest dissent, every gesture of courage and faith and mercy and concern will count; every new awareness will count; every time we defend the human spirit it will count; every time we turn away from arrogance and lies, this, too, will count in the project called Human Being Evolving.

— LILLIAN SMITH, *Killers of the Dream*

Every being, every nature, every modeled form, exists in and with each other.

—*The Book of Mary*

PROLOGUE
Topsail Beach, October 2000

To get its sins forgiven, humanity only needs to describe them as they are.
— KARL MARX

The light on the waves
The light in the waves
Waves break in light
Waves break light . . .

OCTOBER 25, 2000: I am here again by the ocean's edge, and this time I know I am coming as I would to a lover, to deepen an old friendship. The ocean here is a familiar mystery, to which I have returned again and again, drawn like the Zen master to her breath. When I was a girl, the sea was always there, and it remains so clearly bigger than I am, whatever the preoccupations of the year or decade, as I walk down the beach and back in waves, in shards of light—or in sheets those mornings when the sea is calm. There is always the gift of birds, sand, sky, shells, occasional mysterious creatures of the deep, spiked or tentacled, washed ashore or breaking the surface of waves, to pull me back from mental convolution. The sea has whispered softly so many years past a mind not registered to hear: see this clearly, be here now, know that this is home. In those Atlantic, Pacific, Gulf of Mexico, Caribbean waters—always an expanse to which I could surrender.

I was born into segregation in Birmingham, Alabama, on a late afternoon in February 1949—four years after the end of World War II, when my father had returned home from a German prison camp, and five years before the Supreme Court would issue *Brown* vs. *Board of Education*, declaring segregated schools unconstitutional. I was born into a culture in which race colored everything, into a town saturated with anxiety and anger, with fear and hope of Jim Crow dying. That culture did not yet have public language for my deepest impulses, which twenty years later I would recognize in the word *lesbian*. At fifty-something, I am writing this book of travels on the track of capitalism and white supremacy and heterosexism and misogyny. I am trying to get them in my sights from multiple locations to a point of convergence as yet beyond our ken, while a rampant and unchecked free market brutally reshapes the globe. To put it differently, I am trying to peel the onion: to find beneath the political, the economic, and the psychological, the spiritual questions that open into emptiness.

Yesterday I noticed, finally, how waves had edged the shore, fine lines of sand left at their highest point, parabolas, like sketches of mountain ranges, or clouds. The sand was etched with the echoes, with the ghosts, of waves. And this morning I saw the waves break light. I saw not just light on the waves in the path laid down by the sun, but light in the waves ahead or behind me. Not only waves breaking in light, waves breaking light.

I began the travels recorded here in 1995, heading out to Beijing to the largest gathering of women in the history of the world, then to Atlanta to write an article on gentrification and the 1996 Olympics, to Memphis for the twentieth anniversary of Elvis's death, to Honolulu for a gathering on linking queer and sovereignty struggles, to Johannesburg and Harare for the General Assembly of the World Council of Churches, and back and forth to visit my brother Tim, who was dying of colon cancer. It was a serendipitous assortment of destinations, to which I set off on a variety of missions—to attend conferences, to write stories on contract, to remain faithful, and to say goodbye. Only toward the end did I realize that my reflections from these various locations might make something larger, a book.

What I saw, traveling through, was a view at a time of extraordinarily rapid change, a world on the cusp of a new phase of capitalism and a new century and millennium (those arbitrary temporal markers that give us some reflective space to view future and past). The German Jew Walter Benjamin wrote before he died trying to escape Hitler's Europe: "To articulate the past historically . . . means to seize hold of a memory as it flashes up at a moment of danger." I evoke Benjamin—"probably . . . the most peculiar Marxist ever produced by this movement"—as especially relevant in a period when we are reaching for new understandings.[1]

My meditations on these journeys involving memory at a moment of danger are quirky and tentative efforts at a hard-won and fluctuating faith: that neither I, nor you, are born to segregation, separation, domination, subordination, alienation, isolation, ownership, competition, or narrow self-interest. The phrase that most resonates for me in this enterprise is the translation of a South African term, *ubuntu*, which I came upon like a revelation in a Delta Airlines magazine article on Nelson Mandela. *Ubuntu* translates as "born to belonging." It's a simple notion: we are all born to belonging, and we know ourselves as humans in just and mutual relationship to one another. It makes as much sense to me as a political self-description as the term *queer*. It also offers a perspective from which to examine other concepts and practices, such as democracy or the free market. And what might our economic and political systems be like if they were based on an assumption of belonging?

In the following pages, I want to trace the effects of colonialism and of newly unleashed digital capital in (re)shaping cities as disparate as Atlanta and Beijing, Honolulu and Harare. I want to understand the legacies and limits of liberation movements for a new century and these new global realities, drawing on ample material from the locations to which I traveled. I want to mark in a variety of places and texts the understanding of the self that drives capitalism: the isolated, repressed, resentful, individualized, competitive, hyperrational, dominating psyche articulated variously by Descartes, Adam Smith, Hegel, Marx, Nietzsche, and Freud. These were European men who somehow inscribed that self as they described it. Using myself at times as an example, I want to make our often-analyzed alienation more palpable, in order to make us less habituated to its effects in our bodies, our consciousness, and our communities. Thus, perhaps, those effects become more subject to change in an era of globalization when capital is once again intent on shaping a new era.

If I critique the Western self, I do not eliminate subjectivity. Within universities in the United States, bright and progressive thinkers grapple with dismantling the "Western metaphysical roots . . . of an enlightenment discourse on individual rights." They form a critical movement that is "dismantling the very concept of a free-choosing individual and putting into question such notions as identity, agency, reason, and intentionality."[2] My culture-bound *Webster's Dictionary* echoes this narrow construction of the self, its first definitions "a person or thing referred to with respect to complete individuality; one's own self; a person's nature, character, . . . being the same thing throughout, uniform."[3] Yet in questioning (rightly, I believe) the notion of the isolated individual, many theorists seem to throw out the baby with the bath water when they declare the "death of the subject" or discard notions of identity, agency, and intentionality that are crucial to transformative processes and movements. It has also seemed to me that critiques of identity politics have often caricatured various identities to make their points. "What is to be done has been replaced by who I am," is Jenny Bourne's prototypical lament. But, after all, cannot both concerns be retained in some more complex syntax such as, "Given who I am in this particular time and place, what must I do and what must we do together?" Likewise, we can have politics that enable us to see women of color *and* race, blacks *and* whiteness, lesbians *and* heterosexism, and all the multiple positions and identities within each category.[4]

By drawing on ontologies other than those of the West, we can show that the subject is not only or not even primarily individual without thereby eliminating subjectivity or agency—as many people of color make clear. "Are there selves . . . that defy dominant (Western) understandings of identity construction?" ask Jacqui Alexander and Chandra Mohanty in the introduction to *Feminist Genealogies, Colonial Legacies, Democratic Futures*; their implicit answer, "yes." They retain an agency

understood as "the conscious and ongoing reproduction of the terms of one's existence while taking responsibility for this process" as part of "thinking oneself as a part
of feminist collectivities and organizations." *Born to Belonging* is one response to their
next question, "What kind of transformative practices are needed in order to develop
non-hegemonic selves?"⁵ Gloria Wekker in the same anthology comments, "We
need to realize that the 'modern subject' may never have been alive in some Third-
World contexts." As an example, Wekker describes from Surinam a subject "made up
of various 'instances,' including gods and the spirits of the ancestors," all of which
need to be "acknowledged and held in harmony."⁶

At the center of my inquiry is the question of soul, or spirit, and justice. I want to
evoke and experience the self in reciprocity and relationship, the self that most of the
world's spiritual traditions can render as soul and that is, more often than not, the self-
reality, the ontology, of women. At times I will call it an (inter)self, by which I mean
the not necessarily coherent mental or psychological structure(s) of a person who is
already linked to other humans, to culture, to animate and inanimate life, and to an
energy within, between, and beyond that is figured differently in different cultures
and that some call God. The smaller self is personality or ego. This larger self I will
sometimes call soul. Wekker's declension of first-person pronouns in Surinamese
Creole may be illuminating here: "*Mi ik* = my I; *mi kra* = my soul; *mi misi* = my
miss/female part of my soul; *mi masra* = my mister/male part of my soul."⁷ (Clearly,
English lacks the subtleties of Surinamese Creole in mapping psychic and spiritual
junctures.) Help comes from other traditions, too. Buddhists, for example, in refer-
ring to the self, speak of the Five Aggregates: form, feelings, perceptions, mental formations, and store consciousness that "contain everything—both inside us and
outside of us, in nature and in society."⁸

I want to conjure up a space where political and spiritual practice coincide,
those gifts of the last century to the next. I want to explore, imperfectly given my own
cultural biases, nondualistic metaphysical systems encountered and often denigrated
by Europe in its conquest of the world's cultures. They are accessible to us now in the
new migrations and cultural syntheses that are a positive result of the cultural flux
and displacement under globalization. These metaphysical systems offer a different
grounding for our political struggles. They point to new fusions of the spiritual and
the political that offer our best hope in the new century.

To get to the bottom of systems of thought manifest in brutal institutions is surely
one point of any theoretical enterprise. We want to make our institutions and our
thinking more humane. Some of this book's journeys, then, are journeys of ideas. (In
fact, while most of the chapters in this book are travel essays, two are largely theoretical: chapter 2 and chapter 7.) Karl Marx spoke of ideologies as "ruling ideas." In
the next century Antonio Gramsci, writing between the world wars from an Italian
jail, elaborated that ideologies can have "a validity which is 'psychological'" because
they "'organize' human masses, [and] . . . form the terrain on which [people] move,
acquire consciousness of their position, struggle, etc."⁹ Ideologies are the thought

forms of the dominant culture, and they inform not only our thinking but also our feeling and our being. The more awake we are to how we are shaped, the more responsible we can be in our actions. As a young man Marx said, "The reform of consciousness consists solely in letting the world perceive its own consciousness by awakening it from dreaming about itself, in explaining to it its own actions."[10] Paulo Freire, writing from a Marxist tradition in Latin America, called this process *conscientização*.[11] It requires a radical subjectivity, a deepened self that knows itself in solidarity—a result of both spiritual and political praxis. In *Pedagogy of the Oppressed*, Freire defines *praxis* as a "cycle of action and reflection" involving a "deepening of the attitude of awareness characteristic of all emergence." To separate action and reflection is to truncate each process. "Sacrifice of action = verbalism; Sacrifice of reflection = activism."[12]

Everyone should have the luxury, the time and space, to think about what they do. And everyone should realize that their ideas have effects that can be tested in concrete situations. What we have more often now is a truncated process. We have, on the one hand, academics theorizing in universities and think tanks—theories that breed more theories; and on the other hand, we have community organizers and advocates acting in nonprofit organizations, often without resources for adequate reflection. Freire points the way to an engaged action—acting and reflecting as an integral, essential component, not only of what we do but also of who we are (our ontology), of how we know (our epistemology), and of how we act from within our reality to shift it (our metaphysics). This praxis engages us at the deepest spiritual level of meaning in our lives—how we constitute our humanity, what my friend Marta calls our "I AM-ness." Then there emerges what I am calling a praxis of belonging that is both a political and a spiritual practice.

This is the biblical mandate to do justice, to love mercy, and to walk humbly. It is the tradition from the Torah of *tikkun olam*, the completion of a just world, or, by other translations, repair of a tattered world. It is what Jesus meant when he said, "Love your neighbor." Indians brought down the British Empire with the soul-power of *satyagraha*. It is the freedom to which the philosopher Sartre, also part of the French resistance to German fascism, said we are condemned. It is the creative will of Martin Luther King Jr. that enables people to hew from a mountain of despair a stone of hope. It is Audre Lorde's recalling for us the erotic power of our work when it engages our deepest desires. It is what Adrienne Rich meant when she said we must find an end to suffering. It is Alice Walker's reminder that anything we love can be saved. It is the engaged Buddhism of monks and nuns who challenged French then U.S. imperialist wars, some of them maintaining their *zazen* postures even as they burned themselves to death in protest. "Once there is seeing there must be acting," Thich Nhat Hanh explains. "Otherwise, what's the use of seeing?"

For me this book has been a journey of consciousness involving both action and reflection. Its original components were speeches, notes, articles, and readings en route. I have packed my bags in a darkened bedroom, with my partner, Barb, sleeping quietly while I assemble jeans and T-shirts and, hopefully, underwear and shampoo. I have also put too many books in a backpack schlepped through too many airports, their legacy an aching shoulder and these chapters.

So I do not pretend here that ideas are disembodied, cartoonlike phrases floating in clouds above our heads. Ideas also spill out of the books that pile up, dog-eared, by my bed—passages underlined in pencil or ink, highlighted in yellow or pink or red. I search libraries' electronic files for bibliographies, but books also fall out of used bookstore shelves onto my head. I read particular books in particular places: over a cup of espresso, giving Thich Nhat Hanh a particular edge; Hegel in McDonalds, leaving ketchup stains eternally on the page; Adam Smith or W.E.B Du Bois on airplanes, the seats getting smaller over the years even as my hips expand. I read late at night when the house is quiet, or on the john ("Shitting is such an underrated pleasure," my friend Carl intoned before he died).

Sometimes I will struggle to line up the ideas in paragraphs, but at times they intrude on the narrative or leak into my dreams. For if thoughts have a history, they also have a physiology. They are part of the chemistry of our brains, but they also permeate our bodies: emotion and memory encoded in each cell. "Your body is your subconscious mind," Dr. Candice Pert spells out, bringing insights of quantum physics to understandings of biochemistry in one of many efforts to heal our splits. "Mind and body are in fact the same, two ways of perceiving the single indivisible organism that we call the self."[13] So to thoughts or ideologies adhere emotion, and the *thought* is the neighbor to the *not-thought*. *What we know* and *what we don't know* float in the ether of *what we don't know that we don't know* and *what we feel and what we don't feel.* How to travel to *that* realm, *terra incognito*, over a curved and beckoning earth?

My daddy used to tell me of going hunting with his daddy and their friends out in the country, black and white men sitting around a campfire listening to the barks of their hounds running down possums, cadences echoing in the darkness of the piney woods of the Jim Crow South. The point was not to kill possums, Daddy said, as much as to listen to the dogs bay. Maybe I am writing to listen to the hound dogs of the mind track down and tree idea-possums so that then the mutts can sleep it off in front of the fire. Tire that old mind out and let it rest while the spirit opens.

Essay (the dictionary is helpful here): (1) *a short literary composition on a particular theme or subject*; (2) *trial*; *assay*; (3) *to attempt*; (4) *to put to the test*; *make trial of.* Mao, Elvis, Aloha, blues, Martin Luther King, Gandhi in South Africa, Adam Smith, the FMLN, G.W.F. Hegel, Sigmund Freud, the African National Congress, Buddha, Lao-tzu, Captain Cook, Kanaka Maoli, the slave trade, colonialism, Coca-Cola, Jesus—all of it floating through my head in my fathom-long body, as the Buddha used to say, with its perceptions and mind. I am a Pisces, I warn you, but I will try not to make you seasick. I hope my readers will allow me a certain haphazardness. "A good traveler has no fixed plans," the Tao Te Ching instructs.[14]

What's at stake? Let me put it another way. Do you, dear reader, ever feel alienated? Scared? Anxious? Mistrustful? That you don't really belong? Do you have such a profound distaste for that to which you belong that you prefer exile? Have you gone into some form of internal exile already? Do you ever find yourself reenacting those very behaviors that you deplore, that you have set your life to change? Do you ever despair that you have internalized stereotypes about yourself so deeply that they seem to have infected your very soul? Did you ever think that those feelings might be an effect of living in a racist system, a misogynist system, a heterosexist system, a class system, a colonial system shaped for centuries by domination, by masters looking for slaves?

Deep questions. I think many times we are so lost that we don't even know it.

If you are interested in traveling a bit with someone working to get found, then come along with me through the following pages, reader as traveler. For finding our way in such a morass is a spiritual process. It is a spiritual process, as well as a political one, to help create a culture by our brave and conscious actions in which we all know we belong, because that's how we are treated and that's how the institutions of the culture operate. To do this, we need to apprehend that we already live in such a universe, with which we have an indissoluble bond. Nor is this oceanic sense of connection (Freud's term for what he lacked), this spirituality, necessarily what we get within organized religion. In fact, many times we get just the opposite, which can be confusing, and painful, and deeply wounding.

What I trace here is my own path. It begins with the Jesus of my childhood, whom I first met in a segregated Methodist Church and who was reinterpreted for me by the African American theology locked beyond our doors. It also includes an indigenous female spirituality, an infinite Great Mother, through which I know my place in cycles within and beyond me. I am increasingly accompanied by a growing appreciation of Buddhism, especially as transmitted through Thich Nhat Hanh. From this framework I do not have to decide whether "the consciousness of [humans] determines their being" or their social being "determines their consciousness" (Marx argues the latter). I want both consciousness and social being together in a process that Buddhists call *paticca samuppada*, or "dependent co-arising."[15] Joanna Macy's feminist ecology describes such an ontology as the spiritual path that moves from a frame of the world as battlefield or trap, to acknowledge "world as lover" and "world as self": a cosmology that escapes the narrow frames of Western individualism and resulting alienation while it maintains the importance of human choice, of a karma of human intentionality.

The peculiarities of my journey are not intended to negate the power, beauty, or difficulty of other religious or spiritual traditions. We each find a path, and all genuine spirituality, whatever its sources, carries a deep and profound sense of interconnection. Martin Luther King, drawing on Howard Thurman, spoke of an "inescapable network of mutuality" while writing to white racists from his Birmingham jail cell. *Satyagraha*, Gandhi said from his Hindu tradition: cling to truth. *Attend to reality*, the Jewish mystic teaches; *it can be trusted*. Thich Nhat Hanh draws on Buddha's central insight of interbeing for an engaged Buddhism. From the religion of Jesus comes a gospel of love and forgiveness and an apprehension of the presence of God in the midst of us. According to the Taoist tradition from China, our existence is not alien, nor need we feel disconnected, because always, also, already within is the Great Mother, "Empty yet inexhaustible / giv[ing] birth to infinite worlds."[16] Women in most times and places, for biological and cultural reasons, begin with assumptions of mutuality without having them canonized in sacred texts. One remnant from the Gnostic Gospels' *Book of Mary* gives a woman's voice to the spiritual truth of belonging: "Every being, every nature, every modeled form, exists in and with each other."[17] From many points on the globe we can assert our interdependence, a mutuality from which we can (however contingently) know, act, and create with faith that we are always acting and creating both within and beyond what we understand, imagine, or intend. If we are not to replicate and extend the terrible history of human violence from the last century to the next, we will need more grounding in such realities.

Here in familiar calm and solitude I also want to enter again that morning last summer on the office floor when I finally thought: *I surrender all. All my defenses, all my offenses, ego structures held in place with fear, through generations like loops of DNA, inherited, reinvented, calcified.* Some of us have named these structures racism, sexism, heterosexism, classism—projected, introjected as ego. In all the struggle, all the newsletters, press releases, demos, reports, memos, am I searching for moments to let it go, to stop holding on to what doesn't really exist anyway?

Last summer I was trying to explain my surrender to a person I thought already understood: *You know, like the morning you slid into the center of the labyrinth we all walked. Seeing you, I thought, "Girl, you are sliding into the arms of God." Yesterday I knelt on the office floor, CD playing "I Surrender All." And I glimpsed, felt what it is we let go into. It was an experience of deep trust that rose suddenly in the midst of a feeling of bitterness and betrayal. It was like the clouds parted briefly.* I tried to explain it, weeping, searching for words: *as if the clouds part so briefly, and there a full moon, sheer round light larger and closer than it's ever been, as if right out the pitch dark window; or clouds part and there before me, formerly only dreamed, the mountain peak glinting sun. Ahhh, even as the clouds close, ahhh, ahhh. I see that I saw it, I know that I knew it. Ahhh.*

In the outer office, it probably sounded like I was going crazy behind my closed door, the CD blaring, "Wade in the Water," "Take Another Little Piece of My Heart Now Baby," "I Surrender All."

From my thirteenth year, there are two moments that return. I was coming home for lunch. We had been studying atoms, neutrons, protons, electrons—matter as maya, an illusion of solidity when all is space and energy. My foot on the top step, my hand on the screen door's handle. I turned my head to the right, Mrs. Fort's yard beyond the bamboo, oak leaves still lush from summer, azalea bushes, shades and depths of green. Suddenly none of it was familiar but as if in motion. I saw all the whirring molecules, heard a low *oohhmmm.* My eyes widened, I breathed in. It was gone. I turned my head back, opened the door, and went inside.

That moment's vision of molecules in grass and leaves came to me after and because I had recently also finally seen white supremacy as a structure that had shaped me. I saw it because I was looking past its limits to black children moving freely in my segregated school. Alabama, 1963. *Integration*, it was rightly called. How many times have I circled back to that moment lying on my stomach in the grass, looking out through the legs of policemen to the black children integrating "my" school. That moment something shifted: the crack in the cosmic egg, sensation equally delight and terror. I saw that I saw it, the violent limitations of my white culture, and knew that I knew. With that knowledge came a sudden surge: what else was possible?

Through a long gestation, I was a biddy, a chick picking away at lime, pecking her self out. She was dreaming herself beyond the concave shell that seemed to be night to another dome they call sky. Or is the sky an emptiness that comes to us as blue, that comes through us as space?

Here at the beginning of a new century, we are compelled, as Gramsci was, to reenvision transformative work for justice out of any narrow determinisms into which it has been cast. Gramsci saw the necessity of evoking ways to dislodge the state as well as oppressive economies through work in "civil society." In this new century we are called on to consolidate an understanding of the realm of the spirit and its relation to matter and to elaborate its power to dislodge new forms of exploitations embedded in institutions as well as in (our) selves.[18]

Those of us who know ourselves perhaps do not yet have language to explain clearly that what we call justice is the door to wider realities, fuller modes of being. Marx was wrong. All politics, ultimately, is also metaphysics, matter and energy constantly shifting forms.

What does it mean to be a materialist, anyway, after twentieth-century science has shown matter and energy are interchangeable and matter itself in its subatomic forms is either waves or empty space or both? "The arc of a moral universe is long," said Martin Luther King, drawing on Einstein, "but it bends towards justice." King called this basis for his understanding a "transphysics."[19] Seeing that we see, knowing that we know—crack this cosmic egg, and call it revolution.

So I will try to relate to you my recent travels, travails. As the Buddha said: "That the end of the world where one is not born, does not age, does not die, does not pass away, does not reappear is to be known, seen or reached by traveling—that I do not say . . . And yet I do not say that one makes an end of suffering without reaching the end of the world."[20]

1

DIVING INTO THE WRECK

I came to see the damage that was done.
— ADRIENNE RICH, "Diving into the Wreck"

ONCE a semester for my junior and my senior years, I would get blind, stumbling, shitfaced drunk and then I could cry, knowing and not knowing why. Was the unnamed pain my own response to some structure of reality, a world out to confuse me, to make me crazy and break my heart? It was my only excursion into an excessive use of alcohol, but its memory returned to me strongly as I approached this philosophical excursion into the fate of the modern Western male subject, a fate that was in part my own.[1] In this chapter I pause to trace a genealogy, a kind of family history, of the self as European male philosophers from Descartes to Foucault inscribed it. I trace this structure through its male line because it is a masculine autobiography of the self's relations or lack of them that was generalized to the rest of us. Approaching this philosophical excursion, I remembered the summer thirty years ago when metaphysical speculations displaced the reality of my experience, my sexuality, my emotions, my body.

I first encountered formal metaphysics in 1969, the summer before my junior year at Huntingdon College. I took Introduction to Philosophy, and that steamy Alabama summer my brother Tim and I drove together from Tuskegee to Montgomery and back five days a week, he for work and I for school. Each morning in front of the blackboard, Dr. Louise Panigot, her gray hair neat and her thin body stiff in one of several polyester suits, proceeded through all the big questions involved in Western philosophy: ethics, aesthetics, ontology, phenomenology, metaphysics, epistemology. Regarding the latter two, she stressed the relationship of mind and world that has preoccupied modern Western philosophy. *How do we know the world beyond our mind exists, things such as this?* she asked, hoisting her paperweight. *How can I know that my blue is not your green?* Of all the things it had occurred to me to worry about up to that point, the nature of reality was not among them. But I added it to my list, to my pragmatic sister's dismay. Her accurate diagnosis: you think too much.

My new metaphysical anxieties occupied the schism between what I knew and what I denied about my lesbian sexuality (my own personal mind-body problem). That whole next year I would be in love with my best friends, a devotion of mind and heart but not yet the engaging throb of the clitoris or sigh in the labial folds or clench of the vaginal walls. Intro to Philosophy evoked the epistemology of my closet; my sexuality was like Dr. P's paperweight, some *Ding-an-sich*, a reality that existed— *there!*—just beyond my ken. I kept trying to understand the metaphysical thing, tracking the men whose realities Dr. P taught me. I was in some predicament, and I would think myself out of it, reading every summer on the metal glider on the front porch. I had my books and my poetry to protect me—my first woman lover years later would sing to me the Simon and Garfunkel lyrics—but I touched no one, and no one touched me. A rock and an island. Feeling, and not feeling, pain.

My senior year, on my last big college drunk, I bought a bottle of cheap wine and wandered down the backstreets behind the college. A not-yet-lesbian Prufrock, I was quoting T. S. Eliot, longing to roll the balled universe toward my overwhelming question. But I was afraid of the answer Prufrock's girlfriend had given: That is not what I meant at all. By 1971, I was off to graduate school, where I concentrated in modern (twentieth-century) literature, drawn to its poetics of alienation. Should human voices wake me, would I drown?

My memories of undergraduate school help me understand that my challenge in this chapter is to travel through a pattern of alienating ideas without being subsumed in them. Being in a text, I find again, is not the same as being in a body—I do not presume an embodied text as I sit here day after day, fall to winter to spring, tapping out words on a keyboard. But they are congruent difficulties—being in a body and being in a text— with the underlying challenge generating a presence that heals schisms of mind, body, and spirit. Here I'm charting the schisms of the mind, what happened to the self over the last few hundred years of colonialism, when this question of belonging was bollixed considerably by and for the children of Europe. I traverse these texts as a white woman, so they are both my own and not my own. What emerges from this exploration are the complications and contradictions of masculinist self-narration, both its water-eaten log and fouled compass, in Rich's terms. Its ruptures and confusions point to wider realities rooted in other cosmologies; its absences evoke their presences.

Some readers might find this chapter too heady so early on. My suggestion to you is to jump forward to the travel chapters and then circle back around to here.

NO BODY, NO WORLD, NO PLACE . . . BUT PROPERTY

I recently reread René Descartes, whose name is "synonymous with the birth of the modern age."[2] I felt both sympathy and aggravation with this father of modern philosophy, born in 1596 in France (Descartes died in 1650). He was fearful of drawing down the pope's ire as had Galileo with his conviction that the earth is a bit off-center vis-à-vis the universe. The pope had forced Galileo to recant the results of his curious observance of the world because such observations challenged the Catholic Church's traditional authority. Descartes, despite his trepidation, wanted to "reach certainty—to cast aside the loose earth and sand so as to come upon rock or clay." His efforts were part of a collective philosophical project by various European men to free the mind (their minds) by cleaning out the cobwebs of medieval church authority and control. Descartes began a process of radical skepticism, in the pursuit of which he took nine years. During this time, he had "been able to lead a life as solitary and withdrawn as if I were in the most removed desert."[3]

From such a peculiar location he deduced that the only thing he could know for certain was this process of thinking itself: "I am thinking, therefore I exist"—its Latin formulation, *cogito, ergo sum*. It was in the isolated splendor of the acutely doubting self that mind and body parted in his 1637 *Discourse on the Method*: "I saw that while I could pretend I had no body and that there was no world and no place for me to be in, I could not for all that pretend that *I* did not exist . . . from the mere fact that I thought of doubting the truth of other things." Descartes's self, his *sum*, or "I am," is mind as rational process, "whose essence or nature is *solely to think*, and which *does not require any place*, or depend on any material thing, in order to exist . . . *entirely distinct from the body*, and indeed is easier to know than the body" (emphasis mine).[4] What a remarkable pretense—this masquerade of mind without a body—with what a legacy! Descartes's methodology is symptomatic of a Europe setting forth on the colonial conquests that its emerging scientific methods were making possible. The results of that methodology were what I felt in college—a mind trying to think itself out of a body. "That mind-body duality by which he so deftly made sense of us now seems less paradigm than prison," comments John Cottingham on the back cover of his treatment of Descartes. In his more neglected later writing, Descartes does point the way for a mind-body reunion, but by that time the horse was out of the barn, the ghost was rattling in the machine, and the mind-body problem was reverberating through Western philosophy.[5]

What, I ask myself, if Descartes had cultivated a community in the years that he cultivated isolation? What would experimenting with radical belief in human contexts, rather than experimenting with acute doubt in isolation, have brought—besides the wrath of the pope? Would mind then have been more than rationality, his body easier then to know, if faith had not been so terroristic, so repressive, and so out of sync with human curiosity? My lesbian Prufrock thinks that Descartes, and I, would have been a lot better off. Without a body, Descartes realized, there is no place to be, to belong—an insight that would translate into genocidal attempts at annihilation for all those humans with problematic bodies as colonialism played itself out across the globe.

Segue to John Locke. As a junior in high school I won a $1,000 scholarship in the "What Democracy Means to Me" speech competition. Abraham Lincoln might have defined democracy as government of, by, and for the people, but to me democracy assumed first the protection of the individual before the group. I was influenced, no doubt, by my father's John Birch material and his subscription to Buckley's *National Review*, as well as the white zeitgeist in Alabama in the 1960s. But I was also on firm philosophical ground here, knowing from my ninth-grade civics class that the British philosopher John Locke's theory of the social contract in his *Second Treatise of Government*, picked up by Jefferson in the Declaration of Independence, assumed that the individual gave up certain rights to the government in exchange for its protections.[6] If in the course of human events governments violated this contract, then revolution was permitted. This social contract, I understood, protected the individual against tyrannical governments and monarchs. And I was enough of a Confederate to approve of rebellions.

But what I did not realize as a high school ideologue was the degree to which Locke's case for the limited constitutional state was "largely designed to support his argument for an individual natural right to unlimited private property,"[7] starting with his own. I did not know then that Locke (1632–1704) had served on England's Council of Trade and Plantations. I did not know that he had had substantial investments in the raw silk trade and the Royal Africa Company, which meant he was profiting from the slave trade.

In his *Second Treatise of Government* (1690), Locke began his argument by asserting a mythic state of nature, a "state of perfect freedom." It was a freedom for men to "order their actions, and dispose of their possessions and persons." (Males do predominate here, although there were egalitarian elements in Locke's philosophy, given his renunciation of the monarchy and its political institutions.)[8] In this original state, all men are equal and independent. "No one ought to harm another in his life, health, liberty, or possessions" because all are the property of their "one sovereign master," God. With no government yet in existence, "every man hath a right to punish the offender, and be executioner of the law of nature"—a kind of eye-for-an-eye justice. But—Locke asks the big question—given that God "*has given the earth to the children of men* . . . [i]t seems to some a very great difficulty, how any one should ever come to have a *property* in any thing."[9]

Locke solved the difficulty in this way: "The law man was under, was rather for appropriating. God commanded, and his wants forced him to *labour*. That was his *property* which could not be taken from him where-ever he had fixed it. And hence subduing or cultivating the earth, and having dominion, we see are joined together. The one gave title to the other. So that God, by commanding to subdue, gave authority so far to appropriate; and the condition of human life, which requires labour and materials to work on, necessarily introduces private possessions."[10]

Had I read this passage as an adolescent, I might have questioned the assumption that to *cultivate* necessarily meant to *subdue* (I might have assumed it meant *to grow* or *to help to grow*) and that *subduing* gave one the right to *own*. I might have doubted that all of this had happened in "the state of nature" before the social contract that

supposedly protected the individual against government and, presumably, other potentially destructive forces. I knew from Sunday school that the biblical successor
to "an eye for an eye" was Jesus' gospel of love, which (I would have recognized) did
not say a lot positive about property rights.

In fact, I had gotten myself in a bit of trouble my senior year in high school when
I challenged a friend whose father was minister of a Southern Methodist Church that
had withdrawn from the United Methodist Church over segregation. The United
Methodist denomination kept encouraging its local churches to desegregate, and the
Union Springs Methodists were pulling out and trying to take their church building
with them. Fred challenged me when I objected to the fact that our private segregated school would not use the Tuskegee Methodist Church for our baccalaureate
service, because then the integrated Tuskegee High School might want to as well. I
saw nothing wrong with Tuskegee High using the church. I explained that for me (I
had developed this conviction by my senior year) the church should be for everybody. Lynn was explaining how church buildings were not important, that Jesus had
preached on the hillside. "Why doesn't *your Daddy* preach on the Southern
Methodist *hillside*, then?" I sneered. That was what got me in trouble. But I was
pretty clear that Jesus' message had been about people giving up their acquisitiveness
to follow his difficult way—a way so difficult, in fact, that I did not detect anyone I
knew really living up to it, so that Christianity had become a spiritual theory without
a practice, or with its practice so split from its premises as to be painfully ironic and
alienating.

If I had actually read Locke in high school rather than reading about him as I as-
sessed "What Democracy Means to Me," I think I would have seen, even then, that
Locke's—and Jefferson's—social contract would protect *some* individuals (propertied
individuals) more than others. But it was many years later—after watching Barbara
give birth to our daughter, Annie, in fact—that it occurred to me the degree to which
this Original Individual was a ridiculously transparent male fiction. None of us start
out as individuals, but as fusions of sperm and egg, embedded and growing in the
mother's body for nine months. For months after birth, our consciousness is still
merged with its environment, and a sense of a particular and separate self emerges
only gradually. For most of the rest of our lives, we operate in both the more collective and the more particular forms either simultaneously or in alternation. Locke's
fictional individual was also competitive and atomistic and imagined, like Adam
Smith's, as being at the same starting point as other such individuals. What theories
and practices of government and of social change flow from a premise not of original individualism for all, and ownership for some, but of original interconnection?

Another thing Locke made clear: The capitalist individual was also the consum-
ing self—"*forasmuch as we are not by ourselves sufficient to furnish ourselves with
competent store of things, needful for such a life as our nature doth desire, a life fit for
the dignity of man.*"[11] Human dignity became equated with acquiring a "competent
store of things." Inalienable rights were rights to life, liberty, and property, in a social

contract that would not interfere with pursuit of profits—although Locke did set some limits on what it is proper to take from the pool of common resources. But would everybody get a competent store? And how many things do we really need for our human dignity?

In high school, part of my belief in individualism involved a belief in "free enterprise." Democracy goes hand in hand with capitalism (we believed in my family of ardent anticommunists), and free people require free markets. This requires less government; as Thomas Jefferson had pointed out, drawing on Locke, that government is best which governs least. (Of course, less government these days means more room for humongously powerful corporations, but that is getting ahead of the story.) Adam Smith, the absentminded Scottish professor of Moral Philosophy, provided in *The Wealth of Nations* (1776) an early description of and prescription for this emerging market economy, "the outpouring . . . of a whole epoch."[12] Smith's capitalist self—an economic version of Locke's political individual—was driven by self-interest in a competitive system: "Give me that which I want, and you shall have that which you want," he had explained. "It is not from the benevolence of the butcher, the brewer, the baker that we expect our dinner, but from their regard to their own interest. We address ourselves, not to their humanity, but to their self-love, and never talk to them of our own necessities but of their advantages."[13] For Smith, self-interest would balance with the forces of competition in the marketplace to ensure that the maximum number of people were taken care of.[14] Two wrongs would make a right.

MASTERY OF AN ALIEN EXISTENCE

The undergraduate me soon figured out that the self was more complex, the pieces of this "individual" seldom all totally apparent or even individual; and that there were forces that kept some of its parts less accessible. Enter the Other. Years later, I ran across a reference in Simone de Beauvoir's *The Second Sex* to G.W.F. Hegel as the origin of discourses on the Other: "Following Hegel, we find in consciousness itself a fundamental hostility toward every other consciousness; the subject can be posed only in being opposed."[15] What a frightening and remarkable premise, that we know ourselves only in opposition to others, that communities and identities are formed around systems of exclusion! After all, I and many of my organizing friends had by then sought in decades of work to find antidotes to such discourses and practices of Otherness that justify the (mis)allocation of material and psychic resources. As a white girl under Jim Crow, I intuitively understood how white consciousness posed itself in opposition to the Negro. As a lesbian, I later realized as well that the queer is often the Other around whose exclusion heterosexual self, community, and nation form. As a premature antifascist in the Reagan-Bush 1980s, I spent a good part of the decade helping bring victims of hate violence out of isolation, into a community we could not assume but had to construct. Being clear what was at stake, and what the alternatives might be, seemed crucial in this question of the subject and its relationship to community. So I went out and bought Hegel's *Phenomenology of Mind*, carrying it around at particularly masochistic moments.

Turgid as Hegel's prose was, I plowed intermittently on, coming to the seminal "Master/Bondsman" passage. Hegel, I found, situated the self's knowledge of itself in relationship: "Consciousness finds that it immediately is and is not another consciousness. . . . They recognize themselves as mutually recognizing one another." So far so good—this was an intersubjectivity preferable to Locke's and Smith's individual, at least. But then Hegel made a chilling move. At this stage of development, he argued, these two consciousnesses are *always* in relationships of domination and subordination: "The one is independent, and its essential nature is to be for itself; the other is dependent, and its essence is life or existence for another." Consciousness, then, has a dual significance, resulting in a mirroring or splitting. "First, [consciousness] has lost its own self, since it finds itself as an other being; secondly, it has thereby sublated that other for it does not regard the other as essentially real, but sees its own self in the other." In this "self-identity by exclusion of every other from itself," self-consciousness becomes "in the bare fact of its self-existence, . . . individual."[16] Within these severe limits, Hegel argues, there is ironic power for the slave, since the master, his identity based on repression, depends on the slave he *must* master. Hegel draws on slavery in the Greek context, rather than on the more contemporary European enslavement of Africans. He never considers the necessity for the abolition of slavery itself, however—although the international slave trade was, in fact, abolished in his lifetime.[17] Hegel's slave instead gets his freedom in his work, "desire restrained and checked."[18] The slave, in other words, just keeps on slaving, even though he wins the "battle to the death" for authentic consciousness within the master-slave relationship.

Hegel goes on, in a passage I have pondered again and again, to describe the emergence of these two selves as opposites. This polarization is a response to what he calls "this alien element of natural existence." One self tries to dominate the other out of its aversion to the "particularity everywhere characteristic of existence as such" to be "tied up with life." But what if existence were not perceived as alien? And was to be "tied up with life" a *bad* thing? It certainly was what I had wanted as a lonely adolescent struggling with sexual identity.

Hmmm . . . in Descartes, Locke, Smith, and Hegel there seemed to be a kind of autobiography of the self, disguised as metaphysics (which Dr. P had taught me was the study of, or speculation on, the nature of reality). These guys seemed to be confusing the nature of their own male European reality with something considerably larger; or, rather, tracing of the effect on themselves of a particular epistemology (or way of knowing), an epistemology of acute doubt, disembodied rationality, a mania to control and consume, an inalienable right to own something called "private property" that included, without acknowledgment, human beings. The result was a psychic alienation that was becoming synonymous with European modernity. Well, if that was modernity, bring on the postmodern.

Hegel's explanation of a human will to dominance, I came to see, had a particularly personal gloss for me in my ancestors' flight from the emerging modern European state, built on force and repression. Hegel was born during my great-great-great-great-great-grandfather's lifetime. Heini Sigrist emigrated from Switzerland, perhaps from the town of Sigriswil near what is now the German border. He had arrived, perhaps in Charleston, perhaps in Philadelphia, by 1771. His parents, Hans and Madle, were fleeing high taxes, floods, and ruined crops. Perhaps they were also fleeing the conscription of young Swiss men like Heini as poorly paid soldiers in the wars that swept through Europe as the system of modern European nation-states emerged. (Fed by wealth from its colonies, modern Europe, competitive and militaristic not only at home but also around the globe, would distinguish itself in its militarism "from all previous and non-European civilizations of the world," I had learned in Western Civilization.)[19] With the Prussian Hohenzollerns to the east ("not a state with an army, but an army with a state") and the French Louis to the west, the Sigrists took the six-week boat ride down the Rhine, then endured an interminable wait for a ship in Dover, or Portsmouth, England. Then came the Atlantic crossing—stench, dysentery, lice, rats, in a ship climbing waves like mountains—a journey that travelers under seven years of age seldom survived.[20] Perhaps Heini and his parents were fleeing the likes of Frederick the Great, the führer of Potsdam, whose Prussian state would emerge in the twentieth century as a virulent fascism.

In the Europe of this period, as Basil Davidson, among others, has pointed out, the process of culture shaped itself into national consciousness, then nations. The resulting nationalities "duly encased themselves in sovereign states, or at least in states intending to be sovereign; and then, one after another, . . . [tore] each other to pieces. . . . wielding the scythe of indiscriminate slaughter." The Otherness that Hegel articulated between subjects became the reality of relations between and among emerging nation-states. Militarism and state power translated the liberatory impulse of national consciousness to its reverse, acting out the "Janus-like nature of the 'national spirit' that demands freedom with one face and denies it with the other." In the coming century the nation-state would show its dangerous form in the "breaking of the promise of freedom" as a victory of the national over the social (the welfare of most of its people), a dynamic that would become the "central problematic of these European nation-states," as Karl Marx would be the first, the most thorough, and the most eloquent to point out.[21] It would also turn out to be a problematic for anticolonial liberation movements whose newly liberated countries inherited the legacy of the nation-state.

ALIENATION FROM SPECIES BEING: KARL MARX

In the Europe Heini Sigrist fled, Karl Marx was born in 1818 in Germany, in an era of rapid industrialization and modernization that accompanied the nation-state. Marx was kicked out of Germany, then Paris, for criticizing conditions of the poor, ending up with his family in London in 1849. With his friend Friedrich Engels, he put to rest Hegel's concept of the slave as gaining liberation from within his work. With Marx and Engels, workers became the proletariat, their historical role to escape the alienation of capital and to overthrow capitalism itself.

I approach Karl Marx late in what purports to be my political life, a perpetually remedial leftist. Maybe it was that I missed my socialist study-group phase because I was coming out as a lesbian. I was quite absorbed in trying to figure out how to kiss women and what that meant ("The Meaning of Our Love for Women Is What We Have Constantly to Expand," as Adrienne Rich taught);[22] feminism was transforming my life as lesbian and as woman. So I missed the sectarian sixties and seventies when some U.S. leftists were duking it out over their allegiance to Russia or to China and battling over criticism/self-criticism and the correct line. Unfamiliar with the intricacies of the dialectic, I am susceptible to endless instruction. My friend Lenny, both of us engaged in antifascist work in the 1980s, urged: "Just remember, the difference between a communist and a socialist is that communists believe in the dictatorship of the proletariat!!!" (It's a distinction that places me in the socialist camp.)

My own pull toward economic justice came more from Jesus than from Marx, as it had for Martin Luther King. It was harder for a rich man to get into heaven, I recalled, than for a camel to get through the eye of a needle. Then there was the vision of Jesus at the right hand of God, separating the sheep from the goats by whether they had fed the hungry, clothed the naked: "In as much as you did it not unto the least of these," he explained to their soon-to-be-fried perplexity, "ye did it not to me" (Matt. 25:45). Liberation theology would expand this insight into the right of the naked and the hungry to clothe and feed themselves. That much mainline Christianity had somehow turned into a religion of often self-righteous goats was a source of frustration to me, to put it mildly.

My focus on economic justice also sharpened from political work in the 1980s and 1990s that pulled me across class lines to work in organizations in which poor and working-class people, many of whom became my friends, made clear the ongoing exploitation of the poor for the creation of obscene profits. In fact, back from a recent tour of *maquiladoras* along the U.S.-Mexican border with the Urban-Rural Mission, a program of the World Council of Churches, I had issued a ringing call for a "Queer Socialism" at the 1993 Creating Change conference, urging the National Gay and Lesbian Task Force to take a stand against NAFTA (North America Free Trade Agreement). My reading of Marx came after the collapse of communism in China (1976) and the fall of the Soviet bloc (1989). Yet here I was, plowing through texts that for much of the world were thoroughly discredited. I would, apparently, be perpetually out of step. A queer socialist, indeed.

I find that contemporary Marxists, with the benefit of hindsight, distinguish between Marx's later work (writings that tend more toward the economic determinism that became the basis of Stalinist orthodoxy) and his earlier works, which "reveal a more philosophical, humanist Marx."[23] Clearly, the demise of Soviet and Chinese-style communism does not mean that the dangerous excesses of capitalism are over. Quite the opposite—capitalism has more terrain over which to move, into the blocs and crevices controlled by communism over the past seventy years (hence the term *globalization*). One of the projects for a new century is to reconstruct the basis of opposition movements, and this requires taking into account, again, Marx, whose work still "remains the gravest, most penetrating examination the capitalist system has ever undergone."[24] Many of those who seek an alternative to the orthodox Marxism that bit the dust at the end of the last century are searching for understandings that remain "open, nondogmatic, more modest and more tentative."[25]

It is, perhaps predictably, to Marx's concept of the alienation of the self in his earlier work that I am now drawn. Unlike Descartes or Hegel, Marx did not see alienation as inevitable, but as a product of forces over which humans could and should exert control. It is capitalism that alienates humans from their sense of belonging to a wider existence. Alienation under capitalism, Marx felt, was multilayered: humans were alienated from the process of production, from the product, from the family and community of workers, from the self, and finally from what he called one's "species being."

The division of labor under capitalism "does not only produce commodities, it produces itself and the laborer as a commodity," Marx explained. Thus the worker makes a "sacrifice of his life"[26] and his "positive, creative activity" (an implicit critique of the freedom that Hegel posited the slave found in his work).[27] Under capitalism, human work becomes alien, part of an external world that opposes and consumes the self: "The more value he creates, the more valueless and worthless he becomes, the more formed the product, the more deformed the worker, the more civilized the product the more barbaric the worker." The working human thus feels a "stranger" and his work is the "loss of himself."[28]

But alienation extends deeper. The alienation of the worker from the product of his labor at the same time affects his "relation to the sensuous external world, to the objects of nature." And it is human relationship to the objects of nature that helps constitute what Marx calls our species being—an interdependence with inorganic nature, with the "plants, animals, stones, air, light, etc., [that] constitute theoretically a part of human consciousness." Estranged labor therefore turns *"man's species being*, both nature and his spiritual species property, into a being *alien* to him, into a *means* to his *individual existence."* In other words, for Marx, estranged labor estranges humans from all that makes us human.[29]

Marx describes alienation as a loss of belonging—work, he says, becomes an alien activity "not belonging to [the person]," and the worker loses a sense of being "at home." This home to which humans belong is not some "fictitious primordial condition" to which humans long to return, an idea which Marx scorned.[30] So it must be rather some here-and-now sense of connection, some apprehension of external existence, not as fearsome, threatening, or alien, but as home.

Like Hegel, Marx saw self-consciousness as intersubjectivity. But without Hegel's fear of existence, he had a different vision of what forms human relationships might take. "The individual is the social being," Marx explained, "his vital expression . . . therefore an expression and confirmation of his social life. Man's individual and species-life are not two distinct things."³¹ For Marx, the "individual and isolated hunter or fisher who forms the starting point with [Adam] Smith and [David] Ricardo" was a "dreaming platitude," part of the "insipid illusions of the eighteenth century."³² Species life is "life-producing life," but under capitalism "life itself appears only as a *means of life*."³³

For Marx, human consciousness is interactive and always emerges from material reality. Nature is a part of this material reality, and social humans and nature exist interactively as well, not under an imperative (as Locke argued) for men to dominate and subdue: "Society is therefore the perfected unity in essence of man with nature, the true resurrection of nature, the realized naturalism of man and the realized humanism of nature." Material reality itself is primarily shaped by economic forces, the "relations of production" (such as the medieval guild system, the factory system, the modern industrial system). In a famous passage, Marx summarizes how the economic conditions other parts of a society: "The sum total of these relations of production constitutes the economic structure of society, the real foundation, on which rises a legal and political superstructure and to which correspond definite forms of social consciousness." Economic relations also conditioned the self: "It is not the consciousness of men that determines their being, but on the contrary their social being that determines their consciousness."³⁴

Ideas, the content for Marx of consciousness, have a political source and function as *ideology*. Marx relates religion to the derivative realm of superstructure, as opium for the proletariat to distract them from revolutionary work to better their conditions in history. Yet, Marx acknowledged, "Religious distress is at the same time the expression of real distress and the protest against real distress. Religion is the sign of the oppressed creature, the heart of a heartless world, just as it is the spirit of a spiritless situation."³⁵

The point of Marx's historical materialism was to restore to humans their sense of connection and belonging, their species being. Although Hegel and Marx shared a sense of intersubjectivity, Marx, unlike Hegel, had a visceral hatred of relations of domination and subordination. Marx thus "stood Hegel on his head," Marx's historical dialectic being driven not by the contradictions between ideas as Hegel's had been, but by the contradictions between classes. While the end of Hegel's historical dialectic had been the manifestation of an Absolute Idea or Spirit, its political form the Prussian State, for Marx history would move from feudalism to capitalism and eventually on to communism, a society in which the free development of one was the condition for the free development of all.

Marx's methodology for this process of overcoming alienation was class revolution to establish a dictatorship of the proletariat that would seize and collectivize the means of production in order to create new, less alienated human beings. The inevitability of the proletarian revolution became a matter of faith, and there was in the old Karl of *Das Kapital* an element of intolerance to alternate views and opinions that would play itself out in his followers in the next century in authoritarian forms of state power in Russia and China. Stalinism notwithstanding, it's fair to say that overcoming alienation was Marx's intent, an intent that globally we are far from realizing. Overall, Marx was a practical philosopher: the purpose of knowledge for him was its applicability, "not to know history but to change it." Marx advocated a practice in which "man must prove the truth, that is, the reality and power, the this-sidedness of his thinking."[36] Terry Eagleton explains in a helpful way: "To know yourself in a new way is to alter yourself in that very act; so we have here a peculiar form of cognition in which the act of knowing alters what it contemplates."[37]

NIETZSCHE, FREUD, AND THAT OCEANIC FEELING

Thus far, we've been tracing the modern split between self and world, articulated in Descartes and Hegel, critiqued in Marx. This split replicates itself in relationships between and among humans and between humans and nature, as domination, repression, exploitation. It speaks to the question of *why* things happen—why twenty million Africans dead in the Middle Passage? Why sixty million indigenous people dead in the silver mines of Latin America? Why apartheid? Why environmental degradation? Greed, of course, is one big answer—but why greed? It is evil, yes, but what is evil, and why?

The quest for an answer brings us to the spiritual dimension, and to the question of God. It was Friedrich Nietzsche who articulated this shift. He writes of the death of a God that Celie described in Alice Walker's *The Color Purple* as "this old white man . . . [who] wear white robes and go barefooted"; who "act just like all the other mens I know. Trifling, forgetful and lowdown."[38] This is a Calvinist God who dangles sinners over the hot flames of Hell after they have worked themselves to exhaustion. *This* God does not go without a fight, as Friedrich Wilhelm Nietzsche made clear.

Nietzsche died, insane, in 1900, at the beginning of the century that would prove him prophetic about the violent effects of alienation. "God is dead," Nietzsche's madman exclaimed, "and we have killed him. How shall we, the murderers of all murderers, comfort ourselves?" In the midst of a new era of European imperialism, Nietzsche hailed the signs of the imminent arrival of "a more manly, warlike age" and recommended, *"Live dangerously.* . . . Send your ships into uncharted seas! Live at war with your peers and yourselves! Be robbers and conquerors, as long as you cannot be rulers and owners. . . . At long last the pursuit of knowledge will reach out for its due: it will want to rule and own, and you with it!"[39] By 1912, Europe controlled 80 percent of the globe and was poised on the brink of a brutal war. No wonder these sons of a dead God were left with an apprehension of reality that filled them with anguish.

"Whether anyone likes it or not," Aimé Césaire declared in 1955 in his *Discourse on Colonialism*, "at the end of the blind alley that is Europe . . . there is Hitler. At the

end of capitalism, which is eager to outlive its day, there is Hitler. At the end of formal humanism and philosophic renunciation, there is Hitler."[40]

So you get the picture that the Masterful self is under a lot of pressure, having a
hard time holding it together, and generally acting out; in need, in fact, of a talking
cure. Enter Sigmund Freud. The introjected and split consciousness of master-
slave, in fact, structured the modern self, as Sigmund Freud charted. He laid out the
metaphoric psychic drama of controlling superego and rebellious id, with much of
human consciousness lost to the beleaguered ego desperately trying to mediate.
Freud wrote from the standpoint of a Europe on the cusp of fascism, the even *more*
"manly, warlike age" that Nietzsche had beckoned and Césaire recollected, the
Third Reich as the apotheosis of the Prussian State. Freud, like Marx, however, was
a philosopher with a praxis, and he evolved psychotherapy in an attempt to help the
beleaguered ego and to cure the modern self of its afflictions.

Several years ago, I reread Freud's *Civilization and Its Discontents* when I was
pondering issues of sexuality and community organizing. I wanted to remember
Freud's assessment of the relationship of sexuality and culture—his thesis that culture is based on the repression of sexuality. His was an insight that would offer one
good explanation of the difficulty in getting sexuality onto the table, into the open,
to discuss: within a Western ethos, sexuality was not only private, but always prior to
civilization.

In the process, I found something else that struck me. Freud explained in a conversation with a religious friend that he did not feel what his friend considered the
religious impulse, or the "oceanic feeling" connecting a person, an "indissoluble
bond, of being one with the external world as a whole." Freud confesses in *Civilization and Its Discontents*, "I cannot discover this feeling in myself. It is not easy to
deal scientifically with feelings."[41] Thus Freud himself had evidently inherited the
split between self and "the external world as a whole." And it was within this split that
sexuality situated itself. Freud, like Locke and Hegel before him, saw civilization as
being "built upon a renunciation of instinct." The "sacrifice of instincts [to a rule of
law] . . . leaves no one at the mercy of brute force," Freud wrote, echoing Locke's social contract. For these men, sexuality was situated on the cusp between the civilized
and the primitive; and consequently, sexuality also represented those cultures conquered and repressed by Europe: "Civilization behaves towards sexuality as a people
or a stratum of its population does which has subjected another to its exploitation.
Fear of revolt by the suppressed elements drives it to stricter precautionary measures."[42] (If you want to see one terrible effect of such precautionary measures, look
at *Without Sanctuary*, a collection of photographs of lynchings in the United
States.)[43]

Civilization and sexuality, transversing culture and self, replicated relationships of
the colonizer and the colonized, or in Hegel's terms, the master and the slave. And,
sure enough, in India, Africa, China and Indochina, Latin America, and the United
States, political movements against colonialism and imperialism marked what Freud

called "the return of the repressed." That psychotherapy often involved the male therapist with the female patient on the couch also produced its own uprisings.

SARTRE: CONDEMNED TO NAUSEOUS FREEDOM

Contemporary for awhile with Freud, Jean-Paul Sartre carved his existential philosophy of decision and action out of the void left by the demise of God (or, in
Hegel's words, of Absolute Spirit working its way through history). As an undergrad,
I had admired Sartre; he and fellow Frenchman Albert Camus both were antifascists,
I knew, and I appreciated the risk of their engagement against National Socialism,
having grown up in the local fascism known as Jim Crow. Dr. P impressed upon us
that if we wanted to understand existentialism, we had to understand two premises:
(1) existence precedes essence; (2) therefore, we are condemned to freedom. The
self's response to the revelation of such contingent freedom was anguish and nausea.
To me at twenty the anguish was compelling: "There was nothing to prevent consciousness from making a wholly new choice of its way of being." To me at fifty (plus),
this insight presents great possibility.

Roquentin, Sartre's hero in *Nausea,* has a vision while looking closely at a chestnut tree in a garden, a vision in which existence unveiled itself to him: "it had lost the
harmless look of an abstract category: it was the very paste of things, this root was
kneaded into existence." His perceptions come in waves over eight closely observed
pages. "Usually existence hides itself" in categories, Roquentin thinks, "the ocean is
green; that white speck up there is a seagull. . . . It is there around us, in us, it is *us*;
you can't say two words without mentioning it, but you can never touch it. When I
believed I was thinking about it, I must believe that I was thinking nothing, my head
was empty, or there was just one word in my head, the word 'to be.' Or else I was
thinking . . . how can I explain it? I was thinking of *belonging.* I was telling myself
that the sea belonged to a class of green objects."[44]

Roquentin's vision could have yielded a mystic's bliss, an apprehension of expe-
riential belonging beyond rational or linguistic categories. But it never does; he is
constantly pulled back from such a melding. He typically begins: "Existence everywhere, infinitely, in excess, for ever and everywhere; existence—which is limited only
by existence. I sank down on the bench, stupefied, stunned by this profusion of being
without origin: everywhere blossomings, hatchings out, my ears buzzed with existence, my very flesh throbbed and opened, abandoned itself to the universal burgeoning." Then he pulls back: "It was repugnant." His repugnance comes because he
conceives of the material matrix, to which he has a sensuous, erotic response, as female: "All things, gently, tenderly, were letting themselves drift into existence like
those relaxed women who burst out laughing and say, 'It's good to laugh' in a wet
voice; they were parading, one in front of the other, exchanging abject secrets about
their existence." With such misogynist sight, the "perfect free gift" that "could turn
your heart upside down" becomes "rotten filth," and Roquentin's somatic response to

such a perception of existence is nausea, which he generalizes to all humans. Talk about alienation from one's species being! In retrospect, I guess my undergraduate hangover *was* metaphysical. Being hungover (the toilet) was one solution, anyway, to a Cartesian query about whether one was in a body.[45]

Now, Jean-Paul did not have to react this way. Alice Walker's brilliant theological novel, *The Color Purple*, offers us another option. Shug is helping her friend and lover Celie to, as Bob Marley would say, emancipate herself from mental slavery. At the core of this process is Celie's reconception of God. No longer is God that old white guy with the beard whose death Nietzsche had trumpeted. "I believe God is everything, say Shug." Roquentin could have used Shug's instructions, but he would have had to shift his conception of the female body and the erotic. Shug instructs her lover Celie: "My first step from the old white man was trees. Then air. Then birds. Then other people. But one day when I was sitting quiet and feeling like a mother-less child, which I was, it come to me: that feeling of being part of everything, not separate at all. I knew that if I cut a tree, my arm would bleed. And I laughed and I cried and I run all around the house. I knew just what it was. In fact, when it happen, you can't miss it. It sort of like you know what, she say, grinning and rubbing high up on my thigh."[46] Hmmm. Jean-Paul Sartre said we are condemned to freedom. At least the man was taking responsibility, however bleakly. But it sure did not make him grin, laugh, cry, and run around the house!

ENGAGED BUDDHISM AS ALTERNATE PATH

If Shug had a different response to feeling a part of everything, Buddha also did. Roquentin had his chestnut, and Buddha had his bodhi tree from which he looked into the nature of contingent reality. For Buddha, such perception became a door to joy and liberation. Joanna Macy explains in feminist terms the nature of Buddha's insight as it was elaborated in the "Second Turning of the Wheel of Dharma" in the *Perfection of Wisdom* scriptures (approximately two thousand years ago), from which Mahayana Buddhism developed. In these scriptures, Wisdom is figured as a female archetype, the Perfection of Wisdom, Mother of All Buddhas, "very different from the feminine attributes we have inherited from patriarchal thought." She is "freed from the dichotomies which oppose earth to sky, flesh to spirit"; she is "that pregnant zero point where the illusion of ego is lost and the world, no longer feared or fled, is reentered with compassion." (Roquentin had reached that zero point, but he had not been able to stay there; it was too female.) The Mother of All Buddhas points to what Buddha experienced, "to a reality which eludes classifications," a wisdom called *paramita*, "which means 'gone beyond' or to the 'other side' as well as 'perfection.'" From this moment of the Second Turning emerges the figure of the bodhisattva, whose concern is other beings. "The Mother of All Buddhas therefore does not call the Bodhisattva beyond this world, to the final nirvana. She retains [the bodhisattva] on this side of reality, for the sake of all beings." How the bodhisattva acts within contingency is the key to enlightenment and involves *upaya*, "the readiness to reach out and improvise" as the "other face of wisdom." The bodhisattva path is democratized—"for the first time, fully expressed—as a calling and challenge to all persons."[47]

The bodhisattva path is one legacy to the West of anticolonial struggles in Asia, via the engaged Buddhism that emerged during the 1930s in the French colony of Vietnam, as Thich Nhat Hanh's *Vietnam: Lotus in a Sea of Fire* explains. The 1930s brought a patriotic renewal of Buddhism in Vietnam, as Buddhists discussed the engagement of Buddhism in modern society. This renaissance was encouraged in part by Westerners who had come to Vietnam and learned Buddhist practice; their appreciation helped give indigenous people new appreciation for the "profundities of their own faith." "Engaged Buddhism"—explained by some Buddhists as a "Third Turning of the Wheel of Dharma"—emerged in this anticolonial context. While Mao was leading the Red Army and the Chinese Communist Party in the 1930s and 1940s, Ho Chi Minh led the anti-imperialist forces in Vietnam, defeating the French in 1945, making Ho a national hero. "Most people of Vietnam were not aware that Ho Chi Minh was about to establish Communism in Vietnam," wrote Thich Nhat Hanh. Engaged Buddhism then emerged more fully to support "the way of life of a society that aspired to revolutionary change" as an alternative to "mutual liquidation of political parties that had taken an active part in the revolution" that happened in the 1940s in Vietnam. It was both political engagement and engagement with modernity.[48]

He finds the goals of communism consistent with the best in most of the world's great religions. He witnessed how its social and personal idealism drew thousands of people passionately committed to eliminating "the exploitation and inequality that have characterized much of Western society, and to create a form of social organization whose slogan will be 'from each according to his ability, to each according to his need.'" He also finds this goal appealing, and he finds socialism's economic organization of society, "in which the means of production are operated for the good of the people generally rather than for the profit of a minority," consistent with Buddhism.

Nhat Hanh's objections are to communist methodology. In Vietnam he witnessed this as "the suppression of all significant dissent and debate; the liquidation of even the most sincere and committed opponents, violently if need be; the assumption of omniscience on the part of the party, which is a form of fanaticism that is stultifying to the never-ending search for truth—to which Buddhists, for example, are committed; and the willingness to sacrifice the very existence of a small country like Vietnam to the 'larger' interests of the Communist side in the cold war between the great powers." His critique of communism does not displace his original opposition to imperialism. He refuses the "mystical, non-rational, almost religious character" of United States anticommunism and its deep implication in continuing colonial conquests.[49]

It was the scalding dualism in the West's metaphysic that was the root of the war in his country. From his order's Plum Village community in France he continued to teach, write, and do political work, but for years he would not come to the United

States. When he was ready to come, the first workshops he led were with Vietnam War vets. Nhat Hanh summarized: "Opposition to communism within Buddhism has been a development of the past ten or fifteen years, but resistance to Western imperialistic domination is a matter of the past several centuries."[50] Both Sartre's existentialism and the engaged Buddhism that evolved in the same period in Vietnam were responses to French colonialism. The French response reinscribed the very alienation it critiqued.

Other paths of violent and nonviolent struggle come through Africa and Latin America.

MEMMI, FANON, CÉSAIRE: THE COLONIZED (MALE'S) RESPONSE

It was Simone de Beauvoir—Sartre's lover, as you recall—who pointed me to Hegel as the origin of philosophical discourse on Otherness. (Had Shug gotten ahold of J-P, Simone's love life might have considerably improved, I have a feeling.) And it was through Sartre that the discourse on Otherness, begun by Hegel, fed into anticolonial theory and practice (devised by intellectuals from the French colonies who had been trained in France's university system), as it fed into feminist analysis via Simone de Beauvoir's *The Second Sex*.[51]

Sartre wrote an introduction both to Albert Memmi's *The Colonizer and the Colonized*, published in 1957, and to Frantz Fanon's *The Wretched of the Earth* (1959). I can pull Memmi, Aimé Césaire, and Frantz Fanon from my bookcase because I bought copies of these volumes years ago and read them after hearing Joan Nestle of the Lesbian Herstory Archives talk about the influence of anticolonial theory on her own thinking when she was teaching in the open university system in New York City in the 1960s.[52] Their analysis of the need to decolonize the self had inspired (in part) her founding of the archives. My own subsequent work as a lesbian came as much from a glimpse of this concept of decolonization as it did from the feminist edict that "the personal is political."

Memmi was born in Tunisia and interned in a forced labor camp during World War II. After the war he received a degree in philosophy from the Sorbonne. In *The Colonizer and the Colonized*, he translates Hegel's master-slave binary into the terms of colonialism. He paints a portrait of "one of the major oppressions of our time," both to understand himself and to describe "the fate of a vast multitude across the world." His book fueled anticolonial revolts, and police confiscated *The Colonizer and the Colonized* "in the cells of militant nationalists" the world over. In Memmi, as well as in Fanon and Césaire, Hegel's male slave speaks and acts with an emerging revolutionary subjectivity. Theirs is a philosophy that successfully seeks not to know history but to change it: "what help to fighting men [is] the simple, ordered description of their misery and humiliation," writes Memmi.[53]

Memmi's move is what Jacques Derrida would come to call deconstruction, an analysis that destabilizes "the oppositional logic that relies on an untouchable distinction" (for example, between master-slave, colonizer-colonized). By deconstructing the (il)logic of the distinction, it becomes touchable and, in fact, falls apart, "so as to allow for the passage to the other."[54]

Memmi shows the implacable dependence of colonizer on colonized that creates "an obvious logic in the reciprocal behavior of the two colonial partners" and leaves the social self, in its split manifestations, corrupt. Derrida as a literary critic deconstructs the logocentrism, or privileging of the spoken word in literary texts. Memmi's subject is a colonial culture in which inherently unstable identities inexorably decompose. And unlike Hegel, Memmi is "unconditionally opposed to all forms of oppression" and clearly committed to the elimination of colonialism. He draws a detailed portrait of mutual alienation in repressive systems that is similar to Marx's description of the alienation of labor: "For if colonization destroys the colonized, it also rots the colonizer." Their existence is seesaw: "the more freely he breathes, the more the colonized are choked." Here is intersubjectivity on its most destructive terms.[55]

The colonizer's existence is marked by profit, privilege, and usurpation, and in protecting "his very limited interests, he protects other infinitely more important ones, of which he is, incidentally, the victim. But, though dupe and victim, he also gets his share." Mediocrity (the best having left or never arrived) characterizes the colonizer and his administrative mechanisms—this mediocrity "a lasting catastrophe from which the colony never recovers." Nor does the colonizer ever really intend to transform the colony into the image of its homeland, because such transformation "would destroy the principle of his privileges."[56]

The colonizer develops a Nero complex, the response of a "nonlegitimate privileged person, that is, a usurper." He endeavors to falsify history, to rewrite laws, and to extinguish memory; and the implicit guilt of his situation causes him to "wish the disappearance of the usurped." The colonizer is caught in a vicious—Memmi would say a fascist—cycle, given that the more he hurts the colonized, "the more he coincides with the atrocious role he has chosen for himself." The colonizer also has an ambivalent relationship to his mother country, which underwrites his privilege and to which he attributes all the ideal qualities of a superego. Memmi describes the characteristic of this superego as "*not to be a part of things, to control from a distance without ever being touched* by the prosaic and convulsive behavior of men of flesh and blood" (emphasis mine)—not so far from Descartes's mind that "does not require any place" nor from Hegel's reticence to be "caught up in life." The superego is the introjection of the cruel white God-parent that Celie rejects, a God who is not a part of things, controlling from a distance without ever being touched. (As Memmi notes, racism is an inevitable and necessary component of the colonizer's practice and ideology and constitutes "one of the fundamental patterns of colonialist personality.")[57]

Memmi concludes that the cost of colonialism is fascism: "There is no doubt in the minds of those who have lived through it that colonialism is one variety of fascism. . . . It is no more surprising that colonial fascism is not easily limited to the colony. Cancer wants only to spread."[58] Césaire also is emphatic on how Europe's slide toward unspeakable brutality in the colonies came home to roost in the Third Reich. What Europe cannot forgive Hitler for, he concludes, is that "he applied to Europe colonialist procedures which until then had been reserved exclusively for the Arabs of Algeria, the coolies of India, and the blacks of Africa."[59]

Basil Davidson, writing fifty years after Memmi, describes how the opposition to fascism became national liberation of colonial people: "One of the achievements of our blood-stained century, if it may be called an achievement, is so clearly to have revealed the two faces of nationalism: its capacity for enlarging freedom, and its potential for destroying freedom. The rise and havoc of Fascist nationalism in one or the other of its forms were a mortal threat to millions of people, and the threat was made good. But for colonized people, the reality of Fascist nationalism produced the opposed reality of anti-Fascism; and anti-Fascism, unstoppable as it proved, became antiracism; and antiracism led in due course to the end of colonization."[60]

If colonialism warped the colonizer, however, the colonized, too, is disfigured—"into an oppressed creature, whose development is broken and who compromises by his defeat." His internalization of colonialist ideology is reinforced at every turn by his material situation, which accumulates as a "wretchedness—collective, permanent, immense."[61] Two answers for the colonized to such an unacceptable situation are assimilation and revolt. Assimilation—to become "equal to that splendid model and to resemble him to the point of disappearing in him"—is a loss of the colonized's self. And ultimately assimilation cannot work because of the colonizer's racism. Thus the colonized arrives at revolt—doing away with the colonial situation—as the only way out. Now he asserts his differences from Europe, differences that "are within him and correctly constitute his true self." He begins to recuperate his culture, including his religion and his language. But he is not yet out of the master-slave mirror, and thus the colonized develops for himself a countermythology, a positive myth about himself to succeed the negative myth propagated by the colonizer. Still, such a countermythology cannot sufficiently convince him of himself, so "he gives in to the intoxication of fury and violence."[62]

The "painful discord with himself continues," an alienation the end of which must "await the complete disappearance of colonization—including the period of revolt." Here Memmi ends the chapter without answering the crucial question of what will finally make disappear the image of the colonizer in the colonial mind and culture. Concluding that he has no remedies, Memmi does hold out hope that "the liquidation of colonization is nothing but a prelude to complete liberation, to self-recovery." (This self-recovery includes national liberation, but not a narrow nationalism in which self "exists only through his nation" or his religious group, or the past, tradition, or ethnic characteristics.) "Having reconquered all his dimensions, the former colonized will have become a man like any other. . . . A whole and free man."[63] It's not clear at all at this point who these other men are, or how the colonized will join them; but it is clear that they are not women.

However, as the history of decolonization shows, the "whole and free man" as postcolonial actor did not fully emerge. At the end of Memmi's book, the colonized has not located himself fully outside the colonialist mirror, the dance of dualism of the master-slave self. The colonized have not yet emerged from the "blind alley that is Europe."

For Frantz Fanon, the answer was simpler: violence breaks the colonial mirror. Since colonizers conquer by violence, use police and military to keep their power in place, and create a systemic violence that drains the colony's resources, then it will take violence to end such a system: "Violence [is] its natural state, and it will only yield when confronted with greater violence. . . . Only violence pays." Such violence for Fanon is not merely inevitable or pragmatic, it has a positive psychic function: "At the level of individuals, violence is a cleansing force. It frees the native from his inferiority complex and from his despair and inaction; it makes him fearless and restores his self-respect."[64]

Basil Davidson argues from an end-of-the-century perspective unavailable to Fanon and Memmi that the European nation-state model, which the indigenous colonial, anticolonial, and postcolonial elites considered the only path out of colonialism, would betray Africa, as it had betrayed Europe. "You can't think of societies in Europe without armies. . . . That was the instrument which established the state," reflected Julius Kambarage Nyerere at the century's end. Nyerere was first president of the newly formed Tanganyika African National Union (TANU), then he negotiated a union with Zanzibar to form the United Republic of Tanzania, for which he served as president. He also served as president of the Organization of African Unity and helped lead the frontline states in solidarity with southern African countries still under colonial rule. "Once you've accepted the nation-state, you accept the consequences—including armies, including internal security services, bureaucracy, police and the lot. . . . There are misuses of these instruments of state. . . . And every nation under the sun, when they feel that the security of the state is threatened, invoke all these methods everywhere." Kenneth Kaunda, leader of the United National Independence Movement of Zambia who became independent Zambia's first president, echoed: "He who affirms the state affirms violence."[65] The European nation-state (also the basis of the United States as a nation) was a collective reflection of the Master's psyche. The men of the postcolonial state often did not take sufficiently into account the postcolonial woman who had the least access to state power and who was most at the mercy of structural adjustment policies.

MARCUSE, THE CONSUMER ECONOMY, AND MAN'S SECOND NATURE

Memmi was confronting the same question that Marx had—how to create new men from an old system—and in the decade after Memmi wrote *The Colonizer and the Colonized*, Herbert Marcuse arrived at the same impasse from another direction. Marcuse was one of the Frankfurt school, which included Walter Benjamin,

Theodor Wiesengrund Adorno, and Erich Fromm. These critics and philosophers began their work in Germany and (all but Benjamin, who did not escape) immigrated to the United States, fleeing fascism. Along with Antonio Gramsci, they sought to critique the ways that Marxism was evolving in Stalin's Russia.

In *An Essay on Liberation* (1969), Marcuse lays out the new revolutionary predicament and possibility when "the growing opposition to the global domination of corporate capitalism is confronted by the sustained power of this dominion. . . . This global power keeps the socialist orbit on the defensive, all too costly not only in terms of military expenditures but also in the perpetuation of a repressive bureaucracy. The development of socialism thus continues to be deflected from its original goals." Marcuse points to guerilla movements in Cuba, China, Vietnam, and Latin America that "struggle to eschew the bureaucratic administration of socialism," and he lauds student opposition in capitalist countries. He celebrates the 1968 student uprising in France that called for permanent challenge *(la contestation permanente)*, the Great Refusal. In all of this, he sees an alternative that is "beginning to break into the repressive continuum . . . not so much a different road to socialism as an emergence of different goals and values."[66]

Marcuse seeks a "biological foundation for socialism" and a "moral radicalism . . . which might precondition man for freedom." This morality, prior to ethical behavior and ideological expression, is a "disposition of the organism, perhaps rooted in the erotic drive to counter aggressiveness, to create and preserve 'ever greater unities' of life." Marcuse seems to be fusing Freud's instincts with Marx's species being as "an instinctual foundation for solidarity among human beings." He needs to insert such moral radicalism into the generative base in order to produce transformed humans: The "malleability of human nature reaches into the depth of man's instinctual structure [so that] changes in morality may 'sink down' into the 'biological' dimension and modify organic behavior. . . . Unless revolt can reach down into this 'second' nature, into these ingrown patterns, social change will remain 'incomplete,' even self-defeating."[67]

Marcuse is reaching for some different kind of praxis to shift the self from its consumptive patterns: "The so-called consumer economy and the politics of corporate capitalism have created a second nature of man which ties him libidinally and aggressively to the commodity form." For this reason, he concludes that "the radical change which is to transform the existing society into a free society must reach into a dimension of the human existence hardly considered in Marxian theory." Still a materialist, he calls this dimension the biological. I am calling it the spiritual. It requires, he understands, "different reactions of the body as well as the mind." Here he points, I believe, to a fusion of political and spiritual praxis. Marcuse pursues Marx's desire for "a new type of man as the member (though not as the builder) of a socialist society," and concludes: "But the construction of such a society presupposes a type of man with a different sensitivity as well as consciousness: men who would speak a different language, have different gestures, follow different impulses; men who have developed an instinctual barrier against cruelty, brutality, ugliness."[68]

At this historic moment—1969—the limits of *man* as a generic term all but cry out: *Yo, guys?! Maybe the Socialist's New Man is a WOMAN???* Marcuse was pushing toward a Utopian socialism that would involve qualitatively different ways of life, and for him this was the May rebellion in France. But it would also be feminism (with all its varieties and fissions). "Women are the most important new global force on the horizon today with the potential to create a more humane future," Charlotte Bunch would elucidate in Beijing in 1995.

FOUCAULT: DISCOURSE AND SELF-DISPLACEMENT

Let me look at one more masculinist narrative before suggesting an alternative. Marcuse heralded the 1968 uprising in France, in which students joined workers in protesting imperialism, as a harbinger of an emerging Utopian socialism. But the failure of that revolution—a student and worker uprising against the Vietnam War—is what reverberates through poststructuralist writing as a disillusionment with all Utopian narratives and movements. Unable through political movements to free the self from the "blind alley that is Europe," theorists such as Jacques Derrida, Roland Barthes, and Michel Foucault dissolved the subject into text and discourse. Terry Eagleton's trenchant account of this period is relevant here:

> Post-structuralism was a product of that blend of euphoria and disillusionment, liberation and dissatisfaction, carnival and catastrophe, which was 1968. Unable to break the structures of state power, post-structuralism found it possible instead to subvert the structures of language. Nobody, at least, was likely to beat you on the head for doing so. The student movement was flushed off the streets and driven underground into discourse. Its enemies . . . became coherent belief systems of any kind—in particular all forms of political theory and organization which sought to analyze, and act upon, the structures of society as a whole. For it was precisely such power which seemed to have failed: the system had proven too powerful for them, and the "total" critique offered of it by a heavily Stalinized Marxism had been exposed as part of the problem, not of the solution. All such total systematic thought was now suspect as terroristic. . . . The only forms of political action now felt to be acceptable were of a local, diffused, strategic kind.[69]

Michel Foucault set about to re-theorize power, beyond the narrowly economic. As he explains in "Two Lectures," "discourse" replaces the "means of production" as the generative force in a culture, the mechanism that relays power through the social system and at once subjects and subjugates, disciplines and controls. In other words, it is not the accumulation of profit through exploitation of workers that describes power's operation, but the control of truth and the reproduction of knowledge. Foucault distinguishes between two theories of power that historically operated in Europe: a *juridical* theory of power derived from the right of kings, power as a right to be alienated or transferred through contract (for example, Locke, Jefferson); and an understanding of *power as repression*, as a continuation of war by other means (its exponents Marx, Freud, Wilhelm Reich). Sympathetic with the repressive theory, Foucault nonetheless wants a "non-economic analysis of power," which he arrives at in his theory of discursive power.[70]

Discursive power involves the "relations of knowledge" (truth-knowledge-power) more than it does the "relations of production." Power acts primarily on truth, "never ceases its interrogation, its inquisition, its registration of truth." Although discursive power is not independent of "enmeshment with economic relations" and "in fact participates [with them] in common circuits," the production of truth is prior to the production of wealth: "In the last analysis we must produce truth as we must produce wealth, indeed we must produce truth in order to produce wealth in the first place." Furthermore, this discursive power circulates, and "the individual is always in the position of simultaneously undergoing and exercising this power." Discursive power, Foucault suggests, should be interrogated from the ground up, "where it is in direct and immediate relationship with what we can provisionally call its object, its target," rather than from the macrosystem down.[71]

For Foucault, resistance to discursive power comes in an "insurrection of subjugated knowledge"—"blocs of historical knowledge which were present but disguised within the body of functionalist and systematising theory and which criticism . . . has been able to reveal." This is not an insurrection of *people*, we should make clear, but an insurrection of the "concrete multiplicity of *facts*" against the "abstract unity of theory," although subjugated knowledge can also refer to the knowledge of subjugated peoples ("naïve knowledges located low down on the hierarchy, beneath the required level of cognition or scientificity"). Foucault calls his methodology of resistance to dominant discourse *genealogy*: "a painstaking rediscovery of struggles together with the rude memory of their conflicts," "a union of erudite knowledge and local memories which allows us to establish a historical knowledge of struggles and to make use of this knowledge tactically today." If Marx's materialist theory of power privileged the "proletariat," Foucault's theory of discursive power privileges "the critic" who unearths genealogies—who "obviously draws upon scholarship"—an emphasis that has made Foucault quite popular in universities.[72]

Foucault argues that the discourse that subjugates us is different from Marx's notion of ideology: "[What takes place in discursive regimes of power] is both much more and much less than ideology. It is the production of effective instruments for the formation and accumulation of knowledge—methods of observation, techniques of registration, procedures for investigation and research, apparatuses of control."[73] (Here Foucault's description of discursive power does not seem to differ much from Gramsci's elaboration of the "complex superstructures" that "organize human masses . . . and form the terrain on which men move, acquire consciousness of their position, struggle, etc.")

But who or what uses this knowledge tactically is not so clear, which brings us again to the question of the subject. In Foucault's discursive theory of power, it is *knowledge* that has agency, not *subjects* (for example, it is a "whole set of knowledges" that rebel, not a "whole set of subjugated peoples"). In describing the subject, Foucault leads us through the by-now-familiar (and to me a bit tedious) disclaimer that the subject is not "the distillation of a single will—or rather the constitution of a unitary singular body animated by the spirit of sovereignty." Following Marx, Foucault argues that the subject is constituted in a social matrix: "We should try to grasp subjection in its material instance as a constitution of subjects . . . through a multiplicity of organisms, forces, energies, materials, desires, thoughts, etc."[74] But the social-personal self is not alienated from its species being by an economic-political system, as in Marx; rather, the self is displaced onto, because constituted by, discourse.

Foucault deliberately situates discourse so as to de-legitimize inquiries into the subject or self or psyche, a function it has performed quite effectively over the past decades.[75] Genealogies have provided powerful ways to understand discursive power, but—wielded as Foucault prescribes—they have also passed over in silence important questions that have their locus in subjectivity, such as Alexander and Mohanty's query about the "kinds of transformative practices . . . needed in order to develop non-hegemonic selves." While the editors of *Feminist Genealogies, Colonial Legacies, Democratic Futures* clearly draw on Foucault, as is evident in their title, they maintain an analysis/narrative of class and colonialism and insist on an agency that is "the conscious and ongoing reproduction of the terms of one's existence while taking responsibility for the process."[76] Furthermore, some discourse tends to drop responsibility out of its processes, providing a convenient exit from interrogations of the privileges of Mastery. The "death of the subject," in effect, displaces ethics—that crucial question of how we all decide to behave. Gone, too, is Sartre's existential freedom (however nauseous) in an existence that precedes essence—a philosophical practice evolved in antifascist struggles.

The subjugated subject does reappear in Foucault's description of the role of the individual in circuits of power: "And not only do individuals circulate between its threads; they are always in the position of simultaneously undergoing and exercising this power. They are not only its inert or consenting target; they are always also the elements of its articulation. In other words, individuals are the vehicles of power, not its points of application."[77] But such a passage deliberately begs the question of agency (as does the work of Judith Butler, who follows Foucault).[78] If I am an individual who is both the target of power and its articulation—in other words, if I am both abuser and abused—what choices does that leave me, and how do I make those choices? The same question can be asked at the collective level. It was the question that Marcuse had begun to ask. Is there a way, a radical practice, by which we can reroute power through the self and through communities or collectivities of selves so that we articulate power differently—in a more egalitarian, a less brutal way? Can we (in the United States) take ourselves out of the addictive and excessive patterns of consumption around which our very physiology is constructed so that people on other continents, or in the neighborhood down the street, may have more chances? From within systems of power, how do we construct nonhegemonic selves?

How *do* we account for the difference, for example, between the white South Africans who became torturers under apartheid, those who sat passively in their homes being protected from communism by the Nationalist/Afrikaner apparatus, and those who joined the African National Congress? What were the ethical effects of choices, individual and collective, in any of these camps? This inquiry is exactly what South Africa's Truth and Reconciliation Commission spent thirty months sorting through, questions elided in the strictly disciplinary regimes of discursive analysis. Questions such as these require a different kind of insurrectionary knowledge of the (inter)self, disguised by the functionalist or systematic theory of discourse. To that knowledge I now want to turn in this chapter and in our subsequent journeys.

TOWARD A DIFFERENT METAPHYSIC

I had almost foundered on the shores of Introduction to Philosophy back in my undergraduate days. But other solutions were a few miles, if not blocks, away—for instance, at the Dexter Avenue Baptist Church in downtown Montgomery. There in 1955, African Americans had launched the bus boycott and thus the Civil Rights movement, walking rather than riding home from the neighborhoods where they worked, many of which were the very neighborhoods I wandered. They modeled a different kind of engagement with the world, as voiced by the black woman who declared at the end of a long day, "My feet is tired, but my soul is rested." Also, an alternative apprehension of sensuous reality had come to me as a child, in the wet swish of grass on bare feet in the summertime, the hum of the ocean's swell before it embraced me, the tremor of a tadpole's tail in the stream's flow: a countervailing experience of ecstasy that always balanced my anguished speculations.

In the seventies, I was lucky to come out while lesbians of color were mapping a different set of starting points for political work. When Chicana lesbians Cherríe Moraga and Gloria Anzaldúa published *This Bridge Called My Back: Radical Writings by Women of Color* in 1981,[79] I had been doing lesbian-feminist work for four years as part of *Feminary*, a little magazine run by a collective of southern lesbians. *This Bridge* consolidated the "development of women of color as a new political subject" (Angela Davis) and confirmed a multiracial feminism that dealt with race, class, gender, *and* sexuality as "simultaneous oppressions." *This Bridge* incorporated and included "A Black Feminist Statement" from the Combahee River Collective, a black feminist group in Boston formed in 1974. Citing its roots in both the movements for black liberation and feminism's second wave, Combahee's statement announced: "We are actively committed to struggling against racial, sexual, heterosexual, and class oppression and see as our particular task the development of integrated analysis and practice based upon the fact that the major systems of oppression are interlocking."[80]

Moraga makes clear in the book's preface that it was her passion for women that galvanized her to search for and gather together the writings in *This Bridge*: "What drew me to politics was my love of women. . . . I took my lesbianism that seriously."[81] From *This Bridge* emerge women's voices from America's internal colonies, a melding together of the diversely radical subjectivities of women of color. Such intersubjectivity occurs within and across the anthology's offerings: "I am a wind-swayed bridge, a crossroads inhabited by whirlwinds . . . *a third-world lesbian with Marxist and mystical leanings*," Anzaldúa explains. "I believe that by changing ourselves we change the world, that traveling El Mundo Zurdo path is the path of a two-way movement—a going deep into the self and an expanding out into the world, a simultaneous recreation of the self and a reconstruction of society. And yet I am confused as to how to accomplish this."[82]

Both Anzaldúa and Moraga are clear, however, that the task of simultaneously recreating the self and reconstructing society requires a deeply female spirituality. By now, the master-slave chasm has refracted itself into myriad divisions—"we let color, class and gender separate us from those who would be kindred spirits"—and what is called for is to assume "the enormous contradiction in being a bridge" over multiple chasms.[83] In the preface, Moraga struggles with and against the internalized voices that would have her "talking more 'materialistically' about the oppression of women of color," that tell her she "should be plotting out a 'strategy' for Third World Revolution." But she persists: "What I really want to write about is faith. . . . Believing that we have the power to actually transform our experience, change our lives, save our lives. . . . It is the faith of activists I am talking about."[84]

Women of color here relocate spirituality as a generative part of the dialectic. In her own prescient turning away from the metanarratives of liberation, Moraga anticipates the evolution from "Third World feminism" to a multicultural feminism, in Ella Shohat's assessment, that "signals a different historical moment."[85]

I consider myself lucky that it was a multicultural feminism into which I emerged as a lesbian in the late 1970s. This feminism allowed me to acknowledge both the realities of the racism of my childhood and adolescence and the power of my own female and lesbian sexuality. It also led me toward an understanding of class and colonialism, pointing a way out of the blind alley that was Europe and the dead end of unexamined whiteness. *Feminary* was part of a network of feminist presses and magazines, and through that network I became friends with Barbara Smith, Cherríe Moraga, Dorothy Allison, and Elly Bulkin (all connected with the New York–based *Conditions* magazine) and with many, many more remarkable women, such as Harriet Desmoines and Catherine Nicholson from the Charlotte-based *Sinister Wisdom*. Multicultural feminism held white women accountable, and I was lucky to have many white lesbian friends who responded seriously to expectations from lesbians of color of both antiracist solidarity and serious efforts toward transforming white subjectivity and practice. *Born to Belonging*, in fact, is only my latest effort to respond in faith to this charge.

If multicultural feminism emerged collectively from communities of color in the 1970s and 1980s, Audre Lorde provided one of its most compelling expressions. "The master's tools cannot dismantle the master's house," Lorde explained. Although I did not realize it at the time, she answered Descartes and Hegel, Freud and Marx, Memmi and Fanon, providing one powerful poet-warrior's articulation of the emergence of female (inter)subjects as the social actors with the greatest potential to create a more humane future. In "Poetry Is Not a Luxury," Audre Lorde rewrote Descartes's *cogito, ergo sum*: "The white fathers told us: I think, therefore I am. The Black mother within each of us—the poet—whispers in our dreams: I feel, therefore I can be free. Poetry coins the language to express and charter this revolutionary demand, the implementation of that freedom."[86] So much for Descartes, and for subsequent tortured efforts to negotiate the rational while the alternative, the emotional, was cast as irrationally primitive.

For Lorde, feeling was the realm of the self, which she never assumed to be unitary or univocal, and the erotic was feeling at its deepest level—feeling that assumed interconnection. Emotion, for her, was not the antithesis of reason, but rather led to the forming of new ideas: "As they become known to and accepted by us, our feelings and the honest exploration of them become sanctuaries and spawning grounds for the most radical and daring of ideas." Like Marcuse, Audre Lorde seeks to get down to the generative level of species being, and like Marcuse she links this level to the power of the erotic. Unlike Marcuse, however, she does not conceive of humans as primarily rational beings. For Lorde, it is emotion that opens up into the realm of the spirit, and emotion that is politically and psychically generative. Poetry is the language both of feeling and of the future—"not only dream and vision [but] . . . the skeleton architecture for our lives. . . . [Poetry] lays the foundation for a future of change, a bridge across our fears of what has never been before."[87]

It is only in the present moment that transformative reconfigurations of self can occur, and feeling is a sign of our being in this present moment—specifically, a sign that we are bringing the past (with its pain) into the present, thereby making the future fuller and more accessible. Lorde insists on the necessity of deep psychic work that can get at the generative base of action: work focused both on the external sources of exploitation and on the ways in which exploitation has been internalized. This is a process of continuing revolution, the emotional and spiritual work that helps to shift our species being and to produce a deepened humanity.

Possibility is neither forever nor instant. It is not easy to sustain belief in its efficacy. We can sometimes work long and hard to establish one beachhead of real resistance to the deaths we are expected to live, only to have that beachhead assaulted or threatened by those canards we have been socialized to fear, or by the withdrawal of those approvals that we have been warned to seek for safety. Women see ourselves diminished or softened by the falsely benign accusations of childishness, of nonuniversality, of changeabilitiy, of sensuality [of Otherness].[88]

But Lorde insists on the deep psychic work that gets to the generative base (as Marcuse also invoked) of action, and does not hide in the superstructure of manifestation and reaction: "And who asks the question: am I altering your aura, your ideas, your dreams, or am I merely motivating you to temporary and reactive action? And even though the latter is no mean task, it is one that must be seen within the context of a need for true alteration of the very foundations of our lives." This is a process of continuing revolution, the psychic and spiritual work that helps to shift our species being and to produce a deepened humanity.[89]

Women of color or Third World women like Audre Lorde have led in (re)situating an emotional praxis in the realm of the spiritual, turning political analysis into poetry. Gloria Hull's recent book *Soul Talk* identifies 1981 as a founding moment in a new African American women's spirituality, drawing on interviews with Alice Walker, Toni Cade Bambara, and Toni Morrison.[90] Jacqui Alexander's latest book, *Pedagogies of Crossing*, also reflects the maturation of a spiritual praxis that began to emerge for her when she read *This Bridge*.[91] At about the same period, Lorde wrote her amazing essay "The Uses of the Erotic: The Erotic as Power." In the briefest of spaces, she rejected Freud's dichotomy between the erotic and culture and placed the erotic as a praxis to overcome alienation (from work and from species being) as Marx had explained it. To do this, however, required moving beyond what had become a too-binding distinction between material (base) and spiritual (superstructure). It required understanding the link between self and spirit and understanding the spiritual as a source of revolutionary, transformative power: "The dichotomy between the spiritual and the physical is also false, resulting from an incomplete attention to our erotic knowledge. For the bridge which connects them is formed by the erotic—the sensual—those physical, emotional, and psychic expressions of what is deepest and strongest and richest within each of us, being shared: the passions of love in its deepest meaning."[92] For Audre Lorde, the self is a self in reciprocity, and sexuality in its most potent form is a joy of sharing that bridges the sharers and lessens the threat of their differences.

Marx envisioned that, in seizing the means of production, the dictatorship of the proletariat would also alter the human nature that economic production shaped. He conceived of the result as "new socialist man." Fanon affirmed that a part of decolonization was the decolonization of the self, but it was a masculine self he had in mind, resuscitated through revolutionary violence. Memmi as well anticipated the emergence of "the new man" on the "day oppression ceases," although he was not sanguine about what such emergence involved: "The colonized lives for a long time before we see that really new man."[93] For Audre Lorde, women would lead in these rehumanizing processes, and decolonization was necessary for all the aspects of the self. "There are no new ideas still waiting in the wings to save us as women, as human," she wrote. "There are only old and forgotten ones, new combinations, extrapolations and recognitions from within ourselves—along with renewed courage to try them out."[94] It was clear to Lorde that such work drew on a different consciousness embedded in a different metaphysic, a consciousness that was a source of transformative, of revolutionary, power; a spirituality for which the erotic provided a profound expression.

My effort in this genealogy is not to "restore a figure of a choosing subject—humanist"—as Judith Butler disdains.[95] It *is* to retain a figure of a choosing subject—*human*, its South African expression ubuntu. How else can I continue to answer the question from which it was too easy to squirm away, the question that Audre always asked of her audiences: "I am doing my work, are you doing yours?" It also seems to me that Lorde's work has dropped too easily out of many projects of queer theory that have been elaborated since her death.

It was these insights and this charge that Audre Lorde best articulated for me at a formative time, that I took recently on my travels to different continents and cultures. She taught me to look for sources of power in the spiritual, and sources of the spiritual in the cultural, in a spirit of accountability. I have tried to take these gifts along with what other cultural baggage I have packed on my travels, these journeys to belonging on the cusp of a different era and a new century.[96]

2

BEIJING

Mao, the Tao, and the Fourth World Conference on Women

Revolution can change everything.
—MAO ZEDONG

The world is sacred. It can't be improved.
—TAO TE CHING

THE huge China Air jet took off near midnight Sunday morning from New York, following the earth's arc as it rolled eastward beneath us, darkness within darkness extending the night. It caught the lighted curve of dawn at 6:00 A.M. in Anchorage, ten hours into the flight. Later that morning, we crossed the international dateline, Sunday suddenly Monday, our craft a silver needle stitching the sun above the Bering Strait. When we debarked for customs in Shanghai, unfolding limbs and climbing up out of our smell, my first view of China was not the soft implacable countenance of Chairman Mao but the Marlboro Man, too butch in his denim jacket and chin notched to his Naugahyde face. Then we were back in our seats, the plane mounted the sky, turned away from the sea, and headed north.

Its passengers were among the fifty thousand people converging on Beijing for the United Nations Fourth World Conference on Women, which would turn out to be the largest gathering of diverse women in the history of the world. We were meeting twenty years after the 1975 First World Conference on Women in Mexico City helped galvanize a transnational feminism led increasingly by women of color in both north and south—a movement that grew steadily through meetings in Copenhagen and Nairobi. By 1990 any global consideration of the environment, or social development, or children's issues, or human rights took into account women's perspectives.[1] The draft of the Beijing Platform for Action declared bodaciously: "The

NGO Forum rejects the current economic paradigm . . . because it is inherently detrimental to the rights of women." The Marlboro Man in Shanghai made the triumph of the market obvious enough, emblem as he was of China's oxymoronic market socialism, the dreaded capitalist road ushered in by Premier Deng Xiaoping after Mao's death in 1976 ended the Cultural Revolution.

Now China stretched to our vast left and south, four million square miles. In the agricultural plains of the Chang (Yangtze) and Huang (Yellow) Rivers,[2] irrigation systems were worked for centuries by *koo lis*, managed by mandarins, and ruled by emperors, river currents fluid as melting ice in their receptive valleys. The steppes stretched west and south to mountains where pilgrims climbed freed from desire, bandits marauded, and Mao retreated with the ragtag nucleus of the Red Army. He was certain that China's fate was in the hands of its peasants, whatever Marx discerned from the library of the British Museum or Stalin declared from the USSR about the industrial working class as the revolutionary vanguard. And his peasant army did, indeed, make the 4,000-mile-long march across eons of snow-peaked mountains, into eras of swamps, to face the Japanese, then defeat the Guomindang and create the People's Republic of China by midcentury.

In my briefcase was the draft of a speech for a plenary conference on the rise of conservatism. I was invited because I had worked for a decade combating Ku Klux Klan and neo-Nazi movements in North Carolina. I was an organizer raised (as the jacket of my last book politely phrased it) in a "deeply conservative white Alabama family." I flew to China with a heavy heart. I had stood too often on bloody ground.

One day it was a field out from St. Pauls, North Carolina, where neo-Nazis rallied and where one Halloween eve an unidentified assailant dumped the body of Joyce Sinclair, a black woman recently promoted to a supervisory job in a plant. She had been kidnapped from her home by the Klanlike redundancy of a "white man wearing white," leaving her four-year-old daughter sitting on the steps. Another day the ground I stood on was a gravel driveway in front of a small cinder block building. It had been the Shelby III Adult Bookstore until neo-Nazis broke in one midnight and shot five guys in the head to "avenge Yahweh on homosexuals," slipping in blood, viscous, crimson, as they exited the carnage. Then there was the spot in Statesville where the White Knights of Liberty rallied in a suburban community, leaving a cross lying on the ground between weekend rallies, ready for the next outburst. There was the night of the full moon standing in the street outside the jailhouse in Robeson County; inside Eddie Hatcher and Tim Jacobs had seized the newspaper staff as hostages in an attempt to publicize what they saw as the deadly racist complicity of local law enforcement in the county's drug trade. That was a month or so before a midnight assault on a Native American candidate for Robeson County district attorney, three shotgun blasts through his kitchen door that spun a body that was dead before it hit the linoleum.

In the 1980s the proliferation of far-right movements accompanied homelessness as a new identity. Ronald Reagan was elected president on a platform of deficit reduction. Then his administration pumped up the deficit from $79 billion to $155 billion and the national debt from $1 trillion to $2.6 trillion with inflated military spending. Trying to keep up with this arms race bankrupted the Soviet Union, ending the Cold War. It came at the expense of programs for women and children and the poor. Clinton's election in 1992 also left the Democrats with neither funds nor spine to argue for government's role in protecting its most vulnerable citizens. The eighties was a decade of scapegoating gay people and blocking their civil rights with ballot initiatives in states all over the country. As women met in China, the U.S. Congress boosted by extremists elected in 1994 was considering Newt Gingrich's ultra-right "Contract with America," its cornerstone welfare reform. The most vulnerable women and their children would be thrown to the mercy of the market to look for low-wage jobs supposedly created by the trickle-down of unprecedented wealth. Clinton's most progressive policy, health care reform, had gone down in flames along with gays in the military, while his Democratic centrist policies on prisons, police, and welfare reform thrived. This neoliberalism, the peculiar equation of a free market economy with a democratically free society, had caught me off guard.

Let's just say I was bummed.

But the Fourth World Conference on Women in China helped me frame a brutal century at its end as it brought into stark relief the possibilities and dangers of a new era. It also gave me a new kind of hope. In 1995, we *were* at a critical juncture in history, as many of the women at the conference made clear. China's metamorphosis toward the market after Mao's death in 1976 was followed in the 1980s by Mikhail Gorbachev's *perestroika* (economic restructuring) and *glasnost* (political reforms) that signaled the beginning of the collapse of the USSR that brought the Soviet bloc finally out of Stalinist repression and into the vagaries of the market. Sinologist Bruce Cummings in 1983 summarized the effect of these changes on the world's poorest countries: "The Maoist path, it now seems, not only failed but sounded the death knell for any truly self-reliant path to development in our time. Most developing countries now recognize that they must cut deals with world capitalism, usually not on their own terms."[3] With the collapse of communism and the ebbing of Third World liberation movements, a rampant capitalism would inevitably breed other forms of opposition, but on what terms? That was the challenge with which women would grapple.

In a cave, perhaps beneath our plane's shadow, Peking Man (Beijing Person?) had lived as toolmaker and hunter, tending fires kindled by lightning or erupting volcanoes. Were we over the northern wall, each brick mortared with a human life to hold back the hordes of Hun, Mongol, Turk, and Japanese, the grassy steppes, and the Gobi Desert? We landed before darkness caught us, in Beijing, the six-hundred-year-old northern capital, hybrid border city, home to pastoral and nomad Ming and Khan: city of swans.

"We can learn what we did not know," Mao said.

"The more you know," the Tao warned, "the less you understand."[4]

TAXI TO THE TEMPLE OF HEAVEN

Tuesday morning I set out in a taxicab to the Temple of Heaven. The conference did not begin until the next evening, so I thought I might as well start seeing China. The bellhop wrote the name of my destination in Chinese on a small card for the cabbie. Within minutes I was hurtling through the streets of Beijing, joining other tiny cabs, buses, an occasional private car, and the throngs of cyclers who filled the thoroughfares in two- and three-wheeled bikes of every description, carrying families, garbage, produce, merchandise. There are eight million bicycles in Beijing, and they all seemed to be in the street in front of us. At every intersection I held my breath waiting for a bloody pileup. But miraculously the sea of peddlers would part to let us through. I initially attributed this parting of the ways to an automotive tai chi they all understood; but later in the week I began to hear of the wrecks, sometimes the nouveau riche in their newly acquired Jeep Cherokees up against these rusty bicycles, an even worse matchup than a Honda and a Mack truck back home. Along the highway, imperial yellow temple roofs protruded over walls, blurring into newly constructed high-rises. Cab drivers had been warned that all the women at the conference were lesbians who would strip off their blouses and ride bare-breasted through the streets in Beijing taxicabs. If this happened, they were briefed, just throw a blanket over us. Stripping in a taxi cab barreling through Beijing was the last thing this dyke could imagine doing half a world from home.

The cabbie let me off at the corner, and I strolled down a street lined with food and drink vendors and bicycles, the only obvious Westerner in sight. The bus driver on our ride from the airport had told us apartments rented in Beijing for three dollars per month because of government subsidies. There was a noticeable lack of homeless people on the streets or benches and little yet of the huge disparities of wealth and poverty, the apparent despair, so readily visible in U.S. cities, although Chinese millionaires were emerging as a class. The old folks still woke up in the mornings to tai chi while many of the younger ones were converting to aerobics in high heels to the theme of *Rocky*—while back in the U.S. folks were taking up tai chi and meditation in droves trying to find some centeredness in their own hectic, car-driven postmodern lives. On this one street, however, on this one morning, people were going about their business in a city of eleven million without seeming harried.

I paid my admission to the Temple of Heaven and entered the west gate, strolling down a broad walkway lined with trees. Hitting a downdraft of jetlag, I lay on the grass in the shade near a small park to the sound of laughter from young Chinese children playing with their parents or grandparents on swings, slides, and a train going round in circles to the tune of "Dixie." I felt a sudden relaxation as gravity brought the earth up to meet my body, leeching my tiredness into the ground and pulling me deep into sleep. Within ten minutes I woke remarkably rested and began to follow the walkways and signs translated into English. I explored back ways and side buildings with Chinese tourists and even stood in line to climb into a fake emperor's throne to have my picture taken in empress drag for a couple of yuan. I hadn't quite had the nerve to be an emperor for a morning.

Away from the routines and pressures of work, parenting, housework back in Durham, time was slowing down and opening. Intuition, or some other rhythm than habituation, had begun to propel me.

After an hour of wandering, the three-tiered cobalt dome of the Temple of Heaven loomed before me, round, balanced, majestic. It had been built by Yong Le, the first Ming emperor, in the early 1400s, at the same time as the Forbidden City to the west. From that walled city he would journey each winter solstice and climb alone to the topmost terrace of the Altar of Heaven to offer prayers for the year's harvest. The Record of Rites reflected the strong class division: "The ritual does not descend down to the common people; punishment does not extend up to the *chun tzu* [the nobles]."[5] The temple embodied the hierarchical cosmology of a vast, self-sufficient agrarian empire already two thousand years past China's transition from primitive communism to class society. The history of the middle kingdom played out on a huge land mass in relative geographic isolation. Bounded by oceans, mountains, and deserts, the agrarian empires were conquered by, assimilated with, and reasserted themselves over nomadic northern invaders, periods of centralization interspersed with disintegration, but with a remarkable degree of continuity through its cultural and political institutions.

I headed up the nine stairs to the second-tier square terrace, where the four-cornered earth joined the circular heaven of the Red Altar, with its nine rings of nine stones. In the first millennium B.C., raw silk spun from silkworms already clothed emperors and concubines and took the ink of artists and writers. A script both pictorial and ideographic allowed for fine writing and detailed record-keeping and spurred the Chinese to invent paper (and later printing). Silk became one of the country's most sought-after exports, later carried west by camels along the Silk Road at the top of the world. Confucius, who died in 479 B.C., gave expression to the patriarchal Chinese order: "In universe, heaven is the directing force; and in the family, father is the directing authority. In the state the position of the sovereign corresponds to that of heaven in the universe, and of father in the family."[6]

From the third terrace, where the emperor ascended for yearly prayers, I could see back over the trees in the park. Here the emperors united earthly powers with those of heaven. The first emperor, Qin Shihuang, who reunited China in 221 B.C., created a unified political state with a highly centralized government by which the emperor would dominate Chinese life until Sun Yatsen's Nationalist Party overthrew the last emperor in 1911. Qin Shihuang also imposed a single harsh legal code, a legalism that periodically surfaced in Chinese rulers as totalitarianism and cruelty. He marshaled forced labor to build the fourteen hundred miles of the Great Wall from coast to interior and banned most books, to the horror of Confucian intellectuals. The succeeding Han dynasty softened the control of administrative machinery and reintroduced Confucian tradition and a civil service exam for its mandarins in the service of the newly consolidated empire. Chinese emperors built as often in wood as marble, knowing that their immortality rested in the palace archives maintained by succeeding empires. While Mao Zedong had disdained the Confucian order and the imperial system that spread about me, the Chinese Communist Party had drawn on its legacy of centralization and shown its own streak of cruelty.

Was there a deeper source of this layered calm than the elaborate temple, its structure redolent of a hierarchy that gave only the emperor direct access to God? And what God, anyway? The question surfaced on the third terrace of the Temple of Heaven. Right-wing preachers proliferated back home, railing at us homosexuals, their gods cast suspiciously in the image of their own narrow minds. Their rantings were enough to give God a bad name, certainly in the minds of many of the homosexuals against whom they directed their holy ire, for many years me included.

In China, belief in a supreme God had emerged about the same time it had for the Hebrews in the Fertile Crescent when under the leadership of Moses they fled Egyptian slavery. When the Zhou dynasty overthrew the oppressive, slaveholding Shang at the end of the millennium (1027), the Zhou interpreted their victory as the "mandate of heaven," and God (or Ti'en) became moral and universal, not merely a personality God who controlled nature and human destiny as the patron of a particular family or class.[7] I could happily admit justice as an attribute of heaven, I reflected. But these personality Gods tend toward the temperamental, a bit too prone to judgment, and often flailing around as destructively as we mortals do. When my older brother Tim started having nightmares as a child, my grandmother advised my mother to omit reading the Old Testament each night. A God who sent bears to eat children was a bit too severe a fare, she counseled, for sensitive young minds. Tim had recently been diagnosed with colon cancer, caught in a nightmare's bear hug.

Amid all the ornate grandeur of the Temple of Heaven, I recognized my own sensibility more Lao-tzu than Confucius. If Confucius had captured the practical side of the Chinese sensibility, Taoism — the one indigenous Chinese religion — reflected its intuitive and metaphysical side, beyond conventional knowledge and the abstraction of language. Taoism sweetened Buddhism. The Taoist trust in spontaneous human nature made the austere Indian Buddhism more human when it arrived in the fifth century B.C. from India, developing into the stream of Mahayana Buddhism, then, in China and Japan, into Zen.

Could a person step back from her own mind? Lao-tzu asked. Could she allow things to come and go? Could she love the world as herself?[8]

At the bottom of the steps to the three terraces once again, I moved toward the exit. Off to the side, on cobblestones, two boys were spraying each other with water from red hoses that met in the center between them as a mist.

My own spirituality had evolved within and in defiance of the small, segregated First Methodist Church in Tuskegee, Alabama. Martin Luther King spoke of the "anesthetizing security of the stained glass windows" in the segregated southern church, in his jeremiad from the Birmingham jail.[9] But I had watched the morning sun filter through the windows along each side of our sanctuary, where in the last window on the right, Jesus stood knocking at a wooden door, his head cocked to one side listening. That image carried a painful irony for me in those years when white church members locked our doors to the black and white demonstrators on the steps outside. This alienation amplified in later decades as I came to see the church's sexism and as most denominations denied full access to lesbians and gay men. That church had broken my heart, but it had not anesthetized me.

My mother also shaped my spirituality profoundly. She was a teacher and a housewife in a small, torn town. "What to do with a heart always crying after lost desires?" one of her poems began. She kept up with the world through the Women's Missionary Society and periodically fled the church in despair when the congregation voted to buy a second refrigerator or to carpet the sanctuary again rather than send money overseas for mission work. "Give me your Christ," she had quoted Gandhi to me on particularly bad days, "but keep your church." African American theologian and mystic Howard Thurman, who traveled to India two decades before Martin Luther King's similar pilgrimage, put a more sophisticated language to his own adolescent crisis: "Why is it that Christianity seems impotent to deal radically, and therefore effectively, with the issues of discrimination and injustice on the basis of race, religion and national origin [And gender? And sexuality? I added]. Is this impotency due to a betrayal of the genius of the religion, or is it due to a basic weakness in the religion itself?"[10]

I had spent a good many Sundays as a child in classes with teachers who loved me, and on pews waiting for salvation through sermons whose only redeeming feature was their brevity. I learned that the main tenets of our faith as Methodists were itinerate preachers (sent packing at the slightest mention of love and racial justice) and a belief in backsliding. Years later, a perpetually itinerate backslider, I saw a rainbow in a drop of water on a grass blade and realized that revelation was, as much as anything, a matter of focus.

I had run up against questions of human evil and human good, of human depravity and human courage, of the violation of human community and its assertion in the face of all odds in my political work, questions that were as much spiritual as they were political. I had worked across North Carolina, in small towns and middle-sized cities and in the countryside, in communities with organized Klan or neo-Nazi activity where outbreaks of racist or homophobic violence often left survivors terrified and isolated when law enforcement and other local institutions, such as churches, initially refused to respond. Driving down interstates or back roads at various hours of light and dark, a spider crisscrossing a complicated terrain, I felt what we were up against as a web of energy that ran through humans and institutional structures, as if it were some obverse to what King called the "inescapable network of mutuality." The manifestation was violence, but the energy was fear. It was this energy that was at issue, more than the individual people who manifested it.

I also worked with those people across the state who were willing to risk some of their own very relative safety to address violence and its causes, to assert bonds of human community and connection in the face of palpable danger, and I recognized this energy as love. I had seen survivors and the families of victims in communities of color draw on sources of power beyond themselves for courage and for hope when the political and economic power in the local terrain not only did not acknowledge but also seemed complicit in patterns of violence. In those encounters, I was vicariously experiencing something I began to identify as faith.

Here in China I was as far away from home as I had ever been—in fact, about as far away as I could possibly get, given the earth's curve back toward home. I was going to appreciate the perspective, a chance to look again at the familiar from this distance. Approaching my fiftieth year and on the steps to the Temple of Heaven, I knew that I preferred not the emperor center stage, but the tiny human figure in those ink-brushed drawings of the artists of the Tang, in the corner dwarfed by a landscape that was itself as spare and deliberate as the Buddha's mind. Knock and it shall be opened, Jesus had promised democratically in the morning sun that shown through vermilion and ochre stained glass, even as the doors of our church were locked against the demonstrators outside them. To seek *is* to find that which is already present within you, the Tao had already clarified four hundred years before.[11]

Mao had interjected his preference for insurrection into the stasis of empire epitomized by the temple: "In thousands of years of Han history, there have been hundreds of peasant insurrections against the regime of darkness imposed by the landlords and nobility. As for the dynastic changes, *each and every one* has succeeded *only* by the force of the peasant uprisings."[12] Mao had ridden the whirlwind of revolutionary change in the twentieth century.

Was there, I wondered, a tao to Mao?

DEALING WITH A VERY DIFFERENT WORLD

"The meaning of our love for women is what we have constantly to expand," the phrase kept floating through my head, the title of an Adrienne Rich essay circa 1977, as I negotiated the muddy but vibrant scene at the conference site at Huairou, for the Forum on Women for NGOs (nongovernmental organizations). The official UN conference to hammer out the Platform for Action was back in Beijing. Tens of thousands of women thronging around me had me flashing back to when lesbian-feminism was declared (by lesbian feminists) a "wholly new force in history," its goal "not equality but utter transformation." Adrienne Rich had urged us not to withdraw from the "immense, burgeoning diversity of the global women's movement" that moved vibrantly around me now.[13] The scene around me took me back to the day of the "woman identified woman," when we lesbians considered ourselves the "rage of all women condensed to the point of explosion."[14] It took me back to the speech when Audre Lorde, newly diagnosed with breast cancer, electrified us: "Your silence will not protect you," as she continued to teach us about honoring differences.[15] And the differences hit. "With such grace, such blind faith this commitment to women in the [U.S.] feminist movement grew to be exclusive and reactionary."[16] Cherríe Moraga lamented in *This Bridge Called My Back* the grief I myself came to feel as I saw too closely the power of racism and class biases explode the lesbian community. But in Beijing now I felt all this history there with me. As another chance?

The bus let us off on Youth Road, the main drag of Huairou, a self-styled Chinese conference and resort area to boost tourism, in a rural county fifty kilometers from Beijing. Along Youth Road was a bank, post office, radio/TV center, and various restaurants. A Health and Happiness Body Building Center, a multistory shopping complex, and a disco are recent additions to lure *da kuan*, the nouveau riche of China's market economy. Undoubtedly, the China Organizing Committee disrupted things when it announced the previous spring that it was shifting the forum sight from Beijing to Huairou, an hour's bus ride away. The Willow Club—which had been promised for the plenaries—loomed, a half-completed concrete hulk over the other buildings. A typhoon off the coast of Japan that hit the second day of the conference periodically dumped sheets of rain. All of that notwithstanding, what a remarkable community spread out on all sides of me.

The conference site stretched between Youth Road and the Huairou Reservoir, a large lake to the west. Classrooms and exhibition halls held many of the conference workshops in the center of the site. Each continent had a huge tent, the scene of constant conversations and workshops and a fount of information on women's issues in that region. Seven smaller diversity tents were placed in the northwest quadrant, and here the lesbian tent was pitched alongside tents for grassroots women, women with disabilities, older women, indigenous women, youths, and refugees. All along the pathways—now lined with black plastic because of the mud—were food, drink, and craft vendors, mostly the local variety but also the omnipresence of Coca-Cola, with its familiar flowing signature. In the parasol area, bright umbrellas covered hundreds of round tables, offering a place to sit, eat, talk, or rest. Four onsite hotels lined a road and looked out over the reservoir, giving their inhabitants access to all the conference events that Beijing commuters lacked. Ten thousand young Chinese were working as volunteers at the Huairou site, sleeping twelve to a room and rising at 4:30 A.M. for long days helping staff the global village of thirty thousand sometimes disgruntled women—twice as many as the last conference in Nairobi and far more than the Chinese had anticipated.[17]

I soon found that the conference program, stretched out over this muddy site, could be overwhelming: with its offering of workshops and cultural events on a huge range of topics from every region of the globe, plenaries each morning in which four thousand women jammed into a hall made for fifteen hundred, press conferences, demonstrations, informal discussions, all of it advertised by fliers posted along the walls. The bus from our hotel arrived at 9:00 A.M., making it hard to get into plenaries and into the first workshops. The last bus for Beijing left at 7:30 P.M., so those of us staying in Beijing would miss evening cultural events. Choosing any one activity in an hour meant neglecting at least six other good options, and if the first choice had canceled or was already full by the time I arrived, often the other options were on the other side of the site. But these difficulties seemed minor given the richness of all that was available.

The first day of the forum made clear that we were meeting at a critical historic juncture, one fraught with crisis and opportunity. Women from all over the world rapidly set forth in plenary speeches and workshops how the dizzying, unrestrained expansion of transnational corporate activity left nations increasingly vulnerable. Marx had described the power of the market 150 years earlier: "It has resolved personal worth into exchange value, and in the place of numberless indefeasible chartered freedoms, has set up that single, unconscionable freedom—Free Trade." He had predicted that the bourgeoisie would drown "the most heavenly ecstasies of religious fervor . . . in the icy waters of egotistical calculation"; but in the late twentieth century another rapid expanse of capital was creating resistance from those heavenly ecstasies, in the form of fundamentalist movements.[18]

This is a time of transition, Charlotte Bunch of the Global Center for Women's Leadership declared, "when the ways of governing, the ways of living and doing business, the ways of interacting amongst nations and people are in flux."[19] Eva Friedlander, one of the forum organizers, explained: "This forum . . . deals with a very different world than that which existed the time of the Nairobi meeting [ten years ago]."[20] "In Nairobi we used words like *patriarchy*, *capitalism*, and *imperialism*," echoed Irene Santiago. "Spotting enemies was very clear."[21] What remains now, all agreed, are the two big issues: poverty and power.

Gita Sen explained how Third World women organizers and economists had begun in 1985 to map key forces shaping the character of women's lives in this era. The World Bank and the International Monetary Fund, U.S.-controlled global financial institutions, had encouraged leaders of newly independent countries to borrow huge amounts of money for questionable development that did not yield the projected growth. Unable to pay off the debts, the bank imposed structural adjustments when a country's leaders went to refinance. These forced adjustments included lowering their wages, relaxing environmental standards, and selling off precious nationalized resources. Thus burgeoning multinational corporations gained access to natural resources and cheap labor with little constraint. Countries just emerging from colonial status entered a new debt peonage as their leaders sold their souls to the company store, creating a "growing crisis of debt, of food, of fuel and water, and of livelihood." They experienced the immediate effects of "a development model [that places] much higher priority on economic growth over human well-being."[22] The result was only the latest huge transfer of wealth in a long history of colonialism and imperialism. "Between 1960 and 1991, the richest 20 percent increased their share of global income from 70 percent to 85 percent. During the same period the poorest 20 percent declined from 2.3 percent to a minuscule 1.4 percent.

Today more than three-quarters of global income belongs to only one-quarter of the world's population, mostly in the North," Winnie Byanyima succinctly explained the results.[23] These structural adjustment policies were one tool to bring poor countries into line. The other was low-intensity warfare against Marxist insurgencies in countries like El Salvador. Reagan's Cold War spending supported Latin American dictatorships and helped bankrupt the Soviet Union at the same time that it diverted resources from social spending within the United States.

"The Third World—as we used to call it in those simple days of Nairobi—now finds itself almost incapable of acting in global economic fora in a concerted manner." Many voices elaborated the same story. "The demise of the socialist world . . . [and of] superpower politics has opened the way for shifting alliances and new lines of differentiation and conflict." Structural adjustment policies acting as "storm troopers of the globalization process . . . have broken the capacity of governments to impact this process." But they have not "undermined the repressive capacity of the state, which continues to repress its people—particularly when they attack the forces of globalization," Sen explained. The result is new forms of violence—economies of "drugs, arms, and money-laundering . . . and the connected violence in communities, in the street, by the state, and in our homes."[24]

The end of the Cold War has brought a hot peace, Charlotte Bunch explained. "The anticipated peace dividend has turned instead to increased racial, ethnic, religious and gender-based conflict and violence." We are told we have two options, Bunch elaborated: We can "accept the global economy with its homogenized consumerist culture" that sacrifices difference, or we can return to "traditional culture" in which "local identities . . . involve more and more narrow definitions of who they are and what they are about." The second option involves "a narrow, nationalistic ethnic fragmentation into separatist enclaves where all 'others' are demonized and seen as less human." Bunch concluded, "Women are the most important new global force on the horizon in the world today, with the potential to create a more humane future." She called for a third option, an alternative from corporate globalization or rigidly traditional cultural identities. It should be based on belief and practice that "there can be diverse cultures and ethnic identities living together, that there can be tolerant religions that don't have to be in opposition to one another, that we can live in solidarity and respect with those who are different."[25]

Strangely, the accumulating evidence of global patriarchal brutality, old as Peking Man, and the more recent brutality of the unbridled market, were not weighing on me as heavily as they might have. The fact that so many women from points all over the earth had descended in our silver birds to this one teeming muddy place, living brilliantly together for this one week, began to give me more of something I could only identify as hope. It was a web of mutuality that was here in this one part of China this month, quivering, singing, inescapable. As the more linear narratives of revolution had fractured or failed, something more multifocaled and weblike seemed to be taking their place.

FITTING LANGUAGE TO THE SLIPPERY CATEGORY
OF SEXUAL IDENTITY

In my first days in China, I was working madly to finish my speech with the help of a new friend, Laura Flanders, and her laptop. I had met her in a cohort of New Yorkers the night I had arrived in China and found myself assigned to the XiYuan Hotel, a four-star joint venture between Australia and the Chinese government. It was located in a bevy of hotels in the northwest quadrant of Beijing, near the China zoo. The time shift was twelve hours from back home, literally the difference in night and day. I had awakened, disoriented, from a deep sleep after my arrival and descended in a daze to the lobby, to one side a buffet/restaurant, to the other a quartet playing an odd assortment of songs from Mozart to "Home on the Range" to "We Three Kings."

At a tap on my shoulder, I recognized Laura as the tall tousle-haired woman in the black pants and blouse. We had met the spring before at a conference on the queer left, what we were now calling those of us who link our fate as homosexuals to an encompassing movement for justice, a transformation of the culture not to be confused with assimilation. It is at times a discouragingly minority view in the gay community, considering the origins of gay politics that June night in 1969 when, grief-stricken over the recent death of Judy Garland and pushed over the edge by the summer heat, drag queens and stone butches at the Stonewall took on the New York police when the cops raided them one time too many. I was relieved to accept Laura's invitation to join her traveling companions Vivian Stromberg, Lilliana Cortes, and Helen Marden from MADRE, a New York–based international women's organization.[26] All in all, they seemed a lively crew, and by the end of dinner I had perked up about the prospects of the XiYuan as I figured out the bill and bid them good night.

We both spent Tuesday afternoon (I had just returned from the Temple of Heaven) in Laura's room swapping off on her laptop. Out her thirteenth floor window, the city receded rapidly in a haze of pollution, the legacy of China's rapid industrialization in the first years of the People's Republic. Beijing was now an industrial center, producing iron, steel, cotton textiles, and machines. At a stopping place, Laura generously ceded me the laptop. I tweaked the next paragraph of my text: "My grounding is from within the United States, but the U.S. experience both creates and echoes similar phenomena in Canada and Europe."

Although the task of my plenary was to examine the global force of the rise of conservatism, *conservatism* did not adequately capture what was happening globally, if it indicated relationship to the past, to tradition, the preservation of an existing order, or a distrust of change. Today new computer technologies drive the information age, like the steam engine once did the industrial age. Money has become electronic impulse, creating tremendous capital mobility that once again reshapes the globe in its own image. Where once a tax on changing currency (say from dollars to pesos) had made such exchanges more costly, its recent removal meant that speculators could buy and sell currencies, destabilizing whole countries' economies. It also meant that investors could pull out their money overnight, leaving whole regions in collapse—as in the Asian crisis, the Brazilian crisis, the Russian collapse. Free trade, I was coming to understand, is based on the freedom of capital, not of people.

"Permanently revolutionary" was Marx's description of capital—in its power to "[push] beyond national boundaries and prejudices, beyond the deification of nature and the inherited, self-sufficient satisfaction of existing needs . . . and the reproduction of the traditional way of life."[27] Formerly, the comparative advantage of poor countries was raw material exported to mother countries for manufacture—not that it was really an advantage to those countries, former colonies, stripped of their wealth and natural resources; for example, all their gold or mahogany forests or topsoil. Left in a state of permanent underdevelopment, now their comparative advantage is also cheap labor. So jobs flee to the Southern Hemisphere for low-wage workers and unregulated environments, and people flood north, where wealth has accumulated. The Rio Grande demarcates one such Third World/First World border, where Mexicans float over on inner tubes and make a run for it before the Immigration and Naturalization Service (INS) snatches them back. They come because in the United States they can make a minimum hourly wage equivalent to what they make in a whole day at home. We are on the cusp of a new era of capitalism, and its speedy progress creates an opposite drag in conservative movements all over the globe. "Elites move forward with their own agendas," I wrote, "conserving power sometimes in some places but expending it in others, always retaking it."

On the hour, Laura turned the television on to CNN, keeping her reporter's eye on the coverage of the conference. In my first call from North Carolina the night before, my partner, Barbara, had worried about my accommodations, given the bleak conditions being described on the news back home. I described the reassuring splendors of the XiYuan, with its extra phone near the toilet and new toothbrush every day. There had also been a steady drumbeat of criticism in the U.S. media about human rights abuses in China.

Laura was working it right into her talk: "So here you are, twenty thousand or more of the world's more rarely heard-from experts, all gathered more or less conveniently in one place. Being discussed here are some of those key issues, some of them the very issues that the boring men in suits discuss on television every night. . . . I turn on my TV in the hotel room and read a U.S. paper over lunch and what do I find? The same U.S. media that remained tight-lipped when Ronald Reagan approved sales of police equipment to China's internal security force, and praised Vice President Bush's visit here in 1985, are now suddenly concerned about security levels and whether or not Hillary Rodham Clinton is disrespecting human rights by coming to a rights conference."[28]

We traded off on the computer, working in a companionable silence broken occasionally by conversation. I was also trying to figure how to include lesbian issues in a discussion of the economy. The struggle to fit language to the slippery category of sexual identity has been a central preoccupation of my life, as it has been of many lesbians and gay men of my generation. As an adolescent, I was not so much out of sight as out of language. I didn't know the word *homosexual* until I read it when I was eleven or twelve, in the early 1960s, in an article in *Life* magazine, one of the first treatments of the urban gay subculture in mainstream media. In the back corner of my brain, it occurred to me that the word might explain a lot.

My problem, at nine and thirteen and twenty, was not that I was not seen, but more that I was not named—or that the names available carried such lethal stigma. Queer: alone, outside community, outside family, outside love. The only one. Genuine invisibility would have been a relief. Instead, I had my painfully visible efforts at invisibility of my far-too-obvious baby butch self. I had my futile efforts to suck all my energy back in: a child of the universe, trying to be a black hole. I had little means to figure the "curious abrupt questions [that] stirred within me," as the great faggot poet of democracy Walt Whitman wrote, questions of how "I had received identity in my body, / that I was I knew was of my body, and what I knew I should be I knew I should be of my body."[29] Belonging begins in the body, a way of belonging to ourselves.

As an adolescent, with no one available to translate for or with me the language of my body, I began to translate it myself into the language of race. African Americans all around me were rising against ontological erasure as much as they were against Jim Crow. "I am an invisible man," Ralph Ellison had begun his famous novel in the setting of my hometown. "I am invisible, understand, simply because people refuse to see me. . . . When they approach me, they see only my surroundings, themselves, or figments of their imagination—indeed, everything and anything except me."[30]

I saw clearly how race and sex and white people's confusions about both were hopelessly intermingled. Even from my segregated family I could see that the black uprising all around me was deeply spiritual in its challenge to the morality of white supremacist culture. But I heard white people defending that culture by attacking the sexual morality of the Civil Rights movement. They dismissed the Selma-to-Montgomery march as an occasion for white nuns to have sex with black men on the state capitol grounds, leaving used condoms in the bushes. Viola Liuzzo, the white woman from Detroit murdered by Klansmen while driving marchers back from Montgomery, was a whore. Even at thirteen, it was clear to me that part of the struggle was over contending views of righteousness: a prurient and constrictive sexual ethic that could be used to justify murder, against an expansive ethic of liberation that was challenging deep violence in the culture. In the years that followed, I have often found myself puzzled and frustrated at how the movement against homophobia and heterosexism and for gay and lesbian liberation could grow up so seemingly separate from the movement against racism and for the liberation of people of color. I knew instinctively the connection—that we were, in Ellison's words, "simply figure[s] in a nightmare which the sleeper tries with all his strength to destroy." I knew it each time people bumped against me and my aching need to convince myself that I "existed in the world, part of the sound and anguish" of having and being a body.[31] I had consistently found the most holistic understandings in the work of lesbians of color, who offered me models of more unified psyches and analyses. Now, drawing on that legacy, I was trying to link visible sexuality with questions of class and capitalism. This was the challenge of my plenary speech.

If my lens was the rise of conservatism and Laura's was media, we were using them to open a similar critique of corporate control and its attendant ills. "In 1986, when we started FAIR," Laura read to me, "a few months after the Nairobi Conference, media institutions were owned by a small and shrinking number of powerful businesses. Now the number's even smaller. In 1986, twenty-nine corporations dominated broadcasting, publishing and cable. By the end of 1993, the number was down to twenty. Some have estimated that before the end of the century, an oligopoly of about half a dozen hugely profitable giant firms will have consolidated control of the mass media worldwide. . . . If current merger plans go ahead, soon two out of three of the world's richest television networks would be controlled by nuclear power companies, both of which have the U.S. military as their most important client." Working with Laura was fun, unexpected companionship in the often bleak business of lefty lesbians tracking right-wing movements.

Over dinner on Thursday evening with the MADRE crowd we discussed how sex was faring in the Platform for Action being hammered out by the official delegates in Beijing. The challenge to capitalism and questions of gender and sexuality were the some of the hottest sections in the platform. Its construction was the result of a remarkable, contentious global consensus process of regional working groups (in Vienna, Argentina and Chile, Jakarta, Dakar, and Amman) and expert working groups on issues such as gender education and training, and women and economic decision making. A remarkable conservative alliance of the Vatican, right-wing Protestant groups, Islamic fundamentalists, and the Chinese government had worked to substitute the word *sex*—by which they meant biologically determined men and women—for *gender*. The word *gender*, they explained, was, among other things, code for homosexuality and for women's equality.

"*Gender* is still in brackets every time it appears in the text," Vivian reported. She was referencing the marks by which sections were placed in question. Two working groups had reconvened in New York at the UN in late July and early August, removing brackets from a number of human rights and economic issues, but leaving issues of gender, sexuality, equity/equality, and health for the ten-day gathering of five thousand official delegates from 189 countries in Beijing.

I listened intently while awkwardly levering a few grains of rice into my mouth with chopsticks. Supposedly the thumb is part of what allowed Homo sapiens an evolutionary edge, but if my skill with chopsticks was any indicator, I was failing to make the Darwinian grade.

We Cannot Live without Our Lives

The Saturday morning of my plenary on the "Rise of Conservatism," I mounted the stage with sweating palms. I had never been translated, simultaneously, into seven languages. I was proud to be part of the strong lesbian presence at the conference. Under the yellow-and-white lesbian tent, we had been networking, meeting in regional groups and panels, caucusing daily at 5:00 P.M., planning a lesbian rights march that would draw five hundred people, and strategizing on how to effect the Platform for Action.

I was happy to find Marta Benavides seated beside me. She was becoming one of my best friends in the Urban-Rural Mission. It was Marta who introduced me to the *Tao Te Ching*, pulling me aside during a meeting to sit on the sofa and read. Her speech, right before mine, was vintage Marta:

> *Buenos días, hermanas y hermanos de todo el mundo.* I am Salvadoran by birth, a citizen of the world, part of the energy of the universe. I am. I celebrate this, and I celebrate that you also are. . . . This twenty-first century is already here, and it is us! There is no way back, no matter what. Because in spite of all kinds of forces which forcibly try to negate us, we without doubt can proclaim: We are! . . . We must seek clarity of purpose, not for the takeover of power, but for the wisdom of knowing how to reach our goal and maintain it. If we want peace, justice and equality in the twenty-first century, we must start living them now. Consistent practice, not political parties or politicians, will illuminate our path. We must choose to live peace, justice and equality every day in all our ways and for all our needs. This is freedom.[32]

After Marta finished, I began: "I am honored and humbled to be speaking to this global body of women," I began. "I am speaking to you as a lesbian, which might accomplish the 'dislodging of the comfortable' that our Moderator has suggested is part of combating conservatism. In any case, I ask of you a sisterly listening."

There, I had said the word *lesbian.* My strategy was generally to come out in the first paragraph and let the chips fall where they may.

> In a world of corporate homogenization and rapid cultural flux—of Ronald McDonald and Coca-Cola on billboards and street corners in cities all over the world—religious fundamentalism is on the rise as people look for security in ancient patriarchal texts, usually the narrowest interpretations of texts most constrictive of women's possibilities and of human sexuality. From my own Christian tradition, for example, there are plenty of passages about love, but fundamentalists go for the ones about abomination every time, and it makes me crazy.

I was relieved when people laughed. At least the interpretation was working, or a huge percentage of the audience understood English.

At a moment of burgeoning liberation, the "New Right" in the United States was born. After Barry Goldwater's devastating electoral defeat in 1964, the Old Right elites saw they needed a populist base and a new façade—after all there are only so many people you can get to vote for making rich people richer.

I did not share with them where I had been in 1964, wearing a long white dress and carrying a red rose in Crampton Bowl in Montgomery, at a Goldwater rally. My father had turned Republican in 1928, at a time when most people would rather vote for a yellow dog than a Republican in the South.

Conservative business nationalist Nelson Hunt in 1970, for example, donated $10 million to Pat Robertson's Christian Broadcast Network, politicizing Robertson and other evangelical TV ministers with issues of abortion, homosexuality, and prayer in schools.

I had come out in the late 1970s, in the intense climate of backlash created by this strategy. The links between racism and homophobia and sexism had been immediately clear to me. It had taken me a while to realize an underlying economic dynamic.

At the moment when the Old Right moved to defend itself against new challenges, corporate officials also made their decision to de-industrialize the United States. Faced with growing foreign competition, they knew we could either increase productivity and improve our products, or cut labor costs. They went after labor, moving plants overseas or to Mexico, where they could save $20,000 per worker per year, resulting in a loss of 1.8 million manufacturing jobs between 1981 and 1991. One result was a feminization of work in the United States—from higher paying union jobs to work that is low-wage, contingent, part-time, and without benefits. When white people lose their jobs, they are encouraged to believe that it is the fault of poorly qualified people of color hired through Affirmative Action, not that we are eliminating two million jobs a year. If working people have less real wages, propaganda tells us that the problem is not lowering of wage structure, but that people are paying too many taxes to fund the bloated bureaucracy required to run the welfare state. We are facing a society in which 75 percent of the jobs could be lost to automation, yet many Americans have been persuaded that poverty is created by a failure of personal responsibility and that the main drain on the economy is payments to welfare mothers, who are imagined as exclusively women of color, although 38 percent are white women.

The last part of the speech was about sexuality. I took a deep breath.

Homophobia and heterosexism have profound consequences to all of the world's women. They can bracket not only sexual orientation but the whole question of gender as a code for lesbianism in a broader attempt to bar gender from consideration as a category subject to definition by social forces such as the Vatican or Islamic fundamentalists. All the women at the conference have already been branded as anti-family lesbians, so you might as well learn to defend yourselves, by learning to actively oppose homophobia. At stake not only is our right to a broad analysis of gender but also our right to love and pleasure, however they express themselves within the liberative elements of our cultures. And lesbian and gay movements in the United States, deeply divided by race, class and gender, would have much to learn in a global movement that does not replicate our own narrowly nationalistic versions of ourselves as "queer." The stakes of understanding homophobia in this global climate is our ability to create communities in which no one is expendable, to profits, ideology, or rigid community norms; to create communities not based on exclusion. Either we are all born to belonging, or some of us are born to privilege. I don't think we can have it both ways.

We have to take these brackets off. NO MORE DAMN BRACKETS!!! We cannot live without our lives.

I sat down, finally, relieved, as a good many people in the auditorium seemed to be clapping.

The Conference Unfolds

"Gays Don't Have Fun" read the Monday headline on the back page of the daily newspaper of the *Forum on Women*. I guess whoever wrote the article wasn't at the disco last night, I reflected with what was left of my brain. Late the evening before, lesbians from many countries had danced to world beat with young Chinese couples (not all of them straight), overlooked from the balconies by green-clad Chinese police. Clearly, (post)modernization has meant that young Chinese no longer have to curb their libidos for the Revolution. At one point, a black woman and a white woman from the conference had climbed up on the small stage and began a lithe dance together to a slow, bluesy song. I thought, "Well, here's where we get to see the inside of Chinese jails. Harry Wu, where are you?" But, remarkably, the crowd was receptive, charged like we were with the music and the movement.

The Chinese gay activist who had organized the benefit had handed out a mimeographed letter asking for help for a new organization, The Chinese Rainbow: "Chinese homosexuals, though large in number, face much misunderstanding and prejudice from the public, and there are few institutions . . . which are able or interested in helping homosexuals here. . . . Many homosexuals are forced to leave their hometowns and drift, often without jobs, to the big cities where they have a greater chance of remaining anonymous."

At the conference the second week, the International Gay and Lesbian Human Rights Commission produced an impressive report on human rights abuses against women-loving women globally.[33] Lesbians shared information on the first lesbians to come out in the Philippines during anti-Marcos organizing; on Queer Sisters in

Hong Kong; on organizing lesbians in the context of the rights of single women in India; and gave a workshop on flirting.

From the Pacific, facing the resumption of French nuclear testing on the Mururoa Atoll, women declared: "If denuclearization is decolonization, structural adjustment is recolonization," a "remote control of our lives" through global banks and newfound addictions to consumer products.[34]

Testimony from Burma: want and fear drive women and girls to lives of sexual exploitation. "Of what use is a free press in a country where only one half of the people can write and read?"[35]

Winona LaDuke brought an indigenous perspective from within the United States: Forty-seven transnational corporations have annual incomes that exceed the GNP of many countries.

From the eastern bloc of Europe, after five years of multiparty democracy, women reported setbacks in women's condition, loss of state-supported childcare, and higher unemployment.

From India, the number of dowry deaths jumped by 69 percent from 1987 to 1991 because dowries allow for more consumer purchases.[36]

From South Africa: "Women in Africa produce 78 percent of food on plots for which they hold no title, yet receive a puny 2–13 percent of the region's technical assistance."[37]

The same company offers a worker in the Philippines one-twelfth of what it pays a worker in western Europe.

On CNN we watched South African Rainbow, a coalition in opposition to Zimbabwe's President Robert Mugabe who had said gays were worse than pigs and dogs. I did not know then that in three years I would visit both countries.

We were amused to hear that police had given Chinese women bug spray to ward off mosquitoes that might have bitten AIDS-carrying lesbians.

A post-Crusades alliance of Islamic fundamentalists and the Vatican struggled to keep the word *gender* altogether out of the proposed Platform for Action and the word *family* monolithic and singular.

I had brought draft copies of *We Are the Ones We Are Waiting For: Women of Color Organizing for Transformation*, which I left in the grassroots tent for participants. The paper became a booklet published by the U.S. Urban-Rural Mission. It contained edited interviews from thirty-two women of color organizers in the United States, from which Leah Wise and Rinku Sen had begun to name the legacy their organizing entailed. It also contained the careful, thoughtful reflections of grassroots women organizers on strategies to impact local communities from the inside out while also shaping the global environment—the task of so many of the women in Beijing. In the introduction, Leah wrote of the forces converging on women of color in the new global environment: "We are the target of scapegoating and violence by the state, media, corporate interests, white workers and men in our families. Each cut in social programs, each technological innovation, each deregulation, each wage cut, each privatized public enterprise, each debate about abortion rights heightens our vulnerability and threatens our survival. . . . These policy changes that most devastate women of color have been justified through our vilification, cutting us off from material resources and allies at a time of increasing need."[38]

From workshops, posters advertising them, plenaries, and tribunals came a litany of the incommensurable grief and violence of women's lives as old as patriarchy and as recent as the morning paper. At a global tribunal on accountability for women's human rights, organized by the Center for Women's Global Leadership, twenty-two women gave five hours of testimony of mass rape and impregnation, domestic violence, attacks on lesbians and single women, female circumcision, suttee (or bride burning) from fundamentalist cultures, democratic cultures, rich nations and poor.

We all moved through the conference in our foreground while constantly negotiating Chinese culture, landscape, and history in moving from place to place, hotel to conference to dinner to sightseeing. In Beijing I glimpsed the degree to which we Westerners are cultural upstarts. Perhaps it was the view from the Great Wall the afternoon we had the immense structure to ourselves as it rode the curved crest of the mountain range, dipping in and out of clouds that covered the valley below like dragons' breath. From the wall's ramparts it was not hard to imagine Chinese soldiers keeping watch for invaders from the Mongolian plains as they huddled against the damp and the cold in the guard houses that came at regular intervals. Or to hear the clank of horses' hooves along the paved surface, over which men and equipment moved, the wail of wind through the arches like the voices of the dead laborers, one for each brick, legend had it, embedded in its foundation.

ME AND MAO

I was developing an interest in Mao. Maybe it was his picture omnipresent. Maybe it was that I had missed my socialist study-group phase because I was coming out as a lesbian. Back in the sixties, Oakland Panther leaders Bobby Seale and Huey Newton sold Mao's *Little Red Book,* using the proceeds to buy guns and ammo. "Read the Red Book and do it like the Red Guards did it," Seale admonished.[39] Had I been out then, I could have argued as I was being whisked off for reeducation that my sexual identity made me part of the déclassé elements like bandits, soldiers, beggars, and prostitutes, "all those . . . formerly despised or kicked into the gutter . . . who had no social standing," whom Mao recruited for the Red Army and who turned out to be his most stalwart revolutionary troops.[40] Perhaps my interest rose from a need to figure out the relationship between the identity-based movements of the 1970s and 1980s and issues of class and neocolonialism that the 1990s brought into sharp relief after the collapse of the Soviet bloc, the defeat of the Sandinistas, and the transition to market socialism in China. I hadn't expected to encounter these questions in China, but here they were with the ghosts of Marx and Mao—or at least Mao's afterimage, not yet displaced completely by the Marlboro Dude.

I came home and over the next couple of years read Stuart Schram's edition of *The Political Thought of Mao* and a couple of biographies—Peter Carter's *Mentor Mao*, written shortly after Mao's death, and Jonathan Spence's *Mao Zedong*, in the Penguin Lives series (1999).[41] Carter's 1980 narrative presents the heroic Mao, father of the Chinese Revolution; Spence's end-of-the-century Mao is a "Lord of Misrule." Carter's account seems shaded too much by Mao's cult of personality; but Spence's narrative of a tyrant who bumbles his way to power does not account for the remarkable accomplishments (whatever one's ideology) of the Chinese Communist Party. It grew from fifteen delegates in its first Congress in Shanghai in 1921 to a force that could defeat the Guomindang army and unify China by 1949.[42] However present Mao's image, as a historical figure he had not yet come clearly into view. But it was clearer the extent to which his utopian narratives had often been written in blood.

"What should we not fear?" Mao had declared in 1919, "We should not fear heaven. We should not fear ghosts. We should not fear the dead. We should not fear the bureaucrats. We should not fear the militarists. We should not fear the capitalists."[43] I had visited his mausoleum in Red Square that opens to the north, defying feng shui, the geomancy of wind and water that guides the flow of universal *qi* and dictates that all imperial palaces should open to the friendlier south. Even in death Mao is placed askance thirty-five hundred years of imperial Chinese history. The man was taking on a lot: capitalism *and* ghosts, bureaucrats *and* the dead! He set out to dismantle the twin mountains of imperialism and feudalism in China and, whatever else he and the Chinese Communist Party did, they did do that.

European nations had their sights on China in an imperialist and colonizing era. In 1793 Lord McCartney, King George III's emissary, had brought Western gizmos to the Chinese court to trade for silk, porcelain, and tea. The Qing emperor declared to the upstart Brit who refused to kowtow: "We do not have the slightest need of your country's manufactures." Then the British brought in opium, the commodity of imperialist dogs who learned early with rum and sugar and coffee and tobacco that addiction creates a ready market. When the Chinese resisted, the British sent in their gunboats in 1842 and won the Opium War. In the Treaty of Nanjing, the British took Hong Kong; Canton and Shanghai were forced open to foreign trade. Foreign citizens got extraterritorial rights to sections of Beijing that then fell under control of various European countries. British troops stomped into the great within of the Forbidden City and sat on the emperor's throne.

This reversal signaled that the Qing dynasty had lost the mandate of heaven. China's increasingly impoverished masses—her *koo li*s on the brink of starvation as political disruptions increased their vulnerability to flood and famine—took matters into their own hands in the 1850 Taiping ("great peaceful heavenly") Rebellion. The Qing killed more than twenty million people repressing the uprising. Russia took over eastern Siberia in 1860, and France moved fatefully into Indochina. Mao was born thirty years later to a landowning peasant in a country filled with famine and unrest. In the early part of the century Sun Yatsen's Nationalist Party challenged the emperor, who had abdicated in 1911, ending several thousand years of imperial history. But the Nationalists, or Guomindang, had rapidly run into trouble from China's warlords. By 1921, the Chinese Communist Party formed, fifteen strong, at a secret meeting in Shanghai and soon emerged as a bloc within the Guomindang, which was by then fighting the warlords, Western powers, *and* the Japanese presence in China.[44]

It would be Mao's particular genius to make Marxism relevant to what emerged as the Third World. From his youth, Mao advocated for a fusion of Marxist theory and Chinese practice, what he called the "Sinofication of Marxism": "Marxism [in] a national form . . . imbued with Chinese peculiarities." Mao understood that in China's agrarian context the peasants were its revolutionary class, and he evolved a style of guerilla warfare taking strategic advantage of the peasant base in the vast countryside. The Communists staged a failed national insurrection in 1927, after which Mao retreated with the remnants of his troops to the Jinggangshan (*shan* is mountain in Chinese).[45] There, allied with the bandits and outcasts, those déclassé elements he soon found to be especially good fighters, he evolved the tactics of guerilla warfare that over the next two decades defeated his various foes and unified China.

The Chinese Red Army, he declared, was "an armed group for carrying out political tasks of a class nature." He established a soviet, or a people's, government based on land redistribution, laws, and simple rules that kept his army from thieving and looting, winning over the peasants. "The popular masses are like water and the army is like a fish," he explained in what would become a popular dictum of guerilla movements.[46] "The officers do not beat the soldiers; officers and soldiers have the same food and clothing and receive equal treatment; soldiers enjoy freedom of assembly and speech; cumbersome formalities and ceremonies are abolished; the financial administration is absolutely open to [the inspection of] all; and the soldiers' representatives inspect the final accounts." This "democratic process" was "spiritually . . . liberat[ing]," so that "the same soldier fights more bravely in the Red Army today than he did for the enemy yesterday."[47] These strategies applied, Carter says, both in the Jinggangshan (1927–29) and in the Jiangxi Soviet, where Mao set up a base from 1929 to 1934.

His was a strategy that avoided head-on conflict with the opposing force. Mao helped develop insights about force and resistance into military strategy of far-reaching consequences for the liberation movements of the century. "Blockade within blockade, the offensive within the defensive, superiority within inferiority, strength within weakness, advantage within disadvantage, and initiative within passivity."[48] It was a philosophy that I recognized from my years of increasingly remedial karate. There was, it seemed, a tao to Mao.

Mao said, "When the enemy advances, we retreat. When the enemy retreats, we advance."[49] The Tao taught:

When two great forces oppose each other,
the victory will go
to the one that knows how to yield.[50]

Other Chinese Communist Party generals advocated for a more traditional army that fought set battles, a strategy that vied with Mao's guerilla tactics as the Red Army fought its way out of Chiang's encirclement of the Jiangxi base and set out on the first stage of the Great March. When the Communists stopped at Zunyi to rest and assess, they made Mao chair both of the Politburo and the Red Army. Carter says that here Mao made the crucial decision to confront not the Guomindang, but the Japanese. He rightly perceived that the army seen defending China would win its people's hearts and minds.[51] Then the First Front Army led by Mao, Zhou Enlai, and Lin Biao set out ninety thousand strong on the eight-thousand-mile-long march to Shaanxi Province on China's northern border.

By Carter's account, it was an epic journey, with the Red Army chased by Chiang's men, persevering with discipline, cleverness, luck, and courage: across the Chang River into Sichuan. Then across the mountains to the Dadu River, even more turbulent with floods from the spring thaw. A Red vanguard raced the hundred miles up the gorge in three days and took the flaming chain bridge at Luding under heavy machine-gun fire, then the army faced miles of icy mountain ranges, some as high as 17,000 feet. "In the endless void the wild geese cry at the frosty morning moon," Mao wrote of a great mountain pass. "The hills are blue like the sea, / And the dying sun like blood."[52] Then they were out of the mountains and into the tortuous last leg, a month across the grasslands, hundreds of miles of swamp bubbling with mud and infections until finally the remnant of 20,000 (Spence says 8,000) Red soldiers arrived at the Shaanxi soviet to join other Communist troops.[53] The cult of Mao, Spence argues, emerged in Shaanxi during these years. Mao used fellow Communist Chen Boda to get him up to speed as a theorist, generating an increasing confidence that he had the correct line. Mao gave long lectures, after which visitors underwent at times deadly criticism/self-criticism struggles supervised by Mao's growing security personnel.[54]

The long march left Mao and his army winnowed and tempered, facing the Japanese in Manchuria. It brought the Communists back into coalition with the Guomindang as a legitimate part of the Chinese government, against the inevitable and brutal assault of the Japanese that began in 1937. All Chinese fought fiercely against the devastating scorch-and-burn kill-all policy of the Japanese that left twenty million Chinese dead, although Mao stayed in Shaanxi away from much of the fighting, Spence says. Then the United States dropped its atomic bombs on Nagasaki and Hiroshima, ending World War II. For three more years, the two-million-person Russian-armed force of the Red Army outfought and outmaneuvered Chiang's five-million-man American-armed Guomindang force, winning in the north and the south and finally marching triumphant into Beijing. In 1949 Mao proclaimed at

Tiananmen Gate the founding of the People's Republic of China: "Let the earth tremble. We have stood up. We will never be humiliated again. Our nation will enter the large family of peace-loving and freedom-loving nations."

"Practice not-doing, / and everything will fall into place," states the Tao in teaching the concept of *wu-wei*, mastery as effortless action.[55] Less than thirty years after fifteen people founded the Chinese Communist Party in Shanghai, the Chinese Communist Party united all of China. Mao had somehow ridden the whirlwind, harnessed the forces of history. He resided, like the Taoist masters, at the center of the circle.

WAITING FOR HILLARY

I shifted positions as water dripped down my collar. I was standing in a shanty town of umbrellas perched uneasily atop one another on the steps of the plenary hall in Huairou Tuesday morning, waiting with a growing crowd of women to hear Hillary Clinton address the 1995 NGO Forum on Women. I had been standing there since 7:12 A.M. So far the growing crowd remained polite, but people were getting restive as we pressed tighter toward the locked glass doors. I could see the headlines back home: "Local activist crushed in stampede of women."

So what was I doing here waiting for Hillary? She had given a strong speech on women's rights the day before at the UN conference. Mostly, though, I was looking for the point where my experience of the conference would coincide with the media coverage at home. And—whoops!—it began happening as security opened the doors for brief periods to let women through. Word passed back to move forward, and soon I was caught in a riptide of female flesh. "You are antifeminist!" some woman behind me screamed, as if it would help. "The Chinese government will pay for this!" another yelled. There are cultures that line up and cultures that just push, I reflected, as the confluence of the two thrust me through one of the several doors security finally opened to avoid the death by stampede I feared.

Women were streaming into the plenary hall, frustrated and angry, to find most seats taken. We might have our feminist riot yet. I was lucky to get a seat, and I struck up a conversation with my seatmate to the left, who had come in my delegation. She was agitated about surveillance in her hotel, people found rifling through drawers in the rooms.

"And she's taking notes on everything I say," she pointed to the young Chinese woman to the right of me.

"Are you the police?" She leaned over me. "You are the police!"

The Chinese woman recoiled. She quickly handed us a business card, which explained she was a researcher in women's studies at Beijing University.

The woman on the stage had given up on trying to clear the aisles. "We're gonna sing," she explained. "I promise you'll feel better." Then she began a chorus of the forum theme song, "Keep on moving forward . . . ."

I turned to the Chinese woman on my right. "You know, people are very frustrated because of the surveillance."

"I know," she said. "We hate it too. We feel bad when we see things going badly. The opening ceremony went so well, but there have been so many problems since." I remembered the huge red banners along the highway, "BE A GOOD HOST TO THE FOURTH CONFERENCE ON WOMEN," and the hundreds of young Chinese men and women who volunteered daily on the buses, along the roads, at the stadium, and at the conference site.

From the stage, our emcee, Shirley Mae Staten, an African American woman from Alaska, began another song. I wrote out the words and gave them to my new Chinese friend as we sang along. We had the Chinese man sitting to her right take pictures of us together, and then a Latin American woman mounted the stage to lead us in "De Colores." About that time, Hillary's entourage arrived. Crewcut white Secret Service guys mounted the stage and more press streamed in. Our emcee was clearly stalling for time.

"Where's Mrs. Clinton?" someone yelled.

"I'm Mrs. Clinton," she joked. "Don't you recognize me with my suntan?" Then to the audience, "How dare she ask for Mrs. Clinton when you got me up here? Chill, girl, chill." The audience roared. "You got to realize, I'm the only person the Secret Service will allow on the stage," Staten continued, as she announced her candidacy for the mayor of Huairou. "Be sure to vote before you leave."

By the time Hillary got there, the main event had already happened, under the firm direction of the sister from Alaska, who had turned us from a near mob of the tired and disgruntled into a community of women. It was this spirit that carried me through my last morning at the forum, in which, as I reported to friends, "Mab falls in love with the women of the world."

At a restaurant over dumplings, I talked with a woman from Costa Rica who had been at the UN conference the day before. She told me that they had taken the brackets off *gender*. "Some people were arguing there are five genders," she explained to me: "Male, female, gay, lesbian, and bisexual. Thank God they are so dumb. You can trick them, and that's the power of knowledge! They are scared about the power of women, our revolution. We have strong arms. We don't harm people, but we do harm systems. Religion is scared of women, too. Empowered women do not obey."

Then I was off to the regional tents to hear an impassioned plea against structural adjustment. "How will Africa be governed? Will we continue to be used as economic slaves?"

At the grassroots tent, in which all week had been an interesting and lively mix of women from all over the world, music drew me into a chant/dance about saying no to violence against women. Then Mother Freedom, a Filipina vocalist and guitarist, took over as other Filipinas taught us dance steps to songs in Spanish and Tagalog, mixed with "Mona Lisa," "The Twist," and "Those Were the Days." We were all laughing and singing and dancing together, with enough energy and good spirit to float this one tent, anyway, back to Beijing, if not back to North Carolina. For the last song, we stood in a circle holding hands as one of the women translated the lyrics: "Will it be enough to love you and all other women forever?"

I don't have the illusions I had twenty years ago, it occurred to me dancing to Mother Freedom. But I am clearer about what I want these days as a lesbian and a human being: an acknowledgment of a beloved place within multiple and relating communities.

LOSING ONE'S WU-WEI

Over more dumplings on my last evening in Beijing I had tried to explain my fascination with Mao to Laura and to come to terms with the record of the Chinese Communist Party.

"By the end of the 1950s Mao saw the capitalism that the Chinese had struggled against for half a century so easily reasserting itself within socialism. He took extreme measures in the Cultural Revolution, and he lost much more than he gained. He couldn't save the revolution, and he discredited it in the eyes of ordinary Chinese people—'confused right and wrong and the people with the enemy,' in the words of the Central Committee itself! But for a while there, it seems to me the man was on a roll."[56]

I attempted to explain wu-wei, effortless action, which in this case surely involved working with the people, not against them. She looked a bit skeptical as a dumpling dangled from my chopsticks into sauce. I had to admit that I was developing an obsession with Mao.

"You are getting better with your chopsticks," Laura observed. "And what about the Cultural Revolution?"

"OK, so the Communists are in control of the government by 1950. By Mao's own count, 700,000 'counter-revolutionaries' were killed in two years.[57] The Chinese invaded Tibet, which they felt was part of their national territory; although the Tibetans, devoutly Buddhist, had other ideas, the Chinese army crushed Tibetan resistance.[58] The CCP's first strategy was a Soviet-driven and financed command economy. It developed heavy industry with a centralized bureaucracy for state planning. China accomplished land reform and recovered the national economy in only three years. And we know that the Chinese have millennia of history as bureaucrats."

"Yes, we know that," Laura obliged.

"Some say they got overconfident. Some say they panicked. Some say that Mao's Great Leap Forward was wildly utopian and murderously unrealistic.[59] By that time, criticizing his policies was fatal, as other CCP leaders learned. By 1958, there was widespread famine—between the famine, drought, and floods twenty million people died. Natural disasters plagued China, as did the withdrawal of Soviet aid and expertise as China forged a third way for an emerging Third World. By 1962, the Communist Party leadership had split between those pragmatists reluctant to experiment

further (such as Liu Shaoqi and Deng Xiaoping) and Mao's faction that kept press-
ing for continuing revolution. Mao argued that the failure of Chinese agriculture
under the Great Leap was from natural causes, but Liu had a different analysis and
wanted a more open discussion within the party about China's economic path. He
and Deng saw a progressive role for capitalism in this stage of the evolution of socialism. But Mao was ready to take the next step toward communism, wary that the
new Communist Party bureaucracy was becoming a new elite, creating a new class
of capitalists within socialism. He also felt his leadership threatened by Liu.

"So he turned to party-directed mass movement, hoping to 'release the productive
energies of the Chinese people' and create the 'new man.' He was afraid that the
'landlords, rich peasants, counter-revolutionaries, bad elements, and monsters of all
kinds [would be allowed to crawl out] . . . and the whole of China would change its
colour.'[60] He was mostly afraid, many say, of getting ousted. By 1966, Mao's faction
inaugurated the Cultural Revolution to reinvigorate the class struggle, setting loose
the young Red Guards against the capitalist-roaders and against his opposition inside
the party."

"And *did* he . . . create the new man?"

"Well, not exactly. He created a huge mess."

"What about the new woman?"

"The Communist Party tried to bring women out of feudalism, out of arranged
marriages and footbinding.[61] And Mao did *believe* in the process by which serving the
people served the individual.

"But the Red Guards became a Red Terror that played out what Chinese historians themselves called 'unprecedented excesses of collective ethic' for a decade.[62]
They finally ousted Liu from his position as President, detained him and basically
bullied him to death. Mao brought in Lin Biao, People's Liberation Army com-
mander, to take Liu's place. Lin consolidated his own position by escalating the cult
of personality around Mao. He edited Mao's quotes into the *Little Red Book* and
printed a billion copies. Mao appeared in Tiananmen rallies before a million Red
Guards and urged them to destroy the four olds—ideas, culture, customs, and
habits—in order to bring forth the new. The olds included big hair, tight jeans,
T-shirts—everything but green, gray, or navy blue baggy pants. You would have
been in trouble. The Red Guards attacked the five blacks—landlords, wealthy peasants, bad enemies, counterrevolutionaries, and rightists. This included artists and intellectuals, former revolutionary and party heroes, and many ordinary people who
were tortured, shamed, and hounded at times to suicide.

"By 1967, Mao called for Red Guards to overthrow high-ranking and local officials,
but this increased infighting and armed conflict within the guards. Mao eventually
sent in the people's army to establish order and launched the rustification movement
that sent sixteen million urban youth to rural work farms. Lin and Mao predictably got
into a power struggle, and Lin died mysteriously in a plane crash, a death that by that
time fooled few people and contributed to a growing disillusionment with the

Cultural Revolution.[63] Mao was aging. He welcomed Nixon and Kissinger to Beijing while he was still partially coherent. When Mao died in 1976, the ultra-leftist Gang of Four were arrested. Deng emerged as the leader with the old capitalist-road strategy of market socialism based on incentives, consumption, and market forces to drive modernization. Most people were generally disgusted with politics and disillusioned with Communism."

"Mao lost his wu-wei?" Laura offered.

"Yes! Do your work, then step back."[64]

"And here we are in China at the XiYuan, bastion of joint venture capital, drinking Mexican beer and listening to 'We Three Kings'?"

"Well, more or less. I still have a few things to figure out."

The next day, my bags packed and my flight confirmed, I bid my XiYuan buddies and China itself goodbye and headed home. Three days later, in Beijing delegates debated sexual orientation for the first time on the floor of the UN. The phrase was removed from the Platform for Action near dawn on Saturday morning in the final hour of the UN conference, but not until representatives from thirty countries rose to speak against discrimination based on sexual orientation. Delegates did pass a statement on "the human rights of women . . . to have control over and decide freely and responsibly on matters relating to their sexuality."

Beings with Dust in Our Eyes

China did set loose questions in me. Maybe it was being away from the routines and pressures of home and work, so that time did slow down and open. Maybe it was the new friendship with Laura, whom I had found easy to love. Maybe it was our conversations about Buddhism, or my own second thoughts about having chosen to go shopping at the silk market for my nonnuclear family rather than finding the reclining Buddha in one of the city's temples, as she suggested. Once home, I read up some on the Buddha and found what I learned compelling.

Siddhārtha Gautama was raised in India in the fifth century B.C. in the lap of luxury, in a palace with blue lotus pools, no cloth not from Benares, a white sun shade held over him day and night. Siddhārtha's father recognized on his son's body the thirty-two markings of either spiritual or political genius, so he worked to keep his son off the spiritual path by sheltering him from the world. Then one day Siddhārtha ventured outside the palace and saw for the first time poverty, suffering, and death. It shocked and pained him. Deeply affected, he joined a band of ascetics he saw nearby and left with them—the Great Going Forth—on the night of the full moon. For six years he wandered with them, learning meditation and practicing severe austerities until his limbs were like bamboo, his backside like a buffalo's hoof, his ribs like the rafters of a house. Then one day he sat quietly beneath the shade of a rose apple tree, letting his mind settle and recognizing in its settling a potential peace. He resolved not to rise until he had attained complete awakening. It is one of the great brief periods of human history, as Siddhārtha sifted consciousness to touch in some unfathomable way the peaceful, the subtle, the sublime, breathing in and out no doubt the delicate scent of apple and rose blossoms and moonlight beneath the bodhi tree. When the morning star arose, he attained his great insight into suffering, its source in our craving, and the way to its cessation in the Noble Eightfold Path; and he knew with certainty that all beings are connected and are endowed with the nature of awakening.

He was first inclined not to teach such subtle and profound truths to a generation that "takes delight in attachment." But he was approached by the great god Brahma: "There are beings here with dust in their eyes. Pray teach dharma out of compassion for them." Thus was the first turning of the Wheel of Dharma, and thus began the Buddha's forty-five years of teaching, as he wandered in his yellow robe with begging bowl the plains of the Ganges, teaching everyone, regardless of caste and declining the feasts of nobles to take the simple hospitality of peasants and social outcasts.[65]

It was a lovely story. *Beings with dust in their eyes.* Perhaps I knew how that felt.

"Buddha offers an interesting contrast to the emperors of the Forbidden City, royalty who seldom ventured out. You can hardly see Beijing from within the palace walls." I was in another conversation with Laura, post-Beijing, who found my persistence, or perhaps it was my pious southern sincerity, amusing. We were walking across the Brooklyn Bridge, and as far as I was concerned there was a lamentable absence of both piety and sincerity in Manhattan.

"Or it's interesting to contrast Buddha and the emperors with Mao, himself born a peasant, who I guess was also trying to solve the problem of suffering, its manifestations of sickness, poverty, death not so different from what Buddha encountered. Mao saw the cause of suffering as injustice, class oppression, feudal systems, imperialism—all of them, perhaps, manifestations of a kind of craving for profits and power—and the solution working-class awakening, continuing revolution, the dictatorship of the proletariat."

"So should Mao have been a Buddhist, is that what you are saying?"

"Well, you know he *was* Buddhist in his childhood. His mother was, at any rate. But the Communists associated religion with those forces that were holding China in feudalism. So Chinese Marxism became for him the religion of the people. When we say, 'We are the Sons of the People,' China understands it as she understood the phrase 'Son of Heaven.' The People has taken the place of the ancestors. The People, not the victorious Communist Party."[66]

"You mean as in 'Gods are all right for the rich. The poor have the Eighth Route Army'?"

"Yes. Or 'To not have a correct political point of view is like having no soul'—that's Mao as well."[67]

"Mao was so clear about not having to swallow all of European Marxism or Russian Marxist-Leninism. He was clear about the role of peasants in the revolution and the energy for change in the Third World. But he swallowed Marx's flattened

metaphysic hook, line, and sinker. 'Materialism recognizes the independent existence of matter as detached from spirit and considers spirit as secondary and subor-
dinate,' Mao echoed Marx.[68]

"Mao's Red Guards included in the four olds all forms of religion, and they attacked and dismantled monasteries, destroyed centuries-old statutes of Buddha. The
Cultural Revolution was a revolution *against* culture—'a revolution that trampled
culture and civilization.'[69] It represented a Left gone berserk with extracting confessions, 'experimental' hangings, forcing people to kneel on cinders or to stand in awk-
ward positions for hours, burning hair, knifing the buttocks, boiling water baths,
sudden lancings. Not to mention outright beating people to death."[70]

"Sounds like you are over Mao," Laura interjected.

"Well, yes. Under Mao the Red Guards really took the collective part of belonging *way* too far under the unifying effect of Mao's thought. The self was only collective, or it was suspect. 'Every person is a class person,' Mao proclaimed, 'there is no
such thing as a person standing alone, a person in the abstract.'[71] Capitalism—both
capitalist-roaders and the capitalist impulse—became the enemy within, the traitor,
spy, and renegade impulse hiding out in the party. So many of the people became enemies of the state, for both Mao and for Stalin. In a weird way, it's the obverse of
McCarthyism (communism as the enemy within capitalism to be ferreted out).
Rather than these struggle sessions they all could have used a little of the Noble
Eightfold Path. You know, right speech, right mindfulness, right action, right livelihood—Lord, do I know a lot of progressive groups that could use those as ground
rules!"

"So Buddha would not have started the Cultural Revolution?"

"That much," I laughed, "is for sure."

3

ATLANTA

The 1996 Olympics, Co'Cola,
and the Wealth of Nations

We address ourselves not to their humanity but to their self-interest.
— ADAM SMITH, *The Wealth of Nations*

In sorrows, joys, good times and bad, this was the way we lived. We helped each other, and we survived.
— HOWARD THURMAN, *With Head and Heart: Autobiographical Writings*

Atlanta must not lead the South to dream of material prosperity as the touchstone of all success.
— W.E.B. DU BOIS, *The Souls of Black Folk*

In as much as you did it not unto the least of these, ye did it not to me.
— MATT. 25:45

THE hardwood floors and overstacked shelves reminded me of old grocery stores from my childhood, but nostalgia evaporated at the end of the row, when I looked up at the dummy Klansman in hooded regalia with a noose around his neck. If that were too subtle, the National Socialist Party and National White People's Party literature for sale (twenty-five cents) made it clear where the proprietor of Wild Man's Confederate Relics and Herb Shop was coming from. Wild Man's was in *the* Kennesaw, Georgia, whose town council had passed a law *mandating* town citizens to own firearms and appropriate ammunition. One of the first havens for whites exiting majority-black Atlanta, Cobb County has a population that is predominantly white and intends to stay that way. The county has its own transit system and unsuccessfully attempted to require all riders getting off MARTA, Atlanta's rapid transit, to show Cobb County ID. One of Wild Man's bumper stickers staked out the territory of the suburban Right: "MARTA Motto: Come to Cobb and Rob."

It was November, and China seemed much more than three months behind me. Wild Man, alive and kicking, was considerably more primitive than Beijing Person and every bit as contemporary as the Marlboro Dude who had presided over the Shanghai airport. This local avatar of whiteness, this embodiment of European de-volution, was enough to make a person reconsider Darwin, I muttered under my breath as I peeped through the shelves to keep an eye on the proprietor. I needed to finish my casing of this joint and rejoin Pat in her Honda, parked in a side lot. As a self-styled pissed-off black dyke from Georgia, Pat had left the tour of Wild Man's to me, white lesbian incognito.

I climbed back in her car, rolling my eyes.

"See what I mean?" Pat inquired.

"Yep."

Why was I in Wild Man's? I had arrived in Atlanta that morning to research a story I was writing on Atlanta and the Olympics. I had a gig to write a piece on grassroots responses to the Olympics, and I knew plenty of organizers in Atlanta working on a range of issues. Pat Hussain (patient in the car outside) and her friend Jon-Ivan Weaver had mobilized "Olympics Out of Cobb" in response to an antigay resolution passed by the Cobb County Commissioners. Pat and I amounted to one-third of the co-founders of Southerners on New Ground (SONG), an organization we helped to put together to shape a more integrated politic around race, class, gender, and sexu-ality. Jerome Scott at Project South was working with a coalition of antipoverty groups, which included young people from Empty the Shelters, to oppose Olympic development at the expense of Atlanta's poor. People like Beni Ivey and Rose John-son at the Center for Democratic Renewal had tracked white supremacist groups and the Far Right from Atlanta since the early 1980s. I was looking, as usual, for places that identity-group politics (such as those around race, gender, and sexuality) inter-sected, or didn't, with each other and with organizing around class—and how these converged, or didn't, around the Olympics.

Besides, "Hotlanta" had a special place in my psychic geography. I grew up an hour's drive from the Georgia border and a three-hour drive from Atlanta (before the interstate). I remember making my mother leave the segregated Tuskegee movie the-ater during the burning of Atlanta in *Gone with the Wind*; she looked back over her shoulder as I pulled her up the slanted aisle because I was afraid of the enveloping flames from Yankee General Sherman's devastating March to the Sea, an early ex-ercise in what by the next century would be recognized as total war. When Mama flew off from Montgomery to her various destinations for vacations and cures, Delta Airlines always took her first through Atlanta; and the saying was that from anywhere in the Southeast, you'd have to go through Atlanta to get to hell.

In high school I had come to Atlanta with friends to ride the glass elevators in the Hyatt Regency Hotel. In Tuskegee, we were doing well to have three-story buildings, everything but the pine trees being pretty flat. I remember the ascent up the glass el-evator shaft that rose in the middle of the Hyatt lobby toward the revolving café in the dome, from which one could view Atlanta in all directions during an hour's rotation and an expensive lunch. A couple of years later, I experienced another Atlanta ascension, this one up an escalator at Rich's Department Store—one of the largest in the Southeast—when my roommate Jodie took me home with her to Atlanta our freshman year, country come to town. There was more to buy in this one store than in all of Tuskegee! As I turned to look out and down, there spread before my eyes fondue pots, lush towels in brilliant colors, expensive chocolates, and fancy coffee machines, perfumes, furniture, clothes. I will be a lawyer, I thought. I will make a lot of money, and all this will be *mine!* On one of those Atlanta visits I also ate at Pitty Pat's Porch, a *Gone with the Wind*–themed restaurant with a plantation motif, in which we were served southern food by African American women in headrags.

Through it all, Coke was the elixir that got us through steamy summers before air-conditioning turned the South into the Sun Belt—through all those hot August afternoons, after we got too old to sit in front of the fan in our underpants, sucking on ice. We knew Coke's secret formula was stashed away in the vault beneath the Co'Cola building in downtown Atlanta. Of course, Atlanta had birthed and buried Martin Luther King, a prophet against U.S. racism who was not always honored in my own white hometown. The Atlanta University system had also provided an intellectual and spiritual home for the likes of W.E.B. Du Bois and Howard Thurman, as I later came to appreciate.

So I paid attention when the media machine revved up for the 1996 Atlanta Olympics, with everyone from UPS to General Motors to Blue Cross–Blue Shield to Avon to McDonalds to AT&T and Home Depot signed up as Official Olympic Sponsors. In 1992, Atlanta lawyer Billy Payne and former Civil Rights activist, Atlanta mayor, and U.S. ambassador to the United Nations Andrew Young had sold the Olympic Organizing Committee on the Atlanta site. Atlanta's multicultural bid, which beat out Athens, Greece, for the centennial celebration of the Olympics, included a promise that the Atlanta games would not be marred by political protests, as well as the obvious draw of having the centennial in the birthplace of Coca-Cola. Yet when Atlanta made its Olympic bid, Atlanta had the second highest poverty rate in the United States.

Coke, its green contour bottle looming over the Atlanta skyline, is global and transcultural; it is "the most successful product in the history of commerce" and the "most ubiquitous consumer product in the world."[1] Coke has shaped Atlanta, a city that boasts of being "too busy to hate"—a reputation bought and shaped by Coke CEO Robert Woodruff. Coke has also shaped the Olympics since 1928, the "longest running relationship with the games of any corporation."[2] The Coca-Cola Company has also led the way in the emerging culture of what has come to be called late capitalism—the advent of a consumer society in a postindustrial economy, with accompanying electronic media, a proclivity toward spectacle, and the rise of the spatial over the temporal in a culture incapable of dealing with time and history. Postmodernity itself would be in high relief at the Atlanta Olympics. At stake in late July and early

August of 1996 in Atlanta would be more than gold medals and world records, much more than the answer to questions like whether or not track star Michael Johnson would win both the 200-meter and 400-meter races. At stake would be the answers to questions about our future. What kind of economic development will we have, at whose benefit and at whose cost? To what extent do postmodern electronic spectacles like the Olympics depend on the virtual disappearing of the poor? What does Atlanta's plantation-to-postmodern history show us about the racialized and gendered topography of the American landscape? What does it show us about the basis of resistance, and of hope, for the disinherited as well as the inherited?

Cobb County: Nazis, Newt, and Dyke Volleyball

Pat had taken me to Wild Man's as the first stop on my tour of Cobb County. The Cobb County commissioners in August of 1993 had passed a resolution condemning the gay lifestyle and in support of the "traditional family structure [as the] . . . best mechanism for maintaining a lifestyle which leaves citizens independent of their government for support." Pat had handed me a copy of the resolution when we set out from Atlanta.[3]

"Why don't they seek to bar heterosexual widows from getting their spouses' social security benefits if they are so big on getting people off of the dole?" I asked the kind of rhetorical question that Pat knew was for my blood pressure rather than her response. "What ever happened to government of the people, by the people, and for the people?" I mused to Pat. "In a democracy, isn't there supposed to be a bit more, well, belonging, interdependence? And does this vaunted independence of families really result from their lifestyle only—no single mothers or homosexuals? Might it not also have to do, say, with the minimum wage? What about social security?"

When Jon-Ivan had heard in January of 1994 that the Olympic committee was putting a volleyball venue in Cobb County, he was immediately outraged. (Pat continued the account as she pulled out of Wild Man's driveway and headed toward our next site.) Jon-Ivan had tried unsuccessfully to get more experienced organizers to take up a campaign. Then this pissed-off white faggot from Kentucky hooked up with Pat, and the rest was history. In 1994, Olympics Out of Cobb had rapidly mounted pickets, protests, and candlelight vigils. Demonstrating just how big a mess they could make of the city, they organized a traffic slowdown on I-75 at rush hour during the visit of international Olympics bigwigs, to the fury of city and Olympic officials. The Atlanta Committee for the Olympic Games (ACOG) had received thousands of phone calls, faxes, and letters, including six letters of protest from members of Congress.

The crowning blow came when diver Greg Louganis, a multiple Olympic gold medal winner, publicly came out and asked the Olympic committee not to force athletes to go to Cobb County. Atlanta Olympics representative Shirley Franklin had already told Pat and Jon-Ivan that the Olympics committee had surprisingly high estimates of the number of gay Olympic athletes—95 to 99 percent nonheterosexual on women's volleyball, and 40 percent overall![4] That beat even the most self-aggrandizing queer self-census. Perhaps Louganis represented too much of the tip of a lavender iceberg. Too many obviously dyke and faggot athletes would depress the world market for tennis shoes. On July 29, 1994, four days after Louganis's statement, ACOG capitulated, moving volleyball out of Cobb.

Wild Man's easily made Pat's point that Cobb County had a long and varied history of bigoted activities. Cobb County, she informed me, was the site of the infamous 1910 Klan lynching of Leo Frank, a Jewish factory manager. In the early decades of the twentieth century, that lynching sparked a Klan revival and inspired the beginning of the Anti-Defamation League and the NAACP. During the Klan revival of the 1960s, convicted black-church bomber J. B. Stoner launched the National States Rights Party, with its *Thunderbolt* (later called *Truth at Last*) from Marietta. Stoner had mentored Ed Fields, who would himself mentor a new generation of explicitly neo-Nazi white supremacists. With Stoner and Fields as magnets, over the years Cobb County had drawn in the full gamut of Far Right organizations.

I sat in a couple of North Carolina courtrooms monitoring trials in which Fields testified. He and his buddies always gave me the heebie-jeebies, a cold chill along the vertebrae, and a nauseous response to the kind of whiff you might get from pulling out one of those big drawers in a morgue.

I had not realized, until Pat pointed it out, that Cobb County also lay in the home district of Congressman Newt Gingrich, the suburban platform from which he had launched his "Contract with America" as the ultimate assault on the nation's poor and on any remaining sense of public good. The contract, which came in with the 1994 Republican majority in Congress, advertised itself as a "detailed agenda for national renewal . . . [a] historic change that would be the end of government that is too big, too intrusive, and too easy with the public's money."[5] One of its key provisions was the Personal Responsibility Act, or welfare reform, intended to discourage births out of wedlock and teen pregnancy by denying young mothers Aid to Families with Dependent Children (AFDC) benefits and enacting a tough two-years-and-out provision with work requirements for all recipients. I had come off the plane from China three months earlier, fresh from a lesson in the kinds of structural adjustments that were impoverishing women all over the globe, to congressional hearings on the need for more personal responsibility for poor women, which had infuriated me. The money formerly going to AFDC would go into tax cuts, mainly for the wealthy.[6] Another key provision of Gingrich's contract was an anticrime package that included an increase in spending for prison construction—somewhere to put all the poor people without jobs or income. Within a month of my Atlanta excursion, *Time* announced Gingrich its Man of the Year for his conservative revolution that changed the country's center of gravity toward the concept of government as a force for "evil" (*Time*'s word). Ronald Reagan had preached that government was the problem, but Gingrich's contract would finish off Reagan's assault on the legacy of the New Deal and Great Society. "Let them eat cake" were words that sent Marie Antoinette to the guillotine in the early years of the French Revolution. Mr. Gingrich's similar disposition merely sent him back to Congress.

The *Atlanta Journal-Constitution* had recently elaborated on Gingrich's role in this brave new world that business guru Peter Drucker predicted "will inevitably become far more competitive than any society we have yet known." The *Constitution* article continued: "House Speaker Newt Gingrich . . . advocates eliminating all the rules, downsizing government, abolishing what he calls the welfare state and simply standing back and letting this wonderful new world unfold before our eyes. By making people more vulnerable, Gingrich proposes to drive them to new productivity and competitiveness."[7]

Gingrich, not a fundamentalist himself, had distanced himself from the antigay resolution. But his base in the suburban Right, I was beginning to see, was only the latest layer of a deeply sedimented political phenomenon, not too far above plenty of good old-fashioned fascism, of both the European and the homegrown variety.

Pat headed us back into Atlanta while we swapped stories, the traffic flow heavy in the opposing lane, people headed back to the suburbs after work.

ATLANTA AND OLYMPIC DEVELOPMENT

The new Olympic Stadium was rising to completion beside the Braves' stadium on Hank Aaron Drive, inside the Olympic ring of the inner city, multimillion dollar projects cheek by jowl with areas of extreme poverty. Holly Levinson, the twenty-six-year-old director of Atlanta's Empty the Shelters, a national program of students and young people in solidarity with the homeless, was showing me around the city this morning. Holly worked closely with Jerome Scott of Project South, and with a coalition of antipoverty groups in Atlanta such as the Task Force for the Homeless, Tenants United for Fairness, and Atlanta Neighborhoods United for Fairness. Project South was housed with the Georgia Citizens' Coalition on Hunger, an organization of African American women many of whose lives were the subject of welfare reform.[8]

"We are fighting for the future of Atlanta," Holly explained. "And for the future of the country. The Olympics are only accelerating the kind of development happening all across the region and the nation. Some people call it 'urban renewal'; we think of it as 'urban removal.'" Holly gave me a copy of *Misplaced Priorities: Atlanta, the '96 Olympics, and the Politics of Urban Removal*, produced by Project South.

When Atlanta made its Olympic bid, Jerome had explained to me in his office that morning, the city's housing authority had failed 75 percent of federal housing criteria, putting it at the top of HUD's list of troubled housing. The city had fifteen thousand to twenty thousand people without permanent housing, with an average every month of one thousand to nineteen hundred newly homeless people requesting shelters.[9]

Presiding over it all was the Coca-Cola Company. Coke was devoting half of its annual $1.3 billion advertising and marketing budget to Olympic fervor in order, as one spokesperson explained, to "enhance the value of our brands and the value of our investment." Coke had taken its Olympic partnership "to a level no other company has before," according to the *Atlanta Journal-Constitution*. Coke had made the games "the world's premier sports marketing extravaganza."[10]

"In the back of your mind / you are hoping to find / the real thing," went the Coke jingle. But don't hope too hard in the virtual reality of postindustrial Atlanta's postmodern games, I thought, especially since (as Laura Flanders was instructing me) NBC had paid hundreds of millions of dollars for television rights, and Coke was teaming up with the Disney Corporation (which had recently bought out ABC) for its latest line of commercials, with sports, entertainment, and news hopelessly conflated.[11] New technology was supposedly re-creating the world as a global village. But with these increasingly huge media conglomerates as our eyes, would we have adequate information to be responsible global citizens? Decisions in one part of the world were having innumerable repercussions, but would we know what those repercussions were, or care enough to find out?

We got out and walked around the new stadium. If there were sights and sounds of construction all over downtown Atlanta this November morning, the smell in the air was money. There was certainly enough money in circulation in Atlanta to test out Adam Smith's theories, favorites of Ronald Reagan and as current as Newt Gingrich's "Contract on America." Unlike Los Angeles, which hosted the 1984 Olympics, Atlanta lacked the infrastructure for so large a sporting event, Holly explained. The city had to be rebuilt in the Olympic image. The 1996 games were a billion-dollar enterprise. ACOG was the high-powered private corporation in charge of the Atlanta games. The Metropolitan Atlanta Olympic Games Authority (MAOGA) was the public agency supposedly overseeing the project to protect the public's interest. But ACOG and MAOGA, with acronyms like monsters out of Norse mythology, identified the public's interest with private profits.[12] Corporate sponsorships ($40 million to use the Olympic logo as a "Worldwide Sponsor"), broadcast rights (projected to total $559.5 million), and ticket sales (projected at $422 million and going mainly to corporate patrons) were supposed to pay the development bills.[13] But anted up in this public/-private venture was at least $800 million in public money.[14] At stake was even more development—Atlanta's image as a world-class city. Explained one Atlanta Olympic official, "Major decision-makers from all over the world will be coming to Georgia testing the winds and sniffing the air to see what kind of place this is to do business."[15]

Holly drove me to the construction site of the Olympic Village, visible from the interstate. It had already displaced residents of Techwood/Clark Howell Homes, the oldest public housing project in the United States. That month, four hundred units of public housing were boarded up and surrounded with barbed wire, awaiting destruction. One-half of the eight hundred more units were supposed to be converted to mixed-income housing, which means residents must make fifteen thousand dollars—beyond the price range of most former tenants.[16] Relocated residents were given Section Eight certificates for two years, which carry with them a promise of government subsidy for private housing, if they can find it. But after two years they will be on their own. Some were offered a home-ownership plan, but it required two parents in a home—the enforced heterosexual family.[17] Now there was a parking lot where part of the complex had stood, and the mixed-income construction was delayed. In the meantime, many of Atlanta's inner-city homeless shelters and soup kitchens had been closed down or moved to the city's perimeter.

"What will they do with all the poor people in these neighborhoods?" I asked Holly. She drove me to see the first Olympic project completed on time—the huge new pretrial detention center. The Atlanta City Council had passed one of the most sweeping antihomeless bills in the United States in 1991 and changed the sentence for violations of city ordinances from two to six months. One law made it illegal to be in a parking lot if you do not have a car parked there.[18] Police often arrested homeless people on Friday night; if they pleaded guilty on Monday morning, they were allowed time served—effectively making the streets safe for weekend conventioneers. The Task Force for the Homeless planned to file a lawsuit against the vagrancy ordinances, claiming that nine thousand homeless people had been jailed in the city in the previous year.[19]

Ironically, Olympic construction drew on Atlanta's day-labor pool of homeless workers, who get the most dangerous and difficult work at less than minimum wage, and then are vulnerable to being picked up over the weekend for violating antivagrancy laws. Project South reported that the Atlanta Housing Authority had demolished six public housing developments at the same time as the state of Georgia was spending more than $100 million to construct seven thousand new prison beds, Jerome said—a key part of urban development, as the "Contract on America" made clear.

The Selling of the Olympics

In a multipart series in 1992, the *Atlanta Journal-Constitution* had investigated the public-private partnership that was in reality the selling of the Olympics. "Andy Young, the former Atlanta mayor and U.N. ambassador who co-chairs the Atlanta Committee for the Olympic Games, likes to describe the Games as having been 'privatized,' and he believes that's a good thing," the series explained. "'I don't like anybody to think that commercialization is bad,' says Mr. Young, who himself has been privatized with a $350,000-a-year job heading the international division of Atlanta-based Law Engineering."[20]

I was beginning to find *privatized* a peculiar term for corporate takeovers, since both corporations and the state act in the public sphere. I had looked up the word in *Webster's* and found that the *private* "belongs to some particular person or persons; pertains to or affects a particular small group of persons; is confined to or intended for only the persons immediately concerned; removed from or out of public view or knowledge; undertaken independently; not open or accessible to the general public; solitary."[21] Do we as citizens really want our culture's institutions to come under the control of limited numbers of people, outside of public view? Gingrich and Company were busy pointing a finger at the evils of government, but they seldom applied the same critique to the even more powerful corporations.

The Los Angeles Olympics had marked the corporate Olympic watershed, following the retirement of Avery Brundage, the longtime International Olympic Committee (IOC) president who believed in amateur Olympics protected from the corruption of huge amounts of money. Before the Los Angeles games, contributions from governments and U.S. television rights paid the bulk of the bills for the games, but the 1976 games left Montreal a billion-dollar debt. Newly elected President Juan Antonio Samaranch led the IOC in forming the Commission for New Sources of Financing. Horst Dassler of Adidas advised the committee that the Olympic rings were "the most valuable unexploited symbol in the world." Put them on the market was his advice: "To get at the big money nowadays, one has to go international, to the big multinationals."[22]

Travel agency owner Peter Ueberroth was glad to oblige this new Olympic spirit. He pitched the games as a marketing opportunity, and U.S. corporations opened their coffers to buy international sponsorships, opening an Olympics gusher. The Atlanta Olympics, then, were taking wealth and opulence to new heights in a system where "no one keeps accurate and comprehensive books" and the IOC "cannot account for millions of dollars it has spent over the years."[23] Salt Lake City's bid for the Winter Olympics would expose the degree of corruption in the process, including, in retrospect, Atlanta's. That corruption was just what Avery Brundage had anticipated.

WHAT'S COKE GOT TO DO WITH IT?

Booted and dangerously high-heeled feet beat out the distinctive tap of flamenco dance on a table top, on which bounced a can of Coca-Cola. Cut to a Japanese tea ceremony, from guitar strum and clapping hands and feet to the sliding tones, the ceremonial bow, on the table the familiar cups of tea—and Coca-Cola. Again and again familiar scenes: canals in Venice, camels in the desert, an African village, Coke omnipresent in the foreground, or as a backdrop. In the darkened theater the message flashes on the screen: "Coke was global before global thinking was vogue." Holly sits patiently beside me, responding to what must have seemed a peculiar request on my Atlanta Olympics tour to visit the Coke Museum in downtown Atlanta. But I figured the Coca-Cola Company would provide the most apt lens through which to understand the effect of the postmodern, postindustrial economy on the shaping of present and future possibilities. Coke hovers over Atlanta, often the only sign its contoured bottle, and presides over the 1996 Olympic games. (In the back of my mind, still hoping to find the real thing.)

In 1886 an Atlanta pharmacist, Dr. John Smith Pemberton, concocted as a tonic a thick, sweet syrup made up of coca leaves, the kola nut, plenty of sugar, and various oils and extracts. The cocaine, heavy hits of caffeine and sugar, extract of kola, carbonation, and ice made it an instant hit in Atlanta's sweltering semitropical summers—"a [cold] soft drink that could, in theory, compete with [hot] tea and coffee."[24] "Nerve and Brain Tonic, It Cures Headache, Invigorates the System," early ads proclaimed. The tonic found a ready market in Confederate veterans "returned home with aching, lingering wounds and maladies . . . [to] the region's poverty and rural isolation [with its] . . . grinding, dispirited boredom" that had already made them susceptible to little brown bottles filled with laudanum or alcohol. European doctors had recently succeeded in extracting cocaine from the leaves of coca plants; and among the enthusiasts of Dr. Charles Fauvel's wine-and-cocaine Vin Mariani were Sarah Bernhardt, Thomas Edison, Pope Pius X, Emile Zola, and Lillian Russell.[25]

Folks all over the late-nineteenth-century South, like my mama and me half a century later, flocked to soda fountains for a shot of dope, though we all knew that the cocaine was now gone from the secret formula in the bank's subterranean vault. At ten on hot August mornings, my Mama would dig five (six . . . ten . . . twenty-five) cents out of the bottom of her purse and send me over to Hotel Harris, the brick behemoth next door. I'd pump the handle on the red machine, and out would slide our two cokes in those small glass bottles. The first hit, before I got back across the street, brought tears to my eyes. Our morning shot got us both through until about three in the afternoon, when Mama would locate another dime in the bottom of her purse and back I'd run across the street.

Truth be told, Diet Coke has been a faithful companion to me in the last months of writing this book, a 10:30 A.M. dose that gets me right focused on the track of postindustrial capital. I've even gotten to where I *like* Diet Coke, especially with a Toffee Chocolate Chip Harvest Bar. The Coke comes only after an hour's walk, a shower, and meditation as part of my writing ritual. I have every intention of kicking the habit once the book is in. Those little veins in the frontal cortex tend to tighten and whisper, "More, more," and it's easy for a caffeine dose to rise. (I remember the old Doctor Pepper ad—"the friendly pepper-upper at ten, two and four!")

I can testify to the extent that the folks at Coke are this century's experts at marketing. The Coke trademark is the most recognized in the world, and Coke is "the most successful product in the history of commerce."[26] Pemberton's business partner penned the Coca-Cola name, and with the design of the contoured green bottle to distinguish it from cheap imitations, image became the Coke reality as the secret formula that was indeed squirreled away in a bank vault was tinkered with over the years to remove all traces of cocaine. Brilliant use of modern marketing techniques turned Coke into a million-dollar enterprise that first became identified with the American psyche, then went global. During World War II, the company made sure that "every man in uniform gets a bottle of Coca-Cola for 5 cents."[27] Inside the museum, visitors can travel through the twentieth century—with Coke, born on the cusp of modernity, providing "the pause [read: the rush] that refreshes" in moments of work and leisure. (Those of us who have had jobs sitting at a desk all day know all too well that two o'clock slump, when we head out for coffee or a soda instead of taking a nap.) The Coke museum's ten-minute montage shows scenes from all over the globe.

Key to the consumer capitalism that emerged with Coke in the twentieth century was, as Marcuse observed, the creation in people of a plethora of desires for products—John Locke's "competent store of things"—that manifested in stores like Rich's in malls like Lennox Square all over the United States. Marketing is the way of making people want things we don't necessarily need. As both Coke and tobacco manufacturers rapidly figured out, marketing an addictive product helped people get addicted to the idea of products, not to mention guaranteeing a market.

ADAM SMITH AND THE WEALTH OF *WHICH* PART OF THE NATIONS?

"Give me that which I want, and you shall have that which you want," the ghost of Adam Smith seemed to intone over the city. "It is not from the benevolence of the butcher, the brewer, or the baker that we expect our dinner, but from their regard to their own interest. We address ourselves, not to their humanity, but to their self-love, and never talk to them of our own necessities but of their advantages."[28] Wealth, Smith argued, comes from labor rather than from a nation's accumulation of gold or silver. More specifically, wealth comes from the stage where labor is divided into discrete tasks, "reducing every man's business to some one simple operation and by making this operation the sole employment of his life"—thus the transition from the craftsperson to the worker in an assembly line (the source of alienation, as far as Marx was concerned). The human need to barter or exchange, in economic terms to *trade*, is what gives rise to the division of labor, according to Smith. Money eventually became the medium of exchange, but the ultimate value of goods, Smith argued, is always labor, "the toil and trouble of acquiring [them]." The price of goods, however, is altogether another matter. It is the market that regulates the price of commodities, controlled by laws of supply and demand: "the quantity which is actually brought to market and the demand of those willing to pay."[29] Competition over scarce goods makes the price rise; the more goods on the market, the more the price falls—or so Smith argued.

The price of any commodity, Smith continued, has three components, a kind of Trinity: labor (wages), rent (of land), and profit. As trade eventually results in the accumulation of more money in the hands of particular persons, they will begin to hire other people to work for them for wages: "industrious people who they will supply with materials and subsistence in order to make a profit by the sale of their work, or by what their labor adds to the value of the materials." Profit from this labor goes not to the worker (who gets, as Smith explains, subsistence), but to pay the person "who hazards his stock in this adventure" for the use of his money.[30] Rent is payment for the use of land, an expense that can be claimed only after the invention of private property that allows landlords (as Smith admitted) to "reap where they never sowed."[31] But when prices go up, where does the extra money go—to profits (shareholders) or to labor (workers)? And when prices go down, what happens to workers? Smith was silent on these questions, but Marx immediately began filling in the gaps.

And those gaps did seem considerable. Here is Smith's description of American plantations: "A gentleman who farms a part of his own estate, after paying the expense of cultivation, should gain both the *rent* of the landlord and the *profit* of the farmer. He is apt to denominate, however, his whole gain, *profit* and thus confounds *rent* with *profit*, at least in common language. The greater part of our North American and West Indian planters are in this situation. They farm, the greater part of them, their own estates, and accordingly we seldom hear of the *rent* of a plantation, but frequently of its *profit*" (emphasis mine).[32] Hmmm, what happened to *labor* as a factor here? How much does the *gentleman* really farm—a verb that conflates owning the farm with working it? Is it *his* bare black feet in the saw grass as *he* plants rice all day in the Carolina sun, his eye out for alligators? How remarkably easy it is for labor—here slave labor—to drop out of Smith's equations, even after he has named labor the chief source of wealth. When labor drops out of the equation, more of the price of commodities goes to profit—a point that Marx belabored and the point, as well, to chattel slavery.

Right here from Atlanta, with its rich black intellectual tradition, W.E.B. Du Bois took on Smith's failure to calculate the wealth created by the slave labor of Africans. In *Black Reconstruction in America*, published in 1935 while he was teaching at Atlanta University, Du Bois wrote: "The black *workers* of America bent at the bottom of a growing pyramid of commerce and industry. . . . First of all their *work* called for widening stretches of new, rich black soil—in Florida, in Louisiana, in Mexico; even in Kansas. This *land*, added to *cheap labor*, and *labor* easily regulated and distributed, made *profits* so high that a whole system of culture arose in the South, with a new leisure and social philosophy. *Black labor* became the foundation stone not only of the Southern social structure, but of Northern manufacture and commerce, of the English factory system, of European commerce, of buying and selling on a worldwide scale; new cities were built on the results of black labor, and a new labor problem, involving all white labor, arose both in Europe and America" (emphasis mine).[33] "The coming world is colored," Du Bois had foreseen in 1911, when he became as well the "father of Pan-Africanism."[34] Like his contemporary Mao Zedong's reinterpretation of Marxism for China, "Du Boisian Pan-Africanism . . . signified the militant, anticapitalist solidarity of the darker world."[35]

Du Bois's critique of Smith highlights another key concept in Atlanta's Olympic development—that of opulence, which in Atlanta was wealth in an obvious excess. Adam Smith also wrote of that "universal opulence which extends itself to the lowest ranks of people" that is a consequence of the division of labor in a "well-governed society": "Every workman has a great quantity of his own work to dispose of beyond what he himself has occasion for; and every other workman *being exactly in the same situation*, he is enabled to exchange a great quantity of his own goods for a great quantity, or what comes to the same thing, for the price of a great quantity of theirs. He supplies them abundantly with what they have occasion for, and they accommodate him as amply with what he has occasion for, and a general plenty diffuses itself through all the different ranks of society."[36]

In Smith's free market, laborers are hypothetical unitary individuals in exactly the same situation—a fiction that omits slave labor and the poor and the working class and women. Clearly, Olympic opulence was not trickling down to Atlanta's homeless, or the day-labor pool. People in Atlanta were hardly all in exactly the same situation in their ability to get their snouts in the Olympic trough.

If it is "by labour, that all the wealth of the world was originally purchased," as Smith explains, then, even in capitalism's terms, African Americans in Atlanta and elsewhere are owed a good many back wages—considerably more than the forty acres and a mule promised but not delivered to the blacks freed from slavery in the states of the former Confederacy, who headed north and west at the turn of the century in the Great Migration.[37]

Du Bois put his finger on the weakness of capitalism: "In any land, in any country under modern free competition," Du Bois explained, "to lay any class of [politically] weak and despised people, be they white, black, or blue, at the political mercy of their stronger, richer, and more resourceful fellows, is a temptation which human nature seldom has withstood and seldom will withstand."[38]

RACE AND URBAN POLICY IN THE TWENTIETH CENTURY

Project South, Empty the Shelters, the Georgia Citizens' Coalition, and Atlanta's poor were fighting the urban face of the Right when they took on Olympic development. Part of their analysis was an excavation of urban policy in the twentieth century as cities like Atlanta, built and burned in the Confederacy and rebuilt for the New South, moved from industrial to postindustrial economies. What happened to people of color in Atlanta in the twentieth century, I was beginning to see under Jerome's tutelage, is emblematic of what happened all over the country.

In 1910, 90 percent of African Americans in the United States lived in the South. Even then they were fleeing the rapidly industrializing but still rural South of the former plantation system in droves, driven by economic depression and lynching and soon pulled by defense jobs during both World Wars to New York, Chicago, Detroit, D.C., California, and southern cities like Atlanta. The poorest communities of Atlanta's inner city, near where Martin Luther King Jr. was born and lies buried— Vine City, Summerhill, Mechanicsville, Peopletown—are predominantly African American. What blacks in those communities traveled toward was integration into a capitalist economy, the opulence of which was built on wealth from their own labor at the same time as that labor was made invisible. The Great Depression, the mechanization of agriculture, and soil depletion brought more tenant families to cities from more remote areas. These migrants moved into the cheapest (thus the most congested and deteriorating) areas of the cities to which they fled to become part of the urban working class. By the 1960s, two-thirds of the African American population in the United States was metropolitan—three-fifths of those in central cities, places like Harlem, Watts, Newark, and Detroit that erupted into flames in the urban revolts of the late 1960s.[39] King described the cause of these uprisings in an essay published posthumously: "Confronted now with the interrelated problems of war, inflation, urban decay, white backlash and a climate of violence, [the nation] is now forced to address itself to race relations and poverty and it is tragically unprepared. What might once have been a series of separate problems now merge into a social crisis of almost stupefying complexity."[40]

In Atlanta, as in cities all across the United States, the urban renewal projects of the 1950s and 1960s were designed to make profits off the blight of the inner city by buying up depressed property for business development and moving poor people out—a process that came to be known as gentrification. Urban renewal in Atlanta in the 1960s included the expansion of the interstate highway system and the building of the Atlanta/Fulton County Stadium to house the Braves and a new civic center. The poor were relocated to other poor areas, including into public housing, destabilizing neighborhoods. The urban renewal of the sixties displaced one-seventh of Atlanta's population, most of them poor and African American.[41] The residents of the Summerhill neighborhood, still resentful from displacement by the stadium, rioted in 1966 in the aftermath of a policeman shooting a black auto-theft suspect. The riot led to more white flight to places like gun-toting Cobb County, which helped create conditions for the election of Atlanta's first black mayor, Maynard Jackson, in 1973.

During this same period of an increasingly racialized and gendered inner city, Atlanta's progressive reputation as the "city too busy to hate" emerged (eventually to become part of the sales pitch for the Olympics by Andy Young and Billy Payne). Atlanta's liberal reputation had been shaped half a century earlier by William Hartsfield, mayor of Atlanta from 1936 to 1961, and Robert Woodruff, Coca-Cola president from 1923 until his death in 1985. Hartsfield was a white southern politician who early on chose bridge-building over standing in the schoolhouse door or handing out ax handles like Georgia's more neolithic governor Lester Maddox. Hartsfield removed the "white" and "colored" signs from the Atlanta airport, instructed clerks at City Hall to address black citizens as "Mrs." and "Mr." and integrated the Atlanta Police Department in 1948. Robert Woodruff, as CEO of a company that sold Cokes all over the world, thought that race-baiting was "detrimental to an international product because of a sectionalism that has outlived its usefulness."[42] As Civil Rights struggles heated up in the 1950s, Woodruff and other Coke executives realized that a southern-based global company needed a careful public relations strategy. Woodruff began to donate to black institutions, publicizing his generosity only in the black press. Woodruff's influence in 1962 desegregated the Commerce Club, meeting place of Atlanta's business elite, and guaranteed broad business support in 1964 for a dinner honoring King when he won the Nobel Peace Prize.[43]

Atlanta was not an industrial city, so in the 1970s and 1980s it did not suffer large losses from automation and from corporate decisions to send industrial production overseas, both of which had seriously depleted the urban working class and the urban tax base in northern cities. But slashes in social spending and the safety net during the Reaganomics of the 1980s and 1990s hit hard at Atlanta's poor, who had never had access to the kind of unionized jobs offered in places like Detroit.[44] During the Reagan years, public housing nationwide took some of the heaviest of the budget cuts, and the homeless became a fixture of the American urban landscape—targeted now in pre-Olympic development by Atlanta's new vagrancy laws.

As Jerome instructed me, "By the 1990s, the global integration of the U.S. economy meant that Atlanta's workers were competing with 120 million other U.S. workers and the world's 3 billion workers—including more than 900 million unemployed. The race to the bottom had begun." Wages and benefits at their lowest, combined with technological levels of production at their highest, meant that "millions of workers are now human surplus."[45]

Jerome summarized: "The construction and preparation for the Olympic Games in Atlanta quickened the process of the destruction of low-income housing. But the Olympics are not the root cause of it. The root cause of the destruction of affordable housing, of good paying jobs, of the social safety net, and of the social contract itself lies in the globalization and high-teching of the capitalist market economy."

Techwood Homes illustrates the urban trends that racialized and gendered inner cities. It was built in the 1930s for 604 white working families, displacing fourteen hundred units of slum housing (one thousand white, four hundred black), according to Project South. In the 1960s, Techwood was integrated, so that by 1975, 60 percent of its residents were black, with many white residents moving out into homes they purchased. By 1990, 95 percent of the residents were black, one-half with family incomes below $3,200; 9 percent heads of households were employed; 90 percent of the heads of households were women; 65 percent received AFDC.[46] Over this time period, real wages declined, jobs were increasingly automated or moved overseas, and the drug economy moved into inner-city neighborhoods. These trends left poor women and their children in housing developments like Techwood Homes in an economy with fewer decent jobs and increasingly dependent on a welfare system that failed them, but payments from which Gingrich's contract would eliminate because he saw their problems only as a failure of personal responsibility.

Lord help us all.

Andrew Young, one of King's young lieutenants, had another take on the Atlanta economy. Mayor after Maynard Jackson, Young had brought a surprisingly pro-business interest to the job, different from Jackson's more Chicago-style grassroots approach. Young prided himself on having attracted $80 billion in new investment, completed the expressway system, built Underground Atlanta, expanded the airport, and created half a million new jobs during his term as mayor.[47] He pitched the Olympics bid, as he explained it, "based on the notion that people from dramatically different backgrounds can stop fighting, at least for a time, and compete peacefully for the greater good of humanity. We had to learn to do that in Atlanta—to bridge gaps between black and white, rich and poor, between a wide variety of ethnic groups. We did have significant divisions, which we had learned to overcome through competition rather than bile."[48] If decline in housing, decent jobs, and the social safety net were conditions that Atlanta shares with cities all over the globe, this became a bargaining point in the selling of Atlanta: "Billy and Andy sold Atlanta as a Third World City, as the capital of African America—as, in fact, the only African city in the running for the games."[49] Young had morphed from one of King's trusted lieutenants in King's period of militant democratic socialism to his present role as nineties Olympic entrepreneur—a transformation symptomatic of late capital.[50]

W.E.B. Du Bois had already explained his position on opulence in *The Souls of Black Folk*, a passage with which Andy Young, surely, was familiar: "[W]e almost fear to question if the end of racing is not gold, if the aim of man is not rightly to be rich. And if this is the fault of America, how dire a danger lies before a new land and a new city, lest Atlanta, stooping for mere gold, shall find that gold accursed. . . . What if the Negro people be wooed from a strife for righteousness, from a love of knowing, to regard dollars as the be-all and end-all of life?"[51]

POSTMODERN BUT NOT POSTRACIST?

Atlanta and the Olympics offered a view of the postmodern landscape, I argued, but what did that mean? Detroit was the quintessential industrial city, its high-paying union jobs mostly gone now, to automation or to poorer countries with cheaper workforces. Atlanta is a postmodern city, its economy commerce and service, its quintessential product made not with the steel and rubber of Detroit, but with sugar, caffeine, and water.

What is the *postmodern*, anyway, this term that has migrated from aesthetics to politics to just about everything as a sign for the age? In a lecture at the Whitney Museum in 1982, Frederic Jameson (at that time the foremost Marxist literary critic) "redrew the whole map of the postmodern at one stroke," anchoring it in the "economic order of capital itself," not as "mere aesthetic break."[52] When Jameson gave his lecture at the Whitney, the postmodern had been established as something brushed by associations beyond the West, as a cultural system in which space was important, and as an analysis that denigrated grand narratives of Enlightenment progress and (some said especially) of Marxist and other revolutionary transformations. Used as early as the 1930s, its appearance signaled an increasingly strong perception, both politically and culturally, that forces were afoot beyond the modern. In literature, something began to emerge beyond the oppositional and subversive modernist avant-gardes of both Left (for example, British poet W. H. Auden and Spanish poet Pablo Neruda) and Right (for example, Americans Ezra Pound and T. S. Eliot), with their common repudiation of "Victorian taboos and family life, of commodification, and of the increasing asphyxiation of a desacralizing capitalism." Culturally, the newer era seemed to poke out beyond the industrial, the imperial, and the national. Arnold Toynbee explained the postmodern as the destabilized relationship between industrialism and nationalism, the two forces that had shaped Europe since the Middle Ages, as industry burst the bounds of a nationality whose contagion spread downward into tribal and ethnic conflicts—exactly the forces that women had so eloquently described in Beijing. "The rise of an industrial working class in the West, and the bid of successive intelligentsia outside the West to master the secrets of modernity and turn them against the West," are what Anderson cites as Toynbee's marks of the postmodern.[53]

Something newer than what had been declared the new or modern clearly required understanding and articulation, and the postmodern for fifty years had variously marked this need. For some on the left, postmodern signaled an affirmative linking of aesthetic theory with prophetic history—in projectivist poet Charles Olson's words, "after the dispersal / an archeologist of morning." For those on the Right, it became a marker of the triumph of the market over communism and socialism, with the collapse of the Soviet Union in 1989 and an "end to history": "There could be nothing but capitalism."[54]

Jameson's contribution was to link postmodern culture with a "new moment of capital." He drew on Ernest Mandel's *Late Capitalism* for an understanding of a third stage of capital, begun in the 1940s and with the 1960s as a key transition period. Lenin had elaborated on Marx to identify a second stage of capitalism, "the so-called monopoly stage, or the moment of classical imperialism." Mandel elaborated yet another stage when he linked the "emergence of new formal features in culture with the emergence of a new type of social life and a new economic order," variously called "modernization, post-industrial or consumer society, the society of the media or the spectacle, or multinational capitalism."[55] Postmodern culture brought the erosion of modernist distinctions between high culture and an increasingly commercialized popular culture that used the arts for design and advertising. Coke's Atlanta Olympics fit all these specs of third-stage capitalism: consumption, media spectacle, globalization, advertising as art.

The postmodern also brought a death of the subject, as Jameson announced in *Postmodernism; or, The Cultural Logic of Late Capitalism* and summarized in *The Cultural Turn*, "the end of individualism as such," with the subject's unique vision, personality, and style. In an age of corporate capitalism, of organization man, of state and corporate bureaucracy, and of demographic explosions, "that older bourgeois individual subject no longer exists" and perhaps (poststructuralists were saying) never did. The postmodern, Jameson explained, signals a "failure of the new" that brings "imprisonment in the past," and it generates new forms of nostalgia as "pathological symptom[s] of a society that has become incapable of dealing with time and history," hence *Gone with the Wind* and its spawn, Pitty Pat's Porch.[56] If the failure of the new eradicates history and collapses the temporal (past and future into an omnipresent), he argues, what takes the place of time is the spatial. The zooming elevators and escalators of the Hyatt Regency Hotels, for example, signify a "postmodern hyperspace [that] has finally succeeded in transcending the capacities of the individual human body to locate itself, to organize its immediate surroundings perceptually, and to map cognitively its position in a mapable external world"—what I myself had encountered in Atlanta as a teenager.[57] Jameson argued that the process of modernization was all but complete and had effectively obliterated precapitalist social forms, so that culture had become coextensive with the late-capitalist economy itself, turning all to commodity, for sale on the ever-expanding global market—hence "A World of Coke," as the Coke Museum trumpeted.

Jameson might help to explain Atlanta, but Atlanta showed the limits of his analysis as it did of Adam Smith's—and those limits came down to the same thing: race and gender. It is remarkable that in his attention to space, Jameson misses the degree to which the landscape in U.S. cities is so racialized and gendered—exactly what Jerome and Holly and the folks at Project South did such a fine job of pointing out.

"WE HELPED EACH OTHER AND SURVIVED"

Holly dropped me off at the King Center. After our tour of inside the Olympic ring, I was overwhelmed at the degree to which Olympic wealth was rapidly transforming Atlanta. I wanted to spend some time at the quiet pool that lapped around the marble of Martin Luther King's grave, here in the neighborhood where he was born, grew up, preached, and came home from Memphis to be buried.

Yes, I was on another pilgrimage, at the tomb of one of many martyrs to racial justice in the United States. I knew there were plenty of caveats: not to conflate King the man with the movement in a way that made the heroic actions of thousands of grassroots black people (especially women) all over the South invisible; not to fail to credit the bottom-up strategy of Ella Baker and the young Student Nonviolent Coordinating Committee (SNCC) organizers, who worked courageously to build indigenous leadership in working-class communities and who pressed King and the Southern Christian Leadership Conference (SCLC) from the Left; not to forget that King's nonviolence seen from Malcolm X's perspective or that of Black Power came across as a toadying to white people at the expense of black self-respect and self-determination. I knew that King's sexual philandering and his inability to recognize women's leadership had seriously compromised his mission, and that the King family was now full tilt marketing the dream—a process that would net them a $10-million-per-year Time-Warner deal in 1997.[58] All of this notwithstanding, if there was anywhere in Atlanta I might find the spot for an "archaeologist of morning," in Charles Olson's terms, King's grave was still the place.

Theologian James Cone has written that King transformed our understanding of

Christianity by making justice an essential ingredient: "Before King, no Christian theologian showed so conclusively in his actions and words the great contradiction between racial segregation and the gospel of Jesus."[59] Michael Eric Dyson would call King "the greatest American who ever lived" because King "forced the United States to confront its conscience." Dyson concludes: "King's career, with all of its flaws and failures, is simply the most faithful measure of American identity and national citizenship we are likely to witness."[60] By my own understanding, King rerouted the master-slave dynamic, speaking from its downside to descendants of both masters and slaves. With cosmic companionship and a deep faith, he pointed beyond the master-slave dualism to "beloved community" as he mobilized an assault on racist and capitalist structures that institutionalized such relations in brutal regimes of power (deconstruction in the service of Reconstruction). On his own terms he failed, not because those terms were wrong but because the master-slave dynamic is so heartbreakingly entrenched.

I put down my backpack and settled in for the afternoon. I pulled out *A Testament of Hope: The Essential Writings and Speeches of Martin Luther King* and Howard Thurman's *Jesus and the Disinherited*. You never know when you might steal a few quiet moments with the right book. The crisp fall afternoon made this location a great place to read, to ponder, and to meditate.

Howard Thurman, an African American theologian who, like Du Bois, taught at Atlanta University, wrote *Jesus and the Disinherited* to capture his thinking between 1935 and 1949, when it was published, on the meaning of Jesus' message to those with "their backs to the wall." Martin Luther King Jr. had carried *Jesus and the Disinherited* in his briefcase.[61] My friends Mac Jones and Sam Mann turned me on to Thurman, who mentored many decades of black ministers. Mac and Sam were both preachers in Kansas City. I met Mac first in anti-Klan work, when he had rallied the African American community in a little Georgia town against an active Klan. Mac was a big man, and he preached in a booming baritone that reached to the back pew and into the heart. Sam was a dapper white guy who hopped back and forth from one foot to the other when he got wound up in the pulpit, until I thought he would levitate. Sam had been the minister in an inner-city black church in Kansas City for more than twenty years, after getting kicked out of the Methodist Church in the sixties for his antiracist activity. At St. Mark's he was loved and instructed by his parishioners and kept in line by the women of the congregation. Mac was moderator of the U.S. Urban-Rural Mission, and Sam was in its contact group. I had been skittish about working for the church as a lesbian, but I had found their presence reassuring.

At one of my first URM meetings, Mac had caught me off-guard by asking me to pray. After a very pregnant pause, I began, "*Weeellll*, whoever's out there . . ." and then proceeded, I thought, to lay down a pretty good prayer. Afterward, Sam kidded me about it a good bit, but said he appreciated my honesty. I had been mustering a prayer to what I thought was *their* God, who did seem pretty remote from me about then, my own sense of my spirituality being more immanent and internal. "Do you know that poem by Anne Sexton, 'The Awful Rowing Towards God'?" Sam asked. "I always wanted to tell her, 'God is in the boat.'" After a good many years, I have decided that God is the boat, and the water, and the rower, and the stillness of the morning.

Reading Thurman helped me understand more what Sam meant about his God-in-the-boat. Thurman distinguishes between institutional Christianity, about which he had at least as many questions as Marx, and what he calls the "religion of Jesus." Thurman also answers Marx—"the more man puts into God, the less he retains for himself"—with faith in a God that accompanies and sustains.[62]

The point of *Jesus and the Disinherited* is radical subjectivity as an answer to the erosion of self and of human personality under brutal regimes. Thurman did not (as Jameson does) proclaim the death of the subject; instead he suggests ways to restore what he calls the inner life. He radically repositions the religion of Jesus to be *for* rather than *about* the disinherited as he moves Jesus from religious object to religious subject. His approach to Jesus is thoroughly historical: he asks what the life of Jesus—a poor Jew living under Rome—teaches the dispossessed about the terms under which survival is possible. He finds the answer in Jesus' insistent "urgency [about] a radical change in the inner life." Thurman's focus is on how the disinherited can claim more power over seemingly intractable circumstances. "If a man knows precisely what he can do to you or what epithet he can hurl against you in order to make you lose your temper, your equilibrium, then he can always keep you under subjection. It is a man's reaction to things that determines their ability to exercise power over him," Thurman explains. Thus the religion of Jesus grants emotional and spiritual freedom within a repressive order as it builds subjects to challenge that order.[63]

Relations of master and slave were more than metaphor for Thurman, who received his most potent instruction from a grandmother who lived under slavery. She passed on to Howard the necessity of maintaining an inner life in the face of institutional structures—slavery, Jim Crow—that could seem insuperable. "No external force, however great and overwhelming, can at long last destroy a people if it does not first win the victory of the spirit against them," Thurman said, explaining both the religion of Jesus and his grandmother's lesson. "Again and again [Jesus] places his finger on the 'inward center' as the crucial area where the issues would determine the destiny of his people."[64]

What do the disinherited do about Rome, or a white supremacist United States, symbol of "total frustration . . . [and] the great barrier to peace of mind"? Thurman quickly calculates the options available to Jesus: to resist or not to resist. Assimilation involved loss of self-respect. Separatism rose, Thurman felt, from a mood of bitterness and hatred and a deep, calculating fear. Armed resistance might release tension and free people from a "disintegrating sense of complete impotency and helplessness," but Thurman saw violence as a "tragic last resort." Jesus shaped his gospel to give the dispossessed an inner freedom in the midst of outer tribulations, a freedom that not

incidentally creates the energy to assert more just material arrangements. "He recognized with authentic realism that anyone who permits another to determine the
quality of his inner life gives into the hands of the other the keys to his destiny."[65]

Thurman deals at length with three subjective states, the "hounds of hell" of the
disinherited, for which the religion of Jesus offered a solution. The first such hound
is a fear that arises from "precipitate and stark" violence that is "devoid of the element
of contest" and that comes with a "deep humiliation."[66] Here the photographs in
Without Sanctuary float back to mind, almost one hundred pictures of lynchings
from Thurman's lifetime, many of them from Georgia. The photographs were mass
reproduced and used as postcards on which white family members communicated,
then collected among family memorabilia. They are both commodities and public
records of public rituals. They are also representations of lynched bodies, mostly of
African Americans, around or above or below which gather the white mobs posing
proudly for the camera's eye. They bear witness, as John Lewis explains in a contributing essay, to an American holocaust. "Negro Barbecue" one postcard's hand-
written message reads. But even these photographs cannot capture the lynching in
which the white crowd cut off a man's ears, his fingers, his genitals, skinned his face,
knifed him, burned him, then cut out his heart and liver, cut them into pieces, and
crushed his bones into small particles. In other pictures bodies are left to hang, on the
lamp post near the train tracks, off the bottom of the bridge, in innumerable violated
trees, to serve as warning.[67]

Fear of such a horrible fate, explains Thurman, gives people a kind of disease that
eventually becomes a "death for the self." Jesus' antidote to such fear was the message
that "God's eye is on the sparrow"—"God is mindful of the individual." It is a theology to restore the sense of belonging stripped from people by their lack of protection
from atrocity: "The awareness of being a child of God tends to stabilize the ego and
results in a new courage, fearlessness, and power. . . . The individual now feels that
he counts, that he belongs. He senses the confirmation of his roots, and even death
becomes a little thing."[68]

Thurman had learned this lesson from his mother when he was a child. He often
recalled the night she awakened him to go to the backyard to see Halley's comet, a
great spectacle that they watched together in speechless awe. Thurman asked, "What
will happen to us if that comet falls out of the sky?" After a long silence in which he
beheld her countenance, she said, "Nothing will happen to us, Howard; God will
take care of us."[69]

Deception is the second affliction of both the former master and slave still caught
in legacies of slave systems. The unacknowledged pattern of deception "by which the
weak are deprived of their civil, economic, political and social rights" creates the secondary pattern of deception by which the weak circumvent the strong. However reasonable as a survival strategy such reactive deception might be, ultimately "the
penalty of deception is to become a deception." The biological drive of not being
killed must give way to a "complete and devastating sincerity . . . to be simply, directly

truthful whatever may be the cost in life, limb, security."[70] Here spiritual power must act at the level of species being to form a different response than fight or flight.

Hate, Thurman says, is the third characteristic of master-slave relations. Contact without fellowship creates unsympathetic understanding, expressed in an exercise of ill will that becomes hatred walking on earth. Hatred happens on both sides of the power divide; but the hatred of the dispossessed for the powerful can provide a source of validation for the personality and a dynamic energy by which the individual "seeks to protect [the] self against moral disintegration." Jesus rejected such hatred because it was death to relationship with oneself, with others, and with God. His ethic of love meant that "an attack must be made on the enemy status" through a practice of love. Forgiveness was central to this love because it saw that God forgives, that "no evil deed represents the full intent of the doer," and that evildoers do not go unpunished in the "wide sweep of the ebb and flow of moral law [where] our deeds track us down and doer and deed meet."[71]

As a lesbian, I could appreciate Thurman's insights. Holding my own reality in the face of constant heterosexist assumptions was always a challenge, and yet it brought me back to my own grounding. Assumed heterosexuality was itself a deception, against which lesbians and gay men constantly have to struggle, even in the relatively open climate of the nineties. I was having a hard time getting through to my brother Tim and his family, for instance, but his cancer made the task seem urgent. Still, I was not sure I could meet what felt like the conditions of the relationship: to lie about myself.

And I had nothing like the violence of lynching to contend with, but I knew plenty of women and men who had been sexually abused in their homes, a kind of continuing torture, sometimes from the very people who should have been protecting them. The temptation to bitterness and hatred was always there, and it could provide a ready excuse for most anything. I had had a brief separatist period, but pretty quickly decided that it left me in too narrow a world. And I liked Thurman's explanation of our deeds that track us down across the ebb and flow of moral law: a kind of karma that did not require hell's fire to make its point.

Thurman's spiritual lessons came to him through the women in his family: "When my father died when I was little, my mother and grandmother sent me to our neighbors to ask them to help us by giving what they could, and they helped. This was the way of life in our neighborhood. In sorrows, joys, good times and bad, this was the way we lived. We helped each other and we survived."[72] This is a radically different perspective than that of Adam Smith, who addresses himself not to our humanity but to our self-interest.

Thurman's evocation of the religion of Jesus must have resonated deeply with Martin Luther King Jr.—the son of Thurman's friend Martin Sr. "Deep from within that order," Thurman wrote, "[Jesus] projected a dream, the logic of which would give to all the needful security. There would be room for all, and no man would be a threat to his brother. 'The kingdom of God is within.' 'The Spirit of the Lord is upon me, because he hath anointed me to preach the gospel to the poor.' . . . Hatred is destructive to hated and hater alike. Love your enemy, that you may be children of your Father who is in heaven."[73]

The religion of Jesus, Thurman insists, involves "a discipline, a method, a technique, as over against some form of wishful thinking."[74] The Civil Rights movement developed such discipline in the practice of nonviolent direct action. In Gandhi's satyagraha Martin Luther King found the last element of his theology: a method and discipline of love through which people of faith and courage could act within history to change it "Christ furnished the spirit and motivation while Gandhi furnished the method." While Mao and other Communist and nationalist revolutionaries were forging tactics of guerilla warfare and armed resistance, Gandhi, Thurman, and King were shaping the second major path of resistance to colonialism and racism in the twentieth century in an attempt to avoid the tragic last resort of violent resistance to injustice.

What has Martin Luther King meant to me? I pondered, leaning back against the stone. He was the local genius of my childhood. Forty miles away in Montgomery, his voice came to me through the new television that my parents had purchased in the mid-1950s, as the Civil Rights movement came into focus over the next ten years. In retrospect, I can distinguish the complex strands of black struggle that operated in my home territory during my childhood. Already in place was Tuskegee Institute Professor Charles Gomillion's work on voter registration in the 1930s and 1940s, the kind of campaign that happened in counties all over the South and laid the groundwork for the upsurge of the 1950s. The Southern Christian Leadership Conference grew out of the Montgomery boycott, a network led by black ministers such as King who had a profound religious commitment to nonviolence, which had been nurtured as a response to colonialism, with links to Gandhi and the nationalist movement in India. There was the militancy as well of the black airmen at the Tuskegee airbase during World War II. Up near Reeltown, the Share Croppers' Union members shot it out in the early thirties with the sheriff's men trying to repossess their land.[75] The Student Nonviolence Coordinating Committee, the young revolutionaries mentored by Ella Baker, included those who led the demonstrations on the steps of my Methodist Church and who worked with poor black people out in the country. Rumor had it that Black Panthers, emerging from the Lowndes County struggles, had stolen guns from the armory and stashed them somewhere in the county for a coming insurrection. Whatever these not-so-subtle differences, they all cohered in my white child's mind in the voice of King.

Michael Eric Dyson aptly described the psychology King employed on both southern whites and blacks. King's message was therapeutic for southern whites because he understood the nagging inauthenticity of the master whose identity depends on his repression of the slave (and racism afforded such mastery to even the poorest southern whites of all genders). "The sadistic [white] habit of attempting to escape shame by repeating the act that caused it is one that King, a fellow Southerner and

Christian, completely understood." King held out the bracing possibility of redemptive love at a time when we were coming to consciousness about the depth of black anger: "Millions of Southern whites came to depend on a love they really didn't deserve from a figure their culture taught them not to respect."[76] Such a psychology also describes the dynamic between southern white children and the black women who worked as their nursemaids, a dynamic I had explored early on when I started writing, to my mother's dismay.[77] It was a phenomenon Lillian Smith also had explicated in *Killers of the Dream*. Much of my early lesbian-feminist work had come out of a determination to keep a different kind of faith with women's (and, I guess, human) relationships.

Southern blacks, Dyson explains, had a different source of disquiet: their fear that white racist beliefs might be true and guilt at the failure to demand dignity and self-respect. He describes the strategy of the psychic doppelganger, or the shadow self, that blacks constructed to encounter the white southern world, a mask necessary at most points for survival but carrying all the costs of deception that Thurman had elucidated. "Instead of hiding their pain through dual personas and artful duplicity," Dyson explains, "[King] said [southern blacks] must now bend their outer self in a different moral direction . . . to shed the mask of the outer self and reveal in public the inner desire to be free."[78]

King situated himself precisely on the cusp of master and slave, tapping both psychic fields and unleashing a tremendous energy in its most devilish and divine manifestations as this great southern morality play relayed itself through the new medium of television to what I thought of then as "all those white Yankees" who were understandably horrified at what their white cousins were acting out. That such a strategy depended on a high level of northern white hypocrisy was something we southern whites knew then and King would soon enough discover fully, when the movement in its various manifestations won the victory against Jim Crow with the 1964 and 1965 Civil Rights bills and traveled north.

King's faith gave him the nerve, or the naïveté, to take on both sets of psychic forces. After a bomb threat came his "kitchen epiphany" when, in response to prayerful self-doubt, he heard the voice of God say that he would go forward "never alone, no, never alone."[79] In Montgomery, amidst women and men who had already taken on Jim Crow, King experienced a faith that had escaped him in seminary. He could then write: "In many instances I have felt the power of God transforming the fatigue of despair into the buoyancy of hope. . . . I am convinced that the universe is under the control of a loving purpose and that in the struggle for righteousness man has cosmic companionship. Behind the harsh appearances of the world there is a benign power."[80]

Personality linked humans and God, said King, echoing Thurman's insistence on a radical subjectivity for egos that bore the brunt of apartheid. "So in the truest sense of the word, God is a living God. In him there is feeling and will, responsiveness to the deepest yearnings of the human heart; this God both evokes and answers prayers." The self was not limited to the narrow confines of the ego, where hurt was introjected and calcified. "It is certainly true that human personality is limited, but personality as such involves no necessary limitations. It simply means self-consciousness and self-direction."[81]

Sounds of laughter from the streets, kids out of school. It must be three o'clock. I watched leaves hit the surface of the pool and drift toward one end. It occurred to me to be thankful for this moment. I picked up the book again. But I was getting sleepy in the Georgia sun. I began to underline, to keep myself focused.

King saw human nature as neither innately good nor innately evil, a view that throws choice into existential relief. His knowledge of the deep-seated nature of racism in the culture—"the tragedies of history and man's shameful inclination to choose the low road"—led him from a sentimental liberal faith in human nature to an acknowledgment of the degree to which "reason is darkened by sin . . . little more than an instrument to justify man's defensive way of thinking." Early on, theologically, he forged a "middle way," choosing both faith and reason and recognizing humans' innate capacities for both tremendous good and tremendous evil. King called on humans to be "willing to be co-workers of God" through their own "tireless efforts and persistent work."[82] For King, the self may be deeply fractured by the schisms of the culture, yet it reaches for greater freedom and coherence.[83]

Du Bois had prophesied in 1903: Out of "the deep religious feeling of the real Negro heart . . . seek[ing] in the great night a new religious ideal, some day the Awakening will come, when the pent-up vigor of ten million souls shall sweep irresistibly toward the Goal, out of the Valley of the Shadow of Death, where all that makes life worth living—Liberty, Justice, and Right—is marked 'For White People Only.'"[84] One translation of *satyagraha* is "soul force"—spirituality as generative of material transformation.

When the subject is under siege, King and Thurman had seen, then actively *strengthening* subjectivity suggests itself as a valuable project. Neither King nor Thurman understood the African American subject as only unique or individual, given the intensely collective experience of resistance to slavery and complex and often submerged legacies of African cultures to African experiences in the Americas. If transforming the current postmodern and postindustrial late-capitalist reality requires consciousness of an "undreamed of kind," as Jameson observed, then the kind of dreaming from the belly of the beast that is the core of African American theology offers on generative possibility of the "new international proletariat" that Jameson anticipates.[85]

It is warm in the afternoon sun at King's grave. My eyelids droop and lines begin to get wavy. My chin is on my chest, and I am dreaming, I am reading, I am dreaming. The area around King's tomb is bright, warm, glowing—and busy! Atlanta shines behind me, a new Jerusalem, and all its streets are paved with Coke. Karl Marx is trying to walk on the water in the reflecting pool, and Andy Young is being chased down Auburn Street by Red Guards. Yahweh is at Olympic Stadium, competing in the javelin and the shot put, and He has just beaten His own Olympic record for throwing lightning bolts. Then the scene fades again and we are on the track field, and Jerome is running the relay with a baton just passed off by W.E.B. and ahead of them chugs Andy Young on a team with Adam Smith and Newt. And somewhere very else beneath the bodhi tree Martin King sits in a lotus posture, his closed eyes completely peaceful, serene mouth silent now in its faintest smile, his right hand pointing toward the earth. And inside the Olympic ring Buddha and Jesus in their saffron robes with their begging bowls search barefoot for food and shelter, but there is only Coke for $3.75 and there is no room in the inn.

AFTERWORD

It's the Coke image we saw in Atlanta, ubiquitous over the two Olympic weeks, not only in its televised ads, but also in advertisements behind or to the side of athletes experiencing the thrill of victory, the agony of defeat. In spite of the work that Project South, Empty the Shelters, SONG, and other groups did to put together a Progressive Media Center for the Olympics, on NBC (the officially televised Olympics) we did not see the image of Atlanta's homeless men and women, or the 43 percent of the city's children who live in poverty.

A big part of the coverage focused on the pipe bomb that exploded on a Friday night amidst Olympic festivities in the main plaza, killing one woman. The inevitable foreign terrorists were the first suspects, then a security guard who was eventually exonerated. It was, in fact, the domestic Right that provided the terrorist disruption of the Atlanta Olympics. The Olympic bomber has not yet been apprehended, but the current suspect is neo-Nazi Eric Rudolph—one version of Cobb County's Wild Man—wanted for the bombing of a Birmingham abortion clinic that killed one person, and suspected in the bombing of a gay bar and an abortion clinic in Atlanta. Rudolph is probably still holed up in the North Carolina mountains, eluding federal pursuit as a shaggy fascist hermit or a pile of whitening bones.

Adam Smith, realizing the need for some balance to the pursuit of profits and self-interest, found it in the spectator and in what he theorized as a human being's desire for approval by his fellow people: "In the race for wealth, and honours, and preferments . . . [the individual] may run as hard as he can, and strain every nerve and every muscle, in order to outstrip all his competitors. But if he should jostle, or throw down any of them, the indulgence of the spectators is entirely at an end. It is a violation of fair play, which they cannot admit of."[86]

But when the ethical spectator gets too bemused by the spectacle, what happens to ethics? The poor disappear from the streets, from Techwood Homes, from the freeze-frame, the instant replay. What will those of us who think now that poverty is the just due of the irresponsible poor do ourselves in twenty years, when automation may have eliminated 60 percent of jobs as we know them today? Caught in our various spectacles, how will those of us who in those moments are not the poor notice or care? When the spectacle is designed to obscure violations of fair play or, even worse, to promote them, will the spectator know that what she or he sees is not the real thing?

4

MEMPHIS
Received in Graceland

*A commodity appears, at first sight, a very trivial thing, and easily understood.
Its analysis shows that it is, in reality, a very queer thing, abounding in
metaphysical subtleties and theological niceties.*
— KARL MARX, *Grundrisse*

*Colonel Tom Parker has returned to the Hilton, hawking his elixir of unbottled
sex and satisfaction, Elvis Presley. . . . The product up for sale . . . possesses too
much musicality to become the Colonel's mechanized doll—at least on stage.*
—*Variety*, February 7, 1973

I'M trying not to be an Elvis chauvinist, I told myself, waiting for my suitcase to
come down the conveyor belt. Trying not to say I am on a search for the pure Elvis,
just my Elvis. I hoped that I was a less obvious devotee than the woman in the big
white hat with the Elvis bow. We were both in the Memphis airport the first week in
August 1997, the twentieth anniversary of his death on the shag carpet of the upstairs
bathroom in Graceland.

The crowd had just begun to thicken for "Death Week," which would climax the
following Friday with an all-night candlelight vigil past his grave. I planned to be long
gone by then, due to scheduling conflicts and my own ambivalence.

This Memphis pilgrimage began for me on an afternoon in 1957 when an eight-
year-old girl in a very little Alabama town wet her daddy's black comb, shut the
door of her parents' bedroom, slicked back her hair, and crooned into the mirror,
shuffling and strumming an imaginary guitar, "Love me tender, love me true . . . ."
I had just come back from Elvis's first movie, transported. But did I want to have
Elvis, or to be Elvis? Did I want to be one of multitudes of girls screaming up for
him, or did I want to be up there on stage with a multitude of girls screaming for
me?

The closed bedroom door gives a strong clue to the answer. Soon after, the Elvis in me went into a long hibernation. It was hard enough to be female, much less butch and lesbian, in Alabama in the late fifties and early sixties. I lost touch with my body. But a couple of years ago, looking at fifty—twenty years after I'd come out—Elvis resurfaced. I still can't quite account for the change. As near as I can figure, a new friendship with my father had something to do with it. I developed more of a habit of looking in the mirror. I liked Elvis's sexy tenderness, with attitude and energy. My spirit had worn a bit thin, I realized. This Elvis thing, it seemed, first did no harm, and then might just be a lot of fun.

What was that Creole expression: *mi masra*? I guess I was exploring "my mister," the male part of my selves. How else to explain all of these excursions into masculinity? I had spent ten years after coming out hardly reading men. Now I seemed to be in for a return of the repressed. So much for the woman-identified woman.

My Elvis was not the Elvis of the Las Vegas phase: the one with the white jumpsuit and the karate moves in his 1968 comeback performance after eight years of Hollywood formula movies. This Vegas Elvis attracts the impersonators: rapidly aging, mostly white men.[1]

My Elvis would be wearing snazzy clothes he'd bought from Lansky's on Beale Street. Say a black bolero jacket and dress pants with a stripe up the legs, or something in black and pink, walking down the street, combing his hairdo held in place with Rose Oil tonic and Vaseline. All in all, a decidedly un-Bubba look for an eighteen-year-old white guy in 1954.[2]

In Sam Phillips's Sun Studio on Union Street a mile away, my Elvis started goofing around with Arthur "Big Boy" Crudup's blues number "That's All Right, Mama," and hit the million-dollar sound Phillips was looking for: a white man singing black music. Then he took to the stage at Overton Park, hitched up on his toes, started shaking his legs like the Holy Roller preachers at his church, and the girls started screaming. The rest is history, and it's more than rock 'n' roll. Elvis is what happened when black music passed into white bodies, the tremors in his legs like the tremors when those Precambrian African plates rubbed up against the North American continent to make the Tennessee Highlands that spill west into the coastal plains around Memphis. The implications were quite clear to the FBI a decade later: "a social revolution with the racial movement as its core."[3]

My search, intimate as it was, took me across the southern geography of race and sexuality. Memphis seemed to be the place where all the roads crossed. I convinced Dave Perkins, editor of *Brightleaf*, to let me do a travel piece on Memphis, and when he agreed, I packed my bags and went. In the baggage coming on the conveyor belt was another set of questions about this "social revolution with the racial movement at its core." From Atlanta to Memphis traversed Martin King's life, birth to assassination. I was headed to Graceland, but I also wanted to pay a visit to the balcony of the Lorraine Motel. "The King" and Martin King were two presiding spirits of Memphis for whom I would pour libations. King's murder here ended his three-year transformation from Civil Rights reformist to proponent of class struggle, antiwar activist, and democratic socialist—and he had intended to bring the United States along. What had the crack of James Earl Ray's rifle ended? Another coincidence occurred to me between Atlanta and Memphis: Coke and Elvis are two southern products gone global. What "metaphysical subtleties and theological niceties," in Marx's terms, might I encounter tracing Elvis-the-commodity?

LIKE COUSINS MARRYING

Memphis sits on the bluffs above the Mississippi River that flows south through Nina Simone's "Mississippi Goddamned" and on to the Gulf of Mexico. The city was founded by Indian-killer and soon-to-be-president Andrew Jackson and other speculators in 1818. Move the Indians out and the slaves in: that was the formula for the age, and by 1850, 150,000 bales of cotton valued at $7.5 million moved through Memphis as the slave labor system raced the wage labor system westward and toward a cataclysmic war.[4]

I parked my rented Grand Am at the Peabody, a 1930s landmark built in the grand hotel tradition to serve the cotton merchants and planters who traded at the cotton exchanges still on Front Street, just around the corner to the north. I walked south down Main to Beale Street, now a strip of blues clubs and shops in the historical district. Freed blacks poured into Memphis after Lee's surrender, and the segregation established by the turn of the century made Beale Street a thriving center of black life and culture. I was a happy tourist, ready to eat, listen to music, and shop for souvenirs, starting from the Center for Southern Folk Life, a café, museum, craft store, and concert space all in one that sold a deadly mocha milkshake. Around the corner, according to a historic marker, Ida B. Wells began the campaign against lynching from Beale Street in the 1890s when the hanging of three prominent black Memphis businessmen showed her that white violence had more to do with black economic success than with rape of white women.[5]

Here the alluvial swirl of field chants, work songs, and spirituals from the Delta plantations helped birth the blues. Classically trained black Memphis band leader W. C. Handy first heard them sung in juke joints at the turn of the century and composed "The Memphis Blues," a tune with a big-band sound picked up by artists like Bessie Smith and Louis Armstrong. But it was the raw, plaintive notes of blues men and women like Charlie Patton, Muddy Waters, Howlin' Wolf, Memphis Minnie, and Big Boy Crudup that carried into the clubs on Beale Street and into the new medium of radio. That's how Elvis heard it, on the radio in Lauderdale Courts, the public housing complex where he and his parents lived after they joined the great migration from tiny towns like Tupelo, Mississippi, to big cities like Memphis, Tennessee.

When Elvis hung here, Beale Street was already on its way down as a result of a city campaign to close down the clubs for health reasons. The riots that followed

King's assassination a mile to the south finished its demise. The still boarded-up store-fronts testified to how the riots of the late sixties had changed the urban landscape, here as in Atlanta and cities across the country. Beale Street was renovated in the decades after Elvis's death when pilgrims to Graceland showed the city the money to be made in tourist dollars in postindustrial economies. A Hard Rock Cafe will soon go up at the site of the famous saloon where Handy wrote "The Memphis Blues." Even the guidebooks warned me to expect the dissonance that comes when the marketing of a culture displaces the culture itself and the people who created it. Elvis, Ida B., W. C. Handy—all had left the building.

Sunday morning, on an impulse, I drove past Beale Street and over the huge expanse of bridge that reached into Arkansas. When I was a kid, I remembered, my mother would sing "Ol' Man River," the *Showboat* song Paul Robeson made famous, as we crossed over at Vicksburg on our summer trips from Tuskegee to Louisiana, where her brothers lived. We left my daddy at home, hard at work, which he knew how to do from rising at 4:00 A.M. every morning on his family's farm. His "out home" for me was a place to visit my grandmother and wait to go back to the big house in town. Back then, I identified more with my mother's family. I spent the first half of my life spun in a cocoon of my mother's stories. In later life, I developed an appreciation for my father's silences. Perhaps this Memphis trip would help me fill them in.

I wondered who Elvis's people were. "There were times we had nothing to eat but corn bread and water," Elvis's daddy, Vernon, explained to Peter Guralnick, "but we never put anybody down. Neither did Elvis."[6] In fact, Elvis often publicly expressed reverence for the black musical culture on which he drew when the South was increasingly polarized by racism.

I took the monorail over to Mud Island and the Mississippi River Museum. Ten-thousand-year-old stone and pottery artifacts segue into the iron remains of the conquistadors. Then canoes, log rafts, flatboats, steamboats, showboats (with Shakespeare, magic, opera, comedy, songs), the ironclads of the civil war (Memphis surrendered rapidly).

Turn a corner, and we were into artifacts of black culture: a stringed instrument made from a cigar box, a broken beer bottle neck used as a slide. Missing is the record in steel of slavery: iron shackles for wrists, legs, neck. But you can hear it in the sound of field hollers and work songs as these migrate into the twelve-bar, three-line form of blues, with its single clear evocation of love, hate, joy, salvation. I turned another corner, and the next display showed Sun and Stax Records, pioneer labels for R&B and soul, recording among them Elvis, B. B. King, Johnny Cash, Roy Orbison, Isaac Hayes, Ray Charles, Otis Redding. The core blues sound was speeded up for rhythm and blues; added to gospel (itself evolved from spirituals) to make soul; mixed with rockabilly/country to get rock and roll; marketed for white audiences in Motown; and sent back through white bands and called "beach music." (When Motown heir Michael Jackson got together with Elvis's daughter, Lisa Marie, it gave folks an

uncomfortable feeling, like cousins marrying, a bit too close for genetic comfort.)
Built into it all was the tension between Saturday night and Sunday morning. The
blues musician met the devil at the crossroads and sold her soul for his art.[7]

Sitting on the floor of the Mississippi River Museum with other tourists stepping
over me, I was not sure what made me want to cry. Maybe it was memories from college, when white parties gave an audience for soul music, and I listened and danced,
some nights drunk on bourbon and coke, as removed from my own hunger as I was
from women lovers. Maybe it was the memory of those brief years of hanging out
with my brother Tim as friends, a hiatus between the separations during adolescence
and after he got married. Whatever the source, Ray Charles, Chopin's nocturnes,
blues, Irish ballads, and certain arias strike the same deep, sad chord.

RECEIVED IN GRACELAND

I had a bad case of Elvis vertigo. He was all around me this Monday morning at
the Graceland Crossroads, the little shopping mall across the fence from the estate.
Elvis Presley Enterprises tries futilely to control worldwide distribution of Elvis's
name and image. Here in four adjacent shops across from Graceland were contraband Elvises smiling, pouting, sweating, Elvises reverent and defiant, on key chains,
T-shirts, posters, handbags, mousepads, clocks, plates (a full hand-painted set of
eight different versions only $800). Through all this Elvis merchandise bounded Elvis
impersonators in shoe-blacked manes. And over multiple loudspeakers, the voice of
Elvis singing "Jailhouse Rock," "Hound Dog," "Blue Suede Shoes," and "Dixie,/The
Battle Hymn of the Republic." And I hadn't even gotten to Graceland yet.

Queasy, I walked on over and purchased the $18.50 Platinum Tour for maximum
Elvis immersion. It was 1:30, but my tour wouldn't start until 4:00. Not to worry. First
I toured the *Lisa Marie*, Presley's airplane (original cost $250,000, with $800,000
more in extras), then Elvis's car museum (Cadillacs, Studz Bearcats, Rollses, Ferraris,
Harleys).

Next was the Sincerely Elvis Museum. More than a million pictures were made
of Elvis Presley over his lifetime, we were told, and the museum has a good many of
them. No wonder I had vertigo. The museum wall explained, "Everyone shares a
common element with Elvis. He encompasses the daring, the familiar, the spiritual,
the dangerous, the sexual, the masculine, the androgynous, the eccentric, the traditional, the god-like, the God-fearing, the liberal and the conservative in all of us."
The perfect marketing strategy for a man whose life took such remarkable turns and
who had the cash to indulge all sides of himself: an Elvis for all seasons, perfected by
EPE president and ex-wife, Priscilla, that brings in $75 million a year for Lisa
Marie's benefit.

In 1996, when the King family agreed to license MLK merchandise for the
Olympic games, Dexter King paid a visit to Graceland for tips while disclaiming,
"We didn't set out to duplicate Elvis Presley Enterprises."[8]

"A commodity is therefore a mysterious thing," Marx observed of both Coke and Elvis, "simply because in it the social character of [human] labour appears as an objective character." Thus a relation between humans (that is, Elvis and his fans) assumes "in their eyes, the fantastic form of a relation between things." The commodity becomes a "social hieroglyphic."[9] King had critiqued this as "thingification": becoming his fate now as well as Elvis's. Lord, I thought, I was sounding a lot like the posse of cultural critics over at the Elvis Conference in Overton Park, a gathering that had moved up from Oxford due to a schism in scholarly ranks over, among other interpreters of the Elvis hieroglyphic, Elvis Herselvis, a lesbian EP impersonator.[10]

If there was ever a force to alienate a man from his labor, it was Colonel Parker, Elvis's carny impresario who had carefully constructed the multimillion dollar image into which the energetic and talented nineteen-year-old had rapidly disappeared: B-grade movies, mediocre sound tracks, easy cash and women, a retinue of Bubba sycophants, and unlimited access to amphetamines and other uppers and downers, beginning in Elvis's army days in his early twenties. The religious world, Marx believed, was but a "reflex of the real world," and sure enough the mystery of the Elvis fetish seemed to attract pilgrims with religious fervor, seeking their blissful martyr and spotting him everywhere, the eternal Elvis.

"Tell me he's not dead," a new young friend but lifelong Elvis enthusiast had exclaimed when we recognized our shared devotion.

"I'm afraid he was dead before he died," I replied, remembering accounts of him stumbling into the instruments on the stage in his last months, his demise already assumed by the boys in his band, who had watched his long, slow slide.

Elvis-the-Product was kitsch fun, but Elvis-the-Commodity *was* a queer phenomenon. It was not just that the public consumed his art, his singing and acting turned into records and movies, or that Memphis was afloat in Elvis memorabilia. When Colonel Parker heard of his famous client's death, he said, "It won't make any difference." Elvis would keep generating profits because Elvis himself, as the first postwar teen idol, had become a commodity in what was indeed, in Marx's words, a "sacrifice of his life and his creative activity." As Marx described the alienation of the worker/self in a system driven by profits: The more value he created, the more valueless Elvis became; the more formed his product, the more deformed he was as worker, until he became a stranger to everything but his drugs, and his work became the loss of himself.[11] It was as accurate a diagnosis for what killed this king as any I had found.

Now amidst Sincerely Elvis at Graceland, even in this official Elvis there was something to fear. There are pictures of Elvis the gun collector who occasionally shot out the TV and other appliances. There's the Elvis who threw $5,000 cash out a hotel room window to watch the gowned women and tuxed men below leap from their Rolls-Royces into the fountain in pursuit of the bills. And there's the Elvis who showed up to see Nixon at the White House gate looking like Count Dracula in a black cape. He gained admittance, offering to help with the country's drug problem and asking for a narc's badge, causing even Nixon to worry about his credibility. Elvis could have moved the War on Drugs a bit closer to home, of course. After his death, the state charged his doctor with illegally prescribing nearly twelve thousand tablets of uppers, downers, and tranqs the twenty months before his demise, a piece of Elvis history not available in Graceland.[12]

Drugs were a habit he started in the army and continued in order to get him through his exhausting performances and his increasingly vapid life. Perhaps that so many products and emotional states could emerge from "Elvis" shows the degree to which he had emptied himself by the way he chose to live his life.

"You got to be careful what Elvis you latch onto," I scared nearby tourists by saying out loud, "because there's a hell of a lot of Elvises floating out here."

At 4:15, I was loaded up on a shuttle bus for the ride across the Boulevard and through the trellised gates to the house at the top of the hill that Elvis bought his mama and daddy in 1957. "We all will be received in Graceland," Paul Simon's song, backed up by Ladysmith Black Mombaza, sounded in my ears. The grieving Elvis said to his dentist, who came to pay respects the week his mama, Gladys, died: "The newspapers have made my house so laughable. I would love to have your opinion of my home."[13]

I'd read such accounts enough to understand what an easy shot the decor would be, and it was . . . remarkable. The pool room was next door to the TV room in the basement, with Elvis's logo TCB and a lightning flash above the black, yellow, and white vinyl sectional sofa. On the walls, 350 to 400 yards of bright and densely printed cotton fabric were cut, pieced, pleated, and hung. "Eclectic decorating, now popular again, was an 'in thing' in the seventies, and the pool room mixes European, Asian, and American styles of various eras," explains the guidebook. Up the stairwell, lined with angled mirrors, is the den, or Jungle Room: "fake-fur upholstered furniture with its carved wood frames" and a "trendy green shag carpeted ceiling."[14]

The Trophy Room, in a side building, contains the remarkable evidence of Elvis's career as one of the greatest recording artists of all time. Mixed in with the platinum and gold records are cases displaying the evolution of the Elvis outfit, early/surly Lansky's to the oft-impersonated jumpsuit. Here fairly simple white one-piece garments fashioned after his karate gi become increasingly extravagant, climaxing in the jeweled American eagle suit and cape of the Aloha concert and the Aztec outfit of the last year. Toward the end, Elvis approximated his early comic book hero, Captain Marvel, and the extravagant and gay Liberace, who was one of his mother's favorite performers. The fat and trashy Elvis of the last years, according to some.

Finally we arrived at the Meditation Garden, which contains the family graves, the destination of thousands of pilgrims who will file by from dusk until dawn starting Friday. Already, the trellis around the turquoise pool was filled with floral tributes. I joined the suddenly quiet tourists, finally with Elvis and his people. They were his touchstones. If I was in search of some Elvis lost beneath the images of Elvis, I might find him here.

At the Center for Southern Folklore, I had located a Presley family genealogy commissioned by the *National Enquirer* in 1977.[15] The Presleys arrived from Scotland by way of Ireland around 1745, making the trek through North and South Carolina as territory was opened up by Indian removal. Elvis's great-great-grandfather, Dunnan Presley Jr. (the first Presley born in Tennessee), made it through the Mexican-American War then deserted the Confederate army twice. He also abandoned his first of four wives and their daughter, Elvis's great-grandmother Rosella Presley. His total worth at his death in 1900: twenty-three dollars.

Elvis's people, like my father's, were poor European immigrants who settled in the South and became white folks. You may remember Heini Sigrist, who left Swiss Germany and arrived in the colonies by 1771. As Henry Segrest he probably settled in Orangeburg, South Carolina. He fought with the Loyalists, but he nevertheless benefited from the spoils of the Revolutionary War. Records show him gaining two 220-acre plots, another of 150 acres, by 1786—part of the affirmative action program for white settlers on this continent. Segrests apparently needed the civilizing influence of backwoods evangelical churches sweeping the edge of the continent, whose preachers valiantly fought their parishioners' tendencies toward sneezing, coughing, spitting, bringing dogs into the building, horse-swapping, displaying carnal mouths (men) and disorderly walks (women). The Willow Springs Baptist Church records show Margaret Segrest received, Phoebe Segrest excommunicated (for having a "bastard child"), George Segrest censured (for "fiddling and dancing"), and Sarah Segrest condemned (for having dancing in her house). In Four Holes Swamp, up Little Flea Bite Branch, Henry found God in Methodism's short and vigorous services, if not back in the tangled cypress swamps. In 1820 the church found Henry guilty of "dancing and joyousness" practiced on the Sabbath and silenced him for three months, forbidding anyone to speak to him. A year later he was riding for the cypress circuit, and pictures of family relations testify to an austerity that settled into high-buttoned collars and bowed mouths, lips tight and earthward.[16]

Segrest family history, I realized, intersected with a crucial moment in the construction of white identity. As George Rawick and David Roediger argue, blackness came to symbolize the selves that whites were giving up as they were integrated into the wage labor system: it was a lifestyle that gave up "holidays, spurned contact with nature, saved time, bridled sexuality, separated work from the rest of life and postponed gratification."[17] Evolving racism encoded a "pornography of his former life . . . in order to insure that he will not slip back into the old ways or act out half-suppressed fantasies," Roediger concludes. The psychic power of this split self provides much of the percussive force of white racist practices—again the desecrated black bodies in *Without Sanctuary* float to mind—as well as the stultifying effects of white racist institutions and a certain tedium to white culture.

The Presley family, much more trifling than my own, had not adapted so readily to this new ethic, making Elvis a vehicle for the fusion of black and white musical styles that was his original (but rapidly fading) genius. Elvis, like Martin, had situated himself on this psychic black/white divide. They were, in an ironic way, soul brothers.

While the Presleys moved west, sons of Henry Segrest joined the flood of settlers along the Federal Road into Alabama after Gen. Andrew Jackson defeated the Creek confederacy at the Battle of Horseshoe Bend and as president moved out the Creeks in the 1830s. In Macon County, where they settled, the Segrest name became the "most numerous in the county" through Henry's six sons, the Segrests acquiring land from Creek Indian displacement that my family farmed the next one hundred years.[18]

Rosella Presley, the mother of ten children, never married and never had the benefit of indigenous land. She sharecropped all across Mississippi and Alabama, taking in washing and cleaning to keep her and her children alive. One of these sons, Jessie, was our Elvis's grandfather, a "hard-drinking, hard-working hell raiser" who deserted his wife, Minnie Mae, and their son Vernon Elvis. "Owning expensive clothes was [Jessie's] only ambition in life."

If Elvis's trifling ancestor had deserted the Confederate army, mine had not. Thirteen when the Civil War broke, Charles Bosch Segrest served as a private in the Sixty-second Alabama Infantry and walked home from Virginia after Lee surrendered in a final campaign in which the rivers ran red with blood. Charles brought with him pellagra into a region devastated by war. "Gaunt hunger wept beside Bereavement," W.E.B. Du Bois described with great compassion.[19]

This Segrest found God while plowing in the fields. But increasingly he began to display "signs that from some imaginary cause his mind was giving way," according to an obituary among my Aunt May's trove of family papers. May herself told me he saw people shooting at him from trees, probably posttraumatic stress from the battlefields of northern Virginia. He started to shoot back, and by 1902 his family sent him off to "Bryce's"—the Alabama Insane Hospital that stood adjacent to the University of Alabama in Tuscaloosa, on the banks of the Black Warrior River. By the time Charles arrived, the formidable structure housed mostly white people because the Alabama legislature had Jim Crowed insanity along with everything else the year before, when it rewrote the state constitution with the help of another of my great grandfathers. There for three months, Charles Segrest no doubt got neither the straightjacket nor the talking cure that was the fate of some mental patients during this era; at Bryce's patients got instead the moral treatment that ordered the asylum's environment to assert sobriety, cooperation, and order so necessary in the larger society. In the men's west wing, Charles was probably one of the "poor old state paupers . . . who bear the burden of the day . . . similar to that of a poor old private in war, who does all the work and fighting and receives no pay and nothing to eat."[20] Likely, Charles met with women from the other side only in the dining hall. Many of them were not so much crazy as raving and frantic, not with insanity but from grief and trouble, heartbreak, alcohol, their family's embarrassment, sexual peccadilloes, gender violations, or outright crimes that would have landed them in the penitentiary had it not been for moneyed relatives and influential friends.[21] It was the moral treatment of a white psychic order that Elvis's throbbing pelvis would unsettle.

May let me Xerox the correspondence from Bryce's Superintendent J. T. Searcy to my great-grandmother about Charles's death, six brief letters over three months. "I am glad to say that your husband is getting along fairly well," the August communiqué begins. "He . . . has a good many delusions and insane ideas along different lines." By October, Searcy reports, Charles "has an idea that he has made many mistakes and that different people at home want to do him harm." A week later: "I regret to inform you that your husband has been sick for about three days and is now in a rather serious condition. He is suffering from an attack of erysipelas [a kind of cellulitis] involving the face and part of the head. While he is in a critical condition I have hope that he may recover. Today he is partially delirious and very restless. We will give him every attention and in case he grows worse will write you. His body could only be removed at the expense of his relatives in the event of his death." The next day: "I am sorry to say that he continued to grow worse and died this morning about four o'clock. . . . He had nothing to say about dying or any of his people. . . . We have turned the body over to Mr. J. D. Foster, undertaker, to prepare."[22] In this silence ended Charles Segrest's contribution to the Confederacy.

MINNIE MAE PRESLEY is the first grave in the Meditation Garden. Elvis had moved her into Graceland. "You ain't nothin' but a hound dog," Big Mama Thornton sang the blues song that became Elvis's trademark. Elvis's biographer Peter Guralnick had puzzled at Elvis's choice of a woman's point of view.[23] But it's clear to me, standing at Minnie Mae's grave, that those hound dogs were no 'count men like those who deserted Rosella and Minnie Mae. Elvis came by the blues honest, through the women in his family. The hell-raising Presleys highlighted all the more the Methodism in the Segrests' madness, the constraints from which the adolescent Elvis cut loose, inspired by the black culture of the Mississippi Delta. It was this sexuality that had drawn me as a girlchild with queer longings but no lesbian identity. It was a sexual rebellion that Elvis, a product of the 1950s, did not shape into rebellion against white supremacy or against militarism. When he was drafted in 1960, he headed off to the army in Germany, his entourage in tow. Only four years later, American GIs would head to Vietnam.

Then GLADYS SMITH PRESLEY, 1912–1958, read the next tombstone. Gladys was Mama, who held the Presley family together when Elvis's daddy, Vernon, was sent up to Parchman Prison for eight months for kiting a four-dollar check, destroying whatever faith he had in himself to take care of his family.[24] "She was always my best girl," Elvis sobbed the day of Gladys's death. I could almost hear Elvis singing his first big hit at the beginning of rock 'n' roll . . . *That's all right now, Mama,* . . . but it sounded now like a lullaby.

VERNON ELVIS PRESLEY . . ."Elvis, look at them chickens," Vernon had sobbed at Gladys's death, equally transported. "Mama ain't never gonna feed them chickens no more."

"No, Daddy, Mama won't never feed them chickens anymore. She's all we lived for. She was always my best girl."[25]

ELVIS AARON PRESLEY, 1935–1977. His epitaph was written by his father: "He was a precious gift from God."

"That's all right now, Elvis," I wanted to sing over his grave. "Any way you do . . . ."

HEARTBREAK MOTEL

I determined to devote my last day to that other king of Memphis. In Atlanta, Martin King's birthplace and grave is a tourist site, but he is no part of the tourist business in the town where he was assassinated. Elvis was self-evaporating, collapsing under pressures from the culture that defined him even as he shaped it. He stayed a kid all of his short life. King, on the other hand, had taken on the destructive elements in American culture at their generative base, reshaping them even as these forces closed in on him. It was not that King did not have his own demons, including a sexual promiscuity thoroughly documented by the FBI. It is alleged that he was with three different women on the night before his murder.[26] But, still, there was all the distance in the world between the bathroom at Graceland and the balcony of the Lorraine Motel.

Barbara Smith, my Memphis host, got me a copy of *At the River I Stand*, a video of the 1967–68 strike of the Memphis Sanitation Workers, the 1,300-man union on strike against degrading working conditions like carrying barrels of maggoty garbage for starvation wages. Two men crushed to death in garbage grinders had precipitated the strike, which was soon joined by the American Federation of State and Municipal Employees (AFSME) in mass meetings, pickets, and sit-ins at city council meetings as white leadership stonewalled. Against the advice of his staff, King committed his Southern Christian Leadership Conference to Memphis when the strikers invited him in, even as SCLC was preparing for the Poor People's March on Washington.

On the video, I saw an intersection familiar from yesterday's excursions, Main Street and Beale, as King arrived late to lead the march, literally staggering from exhaustion by the forces he was trying to mediate. Then police cars closed in, and the crowd pushed back, in it many of the young black militants whose black power movement had risen so rapidly in the past several years, given white intransigence and the revolutionary consciousness of movements all around the world. The men around King almost carried him away from the melee. Then tanks rolled on the streets of downtown Memphis where tourists now stroll, federal troops with bayonets pointed toward black picketers with their signs: I AM A MAN. The day had been disastrous for King.

When King came back in early April with his full SCLC staff to lead another march, he felt it all closing in. He was a man with a huge and broken heart. The Watts riots—within a week of President Johnson's signing of the Civil Rights Act of 1965—had profoundly shaken King, its flames illuminating both the "imperfections in the civil rights movement and the tragic shallowness of white racial policy in the exploding ghettoes."[27] His Chicago campaign took him into these northern ghettoes, where he confronted a depression in the black community that started in 1964 when automation began to cut into economic improvement. "Fewer and fewer jobs for the culturally and educationally deprived" meant no exit from "present day poverty [that feeds] upon and perpetuates itself," generating a "hopeless despair," he described the emerging postindustrial economy. Unemployment among black youth was 24.8 percent nationwide and as high as 40 percent in some cities.[28] The "flash point of Negro rage" was being fed by a "white failure to comprehend the depth and the dimension of the Negro problem."[29]

King and other Civil Rights strategists had assumed the North would "benefit derivatively" from the southern campaigns against Jim Crow. But, he realized, they had expected "the ghettoes to stand still . . . [and underestimated] the deterioration that increasingly embitters [ghetto] life."[30] Howard Thurman had dismissed separatism and armed struggle as forms of resistance; but Malcolm X, living in the northern ghettoes to which King now journeyed, had conceptualized both as viable spiritual options for the black dispossessed. "The black self must be conceived in the womb of black consciousness even as black culture must be purified in the crucible of self love," Dyson explains of Malcolm X. "From these principles would flow economic control, cultural recreation, social cohesion, spiritual rebirth, psychic regeneration, and racial unity."[31] From the perspective of the North, where the racial segregation worked through informal cures and unwritten rules rather than overt Jim Crow laws, King began to see Malcolm's point.[32]

"The dream I had in Washington back in 1963 has often turned into a nightmare," King lamented.[33] "There is something wrong with our nation. Something desperately wrong."[34] The black revolution, he saw, was "forcing America to face all its interrelated flaws—racism, poverty, militarism, and materialism." These were "systemic rather than superficial flaws," and they suggested that "radical reconstruction of society itself is the real issue to be faced."[35] In response, he shifted positions and ratcheted up his strategy. In successfully reforming southern Civil Rights practices, King realized he had not gotten down to the generative base of racist institutions. He had been dealing with manifestations, with superstructure; he had not "penetrate[d] the lower depths of Negro deprivation." He wanted substantive rather than surface changes, and he directed his energy toward roots causes—"the system rather than in men or faulty operations." He spoke privately of "democratic socialism": "Now this means we are treading in difficult waters," he explained to his staff in 1966, "because we are saying that something is wrong . . . with capitalism."[36] The Poor People's Campaign would get to this root cause, he strategized, by mobilizing the poor of all races to converge on Washington, D.C., in what he called massive nonviolence or nonviolent sabotage. The poor would sit in in Congress, tie up the streets, and shut down the nation's capital in a direct confrontation with the nation's elite.

King's stand on the Vietnam War also moved him toward a more fundamental confrontation with the American economic and political system. In 1966 Congress cut the War on Poverty budget by one-third to pay for the war. That the United States would spend half a million dollars to kill one Vietcong and only fifty-three dollars to bring one of its own citizens out of poverty incensed King.[37] He spoke out decisively against America's involvement in the Vietnam War in a sermon at New York's Riverside Church: "Somehow this madness must cease. We must stop now. I speak as a child of God and brother to the suffering poor of Vietnam. I speak for those whose land is being laid waste, whose homes are being destroyed, whose culture is being subverted. I speak for the poor of America who are paying the double price of smashed hopes at home and death and corruption in Vietnam. I speak as a citizen of the world, for the world as it stands aghast at the path we have taken."[38]

The calling to speak, he explained, was a "vocation of agony," but he spoke from a burning heart to break the "betrayal of my own silences." He was encouraged by other African Americans already opposed to the war, including his wife, Coretta, James Lawson, Hosea Williams, Ralph Abernathy, Andy Young, and James Bevel.[39] He spoke also in response to a plea from a soul brother, the Vietnamese Buddhist monk Thich Nhat Hanh, who had written King a public letter in 1965: "The world's greatest humanists would not remain silent. You yourself cannot remain silent. . . . You cannot be silent since you have already been in action and you are in action because, in you, God is in action, too."[40]

King had read *Lotus in a Sea of Fire*, Thich Nhat Hanh's account of the Vietnam War. According to Andrew Young, the Buddhist monk's influence was one of the main factors in changing King's views on speaking out on Vietnam.[41] Andrew Young remembered "the spiritual inspiration of Thich Nhat Hanh on Martin. His spiritual presence was something that he talked about afterward." Nhat Hanh's third path of noncommunist resistance to imperialism gave King a position from which to take on the U.S. economic system in such speeches as this one: "Increasingly, by choice or by accident, this is the role our nation has taken—the role of those who make peaceful revolution impossible by refusing to give up the privileges and the pleasures that come from the immense profits of overseas investment. . . . We must rapidly begin the shift from a 'thing-oriented' society to a 'person-oriented' society. When machines and computers, profit motives and property rights are considered more important than people, the giant triplets of racism, materialism and militarism are incapable of being conquered. . . . We must not engage in a negative anti-communism, but rather in a positive thrust for democracy, realizing that our greatest defense against communism is to take offensive action in behalf of justice."[42]

So the movement in Memphis invited him, and to Memphis he went, convinced that the city needed to "redistribute the pain."[43] He saw in the struggle there the core economic issues he had determined to address. The FBI had marked him "the most dangerous Negro of the future in this Nation from the standpoint of communism." The fascist homosexual voyeur J. Edgar Hoover was more blunt: "Destroy the burrhead."[44]

Despair about the state of his country pushed King higher, and he followed, knowing the risk. "There comes a time when a true follower of Jesus Christ must take a stand that's neither safe nor politic nor popular, but he must take a stand because it is right." W.E.B. Du Bois, when faced with a similar heartbreaking insight into the intractability and depth of U.S. racism, went to Ghana. Martin King went to God. God had promised to be with him even unto the end of the world, and it was this hope he carried onto the streets of Memphis.[45] He preached at a rally in a Memphis church the night before he was shot: "I've been to the Mountaintop . . . I would like to live a long life . . . But I'm not concerned about that now. I just want to do God's will. . . . Mine eyes have seen the glory."[46]

Perhaps he carried with him the next fateful day his Buddhist friend's words, explaining why monks and nuns in Vietnam immolated themselves to protest the war: "To burn oneself by fire is to prove that what one is saying is of the utmost importance. . . . A man who burns himself too much must die. The importance is not to take one's life, but to burn. What he really aims at is the expression of his will and determination, not death. . . . Their enemies are not man. They are intolerance, fanaticism, dictatorship, cupidity, hatred and discrimination which lie within the heart of man."[47]

The Memphis Civil Rights Museum is a huge concrete structure built around the old Lorraine Motel in a devastated neighborhood south of downtown. I walked across Mulberry Street, where two black women on a raggedy sofa sat talking. The younger woman was Jacqueline Smith, the last tenant of the Lorraine Motel, where she worked as a maid for room and board and fifty dollars a week. After business vanished in 1968, she and the prostitutes who worked the area gave tours of King's room and kept the Lorraine from being bulldozed. She had once been a promising contralto who auditioned for the Metropolitan Opera. Now she is on the 3,499th day of a protest against the city's 1991 decision to spend almost nine million dollars turning the Lorraine into a museum, rather than using it as she feels King would have wanted—to feed the hungry and shelter the homeless. What did she think of Elvis? I asked. Nothing much, except that he should have paid more royalties to the black people whose songs he used—a familiar and justified criticism. I asked her where poor people are now in Memphis, since they are clearly not welcomed near the Peabody or on Beale Street. They are camping out under the bridges, she said.

Then I took the slow walk through the museum that revisits all the southern campaigns, a retrospective leading up to the final destination, the corridor that leads into the bedroom King occupied in the Lorraine Motel the last day of his life. Then the museum visitor steps out onto the balcony from Room 306, as Martin Luther King did at 6:00 P.M., April 4, 1967, and there is the crack of the 30.06 Remington rifle, the bullet that tears into his neck as he steps into the fire.

I got the Memphis blues again.

After King's assassination, supporters from all over the country surged to Memphis for a huge march that forced the city council, finally, to agree to the Sanitation Workers' demands. Ralph Abernathy led the Poor People's Campaign into Washington, D.C. A wave of government repression—perhaps King's assassination was part of it—targeted radical black movements even as the Vietcong won the Vietnam War and the second American revolution failed to uproot the systemic structures that generated the suffering King engaged and many, many others still seek to address. The failure of that revolution has left many black people understandably cynical about the negative effects of integration into a racist system, as I have heard from some black friends responding to my reading and thinking again about King.

"Hmmm, *Doc*-tor King . . . Not that many people where I come from are all that enthusiastic about King," my friend Wendi says, nodding her head emphatically. "Of course, I was a SNCC baby."

King was struggling heroically to bring together race-based and class-based movements; he failed to politicize gender and sexuality, to his own detriment. Those understandings would emerge more fully from the women who had worked in liberation movements of the fifties and sixties. The nonviolent sector of the Civil Rights movement put America to a test that we failed. Perhaps part of what was murdered here on this balcony was a faith in the ability of twentieth-century white people on a mass scale to change ourselves if shown the implications of our actions.

"I got to get out of this city," I told myself as I climbed back in my car and headed toward the airport, passing the unveiling of the new rock-and-roll-king Elvis statue on Beale Street as a raven-haired elderly Elvis impersonator did what looked like karate or tai chi in front of the Orpheus Theater.

TAKING CARE OF BUSINESS

But I was to be drawn once more into the Elvis maelstrom by that one Elvis poster I hadn't bought the day before. I could just scoot by Graceland one last time, since it was near the airport.

I parked my car on the grass of the Graceland Crossings lot and walked across the street and into the first shop, my stride confident. I knew just which Elvis I wanted: a blow-up of a Wertheimer photo from 1956–57, the Brando and James Dean pre-revolutionary Elvis. And there at a table was photographer Alfred Wertheimer himself, autographing posters, pictures, calendars. Perfect.

But it wasn't over yet. On the way out, two black kids handed me a flier: "ELVIS' KARATE LEGACY—the lost karate videos at Hernando's Hideaway, only half a mile off of Elvis Presley Boulevard south of Graceland." I had been a student of karate for five years myself; if I was on the trail of Elvis and the/my body, here was a clue I should not ignore.

After only three wrong turns I located Hernando's Hideaway, a white cinderblock building frequented by the truckers whose companies were on this road and from whom Elvis, who drove trucks himself for a while, got the idea of sideburns. The place was a dive. I was glad I hadn't tried to come at night, although it might as well be, as dark as it was inside the bar. I was shown to a back room, where I joined four guys who sat watching grainy shots of a bleary-eyed Elvis in a white karate gi doing self-defense demonstrations. I tried unsuccessfully to insinuate myself into a conversation about which of Elvis's bodyguards deserted him when. The only other women in this establishment were the waitresses. I ordered a Diet Coke. Wayne Carman, Elvis's martial arts instructor, followed me to his literature table by the bar. (Just about every other person in Memphis has a literature table, and Elvis fans know their bibliography.) I explained to Wayne that I had a green belt in Shoren Ryu. He warmed to the conversation. Elvis planned to use his fame to promote a new martial arts system, he explained. It would be his way to help people all over the world. I purchased the karate patch for five dollars—"TCB FAITH SPIRIT DISCIPLINE" with seven stars and a lightning bolt.

"So with all this training, how come he died so young, Wayne?" I asked the question I had been pondering since learning that Elvis had two eight-degree black belts, no small accomplishment, tenth being the highest possible rank. His 1968 comeback—the one in the black leather jacket—had shown an Elvis in incredible shape.

"His lifestyle," Wayne answered. "The food, the drugs. He was like you and me. He knew what he should do, but he wasn't able to do it. And all the people around him were leeches. He was going to call his martial arts school Taking Care of Business. It was his way to help people get the things in life that he had gotten."

"So TCB meant paying attention to mind, body, and spirit?" I recalled the TCB logo for sale in various forms at Graceland.

"Yes," Wayne agreed. "He called us the New Gladiators."

My heart sank again. Gladiators? Elvis? How the hell would more gladiators help anything?

On the shuttle to the airport, I settled in next to a mother-daughter team of Elvis fans from Montana wearing matching skirts in popular Elvis print. They were on their fourth trip to Memphis (they toured Graceland three times this trip alone). "I didn't make it to Tupelo or the vigil," I confided regretfully. "But there's always next year. And where did you get that lovely print?"

I was back in Durham on Saturday, the sixteenth, Elvis Death Day. I invited friends over for *Aloha from Hawai'i*, the benefit concert for cancer research that beamed Elvis out from Honolulu in the early 1970s. Behind the fading king, "Elvis" was written in neon in innumerable languages: the global Elvis. But I was ready now for the older Elvis, and he was there, pudgier, jeweled cape and all. There was still the soaring, operatic voice but no pelvic thrusts or karate kick sequences. Notable instead were the less aerobic scarf giveaways to women in the audience, a gesture so loved by impersonators and a bit easier to pull off.

By the last half of the concert, his eyes were tired and a sadness washed through. Priscilla had left him, first for her karate instructor, then for her own life, and the heartbreak songs ("Lord, this time you gave me a mountain . . .") had unexpected dignity and poignancy. This was Elvis the Bluesman, down at the end of Lonely Street.

Then came the final sequence, "An American Trilogy," parts of which I had heard but not understood over the loudspeaker at Graceland Crossroads. I flinched at the beautiful, familiar strains: "In Dixieland where I was born in, early on one frosty morning, look away, look away . . . ." But he quickly modulated into the chorus of "Battle Hymn of the Republic": "Glory, glory hallelujah, His truth goes marching on." I started paying close attention. This hymn was sung by Yankee troops marching into battle on southern soil. Now Elvis, great-great-grandson of a two-time Confederate deserter, sings it after Dixie! As fast as I comprehended that, he was off somewhere else, this time a spiritual, "All my trials, Lord, soon be over . . . ." It was like he was looking down on himself in an upstairs bathroom in Graceland. I remembered Wayne saying Elvis had a premonition about his early death, and I remembered King's final prescient sermon, "Like anybody, I would like to live a long life . . . But I'm not concerned about that now." Then Elvis swung back to the Battle Hymn, full-voiced, soaring, continuing the eerie resonance by ending his concert exactly where King's last sermon closed: "Mine eyes have seen the glory of the coming of the Lord."

Elvis at the Mountaintop?

I remembered Guralnick's description of Elvis's spiritual awakening. He and his entourage were driving through the desert when suddenly Elvis gasped and cried out, "Whoa!" The king had taken a metaphysical turn after Priscilla finally left him, and he had a spiritual guide, a man named Larry Geller, to whom he had shortly before said, "All I want is to know the truth, to know and experience God." So, "Whooaa," Elvis said, and all the guys leapt out of the car and looked up with Presley into the sky.

"Do you see what I see?" he whispered. "That's Joseph Stalin's face up there. Why Stalin? Why Stalin?" And sure enough there was Stalin in the clouds. "It's God!" he exclaimed. "It's God. The face of Stalin turned right into the face of Jesus, and he smiled at me." Tears poured down Elvis's face.[48]

"Worshipping the gods," the *Bhagavad Gita* taught, "men go / to the gods; worshipping spirits, / to the spirits; worshipping me, / they come to me in the end."[49] Some of us are more evolved than others, I reflected on Martin and Elvis, but all of us are searching.

It was 1:00 A.M. Elvis Death Week was over in Memphis. All my company was long gone, not having developed my Elvis stamina. I had a strong feeling of compassion for this old-at-forty-two Elvis, and for the older me. I finally saw how most of us use Elvis, do him wrong, make easy fun of him, or shop for one part or another of him in the great contraband souvenir store at the Graceland Crossroads in our lifelong attempts to impersonate ourselves. Maybe instead we should all be doing more of our sometimes inadequate best to take care of our own business.

5

HAWAIʻI NEI
Remembering the Invitation

E mālama i ka ʻōlelo, i kuleana e kipa mai ai. (Remember the invitation, for it gives you the privilege of coming here.)
— Hawaiian Proverb

At six P.M. of the same day I yielded my authority to the superior force of the United States.
— QUEEN LILIUOKALANI, *Hawaii's Story by Hawaii's Queen*

[In the West] the heart has not been trained; it is missing.
— BHAGWAN SHREE RAJNEESH, *The Book of Secrets*

THE invitation to Hawaiʻi came by phone shortly after the Atlanta trip. Kuʻumeaaloha Gomes called to invite me to speak on linking struggles at a conference of the People's Fund in Honolulu the next February. Could I address links between racism and homophobia in the context of the firestorm in Hawaiʻi over gay marriage? My friend Loretta, indigenous Hawaiian and gay, had recommended me.

"I would love to come," I assured Kuʻumeaaloha, stumbling over the pronunciation of her name, even though I had had Loretta coach me on the combination of syllables in a lyrical language with a clear love for the open breath of vowels. I would learn both to pronounce Kuʻumeaaloha and to appreciate the meaning of a name given in a dream to her grandmother: "the place where love comes from."

"Can I bring my family?" After a slight pause that I later came to more fully understand, she graciously consented.

Cha Smith, conference organizer, soon sent me a packet of information on political issues in Hawaiʻi, and I began reading it, as well as other books I could get my hands on. Kuʻumeaaloha, I soon learned, clearly intended to make the most of my visit. I was doing a keynote and a workshop at the conference, then a house meeting with gay folks, then a public meeting at a church.

I was curious to understand why the upholding of gay marriage by the state Supreme Court could happen here and not another state in the United States. Was there something to understand in Hawaiian history about links between gay marriage and Hawaiian culture, or gay rights and the struggle for sovereignty, or between the marriage decision and the labor struggles against the planter class or women's struggles for equal rights? And exactly why do heterosexuals think their relationships need such defending? These opened into larger questions: How do we shape our commitments to one another—erotic, familial, communal, social, and economic? How do we, linking struggles, claim the future?

I would learn from two trips to Hawai'i, in a deeper way than I knew before, to remember the invitation that gives me the privilege of being here. I am a sojourner with a restlessness and a suitcase passed down on my mother's side of the family from a grandfather who died of influenza in the 1918 epidemic, his body weakened by malaria contracted in various adventures and colonial wars. My mother's versions of his travels were usually precipitated by a state she called "being on the verge of a nervous breakdown," a condition that would send her off to Miami, or Mexico, or the Caribbean while I stayed at home, feeling abandoned. There was a difficult comingling of pleasure and pain in her frequent departures—getting sick to get away. She couldn't just say, "I am tired of you all and want a vacation. See ya in a month!" Her departures seemed to require a level of misery to get her out of town that I internalized too easily. My own version of traveling these days was work, which brought its own pleasures and miseries. I considered it anticolonial travel, but in Hawai'i I had to look more honestly at an often failed distinction between what I was doing and what tourists were doing.

> Ku'ia ka hele a ka na'au ha'aha'a
> [Hesitant walks the humble hearted,
> O ke aloha ke kuleana o kāhi malihini
> Love is the host in strange lands][1]

Even more than in Atlanta or Memphis, the effect of the tourist economy here was written in huge letters across the landscape; each year six tourists arrived for every resident, thirty tourists for each indigenous Hawai'ian. "E ao o ha'i ka pua o ka mau 'u ia 'oe" (Be careful not to break even a blade of grass), taught one indigenous proverb.[2] In an era in which colonial adventurers and soldiers have given way to tourists, they trample over golf courses that grow where forests once opened into lo'i (watery taro patches), or they hang out of G-string bathing suits on beaches whose lime and salamander coral reefs are fading to gray, a death that drives fish farther out and makes life hardest on the people who once lived from, and cared for, land, air, water, and fire as intimate relations.

Reading the material that Cha sent, I began to learn of the others who had come to the islands for better or worse. Colonialism there happened with a brutal compactness that made the islands' history a kind of colonial primer. Polynesians from the Marquesas Islands came between A.D. 400 and 800 in their catamarans with sails woven from coconut fibers. Centuries later Tahitians conquered them, bringing divisions between commoner and royalty, women and men. Captain Cook arrived in 1778, in one of the last places on earth to be discovered by Europeans, breaking the *pono* (the balance). The whalers and traders followed, all bringing syphilis and other diseases for which the Hawaiians had no immunity. "Lawe liʻiliʻi ka make a ka Hawaiʻi, lawe nui ka make a ka haole" (Death by Hawaiians takes a few at a time), one proverb explained. Death by foreigners takes many.[3] Shortly thereafter came the missionaries. Hiram Bingham condescended to journey to this "rude, dark, vile part of the world" whose people were "almost naked savages."[4] The missionaries fast became businessmen "who turned amassing wealth into a religious exercise."[5] White plantation owners brought in Chinese and Japanese and Portuguese and Filipinos to work the sugar plantations, deliberately set against each other by the planters' practice of paying different wages to different nationalities. Men in French and British gunboats arrived, and then finally the U.S. Marines provided the force for the missionary-turned-planter elite, who overthrew the constitutional monarchy of Queen Liliuokalani in 1893 in an illegal coup, clearing the way for annexation by the United States five years later. The 5 percent white minority came to control the economic and political resources of the islands. It was, pure and simple, genocide, reducing the indigenous population from 300,000 to 28,718 by 1900.[6] "Na kanaka ōkuʻu wale aku no i kau uhane" (The people dismissed freely their souls and died).[7]

I soon learned that indigenous Hawaiians—or Kanaka Maoli, as they called themselves on Cook's arrival—had a reverence for genealogy that as a southerner I could appreciate. Who a person is connects intimately to where she comes from, both land and people. Barb, Annie, and I would fly to Hawaiʻi, thousands of miles over the curve of the earth. We would need to chart our way by relationships to our birth family and to our chosen family and to our own land, the U.S. South, navigating historic tides, currents, trade winds in the season as the Pleiades set. In my childhood in Alabama, it was a 10 percent white minority that controlled 90 percent African American people and the land, after sending the Creeks on a forced march to Oklahoma.

"Hana ʻiʻo ka haole" (the white man does it in earnest!). "Haole kī kōlea" (plover-shooting haole). "ʻAʻohe paha he ʻuhane" (perhaps he has no soul).[8]

Haole: the Hawaiian word for white person. Loretta told me that *ha* meant "breath," and *ole* meant "not," or "without," translating "without breath, or spirit," the way that Hawaiʻians apparently experienced the whalers, missionaries, and planters whose greeting was a handshake, not the forehead-to-forehead mingling of breath when Kanaka Maoli meet. Jim Crow was one name for separation in my childhood. In South Africa, it was called apartheid, which meant "separation" in Afrikaner. In Hawaiʻi, I learned the equivalent word was *Mahele* (division). In the U.S. South and in South Africa, our separations were acutely racial and geographic: black and white schools, water fountains, churches; black reservations, or Bantustans. In Hawai'i the Māhele was a division of what had been communal land into private property as a basis for a massive land grab by haole settlers in the nineteeth century.

But however else these apartheids and Māheles separate us as humans, they also separate us from our sense of belonging, our oceanic feeling of connection to the world within and beyond ourselves. If the Māhele divided communally held land into private parcels, the various māheles all over the globe over the past five hundred years also split humans from spiritual connection to 'āini. This is the indigenous word for land, but I felt it to mean much more: nature, existence. When we are split from 'āini, we are separate from our species being, as Marx had said, and caught in what Hegel perceived as an alien natural existence that underlies the will to mastery.

DEARLY BELOVED . . .

The invitation from the People's Fund gave me a chance to see up close what was happening in Hawai'i around gay marriage. I knew that early in the 1990s, three gay couples filing for marriage licenses were denied by the state. In 1993 the Hawaiian Supreme Court ruled that the state could not justify discriminating against same-sex couples unless it could show a compelling state interest. Three years later a lower court ruled that the state had failed to meet this standard. Before Hawai'i began issuing marriage licenses to queers, marriages that, under the U.S. Constitution, other states would be compelled to recognize, the ruling was appealed to the Hawaiian Supreme Court. The Christian Right seized the issue and at the national level promoted the passage of the Defense of Marriage Act (DOMA) in 1996, which allows other U.S. states to refuse recognition of gay marriages.[9] DOMA clones swept through state legislatures.

The summer before the invitation to Hawai'i, we had had our own bout with gay marriage when Republican legislators introduced their local version of the Defense of Marriage Act into the North Carolina legislature. It declared that gay marriages legitimized in other states would not be legally recognized in North Carolina. Members of the local lesbian/gay community had planned a wedding ceremony on the steps of the legislature to protest what we knew would be a done DOMA deal, the equivalent of shooting fish in a legislative barrel. No genuine preachers being available or willing, the organizers asked me to preside. It was quite a scene, with the Lesbian Avengers setting up their wedding reception table—punch and cake—in front of the legislature as a nervous couple of grooms and couple of brides awaited the ceremonies. The capitol police moved in to clarify whether this was a wedding or the press conference/demonstration for which we had a permit. We explained that it was a wedding to protest that we could not get married and that, in fact, the legislature was about to vote that only heterosexual marriages were legal in perpetuity.

Demonstrations, they clarified, could happen, with permits, on the capitol grounds, but weddings would have to move across the street. In the meantime, reporters were getting restless, having promised their newsrooms live feed, and they started grumbling about how this was not a press event. Giving up on explaining performance and irony to the police in the minutes before "Live at Noon," we reassembled our wedding/demonstration across the street. Behind us, legislators were peeking through the doors. Many of them had warned that we would set our cause back many years; but since we only had about seven votes, it was hard to see how setting it back from A.D. 2250 to 2275 was much of a concern.

"Dearly beloved," I commenced, and proceeded to try to explain to the cameras and the people who would be watching through them that the wedding vow—to have and to hold, for better or worse, richer or poorer, in sickness and in health—is a social contract for everybody. If the legislature does not protect the rights of workers to safe jobs with decent pay, or provide health insurance and care for everyone, and protect the most vulnerable among us, such as women and children who need public assistance, then all our relationships suffer. Because we are all interdependent. "Do you take this woman to be your wedded wife, richer and poorer, better and worse, sickness and health, from this day forward?" We proceeded to the enthusiastic kisses, then I asked us all to bow our heads as I laid down as much of a prayer as I could muster to open the hearts of homophobic legislators and to strengthen the spines of those who would vote against the legislation. Then I prayed for all people to be happy in their relationships and said "Amen," and we cut the cake.

Several reporters afterward were trying to figure out exactly why I was there in a noon of categorical confusions. "Are you an ordained minister?" they asked repeatedly, to which I replied, "No." I explained how lesbians and gay men have consecrated our own relationships within the community for years without necessarily having access to ministers. When they didn't get that, I finally interjected—"Look, I'm an ordained lesbian." And they left me alone.

What was it about Hawai'i that allowed for even the hope of a breakthrough, I wondered. Now I would get to see.

IOLANI PALACE: YOU DON'T MESS WITH THE QUEEN!

Annie, Barb, and I were waiting on the grounds of Iolani Palace, home to the last Hawaiian kings and queens, to meet Ku'umeaaloha. She had suggested that we meet here as the place to begin getting to know Hawai'i. I knew that the palace had been the location of the 1892 coup, in which U.S. Marines, acting in the interests of U.S. businessmen, had overthrown Liliuokalani, the queen of Hawai'i. It had been a rank display of power and had set the stage for the U.S. annexation of the islands in 1898, when the United States also seized Cuba, Guam, Puerto Rico, and the Philippines after the Spanish-American War. These annexations had marked the United States' first overseas imperial adventures, shortly after the U.S. government had consolidated its hold on the continent. Meeting us here would be a way for Ku'umeaaloha to show us concretely the importance of sovereignty, the right of a people to control their own country and destiny.

As I watched people get out of their cars and approach us on the palace grounds, I tried to guess which of the women was Ku‘umeaaloha. We had had a lively exchange over the Internet in the months before the trip. I had asked her about feminist interpretations of the Hawaiian history I was reading. "Was there a second immigration about 1200 by Tahitians that established more hierarchical systems, the separation of women and men based on female pollution, and more separation between chiefs and commoners? If so, was the culture before then more egalitarian, and does anyone there make those distinctions when reclaiming culture (which will always be complex, with contradictory tendencies)?"

She agreed it was a good question: "Nothing has been written on any observations of what women did when they were confined to the '*hale pe‘a*' during the menstrual cycles, or how they felt, and what they thought. In the same way, while there are ceremonies that are written where men are the ones who coordinate the activity and exclude the women, no one has yet come forth with any research on what the women were doing: whether they had their own ceremonies in which they excluded the men. There are activities today, such as the '*awa* drinking ceremony and *huiwai*, or spiritual cleansing, in the *kai* or ocean—which men conduct and from which women are excluded if they are menstruating. I was at a site recently and had the experience of being excluded, and was I ever insulted—cultural tradition or not! In the same token, some of the women who coordinate *huiwai* also follow this ritual of excluding other women for menstrual reasons."[10]

"So gay in Hawai‘i is genderless . . . what about butch/femme???" I had signed off the last e-mail, having a feeling I knew the answer. Nor was I disappointed when she walked up to introduce herself. Her hair was long, pulled back, she was taller than I had guessed, and uniformly gracious. She extended a warm welcome to Annie, hanging off a parking meter, and to Barbara, and we proceeded together to the palace.

Iolani Palace is a rectangular building, 140 by 100 feet, with large windows opening to balconies and surrounded by palms. With other visitors, we slipped booties over our shoes and entered the downstairs rooms to the right, dining and receiving. I knew how important the palace was to Kanaka Maoli across the political spectrum as a symbol of sovereignty and resistance to colonialism. Loretta had put it succinctly—"You don't mess with the queen!" As the only royal palace in the fifty states, it stood as a symbol of Hawai‘i's former independence. Liliuokalani was not only Hawai‘i's last queen, but a woman who had resisted U.S. imperialism repeatedly on behalf of her people.

All the trappings of royalty, European style, were preserved in Iolani Palace: the dishes on the huge table, fine furniture and rugs, ten portraits of Hawaiian kings and queens. Pictures included Louis Philippe of France, "a symbol of French interest in the Hawaiian islands," the guide explained; and photographs from Liliuokalani's visit to England to participate in Queen Victoria's Jubilee Celebration. Portraits of Kamehameha I and his descendents recorded the Hawaiian royalty that evolved in the nineteenth century, influenced by increasing European and U.S. incursion as tribal leaders became kings and queens and the islands became a modern nation. The Iolani tours focused more on the furniture, less on the contradictions of history, as we mounted the lovely staircase made of Hawaiian woods to the upper bedchambers.

Liliuokalani was considerably shrewder about the dangers of the missionary party than King Kalakaua, the brother whom she succeeded at his death in 1891. In *Hawaii's Story by Hawaii's Queen*, she sees his complicity in a series of actions from the time he assumed the throne in 1874 that "put in peril the independence of our nation."[11] First he supported the Reciprocity Treaty with the United States that allowed Hawaiian sugar and bananas into the United States without tariffs, in exchange for U.S. grains and lumber to Hawaiian markets and U.S. naval use of Pearl Harbor. The resulting U.S. market for sugar produced burgeoning sugar plantations, and so "created a new want in his domain"—labor.[12] King Kalakaua set out on a tour of the world, in search of a source of immigrant labor, finding it in Japan and China. Chinese laborers (fleeing disruptions created by imperialism at home) brought opium to Hawai'i, introduced to them by the British in the decades before Mao Zedong's birth (1893).

"By [Kalakua's] investigation and solution of the problem of labor he gave them the opportunity to raise sugar at an enormous profit." Liliuokalani explained succinctly the results: "The planters were elated, the merchants were encouraged, money flowed into their pockets, bankrupt firms become wealthy, sugar companies declared fabulous dividends." All of these developments made the Hawaiian islands more valuable and thus more a target for takeover; in other words, they worked to "the aggrandizement of the very persons who . . . plotted a subversion of [the king's] authority."[13] By 1887 the planter elite forced King Kalakua to sign the Bayonet Constitution, which handed over the power of the monarchy to the ministry, by this time all haole. In 1889, King Kalakaua departed on his last journey for the planters. His mission was to preserve the free trade that had made plantations profitable. He intended to lobby against the McKinley Bill that would reinstate U.S. tariffs on Hawaiian sugar. But the king died on the trip, to his death, in the trenchant words of his sister, "cheerfully and patiently [working] for the cause of those who had been and were his enemies."[14]

Those enemies rapidly closed in on the new queen, compelling her even before her brother's funeral to take an oath to the Bayonet Constitution. She soon began responding to petitions (6,500 out of 9,500 registered voters) from Hawaiians all over the islands for a new constitution in the interests of the native people. On January 16, 1893, she planned to present the new document to the legislature but was never able to do so. "The troops from the United States ship *Boston* were landed by order of the United States minister, J. L. Stevens, in secret understanding with the revolutionary party . . . for the safety of American citizens and protection of their interests."[15] Faced with U.S. troops in the city, "drawing in line in front of the palace gates, with guns pointed at us," the queen abdicated until "such time as the government of the United States . . . reinstate me."[16]

We walked up the sweeping staircase and into the rooms to the right, where our guide explained the widespread looting of the palace that had taken place during and after the coup, so that its furniture was scattered all over the world. Back in the hall, we approached the bedroom where the Republic of Hawai'i had imprisoned Lili-uokalani for eight months after a failed uprising in 1895. Ku'umeaaloha took over our instruction from the tour guide at this point. In the evenings, Liliuokalani's people gathered outside on the grounds beneath her window and sang to the queen. In a glass-covered case was the quilt she stitched with her companion, into which were stitched pieces of fabric slipped in as well-wishes by visitors. Quilting as protest: an impulse I recognized from the gay community's experience with AIDS. "The first night of my imprisonment was the longest night I have ever passed in my life," she later wrote.[17]

Our tour guide turned to lead us from the room, but I realized that Ku'umeaaloha was crying. I put my arms around her and held her a moment, with a sense that she wanted me to feel what had happened here. This spot was similar to the balcony of the Lorraine Motel in Memphis: something sacred was killed here. Then we joined the others, me with a confirmation of what I had suspected: Ku'umeaaloha and Mab would be friends.

Downstairs, we entered the throne room on the left where Liliuokalani was tried and convicted, with six others, of treason. The sentence was five years' hard labor, never carried out. When she was paroled, she left immediately for the United States, taking up residence in Washington, D.C., and hosting as many legislators and dig-nitaries as she could to strengthen her unsuccessful arguments against the U.S. an-nexation of the interim Republic of Hawai'i that occured in 1898—the goal all along of the U.S. planter class. The Republic of Hawai'i lasted not quite as long as the Re-public of Texas, carved in the 1830s out of Mexican territory. Both republics served the same purpose: holding territory until it could become part of the United States. *Hawaii's Story by Hawaii's Queen* was Liliuokalani's final protest, its appendix con-taining the text of the treaty: "The Republic of Hawai'i hereby cedes absolutely and without reserve to the United States of America all rights of sovereignty of whatsoever kind in and over the Hawaiian Islands and their dependencies . . . [including] all public, government, or crown lands."[18]

After lunch on the grounds and listening to the band play Liliuokalani's compo-sitions, Ku'umeaaloha headed back to work, and the three of us drove south for snor-keling at Haunama Bay. Protected from the fierce tug of the ocean, Annie put on her fins and goggles and leaned over to look at the fish in waist-high water, ecstatic, and we all found a deeper section where we could swim, holding hands and watching fish in the lava rocks.

SEXUALITY AND NEW VISIONS OF A NATION

I kū mau mau!
I kū wa!

The chant went back and forth Saturday morning, echoing off the walls of the Ala Moana Pavilion, where the conference had opened. It was a Kanaka Maoli solidarity chant—literally, a work chant for hauling one of the huge logs from which canoes were made. Kalea, Ku'umeaaloha's partner, led the call, straight from her diaphragm. Kalea had a gorgeous butch solidity. It was easy to see how and why Ku'umeaaloha loved her.

Morning workshops taught me much about various movements in Hawai'i, for which the sovereignty movement provided the heart, or perhaps the spine, and for which questions of land were central. Today, Kanaka Maoli are on the bottom by every measure—health, education, and on the top with imprisonment and homelessness; rents are higher than anywhere in the United States; and 80 percent of the tropical island's food is imported, although it could all be locally produced.[19] The 1848 Māhele cemented this dispossession. It destroyed the *ahupua'a* system of indigenous land management that gave chiefs wedge-shaped districts worked communally from coast to mountains. The *'ohana* (extended family) farmed the mountains and valleys, fishing the coast and waters, and sharing back and forth. The four-month festivals to Lono served to distribute and redistribute food and other resources. By some estimates, land had been a communally shared resource here for two thousand years.

Seventy-five years after Cook's arrival, missionaries-become-royal-advisors were ready for a land grab, for the introduction of full-blown capitalism into islands whose native people had no word for "to own" and for whom generosity was highly prized. From a system in which the people understood themselves to be descended from a common ancestor and related, Hawaiians were expected to "proceed as if they were strangers."[20] Missionary Judd, ensconced as Kamehameha III's chief advisor, honchoed the Māhele. This process parceled out the four million acres on the islands in three segments: to the government, the people, and the chiefs. It left 72 percent of Kanaka Maoli landless, people who were pushed into the cash economy.[21] Missionary and other well-placed haole families made off like bandits with the people's lands and much of the other two portions as well. For example, Charles Bishop Reed married Princess Bernice Pauahi Paki, heir to part of the chiefs', or "crown," lands in 1850. He thus became trustee of 11 percent of all Hawaiian lands in 1884 at his wife's death. By then he had a banking monopoly in Hawai'i and went on to amass a fortune equivalent to the Carnegies and Rockefellers. He established the Bishop Estates for Hawaiian charity and the Kamehameha Schools to return a portion of his wealth as charity to Kanaka Maoli, who, deprived of land and means of livelihood, would increasingly need it.[22]

The Annexation Treaty of 1898, as Liliuokalani pointed out, ceded both government and crown lands to the United States but stipulated that any of these lands not used for the military or local government should be used for the welfare of the island's inhabitants. These ceded lands became the basis for political struggles in the next century. In 1921, with pressure from Hawaiians, the Hawaiian Homes Commission Act set aside 200,000 acres of ceded land for Kanaka Maoli with 50 percent Kanaka Maoli blood quantum. In the next seventy to eighty years, only seven thousand or so families had successfully received these lands, with twenty thousand on a waiting list, some of them for thirty years.[23] After World War II, Article 73 of the UN Charter called for decolonization of all non-self-governing territories, with Hawai'i on the list. The ballot on statehood, however, did not give sovereign independence as an option. The 1959 Statehood Act created a Hawaiian Home Lands Trust, 1.4 million acres of state land to be held in trust, with little actually used for Kanaka Maoli. These ceded lands were instead used for public projects, such as airports and schools, and by the military for toxic waste dumps.[24]

Land issues had ignited the sovereignty movement in the late sixties, inspired by anticolonial struggles in other parts of the world and liberation movements of people of color in the United States. *Hawaii's Story by Hawaii's Queen* was reprinted in 1965 and inspired a new generation of sovereignty activists when they read the queen's account of the theft of Hawai'i and the pains she took to document its illegality.[25] Hui Alaloa fought for access to beaches and against evictions from the beaches of Moloka'i. The bombing of Kaho'olawe Island, also in the ceded lands, by the five-nation RIM-PAC (Rim of the Pacific) fleet, galvanized a vigorous grassroots movement to protest destruction of the island, along with an upsurge of interest in Kanaka Maoli culture and spiritual practices, especially reverence for 'āina.[26] By 1993, a century after Liliuokalani's overthrow, sovereignty groups held a People's International Tribunal.

There were at the time of our visit more than a dozen sovereignty groups with a range of strategies. The state-within-a-state model was currently embodied in the Office of Hawaiian Affairs. Nation-within-a-nation advocates wanted to claim the ceded lands as indigenous territory. This strategy would involve recognition by the United States and international institutions and allow control over assets and the ability to negotiate treaties similar to those signed by Native American nations in the continental United States.[27] Then there were the groups for the islands' complete independence from U.S. control. All of these ideas fermented in community education programs, conventions, *puwalu*, as people discussed such vital questions as the nature of sovereignty, the nature of the modern state, combining traditional with modern cultures. The focus at the conference was decolonization, of self, land, and culture.

On the breaks, I learned more about contradictions between culture and sexuality in Hawai'i from Kalei, Nawahine, Kelaiki, and Ku'umeaaloha. The Hawaiian Christian Coalition was planning to put measures on the ballot to override the Supreme Court's gay marriage ruling and to call for a state constitutional convention.

"A constitutional convention could weaken protection of indigenous land and cultural rights in the Hawaiian constitution," they explained, "and some Kanaka Maoli are supporting the idea of a convention because of homophobia!" It was a wedge strategy familiar from other states, where other people of color were drawn into coalitions around sexuality issues with people who were working to the detriment of communities of color. Hawai'i had become a battleground with predominantly white national gay and lesbian groups pushing gay marriage, and the religious Right rallying against it, targeting Kanaka Maoli communities, with, as usual, gay Kanaka Maoli caught in the crossfire.[28]

The first hearings on same-gender marriage had precipitated the forming of Na Mamo o Hawai'i, a group of indigenous gays Hawaiians. Na Mamo means "the precious ones." They were mostly women, I was finding to my unmitigated delight, preferring the term *gay* because the Hawaiian language does not make the gender distinctions that English does. In 1996 Na Mamo members attended a series of *puwalu* (conventions) of the different sovereignty groups. Inspired by the new South African constitution that protects sexual orientation in a post-apartheid democratic state, Na Mamo member Noenoe Silva wrote of their declaration: "Our freedom to live in our land is linked to our freedom to determine how we live in our bodies, our freedom to live in relationships that may be different from the American culture. Before colonization we lived in a society that accepted diversity, and now we want to propose support for ending discrimination against lesbians, gays and bisexuals."[29]

"We cannot allow a Hawaiian nation to be built that will impose these kinds of oppressions," Ku'umeaaloha explained as we sat around the picnic table, her passion most deeply engaged in imagining a free Hawai'i.

Na Mamo women and other Kanaka Maoli historians had excavated traditional Hawaiian culture to understand its range of premissionary sexual practices that had rapidly become sins when the missionaries arrived. There were practices of *punalua*, in which two lovers could share the same mate, jealousy being discouraged and collective responsibility for children encouraged. Bisexuality, among men at least, was prevalent; *aikane* were male lovers. In general, there was "moe ak, moe mai" (sleeping here and there). Lono, the god of fertility and sexuality, divided the calendar with Ku, the god of war. During Lono's four months there was feasting, celebration, dancing, sports; the absence of war, work, and sacrifice.

Na Mamo members were relatively few in numbers. But they had the kind of courage and vision I had come to expect from lesbian, gay, bisexual, and transgendered people of color. With the least room to stand, they often claimed the widest territory as home. I was moved and honored to be with them. Freud had explained in *Civilization and Its Discontents* that Western culture and civilization are built on the repression of desire. He left the question open that Audre Lorde had so brilliantly addressed: how to have sexual desire more integral to culture. Indigenous Hawaiian culture, Na Mamo members were saying, gave us another model to think about sexuality.

LINKING STRUGGLES

"As a white person I can locate myself in this terrain by great-grandfathers who were settler colonists as rooted in the practices of slavery (although without the slaves) as haole were in colonialism and genocide. But how do I locate myself as a lesbian? I guess that the relationship between Hawaiian sovereignty and gay marriage will be similar to the relationship between African American freedom struggles and gay civil rights. So, again, let me start on what to me is the more familiar terrain of civil rights."

I was in the middle of my speech, after a generous introduction by Ku'umeaaloha. Annie and Barb were smiling in the front row, having joined us from the nearby beach, where Annie had constructed a huge sand house.

"Last year the Supreme Court in *Evans* vs. *Romer* passed a landmark decision that finally gave gay and lesbian citizens of the United States constitutional status. The ruling came in response to Amendment Two in Colorado, the prototype for an epidemic of ballot initiatives that would prohibit states or cities from extending lesbians and gay men protection against discrimination. The opposition argued that we wanted not 'equal rights,' but 'special rights,' and Justice Kennedy faced the issue head on: 'We find nothing special in the protections Amendment Two withholds. These are protections taken for granted by most people either because they already have them or do not need them; these are protections against exclusion from an almost limitless number of transactions and endeavors that constitute ordinary civil life in a free society.' Lesbians and gay men, the court affirmed, were not 'strangers to the law.'[30] Amendment Two was ruled to be a violation of the Equal Protection Clause of the Fourteenth Amendment.

"When I celebrated this ruling last year, part of my gratitude went to the generations of African Americans and their antiracist white allies who struggled to abolish slavery and institute the Thirteenth, Fourteenth, and Fifteenth Amendments in the years immediately following the Civil War. These amendments brought the country closer to fulfilling its democratic ideals. The Thirteenth abolished human slavery. The Fifteenth prohibited denying suffrage on the basis of race, color, or previous condition of servitude. The Fourteenth Amendment defined citizenship for the first time as belonging to anyone born or naturalized within the U.S., guaranteed equal protection and due process, and made the Bill of Rights binding on the states. When lesbians and gay men took up our call for civil rights a century later, we inherited the legacy of this struggle against slavery and the 'badges of slavery.' When we are conscious of this legacy, we can link struggles. When we are not, we seem (and often are) guilty of racist appropriation.

"When lesbian and gay lawyers argue the marriage question before the U.S. Supreme Court, as I am sure they some day will, they will undoubtedly cite *Loving* vs. *Virginia*: 'The freedom to marry has long been recognized as one of the vital personal rights essential to the orderly pursuit of happiness by free men. Marriage is one of the basic civil rights of man, fundamental to our very existence and survival.'[31] Thus in 1967 the U.S. Supreme Court struck down a Virginia law against interracial marriage.

"Questions of race, gender, colonialism and sexuality take us rapidly beyond 'civil rights,' and to the limits of the U.S. Constitution as bases for democratic struggles. After all, the U.S. Constitution in its first seventy-five years did permit human slavery; and in 1893 it did not stop Marines from overthrowing Hawai'i's constitutional monarch. The Fourteenth Amendment guarantees due process to protect life, liberty, and property, and in that last word, *property*, there's a constitutional rub. The Declaration of Independence declared the inalienable rights 'life, liberty and the pursuit of happiness.' This passage from happiness to property is the passage of Hawaiian history between Cook's arrival in 1778 and the Māhele in 1848 that ended the system by which ruling chiefs managed all land for the benefit of all the people. Instead, plots were parceled among commoners, ruling chiefs, royal family, and the government, as the material you sent me explains, dispossessing up to 90 percent of Native Hawaiians of their land and right to vote.

"It is on this slippery terrain of 'native land and foreign desire,' to use the title of a book on the Māhele, that I take my bearing as a lesbian. Last year, the World Council of Churches conducted a study process on 'Gospel and Cultures,' and part of what they asked was, 'When does the Gospel arrive as good news and when does it arrive as bad news in a culture?'[32] Missionaries in Hawai'i brought both good and bad news. The Church, as well, for lesbians and gay men, can be both very good or very bad news. The 'good news' of the Gospel is a spirit of love that redeems the outcast, binds up the broken, lifts up the fallen, tends the poor and sick and pained. When Christianity arrives as bad news, it does just the opposite: breaks, casts out, divides.

"As a lesbian, I feel at home on Lono's terrain. I do believe that if I surveyed any particular group of homosexuals—'Do you want to sign up for Lono or Kū???'—97 percent of us would hunker down in the months of Lono and try to keep the party going for the rest of the year. I think the gays in the military thing was a peculiar aberration, a deliberate working against this grain. I know, like marriage, the campaign about the military was about economics, and for some people it was about patriotism. But I suspect that it was at core some sort of butch fashion statement. Lately in discussions with heterosexual progressives, I get asked what is gay culture? It's a complex question. Partly I want to say gay people *are* culture: We recognize ourselves among the artists and shamans across cultures although there *are* several homosexuals who are not talented or creative or particularly spiritual. We seem to have an affinity for Lono, Mardi Gras, Gay Pride Parades, parts of which are downright scandalous.

"Whalers brought syphilis and missionaries brought guilt. Conflating sexuality with guilt, shame, and disease and narrowing the range of sexual practices to heterosexual monogamous marriage: was this good or bad news? Did the 'missionary position' get Hawaiians screwed in other ways as well? (Let me make clear I am not talking here about heterosexual relationships, the *experience* of heterosexuality, but about heterosexuality as an institution enforced by legal, religious, medical regimes and by brutal random violence.) From an anticolonial perspective, is enforced monogamous heterosexual marriage a Māhele of the body? The sovereign body, sovereign culture, sovereign government: is not there some principle here of self-determination in a context of our essential interdependence that also links Hawaiian sovereignty and gay liberation?

"The enforced nuclear family is part of institutional heterosexuality, as it is of sexism. Lesbian and gay relationships do not make sense within the framework of the nuclear family because it was constructed to exclude us. Many 'welfare mothers' do not either because the nuclear family was also constructed to exclude people of color and the poor. I suspect that lesbian and gay families might fare better in cultures where, as in Hawai'ian, the words for mother and father also mean uncle and aunt or any member of one's parents' generation. And any *keiki* (child) is one's own child.

"Let me make it clear that I raise these questions about marriage as someone in a twenty-year relationship, more than sixteen of which have been monogamous, and I don't foresee changing that agreement any time soon. (Sorry, girls.) If the decision of the Hawai'i Supreme Court became law of the land, it would give me the possibility of access to a right 'fundamental to my existence and security.' The custody of our child would be much more secure. Barb and I could have access to the other's social security when she dies, which, believe me, we will need. Whatever we can scrape up for retirement would pass to the other without taxes taking out another chunk of it. We would signal to our families and much of the rest of the world, in ways they understand, the primacy of our relationship, our intent to be life partners, including the sharing of physical passion and spiritual discovery, a coming together of increased consciousness. Such a ruling, especially, would put lesbian and gay committed relationships on a par with heterosexual committed relationships—as psychologically, spiritually, economically equal. That is exactly where I think they should be.

"Should gay marriage become legal in Hawai'i (and I realize that's still a long shot), the gay community nationally needs to think long and hard about how lesbians and gay men who choose to come to Hawai'i to marry can link with and support progressive struggles here, not become just a homo version of hetero honeymooners, or some new incarnation of gay tourism gone berserk. (I can see it now: lesbians float over on Olivia cruises, getting a choice between getting hitched on the beach or the lava flow; for the guys it's that ritzy hotel with the dolphins in the pool.)

"So how do we, linking struggles and spirits, claim the future? What kind of relationships do we want to have, anyway? We are answering that in many, many ways this weekend. Let me come back again to this question of marriage.

"Barb and I had asked ourselves that question—What relationship do we want to have?—when we had our fifteenth anniversary celebration, which actually came at seventeen years because it took us that long to get up the nerve to do it and get our act together. We invited two hundred friends, hired a band, and told them to bring a lot of good food. Then we set about figuring out what we wanted to promise each other. We affirmed our process, over the years, of 'me becoming you becoming me' and the commitments that, as we follow them, keep our love vital.

Then we made promises, affirmations, really, about how we would live together. They were the last thing we had done for the ceremony:

> I promise
> to honor the spirit in you,
> to protect your freedom as if it were my own,
> because it is;
> to seek abandon and play,
> to honor our bodies' pleasures,
> to speak anger freshly, share pain, allow comfort and release.
> I promise to create joy
> in the everyday tasks of a shared life.
> I promise to nurture your love for Annie.
> I promise to come to find you in the present's blinking eye
> which is the only moment we ever have.
> And when I do not do all these things, perfectly, every time,
> I promise to forgive myself and gently to begin again.

"It's not such a bad strategy, either, for linking struggles."

After I finished, four Na Mamo women presented me with a succession of leis, strung primrose, and braided ginger flowers. With the cool blossoms piled around my neck, it was as if I were in the middle of a garden. They explained later that same-gender lei presentations were a violation of protocols, but they had decided they should be the ones who "lei'd" me, and I had no complaints. Annie and Barb also received leis, and one of Annie's strong memories is our casting the flowers back into the ocean when their petals turned brown.

TRAINING THE HEART

Aloha, from the advertisements for Hawaii Air, in the airport welcoming tourists with leis, from old Elvis movies and concerts. Aloha, commercialized. But underneath, and beyond the mystery of the commodity, I began to feel another reality in our days in Hawai'i.

Aloha is present also in the language, from what I began to glean from '*Ōlelo No'eau: Hawaiian Proverbs and Poetical Sayings* collected and translated as a lifelong labor of love by Mary Kawena Pukui, who was born the year Liliuokalani was tried for treason. Mary Pukui remembers the chants and songs at the queen's funeral procession in 1917. Na Mamo members presented me with '*Ōlelo No'eau* on my second, more difficult trip. The proverbs and sayings are often metaphoric, but always clear poetic images through which sensuous natural forms shine. Imagist poets emulating the Japanese haiku inaugurated English and American poetic modernity—drawing from two thousand years of nature mindfully apprehended.

"Naueue ka hi'u o ka i'a lewai i ke kai" (The tails of the fish that move in the sea tremble), Mary Kawena Pukui translates, then explicates: "Said of fish, such as the *hinālea*, in the cold month Welehu. The tails of the *hinalea* bend as they seek hollows in the corals for hiding."[33] Fragments capture subtle differences, such as these:

> *Ka ua kapua'i kanaka o Pālāwai*
> [*The rain of Pālāwai (which sounds like) human footsteps*]

> *Ka ua kau lā'au o Pāhala*
> [*The tree-resting rain of Pāhala*][34]

"When I was little," said Ku'umeaaloha, "my grandmother used to tell us about Papa and Wākea, the earth mother and sky father. Papa, our mother, supports us every day of our lives and gives us the food from the land; Wākea, father, sends the air we breathe. The mountains on the windward side are dark and deep, like velvet vulva. Clouds settle on mountain peaks, volcanic, still rising, the rain the sweat of their lovemaking that makes all grow. Sexuality for the old ones was not one relationship between one man and one woman for one purpose—procreation; but the energy that joins us to each other, to the land, to *'āina. Mālama 'āina* (care for the land); *Maka 'āina* (eyes of the land)."

In Hawai'i for ten days (and on my second journey as well), I began to apprehend aloha, the love that is shared breath, vital connection. Aloha occurs best in the context of *pono* (balance). From this pono comes *mana* (power). Captain Cook broke the pono in a big way, but imbalance had already started before his arrival, when a burgeoning population brought greater social stratification that precipitated island chiefs into territorial warfare. Capitalism added a pursuit of profits that consumes labor and natural resources for its ever-expanding markets. Aloha, though, was older than King Kamehameha I and his royal successors. *Ubuntu.* Born to belonging: I had pursued it like a mantra. Now Hawai'i was showing me the beauty of *'āina*, that to which I belonged—sky as father, mountain mother, taro brother, all of us vibrating.

Such strong aloha developed here, Loretta helped me to see, because Kanaka Maoli (translated as "the real people") for undisturbed centuries were neither noble nor savage, but close observers of nature in small communities on islands that gave much to sustain them with little terror: without poisonous snakes, or noxious insects, or predatory animals, or frequent invasions, or wars of conquest, although there were sharks and spirits and that powerful ocean. They put their energy into agriculture, worshipping not only Kū, the god of war, but Lono, god of fertility, setting aside work for four months of festivities. At other times they engaged in common tasks of growing taro, staple food similar to a sweet potato, or hauling the logs to make the huge canoes they paddled over seas whose currents could swallow a person or a boat.[35]

"Don't turn your back on the ocean," one guidebook warned, a lesson driven home by an article in the *Honolulu Times*, early in our arrival, of four tourists too near the edge of the sea, swept by a rogue wave into a whirlpool; two were spit back out, two were not seen again. For all the centuries that Europeans hugged the shores even in large boats until some one of them invented the magnetic compass, the people of Oceania set out across the sixty-four million square miles of the Pacific. In their canoes they no doubt deduced from the curved horizon what Europeans did not: a trust that ahead was not an edge over which they would fall, not a boundary between being and nothingness, not a line, but a luminous curve that they also rode and that beckoned them on. For them, there was not an abstract wind, or wave, or star. They learned to navigate across broad expanses by particular constellations shifting with the seasons, by the directions of the winds and the length or taste of a particular wave's swell.[36] All of these acts required not a mind bent on conquest, but the close observation of nature's powers (mana) from which comes a sense of oneness, belonging, balance.

"It is hard for the modern intellectually rigid and extroverted mind to sense the subjective relationships of genuine Hawaiians to Nature, visible and invisible," explained Mary Kawena Pukui when she compiled her observations in the 1930s, "without some comprehension of this quality of spontaneous *being-one-with-natural-phenomena, which are persons not things.*"[37]

"Listen more often to things than to beings." I remembered Sweet Honey in the Rock. Hawai'i could melt that rigid extroverted mind.

The challenge of aloha is to learn the lessons of the heart, "a kind of spiritual ecology," Loretta explained in e-mail, "and yet that's still a Western concept." One sentence from a book Barb had brought, *The Secret Wisdom of the Kahunas*, stuck in my mind: "Western culture has basically emphasized the head centre. That is why in the West a deep concern is felt for man. And the deep concern is with his homelessness, his emptiness. . . . The reason is because only the head has become centre. The heart has not been trained; it is missing."[38] Here again is the devastating legacy of the mind/body split, as articulated so astutely by Descartes, a *cogito, ergo sum* that leaves us homeless, with no place to be because we cannot be in our bodies.

Looking back on this first trip to Hawai'i, I understand more fully why I had wanted permission to bring Annie and Barb. These are the two, of all the beings on earth, with whom my heart has received its most complete training. In the lonely years of my adolescence, my mind had been my refuge. Before I understood the word *lesbian*, I carried a fear that I could never be loved. I read long summer afternoons on the front porch; I was climbing up into my head, as if I could think myself out of the fix in which I found myself. Coming out was to have the heart question called clearly: *Are you willing to lose the whole world, but gain love?* The gift of being queer is the moment we hear clearly the inner voice that speaks through the culture's fear: *This is who I am. She is my heart's desire. I choose us both.*

Barb and I found each other in our late twenties. For both, it was a period of grief from breaking up with first partners and a time of opening. She was a dancer, working as a secretary; I was a writer (just), finishing up a dissertation and teaching. What I loved about her was her spaciousness and her grace. I find still in her body spontaneity, passionate receptiveness, and deep comfort. Over twenty years, our differences have at times loomed maddeningly large. She finds herself in silence; I find myself in language and music. She craves spareness; I crave profusion. Her family washed their cars together. My family never washed our cars. Her parents, in retirement, see the country together in tour buses. I wander landscapes alone with my mother's perpetually half-(un)packed suitcase. I love to read the books that spill out of my bookcases, which she considers clutter. She learns much from early morning prayers, where she listens far more subtly than most and feels the presence of her guardians, of other spirits that some call angels. This is not my experience, perhaps because I have lacked some of her discipline; but I trust it as hers because I have felt its results over the years, as old boulders shifted from both of our backs.

And Annie, smiling from the front row during my speech, was our shared hearts' desire long before she was born. When Barb was almost due, a friend with a toddler told me true: "It will take the bottom out of your heart. You think your heart stops here," she motioned, "but then it drops." And drop my heart did, the first days and weeks of Annie's time with us, a mysterious new creature.

Neither of these women in my life allows me to relate to them through my head. With her quick intelligence, even now Annie refuses to sit in separate chairs reading separate books. When I read with her, it's in our bed or hers, or in the car or plane, reading together aloud. For all her early years graceful and tender, Annie has gained a Scorpio's fire in her adolescence; and she renders her own quick opinions about situations, large and small, in which we have put her.

When she was three, I first explained our relationship. "You are like every other little boy or girl in the world," I explained. "You were made by Barb, who is your mother, and David, your dad. But I am also your mom. Barb carried you in her tummy. I carry you in my heart."

She thought for a moment, then nodded, smiling. "And you in my heart," she replied and kept nodding, as if to her whole platoon of parents, "and you, and you."

Two years ago, we went over the same material again on a ride to Blockbuster to pick out the evening's video.

"You mean you're *not* my *biological* mother?" she exclaimed, alarmed. Good Lord, I thought, don't tell me we didn't make that clear! I groped for where to begin.

"But Annie—"

"Just kidding!" she grinned as I stifled another urge to strangle her. "Why didn't you adopt me?" she asked more seriously.

"Courts in North Carolina are so homophobic," I replied, "we figured it was best not to get them involved."

She sat with the information for a minute, then fixed me in her gaze. "You mean we have been living together all these years, and we have *neither* a biological *nor* a legal relationship?"

I laughed at her precision. "That's right," I said. "It's all love and commitment."

She shook her head as we went inside, and I thought I heard her thinking: I hope these people know what they are doing.

I still feel about her the way I did when I wrote this poem for her when she was four. I was at Windcall, a Montana retreat for burned-out activists:

A Daughter's Questions

Last month you asked me,
"How was the world made?"
I groped around—
"Some say in seven days,
some say in one big bang."
You were hardly satisfied.
"So what do you think it is?"
You fixed me, four-year-old eyes.

I take such questions seriously.
I do not want you snatched in fifteen years
By some cheap grace.

I thought that perhaps in coming here
With deer that rush and fade
Like apparitions in tall grass
And sage enough to cleanse the starkest dreams
I would get my answer.

Annie, I believe
The world is still in the making,
Yesterday I saw it unfold,
In mountains like bear teeth.

I was standing in the bear's jaw
And all around me flowers—lupine,
Yarrow, alpine forget-me-nots.
It answers your bright question
Every day as many ways
As there are grasshoppers on the path,
Or needles on tall firs,
Or moments when your quickness
Takes my heart.

I was increasingly grateful to traditional Hawaiian culture for its expansive view of extended family (*ʻohana*). It honored the full range of biological and chosen relationships: parents, children, friendships. Annie and I had had to explain far too many times, to too many people, what we were to one another.

Having done the work for which they brought me to Hawaiʻi, I spent three days on the Big Island with Barb and Annie. We splurged on a convertible so there would be nothing between us and the tropical breezes, or the orchids in the trees along the side of the road, or the clear expanses of ocean and sun from the highways that ran above the rocky coastline. We spent the first night on the Kona coast, swam where Captain Cook first came ashore, and headed the next day to the tip of the island, where the Marquesans probably first landed. We found the black sand beach, where Barb swam with turtles. We spent a day on the volcano, hiking across the black crater at noon in the tropical sun, following a marked trail, and finding bright red flowers growing up through cracks along the way. Annie built a house out of black lava rock, and we straggled to the other side. I had anticipated a Coke machine and a shuttle bus to take us back to the car, but there was neither. It took us a while to persuade one of the tourists to give us a ride back so that we would not face heat prostration on another two hours of volcanic rock.

We flew back out of Oahu, watching the islands recede over the wing of the plane, leaving behind new friends.

"What did you like best about Hawaiʻi?" I asked Annie as the plane mounted.

She thought a minute. "The people."

REMEMBER THE INVITATION

The second journey to Hawaiʻi came three years later and more tumultuously. Kuʻumeaaloha by then was a member of the URM Task Force on Community, Church, and Sexuality that we had put together to explore liberatory approaches to sexuality and spirituality. Kyle Kajihiro, with whom Kuʻumeaaloha worked in the American Friends Service Committee Honolulu office, was also on the task force. Colonialism's deadly shattering of a richly complicated self, the resulting fractures of mind, body, and spirit, was our increasing focus. Hawaiʻi, we felt, would offer a clearer view of these processes.

> *E hō mai ka ʻike mai luna mai ē*
> *O nā mea huna noʻeau*
> *O nā mela ē*
> *E hō mai*
> *E hō mai*
> *E hō mai ē*

This is the *olʻe* (chant), written by Edith Kanakaʻole, that Kuʻumeaaloha had shared at other meetings of the Task Force and the URM Board. *Grant us knowledge*

that filters from above of the hidden things, the wise things that are concealed in the
chants. Grant us, grant us, grant us.

Knock and it will be opened.

Our group drove over the mountains to a YMCA camp on the windward side of
the island. Mokapu was the place where Kanaka Maoli said the early heroes and
voyager-gods had come; but its more recent arrivals were Starbucks, McDonalds, and
Pizza Hut, offering hundreds of shopping opportunities in the strip malls that lined
the highway running alongside the volcanic spine of the mountain. Hundreds of *'iwi*
(ancestral bones) had been unearthed and removed to a museum during this development. Across the polluted azure of Kaneohe Bay we could see a Marine Corps
base. Everywhere mana, in each direction striking beauty, and everywhere desecra-
tion, in a constant and unsettling conjunction.

Sunday morning we climbed into the vans for our trip to the watery patches of cultivated taro. It was in the *ahupua'a* of Waiāhole, an important site of Kanaka Maoli
and grassroots organizing to resist eviction and keep waters in the windward streams
rather than tunneled through the mountain to plantations and golf courses. We
parked the vans along the road. The thirty-minute walk along the shaded forest path
took us through canopies of *hau* trees, their branches curving with heart-shaped
leaves and trunks used for canoe rigging, floats, and cordage. *Ho'io* (edible ferns)
laced the shaded ground and brushed the path, back from which sat *mamaki*, part of
the nettle family used for tea and medicine. We forded several streams, helping one
another across, wading or using rocks as stepping stones, the occasional call of birds
and insects part of a reverent hum of the heart of the land, *'āina*. Yet even the thorns
along the path showed the impact of colonization, Loretta (also on the task force)
later explained. Even the parrots we heard calling from the trees were fairly recent
immigrants.

A couple of miles in, Ku'umeaaloha stopped us, and we began to chant to signal
our arrival to our host, Uncle Calvin Hoe. "I ka lana wao" (Under the mighty trees),
"I Kū lana wao!" (stand among the tall forest trees!). And we were there, metaphors
becoming realities.

Grant me, grant me, grant me.

As a group, we had two years of experience with rituals, or protocols, as markers
of boundaries and thresholds in our meetings together. They were spiritual practices that strengthen the container (our physical container of mind/body/spirit, our
community, our environment, or nature, or relationship to 'āina). Such spiritual
practices could expand our limits. We had recognized that we needed that extra capacity to get questions of sexuality, its power and its abuses, with all its beauty and
danger, into discussion and view. Such practices also deepened awareness and a
sense of oneness and joy. We had been experimenting with the effects of joining
spiritual practices with political practice: that, in a nutshell, to me, anyway, was the
challenge of these journeys of sex(es) and spirit(s). Some days it worked better than
others.

From the task force's earliest discussions, the prospect of journeying to Hawai'i had raised the ante on questions of boundaries and protocols and trust, given the eight million tourists who flock there yearly to consume paradise, and given the understanding of sovereignty that had emerged in Kanaka Maoli movements over the past thirty years. Issues of tourism and internalized colonialism as they emerged in Hawai'i provided some of the most challenging moments of our time together, in a process that constantly demanded we see ourselves in a mirror, individually and as a group. As a collection of people committed to social justice, we were being asked to take on something even the articulation of which was unsettling: Would we come as tourists? How would we as Americans come to Hawai'i, given the extent to which we are socialized around patterns of consumption, so that Kentucky Fried Chicken can give us a feeling of home?

In the heart of the forest, listening for Uncle Calvin's cry, I understood at a deeper level connections between body politic and the politic of the land: I understood more clearly the need for careful demarcations, for asking for and waiting to hear permission as a way of healing from huge devastation, violence, violation, rape, and abuse. I knew this boundary marking in the bodies of many of the women I had physically loved, all the moments of lovemaking that suddenly became a walk across a mine field—touch the wrong place and the land/flesh explodes with old pain and memory. I had tried to explain this to Barb from my hiatus at Windcall.

> *Yesterday I drove through country*
> *where two years ago a storm of fire*
> *burned off a million acres.*
> *I could see it in the lodgepole pine,*
> *charred trunks fire-sheared of branches*
> *and waiting the first strong wind.*
> *No sane person could deny the damage.*
> *In places heat had scorched the earth*
> *and nothing grew. Others, flame was more*
> *a canopy, flickering limb to limb.*
> *Suddenly I knew this was your landscape,*
> *where amid great ravagement new mosses,*
> *yarrow, lupine now take root.*
> *I know I am not trusted with directions,*
> *which road to turn on, or down how many miles.*
> *I am writing this to say I found the way myself,*
> *saw how heat released the lodgepole's seeds.*
> *Rebirth—the oldest story, but this time it was you.*
> *To say I did not lie down amid the flowers,*
> *and breathe in their sweet breath.*
> *This time, I did not leave a body traced in grass.*
> *I am writing this to tell you: I left it as I found it.*
> *Next time I come here, you will show me how.*

I Kū mau mau! I Kū wā! Uncle Calvin chanted us into the clearing, the forest opening up suddenly into a garden, in its center taro growing in a small lake. After formal introductions and our presentation of Uncle Calvin with a lama tree, sacred to hula practitioners, he put us to work planting ferns in a culvert, tender green in the moist smell of volcanic soil. Then for an hour we weeded an irrigation ditch that ringed the taro patch, feet and hands in cool water and mud until, to our satisfaction, the water in the ditch was running fast and free. Those with open cuts stayed away from the water because it was polluted with leptospirosis, a disease brought by rats that first came to the islands in the cargo holds of ships. Next Uncle Calvin showed us how to harvest taro, its roots looking like sweet potatoes under the heart-shaped leaves. Taro, heart and big brother of the people, this watery taro field at the heart of a people's movement for self-determination, all rippled outward in the noon. Then Calvin pointed us to a stream on the edge of the field, rushing water that pooled beneath a tree. And we splashed and climbed trees above the stream. "You take care of the 'āina," Uncle Calvin observed a certain bliss among us from the work and the play in the water and mud, "it will take care of you."

Back through the forest, I remembered how I had felt as a child, with my brother running in the woods. He had died of cancer four months before, a difficult process for all of us, of pain and separation. But I felt him with me then, walking back to the road from the lo'i. In the lo'i with taro as brother, in the woods with my brother Tim.

The lo'i on Sunday, and a huiwai on Monday at midnight were the gift of Ku'umeaaloha, Kyle, Kakela, and our Hawaiian hosts. The huiwai was a spiritual cleansing in the ocean, which we entered at midnight in a protected part of the bay, fifteen of us silently with ourselves in the water, naked if we chose, for half an hour or more. Diving under the water, I could turn upward and watch the moon. Breaking the surface, I heard others off in the darkness, splashes like fins, or the flippers of turtles. I slipped out of my bathing suit. Here, protected from currents by the reef, I could turn without force in this liquid element, the water on my skin was sensuous after the initial chill, marking where I stopped and the water started, but also enveloping me in a hugeness of ocean and sky. My brother had been with me in the woods, but in the water it was my mother's presence I felt. "When I die," she would sometimes tell me as we walked on the beach at night, "I am just going to swim on that path of light out to the moon." The melding of pleasure and pain that were her travels, it occurred to me looking up at that moon, liquid itself now through Pacific water, was perhaps but one more legacy of guilt, another layer of skin I could shed here in this cleansing.

Back at the camp, in a hall with open windows looking out over the bay, we deepened our conversations. Does decolonizing leave racism behind, or does it allow for the complexities of the way racisms function? Does it leave class and gender behind, as some anticolonial movements and leaders have done historically, or can it give a way to understand how those forces operate together? Does it set up competition over who is more oppressed, or can it clarify and specify how oppression functions in a variety of geographic and political locations? What about the centrality of land, given the way under globalization people are moving around so much that many do not feel connected to a place. What are the implications to people of the African Diaspora, stolen from their land by slavery and forced as chattel to work land owned by their masters? How do we deal with those historical differences in the experience of colonialism? Is there a danger of romanticizing a precolonial past? And where was sexuality in this picture?

"Colonization of the mind-spirit-body begins with the body," Ku'umeaaloha articulated in one conversation. "It begins with the body, then the mind, and then an attempt to colonize the spirit."

I began to see in our rolling discussions and in the specifics of the Hawaiian experience the degree to which colonialism sought to forcefully reorganize all cultural practices: language, movement, worship, family relations, sexual intimacy, ways of knowing and learning. In the nineteenth century, colonial codes had prescribed sexual practices, such as prohibitions against sodomy, setting them into law. The effect was a reorganization of the body at a cellular level, if I understood Barb's work as a polarity therapist. I had also began to suspect that such a forced reorganization will never be complete. Spirit is the thing that is left over, in part at least, both to resist and to dwell apart in a different reality to which colonizers, because of their own tactics and metaphysics, do not have access. But to split off sexuality from spirit—the effect of various mind/body splits—was devastating to both.

I recognized in Hiram Brigham and his cohort of Calvinists his contemporary descendants: the Right-wing preachers railing against *homosexshals* and preaching hell's fire. As a lesbian, I do get kind of touchy on the question of the God in whose name people sometimes approach me, loving the sinner but hating the sin. From a journal entry the year before the Hawai'i trip: "*I am recognizing my stake as a lesbian and a woman in this God naming, which is such a profound mis-naming today in so many respects. Our lack of clarity on this God question is part of what is killing us. Faced with massive economic and cultural changes, people all over are scared and mad and looking for answers and belonging. One place they turn is to these Führer Gods concocted for them by Pat Robertson and Jerry Falwell and their ilk: omniscient, omnipotent, omnipresent, any love modeled on the life of Jesus only temporarily suspending the fires of divine male judgment.*"

Kanaka Maoli , living on volcanic islands, had a different relationship to fire than the hellfire brought by Hiram and his missionary buddies. What the missionaries had called faith was more like idolatry. They continually mistook their whiteness for God, remaking the islands in their own greedy image. Too narrow a vision of God is deadly.

WORLD AS LOVER, WORLD AS SELF

Each evening of this second visit, many of us pulled our mattresses out to the porch (*lanai*) and I slept beside Ku'umeaaloha, Scot, Kyle, Kakela, to a symphony of snores and night calls. As staff coordinator, I spent a lot of time in the emergency room, with three of our people seriously hurt or ill. Judith got off the plane with a strained back. Sky Tears hurt herself in an accident with a boat. Marta ended up with a three-day hospital stay, with cellulitis, a possibly deadly infection on her cheek for which she needed powerful antibiotics. I was exhausted negotiating all of these physical and psychic events, from dawn some days until midnight. Occasionally, I felt compassion for us at the immensity of the forces we had taken on, and pleasure in working with Kuʻumeaaloha on a succession of tasks, hauling that log. "I am following happily in your wake," I laughed at one point, and she didn't seem to mind.

As we grappled with questions of sexuality, identity, and culture, our days were filled with huge ups and downs: moments of happiness and unity, others of tension, pain, disagreement. At times it felt like battling some sense of spiritual scarcity that embeds itself in contested identities; at others as if we had breathed ourselves together into some more abundant, spacious place—if only for moments. All the while around us mountains piercing clouds, rain mists, light off the bay—life.

Joanna Macy writes of the four spiritual approaches that underlie most of the world's religions: world as trap, world as battleground, world as lover, and world as self.[39] In the foreground, some of us acted out worlds of traps and battlegrounds; but what stayed with me from Hawaiʻi and what resonates in Hawaiʻian proverbs and sayings is an apprehension of world as lover, world as self, that to which we belong.

The anticolonial writer Memmi, trained in psychoanalysis, had described the relationship of colony to mother country as one to a superego that existed "not to be a part of things, to control from a distance without ever being touched by the prosaic and convulsive behavior of [humans] of flesh and blood." While this seems more a relation to a father country to me, Memmi's words accurately describe the God brought to the islands by Calvinist missionaries—a separation of people and earth from God, and of spirit from prosaic and convulsive flesh, that played itself out in Māhales of land and body. Private property arrived with eager-to-own missionaries, who also brought a heavy load of Protestant guilt that served, as well, as a separation from belonging. It was an invading worldview that many indigenous Hawaiians— who had no word in their language for "to own," whose fluid bodies and fluid sexualities mirrored their home, who conceived of the elements as their steadfast and loving parents—did not survive. The question from indigenous cultures all over the globe to the rest of us human beings, indigenous to the planet earth, may be: How do we think that *we* can survive such separations?

When I remember Hawaiʻi, I also recall the three Kanaka Maoli girls we met, lined up in a stairstep to greet us. We were visiting the Nation of Hawaiʻi, a homestead of families, about ninety people. They lived on ceded land the state gave them to get them off the beaches, where they had been living. The nation was nestled up against the spine of a mountain reaching ardently, immensely to the sky and drenched in clouds and mist from Wākea and Papa's lovemaking in the falling light. These three girls chanted us in with pride and precision, each taking her turn to lead the call. They played on the mountain many days, they later explained; their mom sent them out with walkie-talkies and let them run. Hawai'i worked my muscles of *belonging*, and I left with many things, not the least of which was a vision down the twists and turns of history of an independent Hawai'i—a Hawai'i like two girls, *keikilanis*, their hair spread black behind them, their eyes like stars, running, running free on the breast of a mountain.

6

REQUIEM
For My Brother

I

Kuʻu ka luhi, ua maha
[He has let down his weariness
And is at rest]

—*Hawaiian Proverb*

IT was the first week of March 1998. I was still on the path with my brother Tim, as I had promised I would be, even though I felt he was throwing boulders at me with the last bits of his strength. It was week three of the month the oncologist gave him. Mourning death is simply hard. It's mourning a life that breaks the heart. Between the morphine and the brain lesions, where did he go, and how could I join him? I knew the way, I was sure of that. I had been back many more times than he, who thought he could leave for good.

Perhaps in his morphine dreams we were running in the woods behind the pool, legs pumping, going at least a hundred miles an hour, faster than the speed of shade, or of the light that filtered through the large sea green leaves of late July when afternoons were swollen with dust and heat. Or maybe we were crossing the creek in the woods near Hilma's house on the sewage pipe that stretched far above the trickle of water: he was balancing ahead of me three years taller, walking across, while I was scooting, not trusting my sturdier body and maybe wanting the cool pipe to slide between my eight—six? nine?—year-old thighs.

Mama used to tell me, "Tim's mind is like a scalpel. He cuts through to what he wants. Yours is like a sponge, soaking up everything." In the years of the late 1950s, after the Russians sent up *Sputnik,* she pronounced our gendered fates: "This country will always need teachers and engineers." Guess which one I became, at one-third the salary, as he had been known to point out as he engineered outer space for NASA, then for defense contractors. Where he saw vectors, trajectories, I saw Orion, Cassiopeia, the Milky Way splashed behind his orbital paths. But I could feel him freer there now, in that space between dying brain cells, between the spacious neutron and orbiting electron, between the meteors and the stars. Now his brain tumors lay beyond any scalpel, and his sponge-brain began to soak up space a different way, wandering the nebulae. However much we engineer, I suspect we all die poets. It comforted me also to think that at some point he would move beyond the peculiar logic of his attitude. "The gay thing makes them crazy," was Daddy's assessment, finally, when I puzzled for the umpteenth time on his distance. It comforted me to think that this homophobia was much more his wife's than his. Perhaps these were my necessary fictions. "Human kind," I remember T. S. Eliot from grad school, "cannot bear very much reality."

I have felt his dying in my body always before my heart or mind: as first a tired anguish, the requiem in the nucleus of each cell. "Tim's in bad shape," Daddy had sobbed to me over the phone in early February three years before. "They operated on him for appendicitis, and his body is riddled with cancer. I'm just grateful his mama is not alive to see this." Ever since than, I've worked at answering his riddle. I imagined I would be there to help sort through the daily doses, large and small, of fear and pain and drips and shots and meals and sleep. Another fantasy I have let go of. I am inept with bedpans, IVs, milligrams. But I was willing to learn.

We came in close proximity, trailing clouds of mucous, blood, and glory through our mother's birth canal. For the first ten years, in my memory we are everywhere together. Our endless nights of kick the can. I would find my favorite hiding place behind the steps on the yard's cool side and settle back against the brick to watch the dusk dissolve the gladiolas, the Studebaker, dissolve the rose arbor and the scuppernong-laden well. I'd see him dodging in and out of shadows. And even then in evening conversations I feared the forms that loosen in the dusk, as his does now, before the back porch light flicked on, and I would lean to catch our voices in spilled kitchen glow as the screen door slammed.

I wanted to be there when he *expired* . . . that last breath that finally lets the spirit go. "I think Mama will be there for you," I had told him during the phone call from his hospital bed, when he knew about the failing liver, but not yet about the wounded brain that let us have one poet-to-poet conversation. His birth almost killed her: too narrow a passage, too long a time, too many women in one hospital having postwar babies. Mama speculated once that the hard labor pitted them against one another early on—the legacy of difficult births, she'd read in some women's magazine. Perhaps we were still living out that karma.

Tim's wife told me once that many of his childhood memories were of protecting me: holding hands to cross the street. I remember sharing the back bedroom for years, comforted by his soft breathing in the other bed when I was awake, fearing to put my foot down to go pee because of the bogeymen under the bed.

He wanted his love to make a difference to his wife. Early in their marriage, Becky drew the line between our mother and her, his present life and his origins, and he let it stand. Tim, our younger sister Dal, and I each took our own distances, from parents and each other. But I have learned from my fifty years that we never really leave anything behind. He seemed to have learned a different lesson. I heard Mama crying over it late too many nights, "What did I do wrong?"

I did my best in the last three years to close the distance, when time was clearly running out. But I had run up the white flag, surrendered to superior firepower, left Becky the utter, final, illusory control over the wreckage of his body. I did not, however, surrender to her my belief in his spirit. It's that spirit for which I still was reaching, beyond any of our control.

Since my brother's diagnosis, I had toiled to rearrange my ratio of doubt to faith, from 97 percent to 95 percent terror and despair, and in that extra space my prayers for Tim, his wife, and his children. Buddhism was my first resort, Thich Nhat Hanh's balm for napalmed spirits, out of the jungles and villages of Vietnam in the blaze and sorrow of imperialist wars:

> *May you be peaceful and happy,*
> *May you be light in body and spirit,*
> *May you be safe and free from harm,*
> *May you be free from anger, affliction, anxiety and fear.*

More recently words have come from closer to home, the lineaments of a faith we learned by rote: "May the Lord bless you and keep you; May the Lord's face shine upon you and be gracious unto you; May the Lord lift up the Lord's countenance unto you, and give you peace." I have prayed this for each one of him, and each one of me, at moments when I missed him most, or I most wanted to kill him. I have worked to cobble a faith in a God who is in the midst of suffering, not inflicting it for punishment; a larger view from which the suffering that we experience, and inflict on one another, is a matter of infinite sadness: "the Great Mother: empty yet inexhaustible." Older, the poet says, than God.

When I put prayers aside and decided to calculate revenge on Becky, I told myself that Mama would have him in the end. "I think Mama will be there for you when you die," I repeated.

"I think she will, too," he replied slowly. "I think I'll need her."

II

He was measuring time in feet of colon: it looked like he needed help.

His first operation was in February 1996, emergency surgery that happened when he had gone in for appendicitis and come out with a diagnosis of cancer. It was the week of Mardi Gras. I drove down to the hospital with Daddy. Tim was depressed, laid up in bed, looking out from eyes in which the spirit was way back, in the midst of great pain and seeing his own mortality in the mirror of his family's need. His sons came bustling in from a shopping spree to find comic books. The older son, Jake, and I fell into familiar company. With Ned I got into an extended conversation about haunted houses in Ohio.

When we were finally alone in the room, I began: "Tim, I feel guilty that the last conversation we had, I called you a chickenshit son of a bitch and now you have colon cancer."

He grinned. "That's OK. I thought it was funny."

It had been a surprising Christmas conversation two years before, when I had answered the phone to his voice, happy that he had called until I realized that he was chastising me for my choice of Christmas gifts for Jake, then sixteen.

"It was inappropriate," he said. I sat racking my brain trying to figure out what about Rilke's *Letter to a Young Poet* would qualify as inappropriate.

"How?"

"You know how."

"No, I don't. You'll have to explain."

"Just like the present last year."

"You mean the art supplies?"

"No."

"Or the year before, the Odetta Christmas record?"

Light finally dawned—the box of books I had sent them five years ago that had included a book on gay issues.

"So what book was it?"

"I don't remember. I put it away where the kids wouldn't see it."

"Where did you put it?"

"I can't recall."

He barreled on to the other part of the conversation that he had obviously rehearsed: "We have bent over backward to be nice to you, but if you think we are going to support your lifestyle you are wrong."

Ah, I thought. Remind me not to mistake a bent back for an open mind. Now I was mad. "Now let me get this right. You call me up to holler at me for giving one book that is inappropriate, but you can't explain why, and another one that you also didn't like but you can't remember the title or where it is? And you are also a chickenshit, because you haven't said this sooner. Daddy told me that your feelings about gay people were what kept you at such a distance. I asked you that, and you lied about it, so you are also a *lying* chickenshit son of a bitch."

"Thanks for making your feelings clear," his voice was lighter, like he was almost laughing.

"Well, what did you expect me to do?"

"We should talk some more like this," he added peculiarly, his energy winding down.

"You go find that book and read it and call me back," I said as we hung up. I wrote him an angry letter that I didn't send. I resolved to send my nephews each Christmas or birthday all the great queer writers. Shakespeare, Woolf, Proust, Whitman, Wilde, Auden, Rich, Lorde, Cather. At least my brother would finally get a liberal education from screening and censoring them. I left it there until Daddy called to say Tim had cancer.

At the Mobile hospital that afternoon, Becky and I had a long conversation on the patio near the cafeteria. I pressed her on the reason for their distance, and she explained that Jake had asked his English teacher, who told him that Rilke was gay. So Jake had concluded, she said, that I was trying to recruit him.

"Why didn't you just tell me?" I asked, genuinely puzzled.

"I guess we're not very good at being close to people."

I explained that I had sent Jake the book because he was coming out of a rough time himself, and he was writing about it. Rilke's observations on using one's suffering and solitude might be helpful, I had thought. They had been for me in difficult younger years. The gay piece had not occurred to me. I wasn't even sure I knew Rilke was homosexual.

She continued that my militancy had stood between us. "You were so angry. You seem peaceful now."

I told her that I had considered us friends, and wanted to be there for her as well as for Tim during this ordeal. She teared up. "Mab, I have maggots," she warned.

"I have a few of my own," I replied.

I left happy that I had made some peace with each of them. I thought we were going to need it.

That spring, Daddy, Dal, and I came to visit at their new house in the country for Daddy's eighty-first birthday, a visit that went well, if carefully. I came again between Thanksgiving and Christmas that year with Daddy. I took Jake and Ned shopping for their Christmas presents. Ned was fourteen that year; Jake, eighteen. I helped Ned decorate the tree with the ten boxes of ornaments we hauled down from the attic, loading the huge tree with layer upon layer. It would take an X ray or an archaeologist to appreciate all of the tree's decor. Becky generously ceded that task to me, giving Ned and me a chance to get to know each other.

When I got home, I sent Tim a copy of Stephen Mitchell's translation of the Psalms. "May goodness and mercy follow you all the days of your life," I wrote as an inscription. The rest of that verse might come later . . . "and may you dwell in the house of the Lord forever."

Then the next October, of 1997, the cancer in Tim's colon recurred. I was scared myself, and not a good listener. I told him how well I thought he was handling it, not able to hear the grief and shock and fear. He was down to seven feet of colon, recovering again from a hole in his gut. When he was better, I got his approval to visit for his and Ned's birthdays. I came alone this time, driving over the mountains. I headed out from Asheville through the Cherokee reservation, where our family used to come for summer vacations when we were little. We would swim in the lake at Junaluska and go to see the outdoor drama *Unto These Hills* that told the story of Cherokee removal in the 1830s. "I will lift up mine eyes unto the hills from whence cometh my help," was one of Mama's favorite psalms. "My help cometh from the Lord who made heaven and earth." Of course, the God that the settlers brought did not offer much help to the Cherokees, whom the U.S. government sent out to Oklahoma on the Trail of Tears, a march in which one-fourth of the Cherokee Nation died.

The drive along the Nantahala River gorge was breathtaking. I stopped by the river, remembering the psalm we learned together in Sunday school: "The Lord is my shepherd, I shall not want. He maketh me to lie down in green pastures. He leads me beside the still waters, he restores my soul." On that perfect fall day, light glinting off the river, I saw the shadow of my brother's death. *I will lift up mine eyes unto the hills, from whence cometh my help. My help cometh from the hills, that join heaven and earth.*

I drove up to his house with a carload of presents: a carving set and two big golden pumpkins picked up on the drive through the mountains; drawing pens for Tim and Ned; Halloween decorations for Ned; two books for Tim. Given the previous ticklishness over presents, I had asked Becky for suggestions. Ned and I carved our jack-o'-lanterns sitting in the driveway. As we watched the sun set, we talked about art and his plans to go to school in Atlanta: "It's a whole town of artists," he declared with a flourish.

Jake drove me around in his truck, both of us in our black leather jackets, still catching up on a decade's missed conversations. He had made a 180-degree turn-around since his father's first surgery: quit an adolescent's acting out and moved into the little apartment behind his parents' house. Clearly he had set out getting to know his father and to make his peace. He was going to school to be an emergency medical technician. He asked respectfully about Annie and Barb, as he had on each of my other visits. He made it clear that he was not the one who had the problem with people being gay. So what was Rilke about? I wondered. Jake also made it clear that he wanted more family. I liked both my nephews immensely.

I think I succeeded too well in getting past the gate and into their new house out in the country and in under the family's defenses. That is my best explanation for what happened next with Becky.

She and I were standing at the kitchen sink the second morning. I had lost some weight. She had quit smoking, and I admired her resolve, which she chalked up to her new faith as a Mormon. I let that one be. I talked some myself about Weight Watchers, and twelve step, and trying to deal with feelings rather than eat them. She implied I'd had a lot to deal with.

"Your mother was so competitive with you," she started in. "It was pitiful to see. I don't think you even realized it. Did you?"

I was surprised by the perception. I have thought a lot about my relationship with Mama, but not on those terms. But I recognized the terrain she was moving us onto: battle.

"Well, I didn't see it that way," I replied. "But I guess when I came out as a lesbian I jumped the track. It wasn't an area in which she had much expertise. I had to get away from home to do it. But I missed her."

"That must have made you feel so guilty."

Jump back and parry, I told myself, grateful for my remedial training in karate. "I guess it did," I replied, "but actually, we worked it out. Before she died, I know that she forgave me."

"And your Dad, you must feel really guilty about him, too."

She wasn't letting up. Parry again. "No, I've worked things out with Daddy, too. Now we're friends."

In the other room, Ned was playing video games: cyborgs whacking luminous swords blade to blade. I silently and prematurely congratulated myself for not being reduced to rubble by her series of observations.

She tried a different tack: "What are you here for? What do you want from Tim?" I have replayed this part of the conversation many times. It is the place where, by answering her question as she asked it, I missed the direction of her thrust. I should have said, " I have come to find out what we want together." Instead I said, "I want to be friends. I would like our families to know each other." She stepped inside my guard and began to punch.

"Why are you bringing your queerness into this household?" The abruptness, and intensity, of the question took my breath.

Thou preparest a table before me, in the presence of mine enemies.

It lasted through the hour car ride to drop off Jake in town, leave his car in the garage, and come back out to the Tennessee countryside. On the drive her anger had escalated: she accused me of not caring about my brother, only about myself. I was lying and manipulative. "If you talk to Tim about being gay," she crescendoed, "I will tear your heart out. I want him to die in peace."

Peace, I was silent by then. Peace. But there is no peace. Was that a line from the Bible or the Gettysburg Address?

I finally withdrew from the conversation altogether, fearful that she would run the car into an oncoming vehicle. I took myself as far away as I could reach. I meditated on the spare gleaned furrows, veined branches of winter trees. Shalom.

When we got back to the house, I went immediately to my car and drove to a Shell station. I phoned Barbara, then every friend I had on the East Coast, but no one was home. I finally left a succession of messages on our answering machine, telling Barb what had happened. I was weeping. "I don't want to stay here, but if I leave now I'm afraid that I'll never see Tim alive again." Just as I was about to drive away, Barb called back to say how terrible it was that this was happening, how much she loved me, how sorry she was. I left the next day, without having a chance to talk to Tim, wrapped in my old silence and invisibility.

I called him the next week. I wanted to discuss with him the vehemence of the argument more than the particulars. I did not want Becky to come between us, which I felt was the motive for her assault.

"Tim, you know Becky and I had a big fight," I began. "I need your advice." His voice softened, but he was cautious. I figured she was in the room. Then he said he'd call me back. Instead he wrote a short cold letter, saying that he agreed with his wife "100 percent." He began it "Mab" and closed it "Tim," not even a "Dear" or a "Sincerely."

An incredulous month later, I wrote back point for point, relieved at least at the chance for honesty:

> You say you don't know what kind of relationship you and I can have. But we didn't know that before, either, did we? Perhaps you mean you don't want to have a relationship with me. If so, you'll have to say that more directly. I have wondered mightily since getting your letter why it is that I make the effort to get through to you. If I thought that you were only the person in the letter, I would not have a reason. I also don't think that your wife is only the person in the car hollering at me. You are both under tremendous stress.
>
> But, you know, we already DO have a relationship. You are my brother, and I am your sister. We spent the first third of our lives together. We swam in the same pool, caught the same tadpoles, dived off the same bridge, built castles in the same sand, ate the same collard greens and tomatoes, had presents under flickering lights of the same Christmas trees from the same Santa Claus, loved the same parents, read from the same books, watched the same TV programs, rooted for the same football teams, bathed in the same tub, walked together to the same school, had the same teachers, sang the same hymns. I guess I had an understanding that your recovery might have to do with more than more chemotherapy, that healing [or dying, I did not say then] requires a deeper level of psychic integration; and that we need what the shrinks call our "inner child" in this process. I know your inner child and his world: I bring him in the door when I come.
>
> Tim, what I wish for you is that you have your life: waking up in a house with the family that you love, watching and guiding the emerging selves of your children, the sight of the meadow in the morning, the sounds of Ned back in his room or on the computer, the drive with Becky to the grocery store, the sight of Jake out the back door going off to classes, work that challenges you, passionate and compassionate touches of love, a clear relationship with a body that experiences more pleasure than pain. I hope that you have this for a long time to come. That's what I feel you would strip from me, any reference to any of these things: my daily life with Barb and Annie, my work, my body, my creative life, my community. I can't check being a lesbian at your door in order not to bring my "lifestyle" into your house. I realize that I have attempted that in the past because of my sense it is a condition that you put on our relationship. But I know now it's neither desirable or even possible. My being lesbian is part of the fullness of who I am; whatever relationship I bring to you needs to be out of that fullness. I don't do such a good job of flattening myself anymore. It just pops out.

Second point about my "chosen lifestyle"—not that you have asked me how I felt about this, either, or how I understand it, or what my life is like. Really, how would you know what "my agenda" is given that we have hardly had a conversation in years and years? Where do those assumptions come from? As to the distinction you make between "accepting" me but not "approving" of me, it doesn't fly. The fact is, you can't really accept me OR what you call my "lifestyle," and she called my "queerness," because it is really pretty inseparable from who I am. I think that what makes you both so angry is the limits to your love, given the depth of your own negative feelings about gay people.

I realize that you want to protect your family, and that is an admirable desire. I just don't think that I am such a threat to them. I think that they are more threatened by isolation, fear and mistrust. Daddy told me that, when he went to see Jake once when he was sick, he told him, "I love you and so do your aunts Mab and Dallas," and Jake responded, "I didn't know anybody cared." I am probably not perfect, but I am not an active alcoholic or a drug addict, I am not physically abusive, I have held down a job now for nigh thirty years, I have a stable family, friends who care about me, a community that loves me, I have work that is nationally respected. Your sons could do worse than me, really. You and Becky could, too.

I have wanted to be available to you and to your family in what could be a terminal illness. But if you want my help, you'll have to ask for it at this point, and you'll need to treat me better.

Love Anyway, and Always, Mab

Many friends advised me to cut my losses. What a jerk he was, they said, reading his letter. But I did not want to let go of him. I wanted to find some way to reconcile the separation, the confusion, the anger, and the differences. In such a disposable culture, I refused to discard a brother. Take it a step at a time, and see what path opens, I would tell myself. *The path into the light seems dark / the path forward seems to go back . . . the greatest love seems indifferent.*[1] The *Tao* of Tim. I sent my letter off to him, signed, sealed, but not sure whether delivered, the week after Christmas 1997. I wrote out a quote from Buddha and put it together with an old photograph of my brother and me—the one in which I am probably two, he is going toward five, I am leaning up against him, and we are both, with all our bodies, smiling. I put this note on our picture:

> *Your brother is like you,*
> *He wants to be happy.*
> *Never harm him.*
> *And when you leave this life*
> *You will find happiness . . .*
>
> *You too will pass away.*
> *Knowing this, how can you quarrel?*

Then I waited. Was this the sound of one hand clapping?

III

The next summer, Daddy called me to say that the cancer had turned up in Tim's liver. I wrote my brother a brief note: I was really sorry about the liver cancer. I didn't know if he wanted to hear from me, because he hadn't answered my letter. If I could help, I wanted to. Please call and tell me how he was doing.

The next week, he called at work.

"Thanks for the note," he said. "I did get your letter. But it upset me a lot. I didn't know what to do with it, so I put it in a drawer. I think you misunderstood my intent. We honor the people you love." I accepted the current sentiment. Then he gave me a detailed, technical account of his liver, the increasingly experimental treatments, possible side effects. "The doctors say that right now, there's no cure. But they are making new breakthroughs all the time. These treatments could buy me time until they can find a silver bullet. It's a long shot, but I can see a path to it. It feels better to have a plan. Do you have any questions?"

"What can I do?" I asked. He said that he wanted to maintain as normal a life as possible, but depending on how things turned out he might need me. I said I had a lot of sick time and could come. To let me know.

"I love you," I said over the phone. "I'll be with you on the path."

"Thanks," he replied. "I will feel you there."

I called Tim every three or four weeks, or when I heard news from Daddy. Most times, I would get reports of the latest drug treatments, an increasing debilitation from the nausea and diarrhea that were their side effects. Then in November, Daddy said the chemo seemed to be failing him, and the colon and liver cancer seemed to be breaking through. I called Tim at work. He talked more openly of dying. He was trying to plan as best he could for his family.

"I think I want to be cremated," he said. "I doubt that Becky and the kids will want to stay here, and I wouldn't want them to be tied to a plot of ground where I was buried. If I'm cremated, they can take me with them." He and Becky were helping Ned get his driver's license. Jake was finishing up his Emergency Med Tech training. What a hard thing to look past your own death, I thought, admiring him greatly.

"Where are we?" I asked.

He waited a minute. "Close, I hope," he answered. Then, after silence on my part, "You know, when Becky gets mad, her anger punches through the floor into some-place else that is not rational. You can't take it personally. She's said really awful things to me, then been crying in my arms twenty minutes later."

I felt a wash of relief and gratitude. It was the conversation I had called him the previous October to have.

"I know that, Tim. It's important for me to know that you do."

"She's like a mother grizzly defending her family," he went on.

"I know that, too. I just don't think you need to defend against me. I don't want her anger at me to separate us in this . . . phase."

"I don't want it to either," he said.

IV

In early February 1998, Daddy, Dal, and I made our final pilgrimage to see Tim, this time in the hospital. The cancer, moving in his colon, his abdomen, and in his liver already, had mounted to his brain. The doctors, finally, refused to order any further experimental treatments and recommended hospice. He said he wanted to see us one last time. I canceled a week's plans. We had our long, slow talk that Sunday night on the telephone. He was still digesting the bad news, as was I. I cried hard, and said I would miss him. I had tried to help, I said, but hadn't been able to. I was sorry.

"I'm sorry . . . I wasn't . . . able . . . to do more . . . to resolve . . . that situation," he said, tortuously slow.

"That's OK, Tim, we all do the best we can."

I drove down on Monday night to Dal's home in South Carolina. The next morning we drove to Tuskegee to pick up Daddy. The journey up the back steps of the house we grew up in always feels poignant, but this trip was especially so as we walked through the yard and entered the house that contains most of the memories of our life together as children. I was happy to be with Dallas and Daddy; the three of us have let one another in our lives again at deeper levels, in part dealing with our impending separation. Daddy had picked baskets of paper whites, the early blooming flowers whose fragrance we always associate with Mama, to bring to Tim. We were in his hospital room that evening for a brief stay, then headed to the Ramada Inn, where we ordered a room service party of salmon and margaritas and wine, leaving space at the table for Mama.

Originally, Tim had invited us for a short visit, just in case something dire happened, and we could come back later for a longer visit when he felt better. Wanting to respond to his wishes, we figured we would leave by Wednesday. But it fast became clear that he wanted us around. A good bit of the time, we had him to ourselves, with Jake. At other times, Becky was a brooding but attentive presence, ready to snap my head off at any friendly advance. But clearly she gave Tim comfort.

"We want to thank you for taking care of Tim," I tried at one point to get through.

"That's just who I am. I couldn't do it any other way. You are virtual strangers to me or you would understand." We all knew we were threading our way through a mine field.

On Wednesday morning, with Becky in the room, Tim shared his wishes with us. He'd been struggling to accept the finality indicated by hospice. He was bald, but beautiful; more of a Yul Brynner skull than I would have imagined. Jaundiced, skinnier, but nothing like the walking cadavers I had become too accustomed to in friends who had died of AIDS. The swelling in his brain had receded, leaving him some brain damage but a formidable portion of right-brain power had still asserted it-self the night before in elaborate instructions about how to get to our motel, in which he laid out the street and highway plan of the city for a grid of fifteen miles.

"I want you guys to know what my wishes are," he began. "I want to be cremated. I want to be able to stay with Becky and Jake and Ned," his voice cracked, and he began to sob. Becky stepped to the bed and gathered him in her arms and held him through his tears.

"I'm sorry," he said.

"You are my hero," she comforted. "I don't know any person braver or finer than you. You don't need to apologize for your tears."

"I'm not ashamed to cry," he answered. "I was surprised when I couldn't stop crying."

"I can't stop crying either," Becky spoke gently into his ear.

His tears subsided, and she stepped back from the bed. "I also want a funeral that is half Methodist and half Mormon," he continued, his eyes filling up with tears again.

"The Mormons have helped us a lot. They are good people."

We accepted his wishes, grateful for the sharing. Mostly, we were happy just to sit there and listen and meet the guys he worked with, engineers who came in bunches and stood at the foot of the bed to talk about work or sports as a way to say good-bye. "Your brother is the brains of this operation, I guess you know," one of them said to me. "Was he always this smart?"

Tim was the chief engineer in his division, having refused to pass over into manage-ment. They were working on land-based missile defense to intercept the new low-flying missiles more likely in the post–Cold War environment. "I find it easier to come home at night when I am working on killing the other men's missiles, not the other men," Tim described his decision to work on defensive, rather than offensive, military systems, a dis-tinction I appreciated. We didn't get into a discussion of the military budget or how a new missile system might upset the nuclear balance and the START Treaty.

Becky was an attentive presence in the hall and at his bed. She and Jake had be-come skilled nurses over the years Tim had been in and out of various hospitals, and he counted on their careful tending—covers, bedpan, IV drips, helping him back and forth to the bathroom, sorting through the doctors' most recent information.

I had one hour alone with Tim that day. We watched college basketball—Auburn was in the running for the South Eastern Conference champions. He was chatty from the morphine, talked about the health care system, his work. I steered the con-versation more personally and asked if there was anything I could do to be closer to Becky. She was still parrying every friendly comment.

"Yes, I noticed that," he said. "Just keep trying. I think it's making a difference."

"Tim, I think your love has made a huge difference in her life," I offered.

I wanted to spend the night with Tim and Jake in the hospital room, but Tim sent me back to the motel. What I wanted was more intimacy, I guess, than we had.

The next day it was time for us to leave. By the doctors' assessment, Tim had sev-eral more days of consciousness before the brain cancer closed in. The six of us sat in his hospital room, awkwardly, aware that we were coming up on the last good-bye. Dal took this last opportunity to explain that Daddy wanted to have a second memorial service, in the Tuskegee Methodist Church, in addition to the one here. Tim's eyes seemed to light up at the idea: perhaps we saw the same image, old pews filled with old friends and memories.

Becky stiffened. "You won't come to the one up here?"

"Oh, of course we will. We'll all be here," Dal reassured her, and I was glad to see that she wanted us.

"We'll talk about it," she said noncommittally.

Then each of us walked over and kissed Tim, tears flowing.

Becky met Daddy at the door. "Mr. Segrest, thank you for lending your son to me. He is a very fine man."

Daddy replied with his usual succinctness, and with more honesty than he perhaps intended: "Lady, it wasn't my choice."

Then we were down the hospital halls, the elevator, into the car, and headed down the interstate out of town, each with our own thoughts and good-byes, but all three of us pleased and hopeful that we had avoided catastrophe and had opened channels to see us all through together till the end.

v

That hope lasted three hours. It was the memorial service that did us in. Daddy was more than willing to go to any service that Tim's family planned. But he needed a Methodist burial. He needed to have a service for his boy, in the church where my brother grew up, with all Tim's old friends and teachers and with his own community around him. We could put a marker up near Mama's grave at the cemetery. It was a reasonable request and not a bad strategy, the two memorials. It was as multicultural as my family gets. But it put us all over the edge.

We had just settled in on the beige-and-brown-figured sofa that had sat in that corner of the living room for years, its cushions with the imprint of each of our bodies. The phone rang, and Dal reached over to pick it up. Her voice lifted, "It's Becky." I figured they were calling to be sure we had made it back safely.

But Becky was into details of the memorial service. What hymns would we like to sing? "In the Garden," I whispered. What was the local florist? But we could provide the flowers here. No, we were not trying to take away her right to grieve Tim. The invitation list? People at the church, old schoolmates, and friends and neighbors. Dal got quiet, then handed the phone to Daddy. "The shit just hit the fan," she whispered, rolling her eyes. "She says that if Annie and Barb are recognized as family, they won't come to the service here."

Daddy put the phone to his ear, and I could hear her voice on the other end, getting higher and higher. I held my breath, not sure what I was waiting for.

"Lady, that's your decision," Daddy said.

Rarrh rahhrr rrhar . . . her voice rose through the receiver, apparently repeating its threats.

"Lady, that's your decision," Daddy repeated. And again the static.

And a final time, like some bad spell in a fairy tale, repeated three times: "Lady, that's your decision." And he hung up the phone.

We all exhaled. I sat there, in the midst of many emotions.

Dal's immediate concern was for me, that I not be hurt. Perhaps she remembered back to earlier of our own interactions. She had come a long way in the past several years.

When recently I asked her husband, Kirk, what made the difference in their shift of attitude toward me, he gave it his usual careful thought. They still don't believe homosexuality is morally right, he shared. But at some point they decided that it was between me and God. Leaving such judgments to God left them more open to love.

"You don't need to take them to that memorial service up there," Dallas said when Daddy hung up the phone. "You just bring them to our memorial service, where they are loved."

So many things happening in one moment. I felt a deep relief and gratitude at Daddy and Dal's spontaneous support. I began to voice how I was feeling, "You know, it hurts my feelings, and it makes me really mad, but mostly I am disappointed in him. Here they have maybe three more days of conscious life together, and they put their energy into something so mean. Maybe it was just Becky's doing," I consoled myself, thinking of his brain lesions.

"Mab, I am rapidly growing up in your presence," Daddy said from his reclining chair.

I took it as a huge compliment and fished for more. "What do you mean?"

"I'm going to get the scuppernong wine," he said, pulling himself out of the recliner and limping on the leg with the bullets still in it from a German attack on his bomber over half a century before. He brought back three glasses and poured us some wine from his stash in the pantry. Dal and I exchanged meaningful glances again, wondering whether this would be our fatal encounter with the botulism that had lurked for decades in the back reaches of the refrigerator or the meat left out on the stove. His wine was sweet, if a little vinegarish.

He settled back. "It's because you come from people," he declared definitively, "who know how to behave."

Dallas and I burst out laughing as he proceeded to explain that he could have married Agnes Wells, she was after him before he went to Germany, but she had been from a family not entirely mentally stable. Dal and I rolled our eyes again over the wine, remembering certain tendencies of Mama's.

"You know," Daddy continued sweetly, "I think we had the perfect family: you girls, Tim, your mother, and me. Even when we disagreed, we could always share our feelings." The remnants of Daddy's perfect family finished up their scuppernong wine in a sweet and companionable end to an exhausting day.

Well, the worst is over, I kept telling myself. But it wasn't yet. The Saturday evening I returned home, David and Royce and Tobi and Betsy came over to dinner to hear about my journey and offer consolation. In their company I realized that with the deaths of many of our friends from AIDS, I had begun to assume that people meet death with the kind of grace to which we had mournfully become accustomed. The phone rang, and it was Tim. Again, I was surprised but glad to hear his voice.

"Mab, Becky told me the conversation she had with Daddy last night. It was totally inappropriate. I am withdrawing my permission for the Tuskegee memorial service."

Had I been less shocked, I could perhaps have asked him what she had told him. But I didn't think to.

"Tim, is that all you have to say to me?" I asked, knowing it could be our last conversation. I heard the phone click.

The next weekend was my fiftieth birthday, and I had planned a big bash for weeks. A party at elin and David's, with the Butchies, my favorite dyke band, not only playing Elvis and Patsy Cline songs but also letting me sing with them, and friends coming in from out of town for the weekend: Laura and Elizabeth from New York, Marta from El Salvador, Pam and Carla from Louisville.

"You sure you want to go through with this party?" Laura asked midweek. She was keeping up with me, and I appreciated it. "How you doing?"

"Today I'm listening to Judy Garland." "When You Walk through a Storm" was blaring in the background.

"That kind of day, huh?"

But I went ahead with the party, figuring he would live past the weekend. I could grieve my brother and celebrate my own life, hold the space for that with my family and my friends. "Love me tender," I sang, and they did.

Tim lived out February. He and Becky were not in touch with Daddy, who was increasingly concerned. My friend Pam's dad had recently died of cancer, and she suggested that I try to track down the hospice nurse. I found her, and she generously gave me information that I passed on to Daddy and Dal every two or three days. March rolled around, its first ten days containing both my father's birthday on March 2 and the anniversary of my mother's death, March 9. I figured that Tim would not live past the ninth. On Monday of that first week of March, I began writing him a long letter, most of which makes up this text. For the next part of the story, I'll speak directly to him.

VI

Wednesday: I just called your hospice nurse to get the day's report. You are jaundiced a deep yellow and your systems are failing. You are talking gibberish, trying to get up and wander the house with what's little left of your strength. You are often semicomatose. I have lit the candles on my bookcase altar at the window, on which I have placed our childhood pictures, tulips and daffodils, a cross made by artisans in

El Salvador, a head of the Buddha, and portraits of Mama and Granny. I've been reading Malidoma Somé on ancestors. He says they are all around, and dying to be helpful. But one has to give them very explicit instructions. So I have a glass of wine out for Mama and Granny, and some chocolate.

"Help him over," I instruct Mama, "but don't do it for him. He has to do this himself!" I remember too many stories of Mama getting in the playpen with you when you were a toddler, it being a bit crowded. One of the photos on the altar is of the two of us as children in a cardboard box in a doorway—half in, half out; half bright, half shade; half brother, half sister. We are exploring the laws of physics: fluid, interactive, two bodies occupying the same space at the same time. Mozart's "Requiem" plays on my CD. *Kyrie Eleison, Christe Eleison.* Lord have mercy. Christ have mercy. *Requiem aeternam dona eis Domine.* Grant them eternal rest, O Lord.

The hospice nurse gives me a daily report because you do not take our calls. Or, rather, Becky told Daddy you did not want to talk with him, after she unleashed another diatribe on homosexuality. "Do you even want to know when he dies?" she asked our father, now eighty-three, struggling to grieve a dying son but refusing to deny a daughter. Friday, 3:00 P.M.: Word has come that you are dying. First from Daddy, whom Becky finally had the decency to call. Then from your boss, who said a priest had administered last rites and only expected you to live a matter of hours. *Dies irae, dies illa, Solvent saeclum in favilla,* the Atlanta Symphony and Chorus sings. *The day of wrath, that day shall dissolve the world in ashes.*

I click off Mozart. I have no stomach for apocalyptic wrath or judgment, which given the magnitude of human suffering in the here and now seems quite redundant. I'll take Sweet Honey for your last hours:

> *Listen more often to things than to beings.*
> *'Tis the ancestor's breath when the fire's voice is heard*
> *'Tis the ancestor's breath in the voice of the waters.*
> *Those who have died have never, never left*
> *The dead are not under the earth*
> *They are in the rustling trees*
> *They are in the groaning woods*
> *They are in the crying grass*
> *They are in the moaning rocks.*
> *The dead are not under the earth.*[2]

You are rising now out of your body, your spirit lifts from the place between your breasts, out the top of your head, the fledgling on the edge of its nest, tentative, as if you are about to take flight, a moment you remember now from dreams, a fear of falling into an abyss, but you are rising, you are rising, you are being lifted up on strong familiar wings, of Methodist, Buddhist, Catholic, Mormon angels, our mother is there first and she cradles you until it falls away, the last of your fear, and

our grandmothers and grandfathers carrying you as well, they are themselves a char-
iot, they have come for to carry you home, and down below in your bedroom is your
soft shattered body, the people you love most—your wife and sons—and the youngest
is weeping, and you see Daddy at Mama's grave with flowers, and here I am at my
typewriter waiting for Barb and Annie, and Dallas in her kitchen with her Kirk and
her children, and out your window the sunset, then the sunrise is blazing for you,
spilling fire over clouds and sky and pasture, and you are rushing now upward, you
remember all of your life in a single moment, it comes to you now, *ahhhhhh*, a revelation, each of the particular, partial broken acts of love, *yeessssss*, that is what we
were trying for, and in this knowledge once again and finally you forgive and are forgiven; you are floating now on currents from the rush, beyond all divisions and all
partial choices, the sinewy wings lifting you toward the Countenance, and everywhere the other hand is clapping, and oh you understand fully what you had once
seen through a glass darkly, for now, now, now you are face to Face, and there is no
longer even language, but if there were, the words would come: *Yes. Yes. Yes.*

VII

The story does not end there with Tim's life, although what I wrote to him does.
It ends with the Tuskegee memorial, which we held in spite of my brother's last
wishes. Dal and I had driven down to be with Daddy the day after Tim's death, and
I took great comfort in the comfort given by family and old friends. When the three
of us walked in any door, people saw the gap there between us: they knew who was
missing. I chose not to attend the Mormon/Methodist memorial. Wrassling Becky to
the carpet over the communion rail—knocking Tim's ashes all over the floor—was
too appealing a prospect. I found the mixture of grief and rage too potent to ensure
that I would *behave* in the way that my father had come to expect of me. Dal drove
Daddy up to their service and I headed back to Durham. We set the Tuskegee memorial for the end of the month.

In the following week I struggled with a fresh grief for which I had no ritual expression. None of my family or friends in Durham knew my brother, because he had
not let them. I was angry at everybody around me for not giving me whatever it was
that I needed. I found myself considering just hanging out in cemeteries looking for
funerals to which to attach myself and cry. During a massage, my therapist played
Gorecki's Third Symphony, a gorgeous piece of music written on the fiftieth anniversary of the Warsaw Uprising with an anguished soprano that did voice my grief.
Then I met my friend Tobi in Duke Gardens for lunch.

"What do Jews do for grief?" I asked, remembering some of the protocols from her
mom's death. She explained about Kaddish, and torn clothing, and the various periods of mourning.

I came home and laid out my yoga mat. I took ashes from the fireplace and covered my face. I put on an old T-shirt and laid Gorecki on the CD player. For the next

hour I tore my shirt to shreds as I sobbed, tears running through the ashes on my cheeks. By the symphony's end, I finally felt more peaceful. That afternoon I joined a Farm Labor Organizing Committee march for the Mt. Olive pickles boycott, yelling for another hour from deep in my belly. Between the ashes, the music, and the yelling that day I turned one corner on my grief.

Barb, Annie, and I drove down to Tuskegee for the memorial service at the end of March. Dal and Kirk brought their kids down to meet us on Thursday to clean up the house and yard, which was in need of a spruce-up, to put it mildly. I was apprehensive. Becky had made such a point of trying to leave my family out, so now we were being included. But how included? And was I ready for it?

Ready or not, the three of us were given a royal welcome. I suspect that Dallas had laid a good bit of the groundwork with the women in town, with whom she had extensive networks. Also, all of Daddy's friends (a huge number) had seen his anguish and heard all the bitter details about how we had been treated, and they were rightly furious. Probably, as well, most folks in Tuskegee had known I was a lesbian for years and some of them had perhaps even read my books about it. But we had never had the opportunity to acknowledge it. I had never given them the chance, I guess.

It was a coming out of another sort for me as well. An old high school friend, Mike Letcher, had produced a video for public TV on the history of Macon County. He had interviewed me extensively and had me pontificating my various race-traitoring opinions. When friends, white and black, stopped by to console us and bring casseroles and pound cakes, they at times drew me aside to say, "I saw you *in the movie!*" their voices and eyebrows going either up, or down, depending on their attitude toward what they had heard. I was out on my own front porch as both a dyke and a race traitor.

So the day of the memorial service, Annie and Barb and I walked down the aisle of the Tuskegee Methodist Church together, the light coming through the stained glass windows and Jesus still up there knocking at the door. We sat on the first row with family, and all of my mother's old friends and my old Sunday school and grammar school teachers made a special point to include Annie and Barb at the lunch they had fixed for us back in the dining hall, as did my Aunt Rob and Uncle John and the four cousins who drove over from Louisiana or flew from Minneapolis. At times it felt as much like a marriage as a funeral to me. It's a southern thing, I guess. At the end of that long memorial Saturday, I went back to find Daddy in the kitchen to thank him.

"I think they're accepted now," he said.

I really don't think that my father chose me over my brother in that moment on the phone. I think he just refused to be bullied, even by a dying son. He stood by what he thought was right, which is what he has always done, even when I have not always agreed with him. I guess I've tried to do the same.

I also reckon that Tim might even have been glad that other people who loved us had given me everything that he needed to deny at a time of great stress. I have found that I have no need to measure our relationship by that last click of the phone. We had already asked for and given forgiveness. People give what they can, when they can. Tim wasn't trying to hurt me, I know that. In fact, in the years since his death, sometimes I've felt him with me. "The dead have a pact with the living," Sweet Honey sings. One midnight on the beach, a full moon laid a huge field of energy at low tide. I walked for an hour, and on the way back I felt my brother and my mother in step beside me, one on each side. We promised to be on the path together, Tim and I, and we are still. I've heard his voice at times when I needed a bit of advice or protection.

Some days, in fact, he still holds my hand when I'm crossing the street.

7

OF SOUL AND WHITE FOLKS

"WHAT therapist would tell us to read history?" I began, looking out over the expanse of people in the large room. The audience was diverse, the racial mix that makes California so rich and complex. African American. Chicana. Salvadoran. Korean. Chinese. Indian. Brazilian. Cuban. Nigerian. White. I had come to the University of California at Berkeley to a conference on "The Making and Unmaking of Whiteness" to talk about the souls of white folk—borrowing from W.E.B. Du Bois's term—assuming that we have souls and beginning with my own. The question of the relation of private emotion to public event to history had been the central preoccupation of *Memoir of a Race Traitor*, my attempt to describe seven years of organizing against Klan and neo-Nazi movements in North Carolina and to come to terms with my own history as a white person. After six years of organizing and four years of writing, all I had was a deeper set of questions, and I had brought them to grapple with at this peculiar and hybrid forum on whiteness.[1]

Each of us in this late-afternoon Saturday panel, "Critical Studies of Whiteness," was intent on making the absolutely necessary connections between academic study and antiracist intent. I was glad I was sporting my blue denim jacket. The queer panel had come right before me. I was the only woman on this panel, so I was butching it up with the guys: David Roediger, David Wellman, and Noel Ignatiev (or his paper, at least). Noel's contribution, a militant call for a new abolitionism, had just been read by a young friend because Noel could not come.

"Good luck," David Wellman had nodded to me as I had stepped into the hot space Noel's friend left behind the podium. I began to make clear that I do not assume that whiteness is monolithic. Its power as a constructed category has been its very historic malleability under the flag of biological determinism. If whiteness is a signifier of power and condition of access in U.S. culture, then women are less white than men, gay people less white than straight people, poor people less white than rich people, Jews than Christians, and so forth. Over the centuries, people of various European nationalities have climbed into and sometimes fallen out of whiteness, the core of which has always been Anglo-Saxon, Protestant, propertied, and male (and now straight).

"Racism normalizes whiteness and makes people of color the problem," I continued "so white people are generic humans who don't have to look at ourselves. We escape scrutiny, and we escape accountability as a group for creating racism and as individuals for challenging it. One response is to begin to look at whiteness as a problem and to calculate its wages. This is the very necessary process of acknowledging white privilege. We can explain and assess the advantage of being white in terms of not going to prison nearly so often, becoming coaches of major sports, more easily and more frequently obtaining home mortgages, buying cheaper cars, dying less often from cancer, more frequently obtaining better jobs, being safer on the streets or when — or if — police pull us over, and on and on and on. But such a calculation can almost be too convincing. Why should anyone give up such privilege?"

I paused here, remembering the many young college audiences with whom I had spoken. I had come to believe that only dealing with white people on giving up privilege was counterintuitive. There must also be some fuller range of loss and gain, some deeper calculus to invoke.

"What we miss when we only calculate our privilege is insight into the profound damage racism has done to us, as if we as a people could participate in such an inhuman set of practices and beliefs over five centuries of European hegemony and not be, in our own ways, devastated emotionally and spiritually. The indigenous Hawaiian term for white person is *haole*—which means 'without breath, or spirit, or soul.'" I invoked Loretta's explanation from my recent Hawaiian sojourn.[2]

Commotion somewhere. A man. Shouting. It took a second or two to pull myself out of the text. To the left of the room . . . about one-third of the way back . . . a bulky white man . . . tall . . . corpulent . . . yelling at the top of his lungs . . . at *me*. I made myself focus on what he was saying, wanting to locate him politically: "white genocide! . . . racial slurs against Europeans!"[3] A Right-wing kook. He hadn't opened fire, I realized with relief, so I figured he had not come armed. This was a scene he had come to make, I registered, and perhaps he felt safer screaming at a woman than at my male co-panelists. But I also knew he was yelling at me now because he thought I had said white people do not have souls. *That's not what I said, brother,* I thought, *what I said is that we need to tend to them.*

People in the room were beginning to respond hostilely. I felt responsible to use my place at the microphone. I knew this rant, this spew, this velocity of raw fury from Klan rallies I had monitored: it was like these guys were channeling; they had become vessels for the furious fear of the culture.

"What's your name?" I focused my attention on him with all the calmness I could muster, wanting to break his rant. "What's your name? What's your name?" I could see some of the people in the audience around him moving toward him deliberately. I assumed they were people with peace-keeper training. They were closing in to de-escalate and get him out of the room.

"What's your name?" After a few more repetitions, my question broke into his tirade, and he was still a minute. Then he answered, "Thorston! My name is Thorston!" He went off again on why he had renamed himself.

Oh, Lord, I realized, he's one of those Right-wing types who's renamed himself after some Norse god. Whatever self I had momentarily evoked was pretty fractured. But by that time three or four people were talking to him from close up, calmly I could tell, and had begun moving him out of the room. Some people in the crowd began to hiss at him. I signaled a request for quiet. We weren't out of the woods yet.

I was hardly advocating for Thorston's free speech. I believe too much in the power of language not to recognize its sometimes violent effects, and I had seen too often Klan marches allowed in North Carolina under the aegis of an interpretation of the First Amendment that allowed officials to dissociate themselves from responsibility for Klan and Nazi violence. As far as I was concerned, Thorston's outburst was at least a misdemeanor. But violent acts can breed other violence. There was enough of his energy afoot in the room to cause a brawl, which was not what most people had come for. I wanted to minimize that possibility as long as I was at the microphone. By now the group around Thorston had moved him out the back door, the sound of his yelling receding down the hall. I said a silent prayer for the people on the street and for any family he had at home.

"Damn!" I said into the mike, "Shake it out!" I flicked my hands at the wrists, wanting to move his energy out of my body. I encouraged people in the audience to do the same. If I had had a little more sense about me, I would have given everybody a couple of minutes each to talk to the person sitting next to them about responses to what had just happened. But I was still focused on my speech, and Thorston had taken about five minutes of my time.

I began again. "Like I was saying, we have a problem with the souls of white folks."

Not Comfort, but Power

W.E.B. Du Bois was one of the first to explore the economic cost of racism to white people, as my co-panelist David Roediger had examined in his own work. For a modicum of economic privilege and a dollop of racial superiority—what Du Bois called the "psychological wage" of being white—white workers gave up class solidarity that could have created better working conditions for all races. But Du Bois also recognizes that the loss here is as much psychological, or spiritual, as material: "[The white worker] began to want, not comfort for all men but power over other men. . . . He did not love humanity and he hated niggers."[4] In gaining power, whites lose comfort of the nonmaterial kind: ease, well-being, consolation, help, solace, and relief. In acquiring hatred, whites lose feelings and practices of love.

I had become intensely interested in exploring what we whites give up as human beings in love of humanity to a racist system, a concern for psyche as human soul, spirit or mind—the larger self. In the United States we have not been able to have a clear conversation about our emotional pain. We substitute arguments about reverse discrimination or immigration or special rights that obfuscate the sources of pain in historical imbalances of power. The business of therapy, both professional and self-help, has emerged in this century in the United States to deal with the psychological damage, which in a culture structured around scarcity and profit happens to people first in the context of our racist, sexist, and homophobic families. But these therapies are highly depoliticized. This failure of therapy to take into account the political causes of personal and family distress is another factor that insulates white people from realizing the damage we suffer from racism and therefore from realizing our own stake in changing racist systems for ourselves, as well as for people of color. We need to balance calculations on the benefits of whiteness (and maleness and heterosexism and the drive for profits) with calculations of pain and loss for all people in this culture; for example, sixty million people suffering from alcoholism, the leading killer in the country; stress that contributes to heart disease and cancer; 50 percent of the population with eating disorders; thirty-four million adult women sexually abused.[5]

These considerations of the personal cost of exploitative systems are not abstract questions for me. My mother was chronically ill and addicted to prescription drugs, from which she died a slow and painful death; my father, Tim, Dallas, and I were left to fend for ourselves amid our mother's periodic bouts of illness. During these times my mother (who was lively and loving when she was feeling good) withdrew almost completely from us physically and emotionally to deal with her pain, not wanting to inflict it on us; or she left home indefinitely for the latest cure. Part of my legacy was a deep sense of pessimism and a distrust for the world in which I found myself. For many years, I carried pieces of her pain. Raised in a segregationist family in Alabama, I had an increasing sense of alienation and difference throughout my adolescence: a growing disquiet about my mother's mental health, an increasing dismay over white racism literally exploding all around me, and a fear that I was both the same as the white people with whom I was raised and, as an unacknowledged lesbian, different in a way that would keep me from ever finding or giving love. Each of us from our childhoods bring our configurations of joy and suffering and this was mine.

This fear, this silence, this sadness: in their thickness they were surely more than one generation old. In my readings about the history of racism, which I incorporated in *Memoir of a Race Traitor,* I searched for the interfaces between my (white) subjective life and history. I found them repeatedly. I had known that part of my mother's sadness came from having lost her father, whom she idolized, when she was three. He died of influenza in 1918, in part because he was in poor health from having caught malaria when he went off as a young man to fight in the Spanish-American War. He was an engineer, a traveler, an adventurer—having caught his second case of malaria from an expedition up some Central American river when he was in Panama working on the canal. I had never considered his relationship to his own father, Judge James

Cobb, who came sharply into focus for me in the process of writing: Confederate officer; Democratic judge who threw Republican Reconstruction officials into the chain gang; and congressman, until he was kicked out of Congress for voter fraud against an insurgent interracial Populist movement in 1894. Before he died, he helped redraft the Alabama Constitution to bring in Jim Crow the same year that my father's grandfather, Charles Segrest, died in Bryce's, the state insane asylum. And, I know from my mother's stories, Judge Cobb beat his children, including my grandfather Ben—who perhaps left home for war and adventure fleeing this rigid father.

Charles Segrest's psychic break seems liked posttraumatic stress disorder, now more familiar to us from Vietnam vets. My aunt explained the stigma under which she and my father had grown up, having a certified crazy person in the family. What I saw was at the root of both my parents' pain: In a very real sense, it originated in my families' involvements in racist wars and their aftermath, racist peace.

Political struggle, like therapy, has been a source of healing in my life. If I was using therapy to pursue more emotional balance, I was also, on a parallel track, increasingly politicized. Coming out as a lesbian in 1976–77 was the first step in my politicization and it opened me up creatively. I began writing seriously and joined a collective doing lesbian feminist cultural work. This soon led me to antiracist activism within the lesbian and gay community. In 1983 I left both a closeted teaching job and what was beginning to feel like ghettoization within the lesbian community. I began organizing against a growing neo-Nazi movement and climate in North Carolina, with many other people, a majority of them heterosexual African Americans. I increasingly focused my anger outward in organizing for social change: of the homophobic world that had so isolated me and of the racism that had dismayed me with its violent fury as a child and an adolescent. I had an instinctive sense that the forces of race and class that white Alabamians had acted out so flagrantly were the same forces that, interacting with a misogynist world, were still destroying my mother's health. This action worked synchronistically with my reflection on family history in therapeutic spaces.

This synchronism also provided part of the framework by which I understood my antifascist organizing. The acquittal of Klansmen and neo-Nazis for the murders of anti-Klan demonstrators in Greensboro in 1979 had opened a floodgate of white supremacist organizing and racist violence. The neo-Nazi White Patriot Party was organizing all over the state, running candidates for public office (free publicity for the most racist propaganda), and marching its battalion, first one hundred, then three and four hundred strong, through little towns. We began to show links between members of the White Patriot Party and The Order, a white terrorist organization in the West. We were doing our best to sound the alarm, but the resistance was incredible. The epidemic of cross burnings across the state were "pranks" or "isolated incidents," according to reports in county newspapers. Patriot leader Miller's boasts of building up a white Christian army to take back the South—a violation of the state's paramilitary laws—was merely free speech, although it was accompanied by increasing acts of racist violence. I kept telling reporters: this man is confessing to a crime (breaking the state's paramilitary laws). What we kept running into felt like the massive denial I had experienced in my community as an adolescent, when most of the whites I knew had refused to acknowledge the reality, much less the moral significance, of the violent white resistance to black freedom movements. I began to formulate a metaphysic of genocide: people don't need to respond to what they can pretend they do not know, and they don't know what they can't feel.

The Anesthesia of Power

What emerged on both the therapeutic and the activist parts of my life also began to show up in my intellectual work, giving me more theoretical language for the nexus of political and emotional states, what I have come to understand as the "anesthetic aesthetic" of racism. "Next to the case of the black race within our bosom, that of the red on our borders is the problem baffling to the policy of the country," former President James Madison explained in 1826. The southern white plantation experience of the "black race on our bosom" is one of many locations that can give us some language for the intimate historical experience of racism in the United States. Our regional black-white experience of racism is not the only racial experience in the United States, of course, or in the South; but it is one of the prototypical ones.

In the South, this experience was captured both in slave narratives (the liberation stories of slaves who escaped the South) and slave apologists (the white southern writers who generated defenses of slavery in the thirty years before the Civil War, when slavery as an institution was under the complex set of challenges that eventually brought it down). The apologists are much more frank about claiming racism than we are today, when much of racial language is coded but racism is still entrenched: the playing field of five hundred years is supposedly evened after three decades by two Civil Rights laws; U.S. culture is supposedly now color blind; and the primary form of discrimination is supposedly reverse discrimination experienced by white men. African American literary critic Houston Baker Jr. has recently made the point that W.E.B. Du Bois and others have made: as the South goes, so goes the nation. *The Mind of the South* (Wilbur Cash's book) is also a study of our national mind, especially where racial consciousness is concerned, says Baker. He writes, "Cash got the psycho-cultural commonalties of southern *ressentiment* and racism absolutely 'on the mark' not only for the Confederate states, but also for the United States at large. He captured, that is to say, the *mind* of America in providing a comprehensive analysis of what he called the *South*."[6]

Reading the unapologetic apologists for slavery can give us insight into the enduring effects of racism on white consciousness shaped within the family—and that's the human family, as well as the plantation family, shaped within our species being. This is the link with Africa for all of us who have grown up in nations built by European settlers on foundations of slave cultures.

On southern plantations, this family was quite a mess. The white father/master/owner was married to a white woman, who bore his white children. But he also raped the African women who were his slaves, who also bore his children. The white children inherited their darker siblings, whom they never acknowledged as kin. The white women got the rap for frigidity, the African woman for promiscuity, a split that justified the white father's rape. When the white father wanted to, he could sell off the black portion of his family, send them down the river, breaking the hearts of African parents and children alike.

I first read *The Narrative of the Life of Frederick Douglass, An American Slave* in 1983 in a National Endowment for the Arts seminar taught by James Olney. Olney provided my first introduction to slave narratives and the black theorizing about them. Over the years, I have returned to Douglass's *Narrative,* as I did when I wanted to explain the identity confusions inherent in the plantation family:

> The whisper that my master was my father, may or may not be true; and, true or false, it is of but little consequence to my purpose whilst the fact remains, in all its glaring odiousness, that slaveholders have ordained, and by law established, that the children of slave women shall in all cases follow the condition of their mothers; and this is done too obviously to administer to their own lusts, and make a gratification of their wicked desires profitable as well as pleasurable; for by this cunning arrangement, the slaveholder, in cases not a few, sustains to his slaves the double relation of master and father. . . .
>
> The master is frequently compelled to sell this class of his slaves, out of deference to the feelings of his white wife; and, cruel as the deed may strike any one to be, for a man to sell his own children to human flesh-mongers, it is often the dictate of humanity for him to do so; for, unless he does this, he must not only whip them himself, but must stand by and see one white son tie up his brother, of but few shades darker complexion than himself, and ply the gory lash to his naked back.[7]

Remarkable in Douglass's explanation of the effects of the "double relation of master and father" is the mirror, the effect of the "double relation of slave and son." Douglass explains in the early section of his narrative that "the whisper that my master was my father, may or may not be true."[8] In the passage cited, he displaces responsibility for the beating onto the white mistress. The father is "compelled" to sell his slave (children); the father is the master who "must" whip them or watch his sons do the same. Douglass must give the father/master either no agency, or no humanity, and it is the agency that goes. Douglass describes his master's beating of his Aunt Hester because she had been keeping company with an African, Ned Roberts. Douglass makes clear the sadistic, sexualized nature of the whipping, the motive for which is the master's compulsion to maintain sexual control: "Before he commenced whipping Aunt Hester, he took her into the kitchen, and stripped her from neck to waist, leaving her neck, shoulders, and back, entirely naked. He then told her

to cross her hands. . . . 'Now you d——d b——h, I'll learn you how to disobey my orders!' . . . The louder she screamed, the harder he whipped; and where the blood ran
fastest, there he whipped longest. He would whip her to make her scream, and whip
her to make her hush; and not until overcome by fatigue, would he cease to swing
the blood-clotted cowskin."[9]

Douglass called this event "the blood-stained gate, the entrance to the hell of slavery, through which I was about to pass." This "blood-stained gate" is also the vaginal
passage into an institution of chattel slavery that "follows the condition of the
mother."

Douglass gives a terrifying description of the way that the near total control of
white plantation men over African bodies created depraved white people of all genders capable of executing, condoning, and encouraging great atrocities. What happens to white emotional life in such an environment? Is there anything left from all
of this that white folks can call a "soul"?

Henry Hughes, a slave apologist writing in 1854, gave some insight into the soul-
destroying dynamic of the plantation. I found the following remarkable passage
reading *The Ideology of Slavery: Proslavery Thought in the Antebellum South*, edited
by Drew Gilpin Faust. Hughes wrote of what he called the "Orderer's [a]esthetic"
and its implications for human relationships. "But the esthetic system is both positive
and negative. It is not for the production of pleasure only. It is for the prevention of
pain. It is both eunesthetic and anesthetic. Warrenteeism [his euphemism for slavery]
as it is, is essentially anesthetic. It systematically eliminates bodily pain. It actualizes
comfort for all."[10]

What remarkable claims! Such accounts as Douglass's of his master's beating of
Hester show how completely Hughes encodes the masters' point of view in his
analysis of slavery as a system that "eliminates bodily pain." Clearly, it does not
eliminate pain in African bodies, who are not considered fully human. It rather in-
tensifies pain beyond endurance. But what does it do to white bodies? What is this
"anesthetic esthetic" that Hughes articulates?

I went to the dictionary. While aesthetics is that branch of philosophy that deals
with judgments concerning beauty, it comes from *aisthesis*, "to perceive." *Anesthesia*
ads the prefix *an-*, signifying a blocked perception translated as "insensibility . . . the
loss of sensation without a loss of consciousness." Sensation is "a perception associated with stimulation of a sense organ or with a specific bodily condition" connected with "the faculty to feel or perceive."[11] Sensation, then, begins in impulses
from eyes, ears, nose, tongue, skin, central nervous system—as the brain "perceives"
or interprets them. These sensations also have associated feelings—localized somat-
ically in the chest and metaphorically in the heart.

I find that Buddhists' insights about consciousness are helpful in unpacking this
anesthetic aesthetic, given that consciousness has been the subject of description and
investigation in Buddhism for twenty-five hundred years. According to Buddhism, five
aggregates compose the human: form, feeling, perceptions, mental formations, and

consciousness.[12] Form, or *rupa*, means our body, including our sense organs (eyes, ears, nose, tongue/mouth, skin, and nervous system)—in other words, our sensations from and of our body. The second aggregate is feelings *(vedana)*, which "are like a river within us, and every drop of water in that river is a feeling." The third aggregate is our perceptions *(samjna)*. How we "notice, name, and conceptualize" often involves distortion, or false perception, which is usually painful. Feelings and perceptions are/become mental formations, the fourth aggregate. These mental formations, if based on distorted perception, can form what Buddhists call knots—the equivalent of neuroses or psychoses in Freudian terms; which is to say, all those places we get stuck. The fifth aggregate is what Buddhists call our store consciousness.

The fifth aggregate is a kind of aggregate of aggregates: it is both individual and collective consciousness that "contains all the others and is the basis of their existence." Each of the aggregates lies as a seed in the store consciousness. Each contains all the others. Using a Marxist metaphor, the fifth aggregate of consciousness is the base, generating the others as superstructure as they rise out of, and fall back into, store consciousness. It is mindfulness, various forms of meditation, the seventh step on the Noble Eightfold Path, that helps one get down to the generative level of store consciousness and find and shift the negative seeds there, transforming painful mental formations such as selfishness, malevolence, malice, and anger into wholesome ones, such as equanimity, self-respect, and humility.[13] Thus meditation shifts *chitta*, the "mind in the mind"—what Marxists might call ideology or generative systems of ideas.

The particular anesthesia of slavery as Hughes celebrates it seems to block what Buddhists call the first and second aggregates—body, or sensory information, and feeling, or emotion—leaving a more abstracted reason, the mental formations of racist ideology.[14] Necessary to the slave system was the masters' blocked sensation of its pain, an aesthetic that left him insensible not only to the fellow human beings he enslaved, but to the testimony of his senses that might have contradicted ideologies of slavery.

The Civil War diaries of Mary Boykin Chesnut provide an equally remarkable gloss, from a white woman's (slave mistress's) point of view, on Hughes's notion of the soul-destroying anesthesia necessary to the maintenance of power. The contradictory position of woman and mistress made Chesnut more vulnerable to feeling the pain of domination and gave her the space to articulate her contradictory status. Mary Chesnut's husband served in Confederate President Jefferson Davis's cabinet during the Civil War, and she enjoyed her status and vehemently supported the Confederate cause. Yet her diary in places makes analogies between the condition of women and of slaves. She felt the schisms in her culture more than many white upper-class women of her day, making her both observer and site of struggle for the forces contending within southern slave society in its penultimate moment. She describes a "tragedy" she observed on the auction block: "A mad woman taken from her husband and children. Of course she was mad, or she would not have given her grief words in that public place. Her keepers were along. What she said was rational enough, pathetic, at times heart-rending. It excited me so I quietly took opium. It enables me to retain every particle of mind or sense or brains I have, and so quiets my nerves that I can calmly reason and take rational views of things otherwise maddening."[15]

Here we arrive again at the anesthetic of slavery. The African woman in her reasonable grief gives voice to her pain, and Chesnut's perception of her situation rends the white woman's heart, arousing dangerous sensation and feeling—"excitement"—which she immediately blocks with opium in a "systematic elimination of bodily pain." She loses "sensation without the loss of consciousness," and her quieted nerves leave her a distracted rationality—the ability to "take rational views of things otherwise maddening." This process also distorts the body's feedback system to let us know that something is dangerously awry.

In Buddhist terms, Chesnut's empathetic response to the African woman's pain was a moment of *bodhichitta*, or "mind of love"—our ability to feel compassion from the pain we share with others. Pema Chodron describes bodhichitta as "our soft spot—our innate ability to love and care about things . . . a natural opening in the barriers we create when we are afraid."[16] This moment of perception had Chesnut on the path to reexamining herself and her culture. ("Looking into one feeling, you can discover everything.")[17] But she has neither the resources, nor the courage, and resorts to opium to short-circuit such a transformative process. Seeing implies action, unless the paths of perception are blocked. Action expands perceptions because it shifts and enlarges our point of view and our capacity and motivation to process bigger chunks of reality.

"Poor women, poor slaves." Mary Chesnut only articulated what Hughes and others explained more dispassionately: "All other people in the State, who are not sovereign people, are subsovereign. To this class belong women, minors, criminals, lunatics and idiots, aliens and all others unqualified or disqualified," not to mention how it might make a person lunatic or criminal to be constantly "unqualified or disqualified."[18]

These passages from Hughes and Chesnut describe and defend the institution of chattel slavery that in concert with the genocide of indigenous people formed the foundation of racism on this continent. They suggest that there is not only a psychology but also a physiology of racism: it encodes itself in our consciousness, closing the doors of our perception. That presence that it partially displaces when it does so is part of that larger self that I am calling soul.

In their frank charting of the psychology of mastery in the U.S. South in the mid–nineteenth century, Douglass, Hughes, and Chesnut articulate a process basic to racist consciousness and to the generic consciousness of domination. As Hughes explained, "In any order there are two classes. These are the, (1) Orderers or Superordinates, and the, (2), Orderees or Subordinates. This, of necessity."[19] The cost to the dominating consciousness is a sense of existence as alien, in Hegel's terms.

These southern descriptions of power also recall Freud's passage where he lamented his lack of connection: "I cannot discover this oceanic feeling in myself. It is not easy to deal scientifically with feelings. One can attempt to describe their physiological signs. Where this is not possible—and I am afraid that the oceanic feeling too will defy this kind of characterization—nothing remains but to fall back on the ideational context which is most readily associated with the feeling. . . . From my own experience I could not convince myself of the primary nature of such feeling."[20] Where Mary Chesnut frankly resorts to opium to contain her feelings, her bodhichitta impulses, Freud (who had his own cocaine problem) resorts to psychoanalysis to justify the absence of his "attempting to discover a psycho-analytic explanation of such a feeling."[21]

What happens to lost sensations and feelings? Freud described a process of projection, which he associated with the state of paranoia: "An internal perception is suppressed, and, instead, its context, after undergoing a certain degree of distortion, enters consciousness in the form of an external perception." The history of racism, colonialism, sexism, and heterosexism (all states of paranoia) demonstrates, as well, that not only are perceptions suppressed, distorted, and externalized, but also emotions: one's fears about oneself, unexamined, become distorted fears about the Other.[22] In the process of repression and projection, distorted feelings migrate, they do not disperse; sexual feelings, or instincts, especially so. By Freud's formulation, in fact, instinctual gratification, and therefore revolt and freedom, all lie outside of civilization, or European culture, which is constituted to repress them and so continually projects them beyond itself. He observes that the human "desire for freedom may be their revolt against some existing injustice" that springs "from the remains of their original personality, which is still untamed by civilization and may thus become the basis in them of hostility to civilization." Here Freud draws on Darwin to code civilization as European, with the original untamed personality coming from more primitive cultures that Europe subdued: civilization and its discontents, sublimation and prior instinct recapitulate the relationship between colonizer and colonized. Repression of instinctual feelings, like conquest of "primitive" cultures, made inevitable what Freud called the "return of the repressed," a kind of psychic revolution congruent with anticolonial national independence movements then active in Asia, Latin America, and Africa.[23] Freud points in these passages to some fundamental characteristics of the "original personality" (species being?) that desires freedom and instigates revolt. I would liken this aspect of self to the larger self of soul, or spirit, which can be reclaimed even within the masterful self if it commits itself to such honest self-scrutiny and (relative) freedom.

Freud's theory of projection provides an illuminating context against which to read his assessment of the relationship between suffering and addiction. He moves here from the macro of civilization to the micro of "our own organism," which surely we can read with reference to Freud's own cocaine problem:

The most interesting methods of averting suffering are those which seek to influence our own organism. In the last analysis, all suffering is nothing else than sensation; it only exists in so far as we feel it, and we only feel it in consequence of certain ways in which our own organism is regulated. The crudest, but also the most effective among these methods of influence is the chemical one—intoxication. I do not think that anyone completely understands its mechanism, but it is a fact that there are foreign substances which, when present in the blood or tissues, directly cause us pleasurable sensations; and they also so alter the conditions governing our sensibility that we become incapable of receiving unpleasurable impulses. The two effects not only occur simultaneously, but seem to be intimately bound up with each other.[24]

"Averting suffering" by chemical means surely induces an anesthesia, or blocked perception, not only to pain but to pleasurable feelings as well, such as the "oceanic" feeling of connection and bonding. This aversion of suffering by intoxication or other compulsive processes is the emotional and chemical basis for addictions. Within the recovery movement, problematic addictions range from heroin and booze to shopping and the wrong kinds of love.

If, as I have argued, anesthesia is necessarily encrypted in mastery, addiction produces anesthesia. The history of colonialism shows the material process through which such encryption occurred.

I first picked up the connection between addiction, with its blunting of emotion, and capitalism when I read Marvin Harris's explanation about how Europeans' acquired taste for the new beverages coffee and cocoa had finally made African slavery profitable. The sugar that went into both drinks came from sugar plantations in the Caribbean. The addictive qualities of sugar, cocoa, and caffeine created enough of a market that the huge losses in the slave trade (which is to say, all the Africans who died in the Middle Passage) could be offset by the new, addictive demand for sugar.[25] The triangle trade from Africa to New England to the Caribbean also had at its center sugar and rum, another addictive substance. The cash crop for slave plantations in North Carolina was tobacco—which also fueled the growth of Durham, my hometown, by robber tobacco baron James B. Duke. Duke liked to brag that he taught the world to smoke. One of the first companies to use modern marketing techniques, American Tobacco sent free cigarettes into the desert of North Africa or gave them away on the streets of Asian cities or handed packs to immigrants coming off the boats in the United States. Duke, too, understood that an addictive demand would allow him to run up his supply. Expanding capitalism had built addiction into the U.S. culture, starting with slavery.

The CIA-backed Contras in Nicaragua sold cocaine in Los Angeles in the 1980s, although *San Jose Mercury News* reporter Gary Webb's story that top CIA officials knew about this was later repudiated by *Mercury News* executive editor Jerry Ceppos.[26] There is only so much twelve-stepping can do by itself in the face of racist, genocidal government schemes that create addiction for profit and control. As Elayne

Rapping argues in *The Culture of Recovery*: "That these [addictive] behaviors, in today's world, do indeed reflect the growing self-destructiveness of people trying desperately to keep up and succeed in a competitive, market-driven world is masked in public discourse by the idea that 'addictive disorders' are genetically—not socially—engendered."[27]

The twelve steps, which I learned in the several years I attended Overeaters Anonymous, gave me a set of emotional guidelines that, when I applied them, could indeed help, in the words of the program, restore my personal emotional life to sanity. But I felt some equally deep need to help restore to sanity the life of my culture. As far as amends go, how does a culture make collective amends for slavery, or genocide? That collective dimension was surely what South Africa's Truth and Reconciliation Commission struggled with. Would folks have a different attitude toward affirmative action, say, or reparations, if they thought politically about amends and saw their own emotional investment in a restored cultural sanity?

The projection that happens in the space between Hegel's dominating self and dominated other, between Hughes's Orderer and Orderee, results in a high state of unconsciousness: in Hughes's terms, *anesthesia*, a stripping away from fuller consciousness a strata of perception. Psychoanalysis was Freud's brave attempt to heal the breech. In Freud's later theory, this dynamic became an internal drama, with the ego caught between the dominant superego and the repressed id. The affective void from which feelings and perceptions have been blocked in oneself and cast onto Others is the space where addictions arise; it is also the psychological space from which whiteness and maleness have been mobilized throughout their histories. This void both justifies exploitation (by projecting onto the exploited all the cast-off fearsome and evil feelings of the exploited—Freud's projection) and holds it in place (the exploiter cannot then feel the violence of his acts, because he cannot feel—Hughes's anesthesia).

Within U.S. culture, various therapeutic movements since Freud have begun to reveal the extent to which exploitative relationships have cost us personally, familially, and socially. They have elaborated the cost of our anesthesia; of how the emotional void, once vacated, is filled again and again with destructive and compulsive thoughts, feelings, and habits. In the past twenty years, also, the Right has made use of what Lawrence Grossberg calls "affective epidemics"—around drugs, the family, nationalism, and so forth. "Questions of fact and representation become secondary to the articulation of people's emotional fears and hopes. This partly explains the new conservatism's 'ideological' successes: they have been able to control specific vectors without having to confront the demands of policy and public action. Similarly, they have been able to construct issues with enormous public passion . . . without leaving any space for public engagement."[28] The current "war on terror" is the latest of these affective epidemics, through which the Bush administration is escalating foreign intervention (domination) and domestic repression. Such affective epidemics are clearly qualitatively different than the revolutionary emotion that Audre Lorde evoked. She writes, "For as we begin to recognize our deepest feelings, we begin to give up, of necessity, being satisfied with suffering and self-negation, and with the numbness which so often seems like their only alternative in our society. Our acts against oppression become integral with self, motivated and empowered from within."[29] The alternative, as Marcuse puts it, "The era tends to be totalitarian even where it has not produced totalitarian states."[30]

This affective void echoes through the terrible, moving, and fascinating testimony from South Africa's Truth and Reconciliation Commission, now available on the Internet. The TRC testimony provides an incredible store of narratives from which to examine perpetrators of political violence, both in their individual and their systemic manifestations. The commission looked at forty years of state-sanctioned violence under apartheid. Many members of the security forces came forward to ask for amnesty during this process. Many of their narratives suggest that even their hottest crimes of torture and dismemberment were cold—that their hatred was experienced (in retrospect, at any rate) not as an intensification, but as a lack of emotion.

Here is one of the killers of Steven Biko: "I am not glad and I am not sorry about Mr. Biko. It leaves me cold."[31]

Or here is an exchange between one of the commissioners and Brig. Jack Cronje, one of the operatives from Vlakplass, the government training center for torturers and assassins:

JUDGE NGOEPE: Now if you were in charge of the operation and, as you have testified, it was an accident that this man was eliminated, why didn't you stop throttling him?

CRONJE: Well, I could have stopped it, but I did not expect that they would throttle him so long that he would die.

JUDGE NGOEPE: Brigadier, really. Did you expect the man to survive being throttled by two men, and after this man had been tortured and assaulted?

CRONJE: I did not expect that they would throttle him that long, so long that he would die.

JUDGE NGOEPE: Well, as the officer in charge, why didn't you watch and when you could see what was going on tell them to stop? You were responsible. You gave the orders.

CRONJE: Yes, I was responsible. But I did not watch all the time. I was looking in front of me.[32]

Or here is an exchange with Colonel de Kock, a member of the elite security force twice awarded the Police Star for Outstanding Service and the Silver Cross for Bravery involved in at least seventy killings during a ten-year period:

ACKERMAN: How would your enemies describe you?

DE KOCK: Cold-blooded.

ACKERMAN: Other words you want to use?

DE KOCK: Determined and persevering.

ACKERMAN: How do your enemies see you?

DE KOCK: As merciless.

ACKERMAN: What else?

DE KOCK: I have not met that many, because most are dead.

ACKERMAN: Have you ever tried to estimate how many lives you've taken?

DE KOCK: One doesn't do it. It's a terrible thing to think about.[33]

For most of the perpetrators, their Christian faith and anticommunist ideology provided their motivation and their excuse. They operated out of their mental formations, in other words, rather than out of their feelings—at least in what they would admit publicly. "I want to use the word 'hate,'" said Craig Williamson (murderer of Ruth First), struggling to articulate his motivation. "It's just virtually impossible to tell you how . . . I don't think it was hate, but how totally and utterly determined we were to win the war and eliminate and destroy the enemy. . . . It was an obsession."[34] Dirk Coetzee, who admitted to six murders and seventeen other serious crimes, explained the feeling of pleasure that came from doing his job well: "I was prepared to kill as many people as I was instructed to kill. I absolutely felt like a hero. I mean, you were there to please your bosses."[35] Former President Botha, under whose regime the most intense state terrorism occurred, testified in a remarkable statement: "I am sick and tired of the hollow parrot-cry of 'apartheid!' I've said many times that the word 'apartheid' means good neighborliness."[36] Here we are back to the anesthetic aesthetic, to slavery that "eliminates bodily pain."

In its final report, the TRC observed: "The white community often seemed either indifferent or plainly hostile to the work of the commission, and certain media [the Afrikaner press] appeared to have actively sought to sustain this indifference and hostility. . . . Often, it seemed to the commission, there was no real appreciation of the enormity of the violations of which these leaders and those under them were accused, or of the massive degree of hurt and pain their actions had caused."[37]

From a position of an anesthetic aesthetic, apartheid, like slavery, is both for the "production of pleasure" and for the "prevention of pain"—it "maximizes comfort for all." Both put the lie to Freud that suffering "exists in so far as we feel it" because it begs the question of *who* feels. Suffering is never an individual phenomenon; and, in fact, denial of feeling in the dominant Self can be literally torture for the Other.

What, then, is the cost to white people of racism? Perhaps now we can more accurately make the assessment, recognizing that racism implicates systems of oppression based on gender and class, on patriarchy, capitalism, and heterosexism:

Racism costs us intimacy.

Racism costs us our affective lives.

Racism costs us authenticity.

Racism costs us our sense of connection to other humans and the natural world.

Racism costs us our spiritual selves: "a feeling of an indissoluble bond, of being one with the external world as a whole," as Freud's poet friend tried to explain.

OUT OF SLAVERY

Of course, not only white people pay this cost. And not only Orderers do. Frederick Douglass knew that he, too, paid the cost of his affective life to slavery when he, like many other slave infants, was separated from his mother, an abandonment over which she had absolutely no control. Douglass reflects: "For what this separation is done, I do not know, unless it be to hinder the development of the child's affection toward its mother, and to blunt and destroy the natural affection of the mother for the child." Douglass never saw his mother "by the light of day." Four or five times, she walked the twelve miles to see him after her day's work. "Never having enjoyed, to any considerable extent, her soothing presence, her tender and watchful care, I received the tidings of her death with much the same emotions I should have probably felt at the death of a stranger."[39]

Douglass's gendered narrative tells the story of "how a man was made a slave . . . and how a slave was made a man" through his process of many years of reclaiming the oceanic feeling of connection. Ironically, this life of feeling was also all around him in his fellow slaves, singing their way through the woods, their spirituals "revealing at once the highest joy and the deepest sadness . . . a tale of woe . . . tones loud, long, and deep." Douglass learns "the pathway from slavery to freedom" when his master forces his mistress to stop teaching him to read because "it would forever unfit him to be a slave." Poor white children in his neighborhood teach him the alphabet, and they "express for [him] the liveliest sympathy." He begins to abhor slavery so much that he wishes himself dead, until he learns the word *abolition*, the light "breaking in on [him] by degrees." He realizes his strong attachment to his young white friends when he is sent back to the country from Baltimore.[39] Back on the plantation, he falls under Covey, the slave breaker, and is whipped severely over a period of months, broken in "body, soul and spirit." He runs away to ask his master for mercy and is refused. On the way back, he is befriended by Sandy, a slave with a free wife. Sandy gives him a magical root that "would render it impossible for Mr. Covey, or any other white man, to whip me." Sandy's solidarity and his medicine prove powerful, and the next time Covey attacks, Douglass fights back, beating the white man soundly. Covey never beats him again. Defending himself gives Douglass self-confidence and a determination to be free. By appropriating violence and the ability to inflict pain, Douglass contradicts the anesthetic aesthetic that slavery "actualizes comfort for all [white men . . . people]." By defending himself, finally, when being beaten, perhaps he breaks his psychic identification with his white master/father and reclaims some identification with the black mother/slave, which augments his capacity for feeling. Up until this point, Douglass has carried the burden of a white masculinity; by using the violence of slavery against itself, he genders himself as black.[40]

He is sent back again to Baltimore, where he teaches other of his "dear fellow slaves" to read in a Sabbath school at the house of a "free colored man." "I loved them with a love stronger than anything I have experienced since. . . . I believe we would have died for each other. We never undertook to do anything, of any importance, without a mutual consultation. We never moved separately. We were one; and as much so by our tempers and dispositions, as by the mutual hardship to which we were necessarily subjected as slaves."[41]

Paradoxically, the "number of warm-hearted friends in Baltimore,—friends that [he] loved more than life," make his final escape both "painful beyond expression" and finally possible. Douglass can escape the slave South when he has completed the making of the slave into not so much a man as a human, by reclaiming his capacity to feel and love (including to love his African self enough to defend himself from white violence).

What does Frederick Douglass's reclamation of his own humanity and his "love of humanity" have to teach white people? Well, for one, he responded to his "family dysfunction" first by escaping, then by changing the structures that created the dysfunction. Douglass's narrative is part of his attack on the slave system that created his and many others' misery. And Frederick Douglass (with the help of a few other people) *abolished slavery* by such efforts. Perhaps if we are really to "systematically eliminate bodily pain" of family dysfunction, as Hughes would have us do, we should systematically eliminate racism, homophobia, sexism, and capitalism. As Marcuse explained in the preface to *Eros and Civilization,* "Private disorder reflects more directly than before the disorder of the whole, and the cure of personal disorder depends more directly than before on the cure of the general disorder."[42]

We can see in Douglass's narratives the evolution of radical subjectivity that Brazilian Paulo Freire called *conscientizacão*, which involved a praxis of action and reflection. This "critical thinking . . . perceives reality as process, as transformation, rather than as static entity . . . [and] does not separate itself from action, but constantly immerses itself in temporality without fear of the risks involved." Thus Douglass learns to act, and reflect, and act, and reflect, until he has gained a fuller humanity for himself and his culture. Consciousness is not only critical *thinking*, as Freire terms it, but, as we have seen, a thick soup of thought, feeling, and sensation, much of which may not always be aware. Such a dialogue requires an intense faith in humanity, in the "power to make and remake, to create and re-create, faith in [the] vocation to be more fully human."[43] It also requires, I am beginning to suspect, a practice of mindfulness.

Mary Chesnut's pain, felt in response to the black woman on the auction block, was her spontaneous biological and spiritual reaction to another human's exploitation and grief, the reassuring mark of her humanity. Then she chose opium. The

Grimké sisters, white southern women of Chesnut's generation, made another choice: abolitionism. The active engagement with real structures, with (in Freire's term) "reality as transformation," not only alleviates future suffering, it is itself therapeutic, because it brings us as humans back to our birthright of "love of humanity" and an "oceanic feeling" of connection, with ourselves, with one another, and with the animate world; it brings us to the palimpsest moment when, or the place where, the fact of love surpasses the fact of death, and we are restored our lost sense of eternity. This moment of eternity is the moment of the present, the moment when all can be transformed, and it's the only moment anyone ever really has.

VIEWING WITHOUT SANCTUARY

The loss of soul I have evoked here cries out as well from the photographs in *Without Sanctuary*, almost one hundred photographs of lynchings in the United States. I had seen one or two of these pictures in anti-Klan educational material. When I heard about James Allen's collection of these pictures, which were reproduced as mementos for the public ritual of lynching, I felt a need to view the entire volume. I found that the Duke library had one copy in Special Collections, not available for general circulation. I appreciated this decision. It would be too easy for anyone to Xerox the photos and use them for various kinds of racist harassment. Viewing the volume in Special Collections also required a level of deliberation. So I caught a bus over to West Campus, found Special Collections, filled out a card, and sat there with the book in front of me. I turned the pages slowly, reading all of the texts before turning finally to the photographs. Then I turned the pages slowly, making notes of my responses:

Without Sanctuary, the title says, *Photographs of Lynchings in America.*

You notice anything first: the grass dead from the bulb's glare, branches caught in the river's bend; you notice the white men's hats—white straw with black bands, fedoras, and there a cap; the frontispiece a sea of white men's white hats.

You notice the white people's eyes looking into the camera beneath, beside, above . . . the glee or pride or vacancy; seldom if ever a shadow of doubt or pain. But you do not notice the bodies hanging there in ones or twos, as many as five; mostly men or what used to be, hanging mostly. But one man is sitting dead at a tree base. They are mostly hanging by rope or chain from limb or lamp post.

Laura Nelson and her son hang from a bridge on which the crowd posed May 25 somewhere in Oklahoma. You notice one white woman's parasol above her white child. You notice the four loops in the noose around the neck of Leo Frank. You begin to notice the angle of the heads above the nooses: some sideways, some forward as in prayer, some faces to the sky.

But, finally, all you can see is the gravity of bodies: the terrible plumb lines.

Suddenly, Frank Embree, July 22, 1899, is alive and looking straight at you, a frontal nude, his wrists cuffed in front, slashes on his black torso. Frank Embree is bearing witness, his eyebrow quizzical. But don't turn the page, because there he is hanging there, from an oak tree this time. Just the page before and unafraid he startled you watching him.

You cannot locate the white child who wrote to an unidentified mother, *"I have seen a man hanged. Now I wish I could see one burned."* But you know Joe, the son who wrote, *"This is the barbecue we had last night,"* because his picture is to the left of the body, white face with an X over it.

Not expecting more from white people, my own relations, it is the trees who disappoint: the oak, loblolly pine, maple, the coniferous, the deciduous—branches, bark, limbs.

Without Sanctuary, the title says.

"In America everything is for sale."

Finally, I notice how the bodies lean toward each other, the ones lynched together—an arm across another's chest, heads on one another's shoulders: a respite there? An *embrace?* Arms cuffed behind backs arch the heads upward: not gravity now but *flight?* The pitch cloud in the book's staple looks as if he burned the photographic plate on his way out. That dark smudge between the trees was never a body; more an ash that marks my forehead. It is this photograph that recurs to me three days later, its charred torso like some third eye, our lashes rain; and finally, finally, finally I can weep.

Without Sanctuary, the cover says. But it is there in the leaning bodies, the glint of light off the river, the witnessing trees. I do not believe there was no sanctuary; only that there was no shame.[44]

8

JOHANNESBURG
Nkosi sikelel'i Afrika

Johannesburg, Johannesburg. Who could believe it?
—ALAN PATON, *Cry, the Beloved Country*

South Africa belongs to all who live in it—no government can justly claim authority unless it is based on the will of the people.
—African National Congress Freedom Charter

It is not surprising that the fight against a people with such deep prejudice should take a long time to bear fruit.
—MAHATMA GANDHI

THE Miami airport's area for international flights was filled with people who were, like me, waiting. Marta Benavides would be arriving from San Salvador any minute, so that this afternoon we could both board the huge South African Airlines plane that would take us on a seventeen-hour flight to Johannesburg on the way to Harare and the General Assembly of the World Council of Churches.

I had avoided the latest revelations in the *New York Times* about the Clinton-Lewinsky scandal, slouching its way toward impeachment this December of 1998. Instead, I was reading the World Council publication *Welcome to Zimbabwe*. Along with a glass of iced cappuccino, it had my mind spinning. "Traditional religion [in Africa] can be divided into two main departments—that of God and of the spirits, functioning in unison but different spheres," I read. God is more remote, concerned with matters of macro importance. Ancestral spirits take care of day-to-day affairs.[1] I had been pondering the passage of Hegel's *Phenomenology of Mind* where he articulates his perception of "the alien element of natural existence" that underlies the compulsion for masters to create slaves, a psychic configuration that shaped my childhood as it did four hundred years of South African history. Sartre's existential response to such perception was nausea—another reaction to a world no longer experienced as animate? Perhaps such profound alienation reflects the absence of mediating spirits? Is it that our European ancestors have raped and pillaged to such an extent that we seriously question whether and how we want them around? Am I ready for South Africa's contradictions—this land of apartheid and *ubuntu*, both three-syllable words that signify states—separation and belonging—that, like physical objects, cannot occupy the same space at the same time?

Archbishop Desmond Tutu provided me a fuller definition of ubuntu, the concept I had tracked across continents since discovering it in a Delta flight magazine. "Ubuntu, a difficult word to render precisely in English, seeks to describe the essence of what it means to be human. . . . It speaks about gentleness, hospitality, putting yourself out on behalf of others, being vulnerable. It embraces both compassion and togetherness. It recognizes that my humanity is bound up in yours, for we can only be truly human together."[2]

"You know when it is there and when it is absent," observed Tutu in a remarkable understatement from a Nobel Peace Prize winner who recently chaired South Africa's Truth and Reconciliation Commission (TRC), which only two months before had presented its conclusions from thirty months of hearings into human rights abuses in South Africa under apartheid. After the first two days of testimony, Tutu put his head on the table and wept openly. "I don't know if I am the right person to chair this commission, because I'm weak. I thought I was tough until today."[3] Over the next two and a half years, victims of police violence testified; then the police perpetrators themselves came forward with first-person narratives revealing their own actions under directives from top levels of government. These revelations exposed, as Tutu summarized, a "depth of depravity [that] was breathtaking."[4] In the profound disconnection of apartheid, Afrikaners, instructed by their leaders that "the [communist] enemy was everywhere" and encouraged to take "whatever steps to deal with the situation," dreamed "the most terrible dream in the world," as Chief Luthuli named it when he received the Nobel Peace Prize, its result a spiraling violence that produced successive states of both political and spiritual emergency.

One piece of the testimony stuck in my mind. "The burning of a body on an open fire takes seven hours," said Capt. Dirk Coetzee while describing to the TRC the security police procedures for disposing of the murdered corpse of Sizwe Kondile: "Whilst that happened we were drinking and braaing next to the fire. . . . The fleshier parts of the body take longer. . . . That's why we frequently had to turn the buttocks and thigh of Kondile."[5]

Again and again the commission and the people of South Africa heard accounts of what happened in the violent force field of separation and alienation as they also highlighted acts of profound courage and solidarity.

Ever since the chance to go to Africa emerged with the WCC's decision to hold its assembly in Zimbabwe, this Africa journey had felt like a pilgrimage to me. It's not that, as a white southerner, I can be going home to Africa in the same way that

African Americans do, I told myself while watching for Marta to appear through the swinging doors. But white identity, I realized a while back, is constituted by all that it represses, so that Africa became a palpable presence in the segregated Alabama of my childhood. What pieces of me might I discover on the continent? I knew I had to go through South Africa on the way to Harare, if only briefly, because of the resonances with southern history in the twentieth century between Jim Crow and apartheid.

I was in search not only of the past but of the future. The most hopeful event for me in the early 1990s was Nelson Mandela's release from Robben Island after twenty-seven years in Afrikaner prison. The subsequent emergence in 1994 of a democratic South Africa offered new possibilities of liberation when many of the old ones had crumbled beneath "new world orders," both military and economic. But the South African majority won its struggle for national liberation in a postliberation age. Ubuntu would not fare well, I expected, in a world of late capital.

I was also grateful to South Africans for including lesbians and gay men in their new constitution. The new South African constitution—the first country in the world to include a reference in its national constitution to sexual orientation—had emerged in a remarkably collective grassroots process to ensure that it was "legitimate, credible and accepted by all South Africans." In a country freed from apartheid by mass movements, the "largest public participation programme ever carried out in South Africa" drafted its new constitution. There were hundreds of meetings at the grass roots level throughout the country to discuss the interim constitution, and people were encouraged to send in their submissions to the Constitutional Assembly. Four million copies of the working draft were circulated in late 1994, and the new South African constitution was officially adopted in 1996. The equality clause protecting lesbians and gay men was thoroughly debated before it emerged as constitutional law.[6]

"Because we have a past of such oppression, we feel the need to list the areas where there is still oppression. . . . Our struggle for the equality clause must be won through large-scale engagement with our communities and not just with politicians," Cheryl Carolus, deputy secretary of the ANC, explained.[7] South African success certainly bolstered arguments that because oppressions are linked, resistances must be. When you are trying to get to something embedded as deeply as racism, or heterosexism, a revolution could help.

South Africa's record contrasted sharply with nearby Zimbabwe's, whose current performance was as discouraging as South Africa's was exemplary. I wanted to understand more fully the difference in the two contexts.

In Beijing, the *Forum on Women* newspaper had carried the story of the disruption of the participation of a brave but small gay/lesbian organization at the Zimbabwe International Book Fair. President Robert Mugabe had called homosexuals "worse than pigs and dogs." The year after the Beijing conference, the World Council of Churches decided to have its assembly in Harare, and lesbian and gay Zimbabweans began to petition the World Council and the global community for help. By summer of 1998, the U.S. Urban-Rural Mission selected six delegates to the Harare assembly. We planned to offer workshops on women of color organizing, on the plight of migrant people, and on sexuality and spirituality in the *Padare* (marketplace) of offerings that ran parallel to the deliberations of the assembly.

Marta's flight was on time, and I had little doubt she had made it. She was skilled in showing up. Over the past several years I had pieced together her history as we became friends. She had worked with Archbishop Oscar Romero in the 1970s as the ruling junta's repression escalated in El Salvador. "Monsignor," as Marta called him, had ordained her—the first woman ordained in El Salvador, even though he was Catholic and she Baptist. Then he asked her to help him start a National Commission for Humanitarian Aid to set up refugee centers and clinics for people being displaced by military and paramilitary violence—the torture, disappearances, kidnappings, mutilated bodies dumped on the roadside that had turned the country, in the monsignor's words, into "the empire of hell." In the three years he was archbishop, Romero increasingly embraced the "preferential treatment for the poor" coming out of the Second Vatican Council and the second Latin American Episcopal Conference in Medellín, Colombia (1968), from which emerged grassroots Christian communities and the "church of the poor." "The cry of liberation of this people is a cry that reaches up to God and one that nothing and no one can stop," he proclaimed.[8]

Marta also worked with Archbishop Romero to set up international committees of solidarity through the National Council of Churches in the United States and the World Council in Geneva. "No soldier is obliged to obey an order contrary to the law of God," he preached the evening before his assassination. "It is time that you obey your conscience rather than follow sinful commands."[9] Monsignor Romero was gunned down the next evening while celebrating mass. Marta herself barely escaped capture and went underground, relocating to the United States but continuing to slip in and out of El Salvador as the Farabundo Marti National Liberation Front (FMLN) was formed amid increasing violence and repression, moving the country into civil war. Marta had returned home in the early nineties when peace accords ended the fighting—about the same time that apartheid was ending in South Africa. I was lucky to have her as a traveling companion and a friend, my funny bodhisattva.

I looked up to see Marta on the other side of the glass, grinning and waving, holding her huge brown suitcase with its familiar silver tape across the belly. She always brings it along, even when it's empty, so that customs agents will be less likely to stop her for drug searches on the flights from Central America. At least she was not traveling incognito, slipping across borders like in the old FMLN days in some peculiar wig and careful not to speak to the person in the seat beside her, who could be CIA. She is an alert traveler, with habits that have kept her alive through years when many of her friends did not survive. I watched through the glass as she negotiated the line in her familiar jeans and T-shirt, her short hair graying. Marta's age is a bit indeterminate—somewhere in her fifties. I get a different number each time I ask her. Now she kidded in Spanish and English with the woman in front of her and the man at the gate. Then she was through the door and we were hugging. "Ohhh, Mob, it's good to see you. We are going to Africa!" We both laughed and headed for the South African Airlines gate.

"MONEY IS THEIR GOD"

Soon we were flying east, speeding toward the sun. I settled into the fleeing afternoon, a water bottle tucked away beside me, granola bars from my bag. The stewardess had seated Marta in another section of the plane when Marta refused to part with the carry-on suitcase that holds her passport and papers. I pulled out of my backpack *The Anti-Apartheid Reader* and my pink highlighter and settled down for the ride. I was reading for parallels in the histories of South Africa and the U.S. South. Apartheid emerged as the policy of the Nationalist Party in its narrow 1948 electoral victory, but the Nationalists drew on centuries of racist practices, a colonial history that links southern Africa and the southern United States.[10] It would be yet another lesson in how colonialism shaped the twentieth century, this time with a sharp emphasis on racial formation, the use of white supremacist ideologies and practices to implement colonial policies.

In 1652, Europeans arrived on the African Cape when the Dutch East India Company dispatched a handful of employees to the Cape of Good Hope to set up a refreshment station for trading ships on voyages to and from Dutch colonies in Asia. Soon Dutch employees settled with grants of twenty-eight acres of free land acquired from the San and Khoikhoi people, who had lived there for centuries and with whom the Dutch were soon at war to extend their territory. The problem of labor followed, as usual, the acquisition of land. The Dutch East India Company allowed van Reibeeck, the settler leader, to import slaves from other places in Africa as well as Asia (25,000 by 1700).[11] Once slavery was in place, its logic shaped all other emerging institutions. On the east coast of North America, the English had arrived in 1613 at Jamestown, also as part of a trading company. English brought the first Africans into what would become Virginia only six years later. Within forty years, chattel slavery emerged with its stamp of inherited and lifelong status, justified by an ideology that saw Africans as subhuman.

In southern Africa as early as 1760, restrictions on movement of Africans emerged, and barbaric practices of beating and torture became a staple of the emerging slave society on both continents. In both places, Calvinism, with its grim predestination, stoked a sense of European racial superiority and a fear-based white spirituality easily manipulated by demagogues. Bringing in slaves entrenched master-slave social relationships. As the Boers (or Dutch farmers) claimed more land, the Xhosas fought back in what would be a century of armed conflict. In North America, English settlers all up and down the seaboard immediately began to push west and were soon at war with the tribes indigenous to the region. They fought back, an open warfare that would be waged across the continent for the next three centuries.

The British invaded South Africa in 1795 to secure a strategic stopover on British trade routes to India. British conquest drew the Cape Colony into global trade, and British presence in southern Africa set up a contest between British and Boer that would last throughout the next century. The British were settled in cities engaging in trade, finance, and manufacturing—not unlike, I realized, the states of the U.S. North, increasingly in tension with the agrarian, slave South. The British had power to extend the range of white supremacy in a slash-and-burn war with the Xhosas that forced the Africans, finally defeated and impoverished, off their land to work for white settlers. By 1807 Britain abolished slavery in its colonies—some argued that wage labor would be cheaper. In the Cape Colony slaves were finally freed in 1834. From then on, capitalist labor systems dominated, drawing even the five powerful African kingdoms into trading networks and thus becoming increasingly dependent on British commodities. Wage labor emerged in the U.S. South thirty years after southern Africa when the passage of the Thirteenth Amendment at the end of the Civil War abolished slavery.

On both continents, I was beginning to see from this vantage point above the Atlantic, victories against slavery led to the reinstitution of white supremacy in other forms in the deadly logic of a settler colonialism. The Masters and Servants Ordinance in 1843 in the Cape Colony made it criminal for a worker to break a contract (as more and more defeated Xhosas joined a tightly controlled labor force). Impatient with British control and abolition, the Boers set out on the Great Trek (1836–46), one in a series of migrations, expansions, and conquests that formed the Boer states of Transvaal and the Orange Free State and drove the Zulus into the growing black labor underclass subjected to pass laws, disenfranchisement, and territorial segregation. *Boers*, who had been *Dutch*, became *Afrikaners* at about the same time that *free Englishmen*, having become *white*, became *southern*.

I looked up as the stewardess arrived with dinner, and I opted for the wine. The clouds colored brilliantly beneath us, sun sinking through them, then night fell and the pencil lights above our seats clicked on. I went to check on Marta, then returned to burrow into my book, at turns for the next two hours alert then drowsy.

In 1870 diamond fields were discovered near Kimberley on Boer land quickly annexed by the British. The discovery changed the region's history forever from strategic backwater to wealthy bastion of empire. As the diamond fields opened, the first sizable black industrial workforce emerged to create huge profits for the English. Cecil Rhodes rapidly amassed control through the De Beers Consolidated Mines Company that became "the most impregnable monopoly in the world."[12] In 1886 the discovery of a vein of gold along the Witwatersrand, also Boer territory, opened the largest known gold deposits in the world—part of a series of gold reefs stretching three hundred miles, and deep under the ground, requiring major capital outlays of the new Rand barons, such as Cecil Rhodes. Mahatma Gandhi, who spent early

years among the Indian population in South Africa, remarked sardonically: "It is related that someone asked the late President Kruger whether there was gold in the
moon. He replied that it was highly unlikely because, if there were, the English
would have annexed it. Many problems can be solved by remembering that money
is their God."[13] Gandhi would soon be leading South Africa's Indians in a campaign
of nonviolent resistance to racist immigration laws, one of his earliest experiments in
satyagraha, or soul force, that along with violent uprisings freed India from British
rule.

With all of this wealth, no wonder South Africa was the last of the African
colonies to win independence, I reflected. Back in Tuskegee, we'd had mainly pine
trees and cotton, with the boll weevil gnawing away on one end and polyester gutting
cotton markets on the other, nary a gold nugget in sight. I remembered Daddy working with a group of people to get a little sewing factory in Macon County, which most
industry avoided because of its overwhelmingly black majority. In nearby Tallassee,
on the other hand, the huge textile mill loomed over the river, cotton flying out its
windows and into workers' lungs inside as they spun cotton to threads.

I drifted off to sleep, tilting back in my seat across the Atlantic waters, deep with
diamond fishes, swimming through reefs of gold in currents of bones. Too soon the
morning light woke me. I brushed my teeth with the miniscule toothbrush supplied
by South African Airlines and picked up the book again, awaiting breakfast.

Below me and to the south, gold and diamonds produced a growing appetite for
cheap labor forced to mine the low-grade ore deep in the ground: for one ounce of
gold, miners must bring four tons of rock to the surface. In 1894 the Glen Grey
Act, or the Native Bill for South Africa, divided up the remaining communal land
into individual tracts to destroy remnants of communal life and drive those people
on it to work in the mines, in a way similar to Hawaiian Māhele or the Dawes Sev-
eralty Act in the United States. "Every black man cannot have three acres and a
cow. We have to face the question and it must be brought home to them that in the
future nine-tenths of them will have to spend their lives in daily labour, in physical work, in manual labour," Rhodes explained, although there seems little question the tenth to which he belonged.[14] A racial division of labor in the mines gave
the skilled and relatively higher paying jobs to whites, who organized into trade
unions that would often wage militant struggles against white capital.[15] Rhodes also
carved Rhodesia, to the north, as his personal empire through his British South
Africa Company, founded in 1889. He called for the "extension of British rule
throughout the world . . . the entire Continent of Africa, the Holy Land, the Valley of the Euphrates," ending with "the ultimate recovery of the United States of
America as integral part of the British Empire"—a grandiose statement even for a
Rand baron.[16]

Out the window in the rising light, through the clouds, finally I glimpsed land, the
southward swerve of the great continent's western hump, like the horizon can evoke
the earth's curve. Africa. I would have only ten days, in two cities of a vast continent,

an abbreviated view suggested by the narrow sketch of shore framed in the plane's window.

The British rapidly consolidated their control of the region's wealth, defeating the last of the independent African societies. They then turned on the Boers in the second Anglo-Boer war with a devastating scorched-earth policy similar to Sherman's March to the Sea that torched Atlanta. British rounded up Boers in what the Brits called concentration camps, one of their legacies for a new century. This war left the Boers the residue of an embittered, defeated white racial identity—not unlike white southerners after the defeat of the Confederacy. I remembered the tags on old Chevy pickups in Alabama that showed an aging Confederate veteran with a stump for a leg and a flag draped over one shoulder. The caption read: "Forget? HELL!"

The British after their victory renegotiated with the embittered Boers, drawing them in 1910 back into the new, white supremacist Union of South Africa closely allied with Britain—similar to the white South/North rapprochement after the removal of Union troops in 1875. Its constitution consolidated white minority rule and the ruthless repression of blacks, Indians, and coloreds by forging an alliance among white landowners, the white working class, and the English-speaking mining interests. It was illegal for Africans to strike; skilled jobs went to whites; blacks were banned from military service; and pass laws controlled travel. Land reform forced blacks, 70 percent of the population, onto 8 percent of the land. Consolidation of agriculture drove many Boer small farmers into urban poverty, creating a poor white problem so that by 1933, 30 percent of whites were poor enough not to adequately feed their families.[17]

Segregation in the U.S. South had not been so stark, a matter of Colored Town or The Quarter on one side of the track, or the highway, or down a hill, where houses segued to shacks. Bathrooms and water fountains were marked "white" and "colored" as if urine, H_2O, and feces were raced. There was no equivalent to the South African policy of homelands or Bantustans, reserves where the white minority forced vast majorities to live and from which Africans could emerge only with permission in their hated pass books, to work in a country in which they were not citizens; perhaps it amounted to the different labor needs in a plantation and a mining economy. Voter disenfranchisement at home had taken other forms: gerrymandering (Tuskegee was drawn with twenty-seven sides), the poll tax, inequitably administered literacy tests, outright intimidation. In South Africa, black demands for freedom of movement, land, living wage, and freedom of association were met by force and increasingly repressive legislation, as well as secret Afrikaner paramilitary groups similar to the Klan resurgence in the 1910s and 1920s in the United States. In South Africa, profits in mining, agriculture, and industry continued to depend on a low-wage African workforce whose movements were tightly controlled.

Afrikaner discontent developed into apartheid with the Afrikaner electoral victory in 1948. Afrikaners had continually been at the bottom of the white economy. Both agriculture and industrial capital were run by local individual proprietors.

Their sectors were profitable only with tariffs and subsidies paid for out of taxation of the imperialist British mining industry and by cheap black labor. During the 1940s many African industrial workers unionized, and their militant action produced a rise in African industrial wages of 50 percent between 1939 and 1948. Afrikaner capitalists (in agriculture), small businessmen, and workers mobilized racist Afrikaner nationalism into victory for its program of apartheid in 1948, promising to push the black unemployed back into the reserves, stemming the "flood of natives to the cities."[18] In the late 1940s and early 1950s, apartheid brought a strengthened prohibition of mixed marriages, making interracial sex illegal, increasing segregation, and strengthening the pass laws—a system that stayed in place, and intensified, until 1990. The need to protect apartheid turned South Africa into a police state.

Apartheid was "the most terrible dream in the world," Chief Albert Luthuli, general secretary of the African National Congress, explained when he won the 1961 Nobel Peace Prize for his work as president general of the ANC. But it was held "not by a crackpot group on the fringe . . . [but was] the deliberate policy of a government, supported actively by a large part of the white population and tolerated passively by an overwhelming white majority." There was nothing new in South Africa's apartheid ideas, but apartheid was unique in the degree to which the practices were "stubbornly defended, extended and bolstered up by legislation at the time when in the major part of the world they are . . . either being shamefacedly hidden behind concealing formulations, or are being steadily scrapped. These ideas survive in South Africa because those who sponsor them profit by them."[19]

"We will soon touch down in Cape Town," the stewardess announced as I adjusted my tray table for the descent. Out the window, the continent's tip was rectangled with streets and houses and a bay beyond the mountains. Ground loomed closer and closer until the bump of wheels announced we had landed. I found Marta again, washed my face, and stretched my legs, relocating for the next, much shorter, jog to Jo'burg, which soon stretched broad around us, an industrial city sprung up out of the bushveld plains and built on fourteen mines—on racist wealth and power—its other name *eGoli* (city of gold, in Nguni). Jo'burg is the largest city in Africa, in fact the largest city south of Cairo, and furnishes 35 percent of South Africa's GNP. Its population is three million; the nearby black township of Soweto, the site of major uprisings against apartheid in the 1970s, another two million. The political capital of Pretoria is a short drive to the north; but Johannesburg served as the financial capital of the South African state, and the apartheid regime.

The airport was huge, we soon found, bustling, bright with glass and metal and neon advertisements for Visa, American Express, and booths for changing myriad currencies. Marta and I waited to get our luggage—mercifully, it arrived! —before going through customs and having our passports stamped "South Africa."

"DOWN WITH THE POTATOSHIP!"

We hailed a cab and headed to a hotel in Yeoville, driving through this city less than a decade removed from the "most terrible dream in the world." Marta and I settled into the large hotel, now a Holiday Inn but obviously formerly much ritzier, in a neighborhood where many white residents have moved to gated suburbs farther out, so that now rates are cheaper. We had supper, and soon it was 11:00 P.M. — but only 4:00 P.M. at home, and who was sleeping?

We turned on the television while I waited for Barb to call. It was World AIDS Day. We had heard Mandela on the radio in the ride in the cab from the airport, urging people to break the silences, to keep from filling more cemeteries. In Zimbabwe, I read on the plane that because of AIDS over the next decade life expectancy will drop from 55.3 to 30.4 years for males, from 58.6 to 31.7 years for females.[20] Since the start of the epidemic, 83 percent of all AIDS deaths have been in sub-Saharan Africa and at least 95 percent of all AIDS orphans have been African. Yet only 10 percent of the world's people live in Africa south of the Sahara.[21] On one talk show there was an AIDS educator from Ghana, which has an excellent program inspired by Cubans. Ghana had sent twenty-seven people to Cuba on a solidarity trip, and the Cuban government tested them for HIV and found that twenty-four were positive. With this information, they urged the Ghanaian government to respond to the epidemic, and they did.

There was also news of the second national election, coming up in 1999. The government had held voter registration over three days the weekend before, with 3.7 million of 12 million voters registered. The African National Congress was trying to secure a two-thirds majority in the legislature, which would allow it to change the constitution. Thabo Mbeki was the ANC candidate for president to replace Mandela. He was running on a platform of anticorruption, the need for democratic government, accommodating tribal differences, and complementing trade with development assistance. Mbeki was now playing a key role in seeking a political solution to the ongoing war in the Democratic Republic of the Congo, where six African armies competed over territory in the wake of the West's abandonment of strongman President Mobuto Sese Seko (of the former Zaire) at the end of the Cold War. Recent polls indicated a decline in support for the ANC, given the slow process in transition and huge job losses.

Other big news was a sex scandal, African style — hardly titillating for this U.S. citizen jaded by what Bill Clinton did with his cigar to Monica Lewinsky. Canaan Banana, former president of Zimbabwe, was apparently recently convicted of sodomy and unnatural acts with a male bodyguard. He had fled to South Africa and just gotten in to see Mandela, seeking asylum. The president's spokesman called Banana's case a "matter of infidelity" and said that it was debatable whether or not in South Africa his transgressions were a crime given the new constitution's protections of sexual orientation. "It's more an issue with his wife," was Mandela's position.

At about 1:00 A.M., we clicked off the TV, turned off the lights, and settled in. It was 6:00 P.M. at home, and I tossed and turned for an hour or two, then finally whispered: "Marta? Are you awake?" "Yess," she whispered back, and we both bolted up in bed laughing and turned on the lights. "Let's order room service," I said, reaching for the menu, and we ordered a sandwich and french fries, eating voraciously our 4:00 A.M. picnic. I took the chance to ask her more questions about her experiences in El Salvador.

"During the civil war in my country," she remembered, "they would have demonstrations in the United States, and my sister would take her children, who were just little things then. They grew up in that time. Before they could walk, they would see El Salvador on the news and crawl up the stairs shouting, '*Salvador! Mommie, Salvador!*' The kids would come home from demonstrations shouting 'Down with the potatoship!' It took Elsie a little while to figure what they had heard—'Down with the dictatorship!' Potatoship," Marta laughed. "Can you imagine that? When I went home after the peace accords were signed in 1992, there was still violence everywhere. People who had lived in violence wanted to resolve everything by violence, especially against women and children. There were rapes, molestation. I almost had a breakdown. I stayed in my house for three weeks. I cried and cried. I sat under a tree in my courtyard, and I got very mad with God. I said, 'How could you do this! After all of the suffering and death, if this is what it came to I don't want to live.'"

Marta shook her fist heavenward, and I could see her taking God on.

"Then one morning I heard a voice call my name. I said, 'Who are you,' and it said, 'You called me.'" Her eyes widened. "And since then I have had this voice in my spirit.'"

It was a story that I liked to hear. It explained much about my friend.

"For years I fought for justice; but now I realize that we have to *be* justice, to *be* peace, to *be* love," she said.

This was familiar to me, Marta's I AM. Marta's emphasis was similar to Howard Thurman's on the need for a powerful inner life, with all the spiritual discipline such a life required. Marta's favorite story was the parable of the one hundred monkeys. Somewhere in Latin America, went the version she told to me, there were scientists trying to teach a colony of monkeys to wash their hands. First they taught one monkey, then two, then four, and fifteen. Those monkeys would go down to the river and wash their hands. Then the numbers climbed, to forty, sixty. And when one hundred monkeys had learned to wash their hands, lo and behold, monkeys all over the world began washing their hands. Those hundred monkeys had performed some evolutionary quantum leap for their species. It was a different approach to cadres—spiritual cadres, I guessed one might say.

Marta polished off the sandwich and fries on the room service tray at about 6:00 A.M. (midnight back home) and snagged a couple of packets of sugar and Cremora for her stash to take back home. Then we dropped off for several hours of sleep before our noon meeting.

A little after noon we were seated in a restaurant in Yeoville with Karin Koen, co-convenor of the National Coalition for Gay/Lesbian Equality. Karin grew up in Capetown but had lived in Johannesburg for three years. The coalition office was nearby in this neighborhood just north of the central city, one of the few mixed-race neighborhoods in the larger metropolitan area. I ordered curry and samp, a corn dish very much like hominy grits and (still sleepy from our night's adventures) strong coffee.

When I had called to confirm our lunch date, Karin explained that Simon Nkoli had died, finally, of AIDS. I had met Simon and Zachie Achmat, one of the coalition's directors, in New York City at the 1996 Black Nations/Queer Nations Conference that Jacqui Alexander helped organize. Simon made the first link between gay identity and the antiapartheid struggle when he came out in prison to his ANC comrades awaiting trial for treason in the mid-1980s. I remembered Simon's parenthetical query at Black Nations/Queer Nations: "we are calling ourselves 'queer' now?" Maybe *we* should be asking *you* what the norms are, it occurred to me. South African lesbians and gays had won protection in the constitution, the labor law, and more recently the country's supreme court had struck down its sodomy laws—none of which queer movements in the United States have achieved with thirty years of organizing. In fact, the United States lags behind South Africa, Norway, Sweden, the Netherlands, Israel, Canada, Denmark, Finland, Slovenia, France, Ireland, and New Zealand in legal protection at the national level for sexual orientation.[22] So much for the leaders of the free world!

Launching the organization in 1994 with the support of the African National Congress and the energy of constitutional reform, the coalition's leadership was determined to encourage a more representative and authentic South African gay movement than the white, middle class, male public face prevalent in the 1980s. More recently, Karin explained, desegregation of cities had led to a more visible black gay presence as young people escaped the more conservative rural areas and townships for the relative freedom of the city.[23] By Karin's account, the coalition, which had begun mostly as white men, was now majority black and 40 percent women. It was made up of seventy-six organizations within South Africa and in southern Africa. I had been interested to get the coalition's position on the Canaan Banana controversy. "In reality, the crime he is alleged to have committed would constitute incidents of rape. . . . NCGLE condemns any form of rape and non-consensual sex. . . . It is ironic that Banana who has been part of an oppressive regime which massacred people in Matabeleland, persecuted trade union activists and remained silent while Robert Mugabe undermined democracy and the rule of law in Zimbabwe, should now seek asylum."[24]

But there was a down side to the current situation in South Africa, we were beginning to see. There's a good bit of general dissatisfaction, Karin said, and much violence and crime. Unemployment was as high as 40 or 50 percent. Whites were angry at the loss of control and what they saw as deterioration in the country.

"What's the source of the violence?" I asked.

Deep anger at the decades of torture and violence, she replied. Poverty, gender destabilization, sexism. It was not dissimilar to the conditions Marta had described in El Salvador after the peace accords in 1992, where death squads and the disappeared gave way to urban gangs, machine-gun toting private security guards hulking over Avon shipments and new supermarkets, an escalation of rape and violence against women and children: a more generalized climate of social, rather than political, terror.

We did not linger long after lunch. Karin was helping to organize a memorial service for Simon, so we parted company, arranging to come to the memorial the next day.

SHALOM ON THE BUS LINE

Marta and I decided to head downtown to the Museum of Africa and the Market Theater. Marta suggested we take the bus. So we stood on the street in Yeoville, watching stores' wares spill out onto the sidewalk in colorful array. A white woman joined us. She was probably in her sixties, dark-haired and fair-skinned, her lipstick not totally congruent with her lips. She turned to us and started to complain, pointing to trash on the street: "It didn't used to be like this," she said bitterly.

"Are you from this neighborhood?" I asked, and she nodded.

"How long have you lived here?" It turned out that she was Hungarian and had moved to South Africa with her husband thirty years ago. They divorced, and she felt stuck in the country. The bus pulled up, and we all climbed aboard. Marta engaged her. "The rand went to hell," the woman said bitterly. Gold prices had fallen in the 1980s due to competition from other continents. "All these people don't want to work," she gestured to the dark faces around us on the bus. "They destroyed it. It was a beautiful city. Now you can't walk around."

From the seat behind, I recognized her familiar, hard-core racism. She was ranting about small brains and no morals. But the bitterness of her complaints about the current state of Johannesburg and South Africa echoed what our black cab drivers had been saying for the past two days. There are too many immigrants and not enough jobs. Crime is rampant, and everybody is afraid. There is corruption in the government. Will the ANC try to fix the elections?

"My heart starts hurting," Marta said to me in the backseat of one of these cabs. "People sound like this in El Salvador now, after all the fighting and suffering. Everywhere it's the same thing over and over." Then she launched into a discussion with the cabbie: "You really must vote," she said. Our second cabbie was going to vote, but swore he would not vote for a black man.

Good Lord, I had thought to myself bleakly.

Now Marta broke the Hungarian woman's diatribe. "Are you a Christian?"

"No, I'm Jewish."

"You are talking about lack of peace. In your tradition, whenever we do justice to all of creation, then there is Shalom."

"So how long do I have to wait for it?" she snapped back. "I am not religious, and I don't steal from anybody, and I don't dirty the streets."

"Stealing is not just taking money," Marta persisted, "but taking chances from people."

We arrived at a corner, where we needed to transfer to another bus. This was the heart of Johannesburg, and the sidewalks bustled with African street merchants, pedestrians, men, women, and children milling around or sitting on the stoops of stores. Vendors' stalls lined the sidewalks. Tomatoes, cabbages, squash rested in pyramids; corn in yellow rows; avocados and onions piled next to cheap hats, shirts, and toys. People thronged here, poor, black, hoping to make their week's livelihood with one or two sales. We approached a bench, on which a light-skinned woman whom I assumed was colored was sitting.

"Would you move over?" our Hungarian acquaintance asked. The woman on the bench began to slide over then thought better of it.

"I was sitting here," she said, settling in more solidly. "Why should I move?"

The Hungarian woman moved to the next bench, and I sat amiably down on the portion of the bench that remained beside its original occupant, my butt halfway off. She was like her Hungarian antagonist in that she began an immediate social commentary with a stranger.

"Look at this dirt," she pointed to banana peels on the street. "It was not like this before the democratic government."

"What accounts for it?" I asked her as she climbed with us onto the next bus and settled into adjacent seats. At the front of the bus, Marta was still working on the Hungarian.

"People have moved to the city from the countryside, and there just are not enough jobs," her voice softened some. "They also come from other countries. There's not work, so they steal. They don't just steal, they kill."

"All roads lead to Johannesburg," I remembered from *Cry, the Beloved Country.* "If you are white or if you are black they lead to Johannesburg. If the crops fail, there is work in Johannesburg. If there are taxes to be paid, there is work in Johannesburg. If the farm is too small to be divided further, some must go to Johannesburg."[25] And that was 1948. I watched out the bus window as we went down Bree Street, also thronged with vendors and people milling. I had also read that Johannesburg has 25 percent of the industrial capacity for southern Africa, which is also drawing people here for jobs.

My companion continued, "Under the pass laws of apartheid, blacks and Indians could only be here in the daytime. I am colored and could move around. But now anyone can come. There are squatters."

We had seen the shanty towns in the parks in a city once tightly controlled by the most racist regime in the world. Shacks built from planks at the hospital left by builders, corrugated iron at the reformatory, sacks at the station neatly in bundles.[26] A century before, mining interests had kept black labor cheap by making it migratory, with women and children living in rural areas and male laborers given contracts for no more than a year. The various control methods over the years were based on the Stallard principle. Africans could come into cities only to "minister to the needs of whites."[27] More than three million Africans had been displaced into Bantustans with supposed self-rule that meant Africans could not be citizens of South Africa or vote in its elections. The pass laws were the target of the defiance campaign in the 1950s. It was organized by African National Congress "Young Turks" like Mandela and Oliver Tambo, radicalized by apartheid. More than eight thousand had gone to jail after entering libraries reserved for whites, or using post office counters, or sitting on railway benches, or camping in open ground in the middle of white cities, and this three to seven years before the Montgomery bus boycott (1956) and the Greensboro sit-ins (1960). The defiance campaign brought the treason trials of 1955 and the Suppression of Communism Act, under which any resistance to the white state was considered communist-inspired subversion.

Now the city built on reefs of gold was teeming with all the people it had exploited, forbidden, and repressed—with their high expectations and hopes, their bitterness and desperation. So many poor people in such a rich country! No telling how many billions had come out of South Africa's gold and diamond mines over the century. I suspected that structural-adjustment-type programs were part of the context for the current economic crisis. I later read on the Web that the new South Africa government had, indeed, introduced its own version of structural adjustment in 1996. The Growth Employment and Redistribution Program emphasized deficit reduction rather than meeting people's needs. Lack of tariffs had exacerbated unemployment with, for example, the collapse of the textile industry when sweatshops moved on to East Asia, where wages were even lower. The ANC, according to antiapartheid activist and poet Dennis Brutus, was installing water meters where once, even under apartheid, water had been free to poor people, and it was preparing to privatize electricity.[28] "Between a Rock and a Hard Place" was the title of Brutus's article; but he indicated that many grassroots people who had once organized against apartheid were beginning to organize against the government. The bus let us off near the museum, and we said good-bye to our traveling companions.

The Museum of Africa was one of the few accessible public places in Johannesburg that recorded and reflected on South Africa's history. The exhibits laid out the context in which the ANC crafted its Freedom Charter (1955), declaring the ANC's program for multiracial democracy: "South Africa belongs to all who live in it, black and white." It was a far-reaching and visionary call for liberation. The treason trials tried 156 leading activists for high treason under the Suppression of Communism Act. In March 1960, South African struggle entered a new stage when police fired indiscriminately into a crowd of thousands of people protesting the pass laws in Sharpeville, killing 67 and wounding 186, an incident that led to worldwide censure of South Africa, whose Parliament responded by decreeing a state of emergency that gave police broad powers.

In December 1961, Umkhonto We Sizwe, "Spear of the Nation," declared the beginning of armed struggle against apartheid: "The choice is not ours; it has been made by the Nationalist Government, which has rejected every peaceable demand by the people for rights and freedom and answered every such demand with force and yet more force." Of the four forms of political violence available (sabotage, guerilla warfare, terrorism, and open revolution), MK chose sabotage because it did not "involve loss of life, and it offered the best hope for future race relations"[29] Mandela and Oliver Tambo left the country to build support and gain resources from independent African nations and, in Mandela's case, to study guerilla warfare. "Nonviolent passive resistance is effective as long as your opposition adheres to the same rules as you do," he later reflected. "But if peaceful protest is met with violence, its efficacy is at an end. For me, nonviolence was not a moral principle but a strategy; there is no moral goodness in using an ineffective weapon."[30] He wanted to learn "the fundamental principles for starting a revolution," and he turned to Mao, Che Guevara, Fidel Castro, Menachem Begin, the histories of Ethiopia, Kenya, Algeria, and the Cameroons, as well as South Africa's past.[31]

After spending several hours in the museum, Marta and I walked around the corner and under the massive highway to visit a community agency that worked with children through art. Their fair was the next week, not this one; but the organizer generously showed us around their gallery, tucked into an open space under the bridges that had once been a warehouse. On the walls was children's art from South Africa and all around the world. Our host's face lit up as he explained their work with children, and I recognized in him one of the many millions of people working daily in South Africa to keep its dreams alive.

SIMON'S FUNERAL

Marta and I took a taxi to Simon Nkoli's memorial. We arrived at the corner of Wanderers and De Villiers Streets, after yet another heated discussion with a cabbie. It was Friday evening, our last in Johannesburg. We walked around the corner to the main entrance, walking past a bevy of black dykes waiting to go inside. I had a feeling of déjà vu, as if I were in Atlanta or sections of New York: the jeans, the baseball caps, the familiar stride. Once inside, Marta and I helped Karin fold programs, then we found a seat in the cathedral, its vaulted ceilings echoing the opening hymn, "I'm Coming Home."

A succession of speakers painted a portrait of Simon as a brave, vibrant man, the "founder of the black gay movement in South Africa." The Dulmas treason trial, in which he had been one of the defendants, occurred in the mid-1980s when the long struggle against apartheid was heating up to civil war. In 1978, newly elected President P. W. Botha had launched a total strategy of cross-border raids and internal political violence, moving the government from repression to torture, abduction, arson, and sabotage that gave the security forces virtually unlimited power. In the early

1980s the ANC escalated guerilla attacks to include military and civilian targets to show that not only MK soldiers bleed. Black youth set out to make the townships ungovernable, defying armed police with petrol bombs and necklacing suspected collaborators by putting gasoline-filled tires around their necks and lighting them. The broad-based United Democratic Front, organized in 1983, carried on mass campaigns of marches, demonstrations, strikes, and boycotts. An international campaign of economic sanctions put pressure on the country's economy. Simon chose to come out to his ANC comrades at this pivotal time in the struggle. When Simon got out of jail and went in search of other gay people, he found the Gay Association of South Africa, a white organization—"which he proceeded, in his inimitable way, to turn upside down." He went on to found GLOW, the Gays and Lesbians of the Witwatersrand.

Many at the memorial service testified to Simon's remarkable effect on them:

"Simon had this amazing belief that things were going to happen."

"I was Simon's lover at the time of the Dulmas trial, and I felt I was the only white man opposed to the Nationalist government. Now there is wider support. Many people were liberated by Simon."

"Simon challenged my view in 1985 that the apartheid judiciary could be trusted, forcing me to confront its gross injustices. It was a political awakening to the magnitude of my own arrogance. Simon and the events of 1985 were my personal turning point, showing me the interconnectedness of all forms of discrimination."

Patrick "Terror" Lekota, one of Simon's treason trial jailmates and now chairperson of the ANC, stepped to the podium to recall Simon's transforming influence on his heterosexual comrades and his "capacity to sustain enthusiasm when all seemed to be lost." Lekota continued: "Over time, all of us acknowledged that Simon's coming out was an important learning experience. His presence . . . broadened our vision. . . . How could we say that men and women like Simon, who had put their shoulders to the wheel to end apartheid, how could we say that they should now be discriminated against?"

Now Zachie Achmat was at the podium. Simon's coming out in prison, Zachie Achmat explained, was the Southern Hemisphere's equivalent to Stonewall, the 1969 riots against police violence that often marks the beginning of gay liberation in the Northern Hemisphere. Zachie, three years younger than Simon, was politicized in high school during the 1976 uprising of African youth in Soweto. Influenced by the Black Consciousness Movement, Soweto students protested Bantu education. When police opened fire they fought back, a kind of *intifada*. "What frightened me more than anything was the attitude of the children," a reporter would recall. "Many seemed oblivious to the danger. They continued running towards the police dodging and ducking."[32] Rioting and burning of buildings spread and intensified, fury fed by heightened military response that spread to other parts of the country and lasted throughout the year. The cycles of violence that erupted in the mid-1970s continued into the 1980s. Zachie heard about Soweto as a schoolboy, and the police shootings of school kids politicized him. He organized his first demonstration and was arrested and beaten by police.

"Simon taught me that lesbian and gay rights are indivisible from human rights," Zachie continued of the man who opened a door that many other South African gays and lesbians walked through. Simon brought both black people and liberation ideology into the gay subculture, giving black gays a political home by fusing the freedom struggle with gay community activism, to provide redemption from personal trauma and family rejection. Zachie gave a passionate call for the South African government to take more of a role in bringing down the prohibitive cost of AIDS drugs.

Simon helped give a face to AIDS in South Africa, said the next speaker, Enea Motaung, from the Township AIDS Project. Simon had been infected with HIV for twelve years. He found public disclosure of his HIV status more difficult than coming out.

The tributes came to an end. We all stood for the familiar strains of the national anthem, "Nkosi sikelel'i Africa" (God bless Africa!) . . . fists raised pew by pew in farewell. Simon, comrade in struggle, friend, generous teacher—rest in peace.

After the service I said hello to Zachie, and he invited me for a drink later in the evening.

A few hours later, a cab dropped me off at a house on a hill above Johannesburg, at what turned out to be Justice Edwin Cameron's house—the openly gay member of the South African Supreme Court. I appreciated Zachie's hospitality and his intensity. Infected with HIV, he was now an AIDS activist, at one time smuggling into South Africa from Thailand 5,000 generic tablets of Fluconazole, used to treat thrush, at 2 percent the South African cost. Zachie had refused to go on antiretrovirals such as AZT because most HIV-infected people in Africa could not afford the drug. He opted for Fluconazole, and his immune system had rallied.[33]

I enjoyed a drink with the guys as we talked about the remarkable advances that the coalition had made in just four years, the upcoming World Council meeting, and the needs of gays and lesbians in southern Africa. It was the coalition's position that it would be very destructive for fledgling lesbian/gay movements in southern Africa should the WCC Assembly split over the question of homosexuality. Late in the evening, I wished them good night and got a ride back to the hotel.

The next morning, Marta and I checked out as Marta joked with the concierge, the bellman, and the maids, who took a second to register her attention before they broke into broad smiles. Traveling with Marta was a bit like floating on a sea of good vibes that she generated by careful, humorous attention. She had increased her stash of tea bags and sugar from the hotel's larders and was carrying a wooden crate she had found on the street, which would become a bookshelf back at her house in Nauizalca. At the huge, shiny Jan Smuts International Airport, we boarded another plane and took off for Zimbabwe. The flight gave me time to reflect on the brief but intense hit of South Africa I'd experienced over the past few days.

I had come to South Africa perhaps naively wanting a dose of hope and courage. I had glimpsed a more complex future than I previously allowed in this country struggling still for its people's freedom. Apartheid might be gone, but racism and economic exploitation and poverty were not. Our three days here had been understated compared to the country's dramatic history; we had taken a bus ride, attended a funeral, and visited a museum and a community organization. In these few days, I had glimpsed frustration on the streets and in taxis. But I had also seen the courage, grace, and hope that carried South Africans through the bitter struggle against apartheid.

"What we need is more presence with the people, not more presidents!" Marta pronounced of both El Salvador and South Africa as our plane lifted off the tarmac in Johannesburg: it was a prescription for the everyday but heroic courage of all people in this emerging new world order who continue to stand between a rock and a hard place, doing the daily work and the dreaming of more humane ways of being.

9

HARARE
Toward a Third Liberation

*Greed, naked, pitiless lust for wealth and power, lie back of all of Europe's
interest in Africa and the white world knows it and is not ashamed.*
—W.E.B. DU BOIS, *An ABC of Color*

*While the Third World is experiencing the immediacy of people's need for
healing in the area of physical hunger, the West is awakening to spiritual hunger
so dramatic as to be almost frightening.*
— MALIDOMA PATRICE SOMÉ, *The Healing Wisdom of Africa*

*A body of local private capitalists, even if they are black, can never free Africa;
they will simply sell it into new slavery to old masters overseas.*
— W.E.B. DU BOIS, *An ABC of Color*

THE South African Airlines jet flew north from Johannesburg toward Harare (formerly Salisbury), the capital of Zimbabwe (the former Rhodesia), one of the smallest countries in Africa, its population 11.3 million. Marta and I nestled into side-by-side seats for this leg of the flight, and I pulled out *Welcome to Zimbabwe* and another WCC publication, *Drumbeat of Life: Jubilee in an African Context*, as I turned my attention to the contradictions we would face at the end of this plane ride. By the time of the WCC Assembly, the unemployment rate in Zimbabwe was 45 percent and human rights abuses were widespread. What was President Robert Mugabe's transit from liberator to demagogue, Zimbabwe's from national liberation and African socialism to a nation-state in crisis under the enforced free market of structural adjustment? To what extent was I equipped to answer these questions?

I noted another fact. Half a century ago, only one-third of the World Council's membership was from the Southern Hemisphere; now it was two-thirds. Clearly the impetus of Christianity had shifted from Northern Hemisphere to Southern. What did it mean that Africa, the poorest continent, was the fastest growing in terms of converts, for Africa, for the church, and for what Howard Thurman called the religion of Jesus?

"The eighth assembly takes place at a time when 20 percent of the world's population controls 84 percent of the world's resources—and the gap is growing," *Drumbeat* informed me. "It takes place in a world where forty thousand people, most of them children, die every day of starvation and of preventable diseases. The economies of the two-thirds world are controlled by international financial institutions such as the World Bank, the International Monetary Fund (IMF), and the World Trade Organization (WTO, formerly GATT). These institutions are in effect modern slave-masters."[1] As we flew north to Harare, Mozambique lay to the east, Zambia and Botswana to the west. Perhaps we were retracing the Pioneer Column of Cecil Rhodes's invasion in pursuit of even more gold. The queen gave him a royal charter for his British South Africa Company in 1889 with powers of government for an area inhabited by Shona and Ndebele people. Four years later, whites had conquered Mashonaland and Matabeleland, and the resulting country became Southern Rhodesia (later Rhodesia). It took only three years for the Shona and Ndebele to rise up against white encroachment in the first *chimurenga* (war of liberation), which white settlers defeated. When white hopes of gold proved chimerical and other sources of profit necessary, the new Rhodesians followed the pattern of Europeans all over Africa. By 1923, the British South Africa Company gave administration over to white settlers and Rhodesia became a self-governing colony with the best land in the country reserved for whites, and with racial discrimination legalized and towns set aside as dormitories for black labor.[2]

By the end of World War II, African resistance was continent-wide and part of a global insurgency. By 1948 the British bowed to the Gandhi-led nonviolent uprising in India, the next year Mao declared a new Republic in China as Ho Chi Minh led guerilla forces in Vietnam. The 1945 Fifth Pan-African Congress (in Manchester, England) helped set in motion people's movements for independence on the continent in the postwar years that were even then being shaped by the Bretton Woods Institutions, the United Nations, and organizations such as the World Council. The century had opened with the first Pan-African Congress ("more pan than African") in London in 1900. There W.E.B. Du Bois—to become both a premier architect of U.S. Civil Rights and the "father of Pan-Africanism"—clarified that the problem of the color line is "the question as to how far differences of race . . . are going to be made, hereafter, the basis of denying to over half the world the right of sharing to their utmost ability the opportunities and privileges of modern civilization."[3]

Attended by Kwame Nkrumah of Ghana, Kenya's Jomo Kenyatta, Northern Rhodesia's Harry Nkumbula, and Peter Abrahams of South Africa, the 1945 Congress saw the torch of Pan-Africanism passed from Africans of the Diaspora to Africans of the continent. Ghana would be the first country to gain post–World War II independence, under the leadership of Nkrumah. There a Positive Action Campaign based on the Free India movement and satyagraha mobilized waves of direct action—"the freedom movement . . . become a way of existence"—forcing the British to call for elections and resulting in Ghana's independence in 1957, a celebration attended by Martin Luther King Jr., himself in the first years of nonviolent struggle in Alabama. "Free at last, free at last!" Nkrumah boomed, a phrase that resonated deeply with the young African American preacher. "The independence of Ghana itself is meaningless unless the whole of Africa is free," Nkrumah proclaimed. Independence worked its way southward, a "logical movement to go down the continent."[4] Du Bois—who "had finally concluded that this weeping woman's promised land [of the United States] was a cruel, receding mirage for people of color"— soon chose to live out his days in West Africa,[5] his death in Ghana in 1963 announced from the podium of the U.S. March on Washington only moments before Martin Luther King rolled into the now-familiar cadences, "I have a dream," resonating between continents linked by deep channels of Atlantic current below the Middle Passage.[6]

As revolutionary and nationalist movements swept southward, Britain granted Rhodesia a constitution that would have included a Declaration of Rights and a multiracial constitution, but the Rhodesian government led by Ian Smith in 1965 refused this offer, unilaterally declaring independence. Four years later the government submitted a racist constitution that was passed by 72 percent of voters, with 85,000 whites and 5,500 blacks taking part. The second *chimurenga*, or war of liberation, was by then under way. Nationalist forces were represented by both the Zimbabwe African National Union (ZANU) and Zimbabwe African People's Union (ZAPU), an offshoot of the African National Congress. After fourteen years of war, ZANU-PF won the first multiracial election, declaring an independent Zimbabwe on April 18, 1980, with Robert Mugabe, ZANU leader, as the first prime minister.

The old Rhodesia left the new Zimbabwe a capitalist mode of production and the British system of public administration. "The only changes made in many restrictive laws were to simply exchange the word Rhodesia for that of Zimbabwe and continue as before," one church document lamented.[7] If Zimbabwe inherited the old colonial system, it added a Soviet-style single-party system modeled on a tightly controlled party leadership.[8] Standards of living for most Zimbabweans did improve in the 1980s under Zimbabwe's version of African socialism. A program of Growth with Equity sought to achieve high rates of growth and incomes and rural development, with social services for the majority.[9] By 1992 literacy was 37.5 percent in rural areas, 92.4 percent in urban areas, and secondary schools increased from 179 in 1980 to 1,529 in 1996.[10] But the foundation for such progress proved short lived, and by the end of the 1980s Zimbabwe bankers reported an underperforming economy. The new government lacked a comprehensive development strategy, and excessive state regulations strangled investment flows, they said. Also, the richest industries and much of the land were still in white hands. The need to protect trade routes against RENAMO rebels in Mozambique and continuing destabilization from still-apartheid South Africa drew off vital resources. All of these contributed to create budget deficits, rising inflation, decline in foreign investment, and balance of payment difficulties—and delivered Zimbabwe to the structural adjustment programs (SAPs).[11]

So Zimbabwe has the worst of both worlds, I shook my head as we circled Harare, an International Monetary Fund–driven free market economy and a one-party state. I put my reading aside to fill out the customs form.

Soon we filed onto the tarmac of an airport about the size of Durham's, but with huge colorful metal birds spread across the asphalt. This port announced itself as different from the glitter and power of Jan Smuts's airport in Jo'burg, as did the ride on the bus into town on a road winding through grassy countryside shaded by huge trees, some of them blooming fire—*flambeau*—or the salmon-flowered and ruby-throated hibiscus, or the roadside livestock, small houses, laundry out to dry. If not Alabama, this was country, slower, familiar from my childhood. The bus meandered into downtown Harare, down streets of high-rises and offices and stores also with a familiar feel except for the palm trees, and finally on to the campus of the University of Zimbabwe, closed down for eight months by Mugabe in fear of student strikes over the price of food and rises in student fees. Finding registration, Marta and I queued up for our packets and to get room assignments in one of the large brick dorms of the university. After what seemed hours, we settled into small adjacent rooms, unpacked our clothes, and ventured out to explore the sprawling campus accommodating the World Council's eighth assembly.

By Sunday, we had negotiated the verdant campus, wet with seasonal rains and muddy trenches being dug to hold new computer cables, into which more than one WCCer would fall over the next week. We found the various cafeterias, the meeting hall for the General Assembly (which as visitors we could not attend), the classrooms in which the Padare would take place, the Internet Café, and a worship tent for morning and evening services, all in tents and buildings dispersed over a sprawling campus. A craft area spread across a swath of lawn, blankets and clothes lines rich with batik, Shona sculpture, brightly painted cups, toy cars and bikes sculpted of wire, African jewelry. WCC staff had arrived the week before, and there were plenty of signs pointing directions to events. The "oasies," tents selling soft drinks, beer, and wine provided a friendly meeting place over the next week. There on Sunday we hooked up with the other U.S. Urban-Rural Mission (URM) delegates—Jacqui Alexander, Carol Zippert, Leah Wise, and Nelson Carrasquillo. We also met regularly with our global URM counterparts to share experiences and track the decisions being made by delegates in the ongoing reshaping of the World Council.

We knew already that the fiftieth anniversary of an organization dedicated to ecumenism, or church unity, was bound to be fractious. "Go ye unto all the world," Jesus had commissioned the apostles. I'm not so sure he had colonialism in mind, however—for example, the missionaries who had marched into what soon became Rhodesia with Cecil Rhodes's Pioneer Column. This was an assembly to which

Christians from the four corners of the world had flocked, and in Harare the WCC would struggle with differences of West and East, North and South, male and female.

The presence of the African Independent Churches highlighted the North/South differences. These churches, founded by African spiritual leaders as a way to avoid colonial domination by Western missionaries, drew on indigenous forms. In them the earth-keeping spirit of indigenous culture and the presence of African ancestors blended with the Holy Spirit of the Christian Pentecost in what some Western (and Eastern) theologians charged was syncretism—the heretical attempt, as they saw it, to merge opposing principles. Reading these debates in WCC material, I decided that all culture is syncretistic, the most interesting spiritual developments consciously so. But, syncretistic or not, these churches had fifty million members, which included half of all Christians in Zimbabwe, with projections to include more African members by 2000 than the Roman Catholic and all the Protestant denominations together.[12] Theological purity is one thing. Folks in the pews is quite another.

Korean feminist theologian Chung Hyun Kyung had taken the syncretism question over the top in the previous WCC Assembly in Canberra, Australia, with her multimedia presentation on the gospel, drawing on Buddhism and shamanism from Korean culture. "This is taking things too far," the traditionalists had sputtered. "But we have just begun to speak!" the indigenous upstarts had replied. The result was a global "Gospel and Cultures Study Process" to explore the ways in which the empire was praying back. Its import: the gospel is incarnate in cultures, and in various cultural expressions gospel finds its fullest form. Chung soon showed up in Harare unrepentant. "I think that my Christianity, which is meaningful, which is incarnated in a specific people's history, is sure to be syncretistic. . . . Who wants to see a museum piece?"[13] African theologians were seconding this conviction: "The challenge to the church in Africa in the next millennium is to develop a theology which will enable African Christians to *own* the church instead of being custodians of it. . . . Africans cannot own Eurocentric or ethnocentric Christianity unless it is entirely immersed into African spirituality and is born again. That is what 'incarnation' is about."[14]

Then there was the Orthodox problem, or the East/West split. Prior to the assembly the Georgian and Bulgarian Orthodox churches had withdrawn from the World Council; the Orthodox Christians who did arrive, as one explained, had "come to regard the Council as a Western, Protestant and liberal movement" in need of radical reform. The threat of an Orthodox walkout on their fiftieth anniversary had apparently given WCC officials in Geneva sleepless nights. Then there was the Roman Catholic Church, which refused to join the WCC but wielded considerable influence in ecumenical circles, given that its nine hundred million members doubled the number of Protestant and Orthodox churches combined. The Pentecostals were showing up in Harare as well, announcing themselves as the fastest-growing churches in Latin America, Africa, and Asia. Then there was the issue of proselytizing—Christians were obligated to convert heathens, but when Baptists began converting Methodists, or Presbyterians went after members of the Orthodox churches, things were going too far.

While Catholics, Orthodox, and Protestant Pentecostals might differ on liturgical issues such as baptism and Eucharist, or communion (for example, who was *really* saved), they converged in opposition to the ordination of women, inclusively gendered language about God, and homosexuality. Issues of gender and the role of women in the church—the feminist challenge to patriarchal Christianity—seemed, in fact, to be the most deeply divisive issue within Christianity. Women who attended the celebration of the Decade on Women prior to the assembly reported resistance and opposition as well as openings over the past ten years. They demanded exposing of sexual abuse by those in church leadership, processes of restorative justice, the critical examination of theology that sanctions violence, and denunciation of war.

Add to all of this commotion a decade of financial crisis that had begun in 1991. The WCC's major funder, the German government, began to withdraw financial support because of its need for development money in East Germany after the fall of the Berlin Wall. Money woes led to downsizing of the WCC, with huge cuts in staff and program funds. Throw into this mix a restructuring proposal for the next seven-year period, which would come up for an assembly vote along with new officers. Much was up for grabs. URM assembly delegates were part of a larger contingent who wanted to ensure that WCC's commitment to marginalized people survived these changes intact so that the meek might have a chance to inherit the earth sometime this side of the Rapture.

Under such multiple pressures, homosexuality became once again a love that dared not speak its name, at least on the floor of the assembly. "Any move to develop a homosexual agenda would severely jeopardize Orthodox participation in the WCC," Vladimir Shmaliy of the Russian Orthodox Church had threatened.[15] A challenge letter from participants in celebration of the WCC's Ecumenical Decade in Solidarity with Women did manage to affirm "human sexuality in all its diversity" and condemned any violence because of these differences. But this evasion guaranteed that "no document put before the delegates included the words 'homosexual,' 'gay' or 'lesbian.'"[16] The discussion of (homo)sexuality would be left to the workshop in the Padares—workshops by both official assembly members and assembly guests, such as ourselves.

SEX AND THE SPIRIT

Monday was U.S. URM's Padare on "Sexuality and the Fullness of Life." It was the first of eleven Padare offerings on sexuality and sexual orientation. The classroom was crowded with about forty people, including media. We had a good representation from the project: Marta, Leah, me, Jacqui, Rebecca Voelkel-Haugen from Spirit of the Lakes United Church of Christ (Minneapolis), and Joe Leonard from the National Council of Churches. Jacqui Alexander, who was chair and chief facilitator of the project, would facilitate the workshop.

Jacqui and I had become friends when we worked together on a feminist anthology on racism in the late 1980s and early 1990s.[17] That collective process had aided me in framing my own analyses in international terms and in the historic context of colonialism. Jacqui grew up in Trinidad in the 1950s, and she taught then at Connecticut College. *Feminist Genealogies, Colonial Legacies, Democratic Futures,* which Jacqui edited with Chandra Mohanty, has helped shape a transnational feminism, as I reflected in the prologue. Jacqui brought her intellectual gifts as well as a deep spiritual grounding to our inquiries into sexuality, spirituality, and culture. Now in Harare, she gathered participants into a circle to center the group, having each person introduce her- or himself, before beginning.

Jacqui took about fifteen minutes to lay out the premises of the project, which examined sexuality as a force operating behind both practices and identities. "What *is* the link between sexuality and spirituality?" she began. Certainly this nexus was the point of contention here in Harare. "Can these be used in the same sentence, when they have often been placed so against each other? What is their relationship to social justice work? Our process in addressing these questions has been neither neat nor linear. All twenty-seven of us on the 'Community, Church and Sexuality' task force initially came together after decades of involvement in social justice work. We came from several decades of living the geographies of Hawai'i, El Salvador, Trinidad, Puerto Rico and these United States of North America, from New York to Portland, Atlanta to Philadelphia, North Carolina to Minnesota, California to Boston. We on the task force have come to understand that the framework of colonization is useful to our understanding. We have also seen that we can't understand sexuality without understanding the operation of violence, which happens to different people in different ways.

"As we grappled with the division between sex and the spirit, we understood how an ideology that has steeped sex and sexuality in sin, shame, and a general disavowal of the sacred is sustained. This very ideology has attempted to contain all of what is of spirit and spiritual within the structure of colonizing religion, all with predictably devastating consequences. Splitting sex and the spirit, body and spirit, meant that people were sexualized in different ways: for example, native people were considered oversexed, we had too much sexuality. Lesbian and gay people's sexuality could corrupt a nation; we were not loyal citizens. Welfare mothers had too many children and ran up the nation's bills. In the Third World, too much sex (especially by women) impedes progress by increasing population. In this process, people learned that sexuality was not to be trusted.

"We came to understand that sexual colonization involved a profound split of mind, body, and spirit so that each became a separate, discrete thing. Only certain people had 'minds'—people in the First World, who were white and men. Natives had bodies, especially Third World women. Lesbian and gay people also had only bodies, for only perverted sex. And spirituality was based on 'religion' and could only be practiced within certain confines, usually not on our own behalf.

"To this process of fragmentation of mind, body, and spirit we gave the name col-onization—a set of exploitative practices usually understood in political, ideological, and aesthetic terms. We saw its minute operation in dualistic and hierarchical think-ing—divisions among mind, body, spirit; between sacred and secular; male and fe-male; heterosexual and homosexual; rich and poor; the erotic and the Divine. It is a thinking always in negation, often translated into singular explanations for oppres-sion, such as racism versus sexism, with less attention to how all these systems work together.

"Internal colonization leaves us dealing with alienation from the body, from the self—the 'other' is in the self. It is the othering of ourselves. So we exist for them, not for ourselves. For some kind of them. It produces a love/hate relationship with our oppressors. We want to be sovereign, but don't let us be too sovereign. Instead of tak-ing out the pain and examining it, we act out of negation. It's the lateral violence we visit on each other.

"We also knew that the moment of colonization is also the moment of resistance. But there are many ways to resist, and resistance is not all of what the self is: to peren-nially oppose. Nor is spirituality only resistance. Breaking down these divisions and hierarchies, indeed making ourselves whole again, is the work that occupied us throughout this leg of our entire journey."

Around the circle, heads were nodding.

Then Jacqui asked people to name a part of her or his body from which the per-son felt separate. *My breasts*, one woman called. *Vagina, I never knew the word until I was an adult woman. They told me my anus was filthy. Don't touch your penis; it's too small. My skin; I had acne. Clitoris. Big thighs and butt. Pubic hair. My face. My brain; it was not a part of my body. My eyes blinked a lot; I was made fun of.* Then Jacqui opened up the discussion, and people responded fully from their own experi-ences from different places in the world to the frameworks we had offered.

I looked around the crowded circle at each person's face; they were all engaged and moved. I breathed a sigh of relief.

THE BANK AND THE DEBT

In an assembly disputatious or silenced on questions of gender and sexuality, there was remarkable unity on questions of economic justice and the need for a more hu-mane global order. Calls for debt relief in Harare echoed women's calls in Beijing at the UN conference, but they were given special urgency here in sub-Saharan Africa, a continent that on the cusp of a new century had fallen, some said, into a Fourth World.[18] The Physiocrats had argued that money circulates like blood through the body politic. If so, Africa, with only a 2 percent contribution to world trade and trapped still as primarily an exporter of raw materials, was a continent cut off from capital flow and experiencing a dangerous anemia. Much of the cash that came in from trade went out again as payment on its debts. Fifty years after the World Bank's founding, sub-Saharan Africa had an external debt of $313 billion, up from $84.3 billion in 1980—representing four times as much as countries could spend on health care each year. The debt burden sucked up public funds that could go for education or health care or housing, or for response to the huge AIDS crisis facing African countries. W.E.B. Du Bois had seen it coming. He had warned African male leaders in 1958:

> Here then, my Brothers, you face your great decision: Will you for temporary advantage—for automobiles, refrigerators and Paris gowns—spend your income in paying interest on borrowed funds; or will you sacrifice your present comfort and the chance to shine before your neighbors, in order to educate your children, develop such industry as best serves the great mass of people and make your country strong in ability, self-support and self-defense? . . . The capital offered you at high price by the colonial powers . . . will prolong fatal colonial imperialism, from which you have suffered slavery, serfdom and colonialism.[19]

The World Council announced the biblical theme of Jubilee when it chose Africa as site of the fiftieth anniversary assembly. The reference was to Leviticus 25: every fiftieth year, "return every man unto his possessions, and ye shall return every man unto his family." In this Jubilee year, land and animals rest, debts are canceled, land is returned to its original owners, and slaves are freed. Jesus had inaugurated his own ministry in a synagogue in Nazareth with the Jubilee promise: "The spirit of the Lord is upon me, because he hath anointed me to preach the gospel to the poor; he hath sent me to heal the broken-hearted, to preach deliverance to the captives and recovery of sight to the blind, to set at liberty them that are bruised. To teach the acceptable year of the Lord."[20] The intent of the Jubilee was forgiveness and atonement. It provided a means to break cycles of accumulation and impoverishment—the theological basis for the church's call to the international financial institutions to cancel Third World debt.

Fifty years ago the World Bank's mission to provide loans to developing countries might have appeared relatively benign; but the evidence now is increasingly damning as to the bank's intent and its effects. Therefore, it is worth taking some time here to trace the history of the World Bank, an institution as old as the World Council, which emerged in the same postwar environment. I acquired some of this history by attending workshops at a Padare in Harare and over the last decade in various meetings of URM. *Masters of Illusion: The World Bank and the Poverty of Nations*, reporter Catherine Caufield's history culled from public documents and private leaks from bank officials themselves, also provides a coherent narrative of the bank's problematic history.[21] A Kenyan theologian underlined for me in a lunchtime conversation in Harare the illogic of the bank's processes: "They force our countries to follow their advice to get loans. The advice ruins the economy. They make you renegotiate the loan and give you more bad advice. Our countries still owe the loans and the interest." This background on the World Bank is also key in understanding the political and social crisis in Zimbabwe.

In 1944 President Roosevelt called a meeting of forty-four Allied countries in Bretton Woods, New Hampshire, to consider how to reform international trade as a means for postwar global security. The International Monetary Fund (IMF) and the International Bank for Reconstruction and Development (the World Bank) emerged as the Bretton Woods Institutions that would control global finance for the rest of the century.[22] The World Bank would issue high risk loans "only for proper purposes and in proper ways after due inquiries," they explained. The United States and Great Britain had majority control with the bank's headquarters in the United States and the IMF's in Britain. In 1949, Truman's Marshall Plan made the bank's original role of reconstructing Europe obsolete, and its focus shifted solely to development in Asia, Africa, and Latin America. While the Marshall Plan gave Europe a $12 billion grant outright, poorer continents received development loans. The World Bank in the next fifty years became the premier lending agency for poor countries, the biggest single lender to the Third World, with loans of a third of a trillion dollars—more than 11 percent of long-term debt. But even more, it became a dominant influence not only within the countries to which it lent, but also in the decisions of other funders.

During its formative years (1949 to 1963, under President Eugene Black) the bank developed a procedure of making loans only for giant infrastructure projects such as dams, ports, and roads (rather than, for example, education or health). Its goals were to create markets for U.S. trade and to stop communism by shoring up poor countries for whom communist ideology had special appeal. There was little local consultation and no evaluation of projects, remarkably, for the first twenty-five years.[23] Bank officers had to work initially to get countries' leaders to take loans, and bank officials helped set up agencies within debtor countries to administer loans. The postwar years saw the success of national independence movements all over the globe. These countries emerged from colonialism into this international banking system through which they had to give up much sovereignty to have access to development capital. Between 1954 and 1964, membership of the World Bank doubled to 102 nations, reflecting the number of African countries that were gaining their independence.

One of the bank's early projects in Africa was the Volta River Dam in Ghana, and it illustrates many of the loans' disastrous effects. The bank granted a $47 billion loan in 1961 in spite of warnings from its own mission teams who visited the site. Kwame Nkrumah promoted the loan, seeing it as newly independent Ghana's means for industrialization. The dam created the largest reservoir in the world and displaced eighty thousand villagers. When these people did not get promised seeds and tools in their new location, widespread starvation eventually meant that two-thirds of these refugees moved to Ghana's cities. The dam's environmental impact was also devastating: it brought saltwater into estuaries, destroyed clam and sport-fishing industries, and created a breeding ground for disease-carrying snails and for a fly that carried river blindness. By 1980, one hundred thousand people were infected and seventy thousand became blind. Its economic and political impacts were equally destructive. The Volta River Dam's biggest customer was Kaiser Aluminum, which paid one-twentieth the rate for electricity that the people in Ghana did. At Kaiser's behest, the dam had been designed only for electricity, not for irrigation. Popular discontent about the dam was a factor in Nkrumah's overthrow; he was ousted in the first of a series of military coups that contributed to political deterioration in Ghana.[24] Dr. Eboe Hutchful in *The IMF and Ghana* argues that the monitors of international governments needed a means of manipulating African governments run by radicals and used Ghana as a test case.[25]

When President Black stepped down in 1963, the Third World was dangerously in debt. Debtor nations could not repay their loans, which made them uncreditworthy for new loans—a threat to the bank's continued existence, since its purpose was to make loans and thus earn interest. The gap between the rich and the poor was not closing but widening. In 1947, per capita income in the United States and in poor countries was at a ratio of 6.5:1. By 1966 it was 16:1, with a widening gap between rich and poor within poor countries. The bank's policies were not eliminating poverty but increasing wealth. In 1965, half of what poor countries were taking in from export sales and aid was going back in the form of debt service payments, a debt that was growing three times as fast as their gross domestic products (GDP).[26]

"We simply made a major misjudgment—a mistake—when we assumed that the conventional banking terms and conditions could be applied to such countries—India, Pakistan, countries in Africa,"[27] one bank official admitted belatedly. But when George Woods became the next president, his strategy for this debt crisis would be, remarkably, to make more loans, beginning a policy of exponential increases in the amounts of loans to countries already struggling with debt payments.[28] Soon debtor countries began rescheduling their debts—between 1957 and 1969, twenty-one countries rescheduled, stretching out the loan period for lower monthly payments.[29]

Robert McNamara took over from Woods in 1968, after resigning his post as secretary of defense during the Vietnam War. McNamara's line was that the "rich and powerful have a moral obligation to assist the poor and the weak," and to this end he increased bank spending from $1 billion a year to $12 billion annually in 1981.[30] But this money did not go to the poor and the weak within borrowing countries; it went to the wealthy on the premise that wealth creates wealth. (Remember trickle-down economics?) McNamara escalated investments beyond infrastructure into social spending. But bank loan officers were under such pressure to fill quotas that their hasty loans went to the more questionable projects and were poorly prepared. The bank under McNamara's tenure also encouraged private banks to get into the lucrative business of high-risk, high-interest, high-fee loans. They were glad to comply, sure they would be bailed out if countries should threaten defaults.

The huge and carelessly made loans to Third World leaders began to find their way into the private accounts of national elites, who siphoned off the loan money into Eurodollars laundered into Swiss bank accounts in a huge wave of graft and corruption. Increasingly, the country's leaders, elected or not, got the money, and the people were still left with the obligation to pay the debt. Between 1976 and 1984 in Latin America the capital flow out of the continent equaled the increases in external debt, and this money was then reloaned to developing countries in an escalating cycle. In 1983 alone, the president of Mexico deposited $163 million in a Swiss bank![31]

I began to understand more Marta's emphasis on sustainability—doing what you can pay for and control yourself. She lived on a small stipend and structured her work to rely on local resources well deployed, rather than applying for grants, either private or government. A growing understanding of such widespread financial corruption also gave me more of a context in which to place Mugabe's political and ethical decline over the past twenty years.

McNamara had emphasized the need to help the poor. But he had instead thrown money at the rich, at big landowners, ranchers, corporations, banks. Did this loan money help the countries that were becoming increasingly indebted? No. The bank forced a nation's economy to gear itself to produce a cash crop in order to earn foreign currency with which to pay back, or pay interest on, the loan. For example, bank officials encouraged Zimbabwe farmers to produce tobacco in a cash economy instead of the maize that subsistence farmers had produced for local consumption.

Such policies have devastating effects on women, as Women's Education in the Global Economy (WedGE), a workbook growing out of collaboration from Beijing, explains. "African women produce between 60% and 80% of the food used for family and community consumption. Yet agricultural policy discriminates against women. Men often own the land, tools, and resources. Men have greater access to training in agricultural techniques, aid, and payment for export crops." Export crop production, then, means that women lose access to land that grows their family's food. They shift to work as maids, vendors, or cooks. Some turn to prostitution to survive.[32] This policy also inflated food prices, because Zimbabwe's people had to import maize at higher prices when small farmers (most of them women) went out of business. Disaster piled on disaster, with women and their children at the bottom of the pile.

The bank's solution was not land reform—redistribution of land. Rather, it advocated opening new lands by deforestation of tropical rain forests, draining wetlands, and building roads. The environmental consequences were so disastrous that they finally brought the World Bank under fire in the 1980s, with well-funded environmentalists taking the lead. By then, half of sixty-four area development and resettlement projects had failed—and the countries still owed for these projects![33] What price did poor countries pay? Between 1972 and 1980, their external debt rose from $100 billion to $600 billion, bringing Zaire, Peru, Turkey, Iran, and Poland to the brink of financial collapse.[34] To avert collapse, McNamara then devised a new version of large, quick loans. These loans would convert short- and medium-term debt held by private banks into bank-held long-term debt, shifting the risk off of private banks. But the borrowing countries would have to agree to reform their economies—again. McNamara stepped down when Ronald Reagan became president, appointing Tom Clausen to respond to the latest debt crisis.

Clausen soon made it clear that "the only constituency that mattered was the United States."[35] By this time, countries in default could precipitate a world financial crisis, given how widespread the loans were. Clausen's bank would use the loan process to apply Reagan's supply-side economics on a global scale. This was the economic theory we had seen at play in Atlanta, written large for Olympic development. The supply-side premise was that economic growth trickled down from rich to poor—not exactly a premise that the bank's funding had proved for thirty years. Supply-siders held that the private sector stimulates growth rather than the demand side, or government, which means curtailing government programs, power, and influence, leaving corporations free reign in national economies. India by itself changed over twenty laws at the bank's requests. This was the broad policy of privatization that began to operate, locally to globally, in the 1980s and afterward. Promoting economic growth through the private sector became the bank's goal. The magic of the marketplace would then solve global problems from inflation to unemployment to underinvestment to poor public services to inefficient public bureaucracies to lack of personal freedom by having governments reduce public spending, lift trade restrictions, remove price subsidies, and lower wages and environmental standards.[36] If they did not achieve these goals, too bad, because most politicians would be afraid to raise taxes anymore, and countries needing development funds would be cut out of the capital loop. By the new plan, debtor countries would get no more than five loans in no more than five years with the expectation that within another two years they would have a strong enough balance of payments to get development back on track.

Did this scheme work for the countries loaned the money? No better, really, than the other strategies had. By 1995, eighty-eight countries had received bank-funded adjustments, and not a single one had kept to the projected timetable.[37] Ghana by the 1970s had a debt of $500 million, and since 1983 Ghana has undergone sixteen different stabilization and structural adjustment programs.[38] That's a lot of adjustment, but not a lot of stability. Adjustment lending the world over, in fact, intensified under structural adjustment, and the collapse of Mexico's model neoliberal economy required President Clinton to arrange a $20 billion bailout to keep U.S. banking institutions afloat, paid for by the America taxpayer. The Mexican people took the brunt of the austerity program the bankers imposed: a wage freeze, cuts in government spending, and tax increases.[39]

How does this whole dismal history add up? In 1972, there were 800 million people worldwide in absolute poverty, a figure that had increased to 1.3 billion—or 60 percent—by 1996. The income gap between richest and poorest countries had also grown, from 16:1 in 1948 to 23:1 in 1993, and it was widening by the end of the century, when nineteen countries had lower gross domestic products in 1996 than they had in 1960, an increase from seven such countries in 1992. By the end of the century, the wealth of the top 20 percent was 150 times greater than the poorest 20 percent globally. Developing countries were taking in $167.8 billion in loans, but paying $169.5 billion in debt service each year, a net loss of $1.7 billion a year. "It is hardly too brutal an oversimplification to say that the rich got the loans and the poor got the debts," UNICEF concluded.[40]

The World Bank's lending policies over its fifty-year history had created a debt peonage for the world's poorest countries, a staggering burden borne by the most vulnerable humans on the globe. It was not a new tactic for colonialism or capitalism. A couple of centuries before, Thomas Jefferson had explained his strategy for obtaining Indian land: "To promote this disposition to exchange lands, which they have to spare and we want, for necessaries, which we have to spare and they want, we shall push our trading uses, and be glad to see the good and influential individuals among them run in debt."[41]

A year after the Harare assembly, demonstrators in Seattle closed down a meeting of the World Trade Organization, signaling the maturation of a new global movement against global financial institutions. "Turtles and teamsters together at last!" read one of the placards. A series of protests beginning in Seattle would flush WTO delegates out of the obscurity of anonymous high-level meetings and into more public scrutiny. The ingenuity and determination of Seattle demonstrators caught the global and local police forces off guard. They rapidly retaliated as Seattle's police morphed within a twenty-four-hour period from its warm, fuzzy community policing image to a crack-down mode complete with Darth Vader outfits, teargassing of Seattle neighborhoods, and broad and unconstitutional sweeps of demonstrators. Nineteen months later, police protecting a G-8 economic summit in Genoa, Italy, shot to death one young protestor, then ran over him with a jeep. They also attacked reporters at an independent media center and rounded up demonstrators into Italian jails, where they were forced to pay homage to "Il Duce" (Mussolini), making explicit the fascist tenor of this emerging global police force, making the fascist proclivities of their policies particularly clear.

A CALL FOR A THIRD LIBERATION

If African hosts urged the WCC Assembly to focus on debt relief, they also were looking inward. Many African speakers were calling for a new moral imperative on the continent itself. "Corruption is theft from the poor," one speaker had exclaimed, an issue I understood more after exploring more fully the history of World Bank loans to the new colonial elites. Speakers at the African plenary had called for a third liberation against an indigenous oppression from these leaders—in addition to liberation from slavery and colonialism, and from poverty and international debt. Speaking at the African plenary, Barney Pitanya had warned of the dangers of a "theory of vic-timology" by which "one is inclined to blame everyone else for the fate of Africa ex-cept Africans themselves."[42]

I began to see from Harare how African countries struggle with the complex re-alities of a post–Third World. "In many regions the powerful frameworks of nation-alism, which once held such enormous liberationist promise, have begun to fall apart," Ella Shohat summarized at the end of the century.[43] Basil Davidson, whose *Black Man's Burden* was recommended to me by my Kenyan lunch companion, saw Africa's problems circa 1992 as resulting from a crisis in institutions that had been in-herent in the European nation-state form adopted by newly liberated countries. Women in Beijing testified as to this shift over the twenty years of the UN Women's Conferences. Spotting enemies was clearer twenty years ago, the women in Beijing testified. What was left were the two big issues: poverty and power. It was against such a backdrop that Robert Mugabe and the situation in Zimbabwe came more clearly into focus.

A coalition of fifty churches in Zimbabwe issued *A Call to Prophetic Action: To-wards the Jubilee Year 2000* in time for the assembly. "We are . . . a society in which fear prevails," it concluded. "This is our critical moment of truth. . . . Zimbabwe has been plunged into a political, economic, and, above all, moral crisis that is shaking its very foundation."[44]

In 1987, emergency regulations strengthened the dictatorial role of the president, the Kairos document explained. The government (for example, the ruling party) owns and controls the media. President Mugabe cannot be questioned by the legis-lature, nor is he accountable to the courts. Zimbabwe citizens are among the high-est taxed in the world, with a president whose conspicuous consumption, including expensive foreign travel, contrasts starkly with the realities of poverty for most of his black countrymen. Citizens live in "real and constant fear of those in authority and the apparatus which surrounds them to keep them in power"—the government of-ficials, police, the Central Intelligence Organization, and the ruling party, all of which subject people to harassment, arrests, disappearances, and even death.[45]

Structural adjustment, which Zimbabwe accepted in 1990, increased the eco-nomic pressure. By 1998, the country's debt burden was 90 percent of its GNP and the economy was divided along racial lines, 75 percent of it controlled by multina-tional corporations and white-owned commercial farms. This sector has high in-comes and a state-supported infrastructure. At the other end of the economy, the black community provides a reserve of cheap labor with an unemployment rate of above 40 percent.[46] Neoliberalist economic policies in Zimbabwe, as in China, did not bring increased political freedoms. Economic decline and political repression brought strikes and other outbreaks, which were met with resistance by the police.

In 1996 doctors and nurses went on strike, and the government sent in riot police to attack their union. As a result, the country's health care system is in shambles, contributing to astronomical rates of HIV, the highest in the world. A year later demonstrations against food prices (high because of the shift from subsistence maize to tobacco as cash crop) met government tanks and bullets, and early in 1998 violence spread in which many people died.[47] At the assembly, unions asked the WCC to speak out against the government's ban on strikes and demonstrations. Mugabe's attacks on gays were clearly part of a much larger fraying of Zimbabwe's social fabric.

Part of Zimbabwe's problem was a one-party state. But how democratic is the two-party state within my own country? I came to wonder over dinner table conversations. Multiparty systems were part of the neoliberal formula of structural adjustments. But did those systems in themselves guarantee democracy? How much latitude did any elected leader really have when he (rarely she) had so little say over the functioning of the economy?

A year later I certainly would have a month to reflect on the two-party democracy in the United States during the long month of November 2000. The outcome of the presidential election between George Bush and Al Gore for the leadership of the most powerful country in the history of the world hung, finally, on an official balance of a little more than five hundred votes. During the campaign, both major party candidates had tacitly agreed to discuss only the welfare of the middle class and above. Ralph Nader, a Green Party candidate who critiqued corporations, was locked out of national debates, figuratively and literally not even allowed in their audience.

In the Florida election itself there was gross discrimination against communities of color. The state of Florida was headed by George Bush's brother Gov. Jeb Bush and was clearly a swing state from the beginning. Secretary of State Katherine Harris paid a Texas firm called Choicepoint ("run by a bevy of GOP corporate funders") to purge the voting rolls. Florida prohibits people who have had felony convictions from voting, a law which disproportionately affected black voters. Secretary Harris compiled a list of 700,000 Floridians permanently disqualified from voting. The move eliminated 7,000 people who should have voted, 54 percent of whom were black voters. Human Rights Watch estimated that, overall, 31 percent of black voting-age Florida men were disenfranchised. In Tallahassee, police roadblocks in black communities intimidated voters. Haitian voters were turned away or denied translators.[48]

For the election count, things went from bad to worse. Gore refused to look at the civil rights issues when he contested Bush's narrow vote count, instead narrowing the range of his focus to recounts of ballots in four southern counties. We saw the grossest political patronage when Republican Secretary of State Harris closed the deadline for a vote recounting that looked like it would have put Gore ahead. Many elderly Jewish voters mistakenly cast ballots for white supremacist and anti-Semite Pat Buchanan. Journalists reported disparities in voting machines all over the country, varying county by county, with the poorest counties having the least accurate machines.

This is democracy? I thought night after night, tuning in to CNN. Then the Republican-controlled United States Supreme Court made Bush the winner by a partisan vote that used the Fourteenth Amendment's guarantee of equal protection to give Bush the vote. They declared, "the individual citizen has no federal constitutional right to vote for Presidential electors."[49] And it was over. Bush won the Electoral College with the Florida vote, but lost the popular ballot to Gore. That had not happened since the Hayes-Tilden Compromise of 1876 resulted in federal troops pulled out of the South to end Reconstruction.

When both Republicans and Democrats explained how the outcome showed that the system works, I was flabbergasted. Is that what the outcome showed? Pundits in November had speculated that Bush would need to pursue a path of compromise, hindered by the fact that he did not receive a majority of the popular vote. But determinedly retro, he was unhindered by any of these restraints as he pushed through another massive Reagan-era tax cut to eliminate much of the budget surplus built up during the flush 1990s. A faltering economy provided the rationale, but the cuts effectively limit the amount of money available for social or any other spending in the immediate future. In addition, the new administration rapidly isolated the United States by its stances on global warming, small arms, biological warfare, and the ABM treaty. It was déjà vu, boy-Bush a reincarnation of his daddy, Ronald Reagan, the Marlboro Dude, and Wild Man.

The system works, yes, but for whom?

HUMAN RIGHTS

Wednesday evening I hopped another cab to the Gays and Lesbians of Zimbabwe (GALZ) reception, held at its community center in one of Zimbabwe's suburbs. A brick wall surrounded a courtyard with a huge tree covering the tent set up for the evening's festivities. Inside the walls a packed crowd of lesbians and gays from Harare and their international guests partied, with a swish and snap almost shocking in its familiarity. There was a freedom, an easy banter and ready humor in gesture and in conversation within the courtyard that few of us felt at the conference and certainly not on the street, in Zimbabwe or in Durham. I found the drinks and hors d'oeuvres under the tent in a party that was already in full swing. I struck up a conversation with two African women from Harare, one elegant in pants, the other in a long skirt with a slit up the side. The more femme of the two, I discovered, had a master's in development from a university in England, and we discussed the way that issues of international debt played out in Zimbabwe.

"Unemployment in Zimbabwe is upwards of 50 percent," she said over her wine. "Inflation is at 35 percent and interest rates at 40 percent. Interest alone on Zimbabwe's debt was $1 billion per year, or thirty-seven cents on every dollar of government spending. It all puts huge pressure on people and on families. More people are without income than ever, and the price of basic goods has increased as much as 70 percent in the past six years. People are hungry because they can't eat the tobacco that is our cash crop, and now there's not enough maize."

I had not yet figured out how to flirt and discuss the World Bank, nor would it have been the best move (the flirting, that is). These two made it clear that they were not sexual partners or lesbians, in spite of the familiar air between them. Soon the so-cial rotation of such parties sent me back to the bar, and I went out onto the patio and found Keith Goddard, with whom I had been in communication via e-mail. I con-gratulated him on GALZ's presence at the assembly and the obvious risky work they were doing in raising issues of homophobia in the current Zimbabwe climate.

Keith explained how the International Book Fair incident that caught our atten-tion in Beijing had brought GALZ substantial support in the intervening years. Mugabe's opening address to the fair had set the tone of homophobic diatribe: "I find it extremely outrageous and repugnant to my human conscience that such moral and repulsive organizations like those of homosexuals, who offend both against the law of nature and the morals and religious beliefs espoused by our society, should have any advocates in our midst, and even elsewhere in the world."[50] Some guests walked out on the opening ceremony, given the vitriol of his speech, and Nobel Prize winners Nadine Gordimer and Wole Soyinka issued statements in support of GALZ.

After the book fair Mugabe escalated his attacks, calling for a worldwide anti-homosexual campaign and for patriotic youth to arrest perceived homosexuals. He had the support both of the Parliament and of the Zimbabwe Council of Churches. The debate in Zimbabwe's Parliament was mainly vitriol: "The homosexuals are the festering finger endangering the body and we chop them off."[51] "African culture ab-hors homosexuality and considers it abnormal," explained the Zimbabwe Catholic Bishops' Conference in a familiar equation of homosexuality with Western deca-dence.[52] In a culture experiencing such stress, queers provided a handy target. Africa's colonial history made clear the risk of reliance on Western imports. But Keith and I puzzled over the irony of calling on a Christian theology that was itself a Western im-port to condemn homosexuality as a tool of colonization.

"In Africa homosexuality might be a Western disease," I reflected. "In the West, it is merely a disease."[53]

Keith explained that the publicity after the book fair helped GALZ get interna-tional support from some mainline Christian denominations such as the United Church of Christ and from the Dutch. The Zimbabwe Council of Churches, al-though publicly supportive of Mugabe, moved behind the scenes to assure the WCC that gay and lesbian assembly delegates would not be barred entry or harassed within the country. GALZ protested the obvious hypocrisy of protecting only WCC gay people: "What is it that makes Zimbabwean gay men and lesbians deserving of a persecution from which foreign delegates should be protected?"[54]

Keith was white, but the majority of the GALZ members present were African. He explained that Mugabe's persecution had brought more Africans into the organiza-tion, politicized by the repression and informed by the publicity. But the economy made it harder generally for people with fewer resources to be more open about same-gender attractions, given that the high unemployment rate was forcing people to live with their families for longer periods of time. Queer theory makes much of the difference between homosexual acts and homosexual identities. The emergence of gay and lesbian identities, it seemed to me, is more a function of urbanization than of Westernization. It is moving to the city that brings people out of kinship networks and provides them with more anonymity to form alternate communities and to experiment with attractions and desires.

It was getting close to midnight, so I soon piled into a cab with four other women to return to the university. Back at the dorm, Marta was still up, and I sorted through with her some of the past days' experiences. She let me talk through the difference here and in South Africa.

"South Africa was the last African country to free itself from colonial domination. In the long, grueling gestation of its liberation struggle a more complicated, flexible form of African nationalism seems to have evolved. The emphasis on human rights, so needed in the escalating brutality of the decades of apartheid, carries with it more recognition of respect for various forms of minority rights. With the new democracy, more groups are making claims—not only lesbians and gays, but women, the disabled, shack-dwellers, people in various ways on the outs."[55]

The generosity of the South African experiment moved me, as did its vulnerability.

I asked Marta about her work on sustainability. "How do you define it?" I asked.

"It's the ability to have our sustenance, that which will nourish you. Is it money? If you believe so, that's capitalism. Or you can find that we are our own answers, we are the solutions. We don't need all these billions of dollars of loans for projects we never asked for. At home, my programs with the people have four levels: the physical (what we need each day of life), the mental (which involves education), the emotional (when we are so full of fear or self-doubt), and the spiritual."

"And what does *spiritual* mean to you?" I asked again.

"I know that spirit is eternal, and it manifests the highest dreams and aspirations. In people it manifests as gifts of the spirit—love, patience, tolerance, caring, forgiveness, sharing, understanding. The spirit illumines all of them and helps to bring out the humaneness within our humanity."

"Here we are at ubuntu again," I grunted.

"People say of cruel acts that they are inhuman, but are they really? In a way, they are fairly characteristic of humans, unfortunately. But the torture of apartheid, or what the death squads did to people in my country, or what the World Bank does to poor nations, is in*humane*. Humanity needs more humaneness—but how many people are willing to walk that road?"

Marta was about to segue into her theory of The Vibrations and the One Hundred Monkeys, but I had enough to think about from this long day.

"Mercy, mercy," I pleaded from the exhaustion of the material plane, and she laughed and said goodnight.

On Thursday, December 10, I decided to join the march downtown in commemoration of the fiftieth anniversary of the Universal Declaration of Human Rights. It was sponsored by a coalition of Zimbabwe's human rights groups—Zimbabwe Lawyers for Human Rights, the Catholic Commission for Justice and

Peace, the Zimbabwe Council of Churches, the Zimbabwe Congress of Trade Unions, and Gays and Lesbians of Zimbabwe. The sponsors had gotten government permission by explaining that it was a march, not a demonstration; but we still were not sure what might transpire. The open presence of GALZ also raised the ante.

I climbed out of yet another yellow cab at the designated intersection. There were about four hundred of us gathered, with no police in sight. Was this a good thing, or a bad thing? We later learn that a promised police escort withdrew when police learned of gay activist participation. And here we were, "Out and Proud in Zimbabwe," a huge rainbow banner read. "Ngoni Chaiza" (Honor Our Relationships), in Shona, another. Keith and the GALZ folks gathered behind the banner, as we proceeded through downtown Harare, past flower vendors, apartments, taxis, kids on the street, shoppers. The march was, I later heard, the largest and most public presence for lesbians and gays in the country's history. Police neither protected nor harassed us, so we probably got off pretty well in that exchange.

For part of the march, I handed out copies of the declaration (an $8\frac{1}{2}$-by-11-inch sheet, folded twice) to people along the side of the road or on the sidewalk, to shoppers and vendors and a couple of interested boys who let me snap their picture, alert, open-faced, and curious about the crowd. The declaration had been passed by a newly formed United Nations in 1948 in recognition of "the inherent dignity and of the equal and inalienable rights of all members of the human family . . . as the foundation of freedom, justice and peace in the world." It was another of those postwar frameworks and institutions that had shaped the last half of the century.

I took time to read the declaration over again myself. Its first provisions were familiar, similar to the U.S. Declaration of Independence and Bill of Rights: "All humans are born free and equal . . . Everyone has the right to life, liberty and security of person . . . All are equal before the law . . . No one shall be subjected to arbitrary arrest, detention or exile . . . . Everyone is entitled to a fair and public hearing . . . everyone charged with a penal offence has the right to be presumed innocent . . . All have the right to freedom of thought, conscience, religion, opinion, expression, and peaceful assembly."

Further on the list, I noted principles less familiar to me as a U.S. citizen: "Everyone has the right to work, to free choice of employment, to just and favorable conditions of work and to protection against unemployment." The declaration, unlike the U.S. Constitution, views economic rights as human rights. "Everyone has the right to equal pay for equal work . . . Everyone has the right to just and favourable remuneration ensuring for him [or her]self and his family an existence worthy of human dignity, and supplemented, if necessary, by other means of social protection." These were rights of workers, not of property owners. They were hardly guaranteed in the U.S. economy that over two decades has moved toward low-paying, insecure jobs with no benefits and toward dismantling the safety net put in place by the New Deal's social programs, post-Depression.

"Everyone has the right to a standard of living adequate for the health and wellbeing of himself and of his family, including food, clothing, housing and medical care and necessary social services and the right to security in the event of unemployment, sickness, disability, widowhood, old age, or other lack of livelihood in circumstances beyond his control." I had friends in the Living Wage Campaign back home who were advocating that people working full time should have wages that never fall below the poverty line. The minimum wage in the United States, in spite of all the talk of a rosy economy, is a quarter lower than it was in 1980 with adjustments for inflation, and in a context of rising consumer debts and eroded living standards for all but the 30 percent of the population with money in the stock market. "Everyone has the right to rest and leisure." But a growing number of new jobs at home are temporary or part-time with no health insurance, retirement, or vacation. Two out of three new private-sector jobs are temporary, and our largest employer is a temp agency: Manpower, Inc.[56] We should be handing these declarations out on the streets back home, I thought as our march turned into the Harare Gardens, the destination of the march.

The day before, President Mugabe spoke to the assembly, evoking memories and sounding themes of national liberation and calling for an end to the "global conspiracy against poor nations." A few days later, unions and human rights agencies demanded that the assembly condemn Mugabe's ban against the opposition. "When people riot against food prices in the next months, we hope the WCC will be here to protect us from the government's police and military thugs," one NGO leader remarked.[57]

TRUTH AND RECONCILIATION?

On Friday I chose a Padare on South Africa's Truth and Reconciliation Commission. Its controversial report had been issued in October, after two and a half years of testimony. I was eager to hear from closer up its findings and South African responses. This Padare was in a classroom amphitheater, its seats stacked up in rows, with the lecturer in front of a green board below. She was one of seventeen commissioners appointed by Mandela to chair the TRC.

South Africa's Truth and Reconciliation Commission had a formidable task, she explained, "to look the beast of apartheid in the eye," in Bishop Tutu's words, in a political climate of transition from Afrikaner to majority rule. Over thirty months, the commission heard testimony from 21,000 victims and received 7,000 applications for amnesty, 150 of which were granted. Two thousand more are pending. At both the beginning and the end of the process, the most controversial provision was amnesty. President F. W. DeKlerk had insisted on amnesty as part of the Nationalist Party's agreement to move toward democratic elections. Mandela insisted, in return, that truth-telling be a condition of amnesty. This compromise, written into the provisional constitution, meant that anyone who came forward and made a full disclosure of crimes against humanity would receive immunity from civil or criminal prosecution.

"For many victims of apartheid, this has not felt like justice—to see a confessed murderer walk free. Stephen Biko's family's opposition was the most publicized in this regard," the lecturer explained.

In setting up the TRC, South Africa was able to draw on the experience of other countries who rid themselves of dictators in the 1980s and 1990s, then had to deal with their crimes. Argentina had the first truth commission, its National Commission for the Disappeared, which investigated the twelve thousand deaths and disappearances during Argentina's Dirty War. Chile, El Salvador, Guatemala, and Haiti all chose truth commissions as well, because of the continued power of the military in those countries to block prosecutions. Continuing political conditions in those countries meant their commissions brought only a few, high-profile cases; they were not able to get perpetrators to testify, and, often because of fear of reprisals, hearings were not public.

"In South Africa, we had and took much wider latitude," the speaker continued. "Our hearings were public and widely covered in the media. The commission had subpoena and seizure power and an investigative unit. We did not operate under normal rules of evidence—so victims were not subjected to cross-examinations. People were allowed—in fact, required—to name names. We heard thousands of cases, and because of the threat of prosecution, hundreds of perpetrators testified about their crimes. Their testimony confirmed the UN's assertion, and our finding, that apartheid was indeed a crime against humanity and that the war against apartheid was a just war. The testimony of police proved that death squads operated as part of government policy at the highest level, Nationalist leaders who also approved systematic use of torture. It proved that the deadly violence between the ANC and the Inkatha Freedom Party was encouraged and financed by the Afrikaner government. It showed that apartheid included offensive chemical and biological warfare. It solved the murder and disappearance of many people. Those are our accomplishments.

"The process involved failures and disappointments as well. One of the disappointments was how much apathy, or outright hostility, that white South Africans showed to it. Former President P. W. Botha—the architect of the most deadly total strategy of the 1980s—repeatedly refused to respond to the commission's subpoena. Archbishop Tutu offered to accompany him to the hearing and pled with him publicly: 'If Mr. Botha is able to say, "I am sorry the policies of my government caused you so much pain"—just that—that would be a tremendous thing.'[58] To no avail. The commission found him guilty of criminal misconduct. President DeKlerk—who had dismantled Botha's national security management team when he came to office in 1989—apologized for the pain and suffering caused by Nationalist Party policies, but refused to accept responsibility for security force abuses, dismissing them as the work of 'mavericks.' The commission found that DeKlerk had failed to make full disclosure—a passage that he successfully sued to have removed from the final report. The larger white community often seemed either indifferent or plainly hostile."[59]

The second source of controversy after amnesty for many black South Africans, she explained, was the decision to investigate ANC activities as possible human rights violations, even though the ANC's struggle against apartheid was declared to be just. "A just cause does not exempt an organization from pursuing its goals through just means," the commission found. It censured the ANC's bombing and land mine campaigns in the 1980s that resulted in civilian casualties and its policy during the same period of regarding informers and collaborators as targets for assassination. The ANC was also guilty of serious abuses in its camps in Angola. The TRC had similar criticisms of Pan-African Congress strategies targeting civilians. The ANC responded strongly, accusing the commission of criminalizing the struggle against apartheid. ANC President Thabo Mbeki applied unsuccessfully to the high court to block the commission's publication.[60] President Mandela accepted the report "with all its imperfections."

Bishop Tutu responded to criticism of the TRC report, "We can't assume that yesterday's oppressed will not become tomorrow's oppressors. We have seen it happen all over the world . . . . We so easily jettison the ideas we had when we were struggling. It is important that we retain the vigor of our civil society organs that were part of the struggle. . . . We've got to retain the same capacity to smell out corruption, the abuse of power."[61]

The Truth and Reconciliation process also left the profound economic inequities from South Africa's long colonial history untouched.

"What happened with El Salvador's truth commission?" I asked Marta over lunch. We had filed through the line full of meats, vegetables, fruits, and bread brought in by a local Sheraton on contract with the council. For meals we all sat at long tables covered with white tablecloths.

"The process was very important," she replied. "It took a long time and was worked in much detail. It was a confidential process, in order to protect those who came forward. They issued a very thick report at the end. Many people didn't necessarily trust the process, because they had never been respected, but they went to testify anyway. The government kept postponing the date to put it out. It was clear to the people who had led the massacres that they were going to look bad. At least one of the generals resigned and apologized the Saturday before it was released. He was crying and everything. The people said that he was 'killing his dog in time'—getting ahead of the process to protect himself from it. He dropped out of public life for a while, then he became a big businessman."

"What effect did it have?" I asked.

"There was a general amnesty," Marta said. "It was important to release anger for the people, and forgiveness is good, but no one took responsibility, there was no accountability. And not the best use was made of it to systematize its findings and create processes to do justice and healing."

"Was this out of fear that the military were still around?"

"Yes, in part. The healing has never really been done. So there is still much pain in the people. But it was good as far as it went. You know, the UN was very helpful.

There is an international criminal court, a treaty signed by 120 nations last July that is now in a process of being ratified, that would allow an international criminal court to bring human rights violators to trial internationally, although it would have to be with the permission of the country in which the violations occurred, or the perpetrators lived. Still, it's a step. But the United States does not support it."

"Because U.S. leaders don't want to be brought to trial?" I asked and she nodded. "What about the links between human rights and structural adjustment, or the World Bank? One position seems to be that liberal democracy has won out in this century over communism and fascism in both Europe and Latin America, and with liberal — or Western — democracy comes the concern with human rights. It lauds all the countries (by some counts half the world's nations) that have moved from war or dictatorship to democracy or peace. El Salvador was one of those countries. What do you think?"

"People often aren't seeing the linkages. We need holistic ways of looking at things, and we have to understand all the forces at play in a society. What is called liberal democracy means a free market, but free for what? To make profits! Bill Gates is worth the budgets of forty-six impoverished countries in the world. But there's a relationship when we don't use profit to benefit the people and the planet, not whoever can make it. This system of profits creates human rights violations. It often requires militaristic governments to keep it in place. In Latin America, we were governed by force by military dictatorships for many years. And who trained them? They were trained by the United States government."

All around us sounded the clink of silverware and differently accented voices in similar conversations.

"We need to look holistically and live reflectively," Marta continued. "The way we live personally is linked to what's happening in the world. It *is* important to live well. Quality of life is one thing, but it's another to be like a hog. All the people who want a difference in the world, we have to have clarity on how that difference happens, and then live it."

UBUNTU IN THE MIDST OF US

Saturday morning, my last in Harare, I got up early to walk around the campus for one last time, to smell the red mud, feel the dew in the grass, the flame of trees in bloom in the quiet of dawn. The problem of suffering and the miracle of hope, I reflected, they were not so different in Harare as in Beijing or Honolulu or Atlanta. The assembly had presented the dilemma in Christian terms, with the cross as a reminder of the pain of this world in which Christians believe God took human form. Jesus might have said that the poor would be with us always, but I do not think he had in mind that 80 percent of the world's people would be caught in deepening cycles of poverty, while the upper 20 percent accumulated unprecedented wealth.

I was proud that the final World Council report on the debt issue was strong and visionary. "We are called, through a process of discernment and response, to seek new ways to break the stranglehold of debt. . . . This can only be achieved through a new, just global order." The assembly called for:

> Debt cancellation for severely indebted, impoverished countries and substantial debt reduction for severely indebted middle-income countries;
> Participation by civil society in deciding and monitoring how funds made available by debt cancellation are used to restore social and ecological damage;
> Establishing an independent, transparent arbitration process for debt cancellation, and ethical lending and borrowing policies to prevent future recurrence of the debt crisis;
> Ethical governance in all countries and legislative action against all forms of corruption and misuse of loans;
> A new just process of arbitration for debt cancellation, such as an international insolvency law, which ensures that losses and gains are equally shared;
> A tax on financial transactions that can be used to support development of alternative options and limits to the unregulated flow of capital.[62]

The report repudiated neoliberal ideology. "The credo of the free market is the firm belief that through competing economic forces and purposes, an 'invisible hand' will assure the optimum good as every individual pursues his or her economic gain. It views human beings as individuals rather than as persons in community, as essentially competitive rather than cooperative, as consumerist and materialist rather than spiritual. Thus, it produced a graceless system that renders people surplus and abandons them if they cannot compete with the powerful few."[63]

I was not outside of this loop: money ran from my taxes through the U.S. government into the World Bank into not-really-developing countries and back out into private accounts that were reloaned by banks to countries so that, when the countries' economies collapsed, the banks were also bailed out by my tax money. Or my small pension fund made private investments that operated a similar way. Part of what it all financed was a pattern of wasteful consumption and a higher level of health and well-being for a small minority of the world's people. If my journey unraveled at institutions like the World Bank, to presidents and corporate boardrooms, G-8 and World Trade Organization gatherings, it also unraveled right back to me, every time I climbed in my car, or switched on a light, or accepted too narrow a range of choices for my vote. Gandhi had warned, "Remember that their God is Money"; and money, sacralized, was flowing in a global network that did seem *almost* inescapable. But it was hardly a network of mutuality—to use Martin King's terms; more *dis*mutual, because of its initial assumptions of individuality, competition, ownership, and profits.

"We have no temples, no stone architecture, no holy places or holy dress," I had heard at the African plenary. "European missionaries thought that we had no sense of God. But the entire activities of the people were devotion to the deity who is their

Creator. And the God of Africa is coterminous and coexistent with the people of Africa. Africa IS the footprint of God."[64]

I had come looking for ubuntu, and everywhere at the assembly it was evoked, a cry of the spirit from across a continent, offering a continuing measure of humaneness as always more powerful and poignant because of its contradictions in humans' cruelty, selfishness, corruption, and greed. It was here, and on every continent, in the spirit of peoples who make a way out of no way; who do not give up, but work for third—and fourth and fifth—liberations.

I was beginning to think of ubuntu as an organism, maybe like the ozone layer, our inescapable network of mutuality, tattered, torn in places, with some gaping holes; but at least partially regenerative, still protecting us, holding us together in spite of ourselves. If we could color the air, say with metal filings, we would see it there, I was sure, similar to our magnetic fields. Each act of decency, kindness, courage, and solidarity strengthened it; just as each act of cruelty, oblivion, greed, or hate knocked out another hole. Collective actions for a common ethical good boosted its power because of the increased intentionality such community-building requires.

"The Kingdom of God is in the midst of you," Jesus explained—but I had come to feel at times not a kingdom but a sacred company, or presence, energy within and between people as well as beyond. One of the most consistent forms of such union was sexuality, which is why it is so vulnerable, so maligned in a culture so fraught with alienation. That presence was here in the beat of drums on the dancing floor. It was in those moments when bodies align with minds and spirits. It was in the courage of activists and organizers in communities all over the world who worked for more humane systems and practices.

Malidoma Somé, concluded that the indigenous and the modern have been brought together in this era because of the profound truths each can learn from the other about the need for more balance in the distribution of material and spiritual resources. He reflected: "Africa's material scarcity may be symptomatic of a deeper global problem pertaining to soul and Spirit. While the Third World is experiencing the immediacy of people's need for healing in the area of physical hunger, the West is awakening to a spiritual hunger so dramatic as to be almost frightening. . . . The converging paths of these two worlds may ultimately enable material abundance to silence the Third World body's cries for nourishment and the cries of the Westerner's hungering for soul."[65]

I settled myself beneath the flambeau tree, breathing in clear air as the morning sun began to filter through rows of tiny leaves that, when touched, closed like praying hands.

There were no perfect solutions, no perfect social systems, any more than perfect cultures or perfect people. It is not utopia, but ubuntu, humaneness, that is our goal, and justice one of its beacons, compassion its practice, sharing and reciprocity its primary mode. "African people never blame God for their suffering," I remembered one plenary speaker explaining. The alternative is a radical accountability, a refusal to give up, and an incredible hope sustained by a belief that we are never alone. Our personal and our collective acts begin to shift our karma.

African philosophy was not so different from Marta's views on energy. I could hear her voice: "Einstein said all is relative, and we are all energy, which can never be destroyed, it can only be transformed. This is the law of the universe. If we believed that, we would not be about destruction, but transformation. We would align ourselves with the universe."

It did seem that the orange mud vibrated to the shrill of a bird in a blossom-drenched branch above me. The Innate Great Perfection, Tibetan Buddhists might say, even as Mao's troops closed in. There are sanctuaries of spirit even in forests where the strange fruit of lynched bodies makes terrible the trees. Presence as God in the midst of us. Do everything, Gandhi's beloved *Bhagavad Gita* preached through him to the struggles in Africa as well as to Martin King, do everything as if it is worship.[66]

The opposite, all around us, are our various apartheids, Māheles, Jim Crows, played out on such a bloody canvas in the history of the closing century. People all over the world are shaping their faith into new structures of resistance and transformation. These will take a while, I suspect, to come to fruition in collective global practices and consciousness to challenge and transform brutal systems. If the great male revolutionary narratives of the nineteenth and twentieth centuries have run their course, emptied their plots of history, people all over the world are always already speaking, singing, drumming, dreaming, and writing new stories that will eventually weave into a strong enough narrative web to catch our deepest common longings and the new strategies that can transform our new realities. Birthing such new structures will require both great patience and great impatience. The people who create these stories and these processes will be the ones who know that spirit, energy, is generative, is formed and transformed in the material realm.

The more extreme the circumstances, the more the presence of the sacred, which sometimes I have felt more as an absence or betrayal, as if a shadow could belie the sun, or the trough of a wave the reality of water. The meek do inherit the earth. Perhaps I finally understood what Jesus meant.

Marta's voice continued: "There is no enemy, only oneness. There is no Other, only various manifestations of energy. When you see this, you don't need to have faith any longer, because you know."

I appreciated Marta's conviction, but I recognized I was still just getting around to faith. That was enough for now. I was ready to go home.

EPILOGUE
Durham, North Carolina, November 2001

I

As I completed this manuscript to send to Rutgers University Press on August 31, 2001, activists from all over the world gathered in Durban, South Africa, for another UN conference, this one a world conference against racism, xenophobia, and other forms of discrimination. The Bush administration pulled its high-level delegation, boycotting over the issue of whether Zionism is a form of racism and over the question of reparations for slavery and colonialism. Many U.S. nongovernmental organization participants also raised the issue of the racist criminal justice system in this country. Grassroots groups in South Africa used the conference to protest the neoliberal policies adopted by the African National Congress, leaders of the new South African government. The new Durban Social Forum included the Soweto Electricity Crisis Committee, fighting electricity cut-offs; the Concerned Citizens Forum, which fights evictions and water cut-offs; the Landless People's Movement; Jubilee 2000; the Anti-Privatization Forum; the Treatment Action Campaign for government provision of anti-AIDS drugs; the Alternative Information and Development Centre; and the National Consultative Forum on Palestine. At the grassroots, South Africans are once again mobilizing, resisting evictions, turning power back on.

"If we find ourselves in a situation where the government of the day does not deliver and we believe that the government has the capacity to deliver, we will demand that it delivers," said Fatimeer Meer, anti-apartheid activist and Mandela's official biographer.[1]

One week after my manuscript reached Rutgers University Press, terrorists hijacked four airplanes and crashed them into the twin towers of the World Trade Center, the Pentagon, and a field in Pennsylvania, killing more than three thousand people at the current count. In the wake of huge shock, grief, anger, and confusion, commentators on each of the major networks announced that now, after September 11, everything has changed. But has it?

As I grieved the deaths in Manhattan, Pennsylvania, and D.C., I also braced for my government's response. As President Bush quickly declared a "war on terror," I could see in the flames of the twin towers the coming flames over Kabul. I fumed as all the major television networks shaped the shock, anger, and grief in response to the "Attack on America" into a jingoistic call for revenge. They declared the attacks to be the "end of American innocence." What innocence? I wondered. Spending late nights and early mornings surfing channels or the Net for any real news, I despaired of a national memory that seems always already encrypted with amnesia, a national emotion laced with anesthesia, a media-guided grief that would have us track our tears like its bombs in the gun sights of its empire. I have protested as the Bush administration encourages what Lawrence Grossberg calls "affective epidemics" to the terrorist attacks to institute a range of unconstitutional practices, from use of military tribunals to holding immigrants without habeas corpus to reinvigoration of domestic surveillance on political or religious groups deemed subversive, to giving even more money back to corporations as tax breaks to jump-start the recessional economy. In the midst of all of this, who is noticing that women on Temporary Aid to Needy Families are about to max out their five years in a welfare-reform process that assumed a full economy?

Bush can now make oversimplified arguments to justify these regressive foreign and domestic policies because of thirty years of careful propaganda and political work by the Right that has constantly rerouted conversations about class and power, race and power, gender and power, and sexuality and power into narratives of "reverse discrimination" or "special rights" or "right to life;" or conversations about colonialism, or neocolonialism into support for "freedom fighters" and "free markets." U.S. Right-Wing leaders over the past two decades have used religious arguments in a culture war, a strategy that boasted of turning cultural fault lines into battlegrounds. They have waged popular campaigns against affirmative action, AIDS funding, all art that functions as cultural critique, immigrants of color, women's right to control their bodies, and civil rights for lesbians and gay men. It is as if causes and effects have been so scrambled and distorted, the radar over our causal fields so jammed, that events come to us, quite literally this time, out of the blue and crashing into national consciousness.

If, deep within the earth, the explosions shifted tectonic plates so that volcanoes erupted in our families, or schools, or neighborhoods, or legislatures, separating sister from brother, parent from child, it was of no matter, because it fed the launchers' long-term strategy and their immediate gain. And if these depth-bombed tectonic plates also shifted far away and threw up bloody little generals, like volcanoes whose lavas cover villages, caused earthquakes to slide mud over people and goats and dogs and parrots in thatched or adobe houses in countries remote from our imagination, it was no matter, either.

Now U.S. bombs fall on Afghanistan, literally shattering bodies, houses, towns, a landscape already nearly obliterated by war. Bombs fall, figuratively as well, into that region's cultural fault lines, turning them increasingly into battlegrounds. And if the quakes are felt in Muslim communities across the globe as riots in Nigeria or Pakistan or Palestine or Delhi, as shelling in Kashmir, that does not seem to matter, either, because these subsequent tragedies and violent disruptions are not in the U.S. plan for infinite justice. As Colin Powell explained to Indian leaders, it is time for their conflict with Pakistan now to stand down in favor of the American empire's new and noble and seemingly endless war—on terror?

Indian novelist Arundhati Roy captured the eerie double entendre between George Bush and Osama bin Laden in her brilliant and searing "The Algebra of Infinite Justice" in *The Guardian* in a passage resonant of Hegel: "Now Bush and Bin Laden have even begun to borrow each other's rhetoric. Each now refers to the other as 'the head of the snake.' Both invoke God and use the loose millenarian currency of good and evil as their terms of reference. Both are engaged in unequivocal political crimes. Both are dangerously armed—one with the nuclear arsenal of the obscenely powerful, the other with the incandescent, destructive power of the utterly hopeless."[2]

We know that the Taliban equals bin Laden's fundamentalism. But what constitutes Bush's? In 1979 New Right architects Richard Viguerie and Paul Weyrich made the trip to Lynchburg, Virginia, to visit Jerry Falwell, who had a large church and television ministry. They persuaded him that Christian evangelicals had responsibility this side of the Rapture and that he should mobilize the evangelical base into a moral majority to shape the Republican platform in the 1980 election. He agreed, and he did. This Religious Right would build on Phyllis Schlafley's brilliant campaign against the Equal Rights Amendment (passed by Congress in 1972), opposition to 1973 *Roe vs. Wade*, and reaction to a growing movement for lesbian and gay rights (organized first in Anita Bryant's Florida campaign and in the Briggs initiative in California). Christian fundamentalists brought into New Right politics their extensive grassroots organization and religious broadcast networks. By 1979, Pat Robertson's Christian Broadcast Network was spending $50 million annually, reaching five million people. The network's larger effort was to tap into the 20 to 33 percent of the U.S. adult population, some fifty million people by some estimates, who professed to be born again—meaning they accepted Scripture as authority for all doctrine and felt an urgent need to spread their faith.[3]

In 1980, anticommunist activists within the Republican Party called for a New Inter-American Policy for the Eighties. It included an agenda to "counter . . . liberation theology" and to replace human rights ("a culturally and politically relative concept") with a "policy of political and ethical realism." In January of 1981, Reagan's Secretary of State Alexander M. Haig announced that a concern for human rights would no longer dictate U.S. foreign policy; human rights concerns were replaced by concern for the threat of international terrorism—the situation in which we find ourselves today. Pat Robertson used his Christian Broadcasting Network to raise money for the Nicaraguan Contras ($3 million), as did Rev. Sun Myung Moon's Unification Church. Robertson also used his network to lobby for military aid for the junta in El Salvador and for Gen. Efrain Rios Montt, dictator of Guatemala converted to Protestant Pentecostalism by Gospel Outreach. Sara Diamond quotes a Gospel Outreach pastor defending Rios Montt's killing of indigenous Guatemalans: "The Army doesn't massacre the Indians. It massacres demons, and the Indians are demon possessed; they are communists."[4]

In the same year that New Right leaders approached Jerry Falwell to help in politicizing Christian clerics into a militant moral majority, the CIA and Pakistan's Inter Services Intelligence (ISI) "launched the largest covert operation in the history of the CIA," in order to "harness the energy of Afghan resistance to the Soviets and expand it into a holy war, an Islamic jihad, which would turn Muslim countries within the Soviet Union against the communist regime. . . . Over the years, the CIA funded and recruited almost 100,000 radical mojahedin from forty Islamic countries as soldiers for America's proxy war. . . . The jihad spread to Chechnya, Kazoo and Kashmir. The CIA continued to pour in money and military equipment, but the overhead had become immense, and more money was needed. The mojahedin ordered farmers to plant opium as a 'revolutionary tax.' The ISI set up hundreds of heroin laboratories across Afghanistan. Within two years of the CIA's arrival, the Pakistan-Afghanistan borderland had become the biggest producer of heroin in the world and the single biggest source of the heroin on American streets. The annual profits, said to be between $100 billion and $200 billion, were ploughed back into training and arming militants."[5] So, domestically, in Central America and in Afghanistan there was an active U.S.-based Right-Wing policy—by movements and by the state—to radicalize clerics for political ends. It was the same year that death squads murdered Monsignor Romero in El Salvador.

Let's be very clear about one of the effects: Having been traded for arms, drugs showed up in U.S. inner cities suffering economic devastation, hitting families whose women—who were expected to hold the line in neighborhoods like those in Atlanta, or Memphis, or my town or yours, crumbling from structural unemployment—would be pilloried by Ronald Reagan as welfare queens and instructed to assume more personal responsibility by the welfare reform legislation of 1996, which touted these women's forced participation in a full economy. And all of this is called family values.

In the midst of the war on Afghanistan, the U.S. government signed a $200 billion contract for a new fighter jet—the other side of the dialectic of terror from the five-dollar box cutter and the thirty-four-cent stamp. If we in the United States are declaring war on all that terrifies us, let me register that AIDS in Africa terrifies me. Structural adjustment and the deliberate impoverishment of continents for the greed of a very few terrify me. A police state that interrogates and imprisons all it suspects as Other terrifies me. But, however afraid I might get about any of these phenomena, I know that it is not fear, but love, that will answer them clearly and fully. A recent

World Health Organization report explains that the total cost of providing safe water and sanitation to everyone in the world who needs it would be only $10 billion.[6] The entire external debt of sub-Saharan Africa is $230 billion. I say we take the $200 billion, dump the jet, and cancel African debt.

Citizens of the United States can never win a war on terror, because war itself is an act of terror and because war is terrifying. Military contractors will win it; those who hold stock in privatized prison industries will win, too. For the rest of us, we may not believe that we suffer ourselves the grief and fear that our military calls down on Afghans now, perhaps Iraqis next, because ABC and CBS and CNN (owned themselves by a handful of multinational corporations) do not make it into spectacle: they do not daily subject us to vignettes of their dead, to smoking scenes of rubble at Jalalabad Ground Zero, to weeping Afghan widows and their orphaned children, to narratives of the brave people, Taliban or Northern Alliance, who rescue the wounded, carry out the corpses, and put out the fires. But that does not mean they do not exist or that they do not feel this history, which is theirs and ours.

The events on and subsequent to September 11 are our threshold to the twenty-first century, which we are on the verge of making even bloodier than the twentieth. I think that Carolyn Forché, fresh from the wounded ground of El Salvador's civil war, got it right:

> It is either the beginning or the end
> Of the world, and the choice is ourselves
> Or nothing.[7]

It is time, again, in Forché's words, to "go after all that is lost," to shape a post-modernity in which *humaneness* and *justice* and *democracy* are more than ironic doublespeak. In such a situation, if there were not already a transnational feminist analysis and movement, it would be necessary to invent one. Fortunately, we do not have to.

It is time to say to the multinationals: Share the profits of modernity with all the communities and the continents that capitalism has sucked dry.

It is time to say to the patriarchs: Women will shape a humane future beyond your control. Join the rest of us when you learn to behave.

It's time to say to the homophobes: There are many ways to love, and we will use them all, driven by a deep desire for justice and relationship.

It's time to say to the racists: We are finally dismantling the legacies of slavery and colonialism, and together we will repair the damage that was done.

It is time to say to all the warmongers: You cannot have this century. Stand down.

II

Writing this book is a process to which I have surrendered myself, most days, for the past year. I have rolled out of bed at 6:45, walked for an hour, showered, and meditated before beginning work at 9:00 A.M. at my desk, or at a table on my front porch in lovely weather. There were days and months when I was not sure at all of the outcome: of whether I would be able to do the complicated combination of research and personal reflection that the project required, in the time I had to do it before my money ran out. Writing *Born to Belonging*, then, has been a daily practice of faith and discipline. Sufficient unto the day was the writing thereof, most days anyway.

Do your work and step back: the secret of *wu-wei*, effortless action. This detachment is not a polar opposite from engagement, as perhaps I once suspected. On the contrary, I have learned, such detachment allows for deeper engagements because I know that the effects are not really up to me, though the work itself is. Do each thing as if it were worship, and the rest should more or less take care of itself.

Stepping back from this work at the end also means letting go of you the reader, whom I have imagined and conversed with on the other, silvery side of my computer screen through hot days and cold, dry and wet, in dark and in light. There is some imagined intimacy now that I find hard to surrender. I have found it a good conversation. I console myself that I will meet my reader, in your many faces, over the next few years. I have found that each book I have written has brought new friends into my life.

Perhaps the hardest letting go is the letting go of language itself. This is especially difficult now that I have gotten past the hard labor of getting drafts onto the page in sometimes tortured sentences, then gone back through to reshape, and reshape, and reshape. Writing is mainly rewriting, I tell my students when I have them. But at the end, when it all starts coming together, there is an aesthetic rush, a falling in love again with language itself. Here in my hesitant grief, I am humored by Malidoma Somé. He reminds me that trees and plants are the most intelligent beings because they do not need words to communicate, as we humans do. Plants and animals other than ourselves live closer to what he calls "the world of intrinsic meaning."

Here we are again at "natural existence," "reality," the "oceanic," and by now I hope I have evoked sufficiently what our loss of contact with that existence feels like and its costs. "The tao that can be told / is not the eternal Tao," Lao-tzu begins. The world has its own intrinsic meaning, which we cannot capture or control, with rationality or language or violence or cold cash. "To utter," Somé continues, "means to be in exile. . . . We are confessing our distance from the source. . . . We are far removed from the vast array of meaning that is our home. For if we were home, we would not feel the need to journey there."[8]

There are roughly one-half million characters in this manuscript. Like matter, the text itself a thin line of ink squiggles suspended in mostly empty space. That space evokes the world of intrinsic meaning to which we all belong. It is a world I have journeyed toward but never captured, my words merely the finger pointing to the moon. It is this silence, this emptiness, this belonging, to which I finally surrender.

NOTES

PREFACE

1. Zora Neale Hurston, *Dust Tracks on the Road* (New York: Lippincott, 1942), 36–37.

PROLOGUE

1. Walter Benjamin, "Thesis on the Philosophy of History," *Illuminations: Essays and Reflections*, ed. Hannah Arendt (New York: Schocken Books, 1968), 11, 255. Frederic Jameson elaborates this contemporary "moment of danger": "There has never been a moment in the history of capitalism when this last enjoyed greater elbow-room and space for manoeuvre: all the threatening forces it generated against itself in the past—labour movements and insurgencies, mass socialist parties, even socialist states themselves—seem today in full disarray when not in one way or another effectively neutralized; for the moment global capital seems able to follow its own nature and inclinations, without the traditional precautions" (Frederic Jameson, *The Cultural Turn: Selected Writings on the Postmodern, 1983–1998* [London: Verso, 1998], 48).

2. Elizabeth Weed, "Introduction: Terms of Reference," in *Coming to Terms: Feminism, Theory, Politics*, ed. Elizabeth Weed (New York: Routledge, 1989), x.

3. *Random House Webster's College Dictionary*, s.v. "self." Much of contemporary theory aims itself at this completely individual self, which I hope to suggest is too easy a straw self for certain kinds of arguments. I hope to show that a person's nature in other metaphysical systems is never considered completely individual; that the completely individual self is, in fact, a highly Westernized fiction.

4. Jenny Bourne, "Homelands of the Mind: Jewish Feminism and Identity Politics," *Race and Class* 29 (summer 1987): 1–24; cited in Ellen Rooney, "Commentary: What Is to Be Done," in Weed, *Coming to Terms*, 231–232: "Identity Politics is all the rage. Exploitation is out (it is intrinsically determinist). Oppression is in (it is intrinsically personal). What is to be done has been replaced by who am I." Weed echoes, "It is the politics which ask 'what is to be done?' rather than 'who am I?' which attempts to avoid the identifactory structures available everywhere, those structures which enable us to see women of color but not race, blacks but not whites" (xxi). In this book I ask both of those questions together rather than prioritizing one over the other.

5. M. Jacqui Alexander and Chandra Talpade Mohanty, "Introduction: Genealogies, Legacies, Movements," in *Feminist Genealogies, Colonial Legacies, Democratic Futures*, ed. M. Jacqui Alexander and Chandra Talpade Mohanty (New York: Routledge, 1997), xxviii, xviii.

6. Gloria Wekker, "One Finger Does Not Drink Okra Soup: Afro-Surinamese Women and Critical Agency," in Alexander and Mohanty, *Feminist Genealogies*, 331, 333.

7. Ibid., 352.

8. Thich Nhat Hanh, *The Heart of the Buddha's Teachings: Transforming Suffering into Peace, Joy and Liberation* (Berkeley, Calif.: Parallax Press, 1998), 164.

9. David Forgacs, ed., *An Antonio Gramsci Reader* (New York: Schocken Books, 1988), 199. Gramsci, writing from prison, critiqued the deterministic forms of Marxism by elaborating the "sphere of the complex superstructures"—all those realms relegated to secondary status by Marx's "economism" that deterministically reduced understanding of reality by the "theoretical separation of the economic dimension from a social and political ensemble . . . [and] the reduction of this ensemble to its economic causes" (422). Gramsci explained that ideology is what holds the "superstructure" of culture in place and makes its subjects complicit. Ideology is "real historical facts which must be combated and their nature as instruments of domination revealed . . . for reasons of political struggle: in order to make the governed intellectually independent of the governing, in order to destroy one hegemony and create another" (196).

10. Marx, Correspondence from 1843, David McLellan, ed., *Karl Marx: Selected Writings* (Oxford, U.K.: Oxford University Press, 1977), 38. In *German Ideology*, Marx writes: "It does not explain practice from the idea but explains the formation of ideas from material practice; and accordingly it comes to the conclusion that all forms and products of consciousness cannot be dissolved by mental criticism, by resolution into 'self-consciousness' or transformation into 'apparitions,' 'spectres,' 'fancies,' etc. but only by the practical overthrow of the actual social relations which give rise to this idealistic humbug" (quoted in Terry Eagleton, *Marx* [New York: Routledge, 1997], 14–15). I am suggesting here that it's not an either/or: an increased self-consciousness collectivized *can* help the "practical overthrow of actual social relations." Eagleton describes Marx's practical philosophy—"not to know history but to change it"—in a way that also emphasizes the importance of consciousness: "to know yourself in a new way is to alter yourself in that very act; so we have here a peculiar form of cognition in which the act of knowing alters what it contemplates" (4).

11. Paulo Freire, *Pedagogy of the Oppressed*, trans. Myra Bergman Ramos (New York: Herder & Herder, 1970), 101.

12. Freire, *Pedagogy*, 75, 101.

13. Candice Pert, *Your Body Is Your Subconscious Mind* (Boulder, Colo.: Sounds True, 2000). This is from the transcription of the taped lecture and interview.

14. *Tao Te Ching: A New English Version*, trans. Stephen Mitchell (New York: Harper-Collins, 1991), no. 27. All other references are from this text.

15. For an explanation, see chapter 5 in Joanna Macy, *World as Lover, World as Self* (Berkeley, Calif.: Parallax Press, 1991), 53–64.

16. *Tao Te Ching*, no. 6.

17. "The Gospel of Mary," *The Complete Gospels: Annotated Scholars' Version*, rev. ed., ed. Robert S. Miller and Robert W. Funk (San Francisco: HarperCollins, 1994).

18. Leela Gandhi explains in *Postcolonial Theory: A Critical Introduction* (New York: Columbia University Press, 1998) that the postcolonial critic "has to work toward a synthesis of, or negotiation between" the "poststructuralist critique of Western epistemology and . . . materialist philosophies such as Marxism" (ix). But perhaps neither offers enough, and perhaps both together could be seen in some dialectical relationship to the various realms of spirit embodied in the range of cultures that Europe attempted to subsume as colonies.

19. The phrase about the "moral arc of the universe" is from "Remaining Awake through a Great Revolution," in *A Testament of Hope: The Essential Writings and Speeches of Martin Luther King, Jr.*, ed. James Melvin Washington (San Francisco: HarperCollins, 1991), 277. King used the expression *transphysics* in his last sermon in Memphis, the night before he was killed: "And as I said to you the other night, Bull Connor didn't know history. He knew a kind of physics that somehow didn't relate to the transphysics that we knew about. And that was the fact that there was a certain kind of fire that no water could put out. And we went before the

fire hoses; we had known water. If we were Baptist or some other denomination, we had been immersed. If we were Methodist, and some others, we had been sprinkled, but we knew water. That couldn't stop us" ("I See the Promised Land," 281).

20. Samyutta Nikāya i. 61–62, Aṅguttara Nikāya ii. 47–49. Quoted in Rupert Gethin, *The Foundations of Buddhism* (Oxford, U.K.: Oxford University Press, 1998), 126. The entire quote: "Rather in this fathom-long body, with its perceptions and mind, I declare the world, the arising of the world, the ceasing of the world, and the way leading to the ceasing of the world."

CHAPTER 1

1. Thanks to Aime Carillo Rowe for a walk on a Connecticut beach and a great conversation in which some of these memories converged.

2. John Cottingham, *Descartes* (New York: Routledge, 1999), 3.

3. Descartes, "Discourse on the Method," in *The Philosophical Writings of Descartes*, vol. 1, ed. J. Cottingham, R. Soothoff, and D. Murdoch (Cambridge, U.K.: Cambridge University Press, 1985), 125–126.

4. Descartes, "Discourse," 126–127.

5. Thanks to feminist philosopher Jennifer Manion at Carlton College for providing cyber-consultation for a more subtle reading of Descartes than I originally attempted.

6. John Locke, *Second Treatise of Government*, ed. C. B. Macpherson (1690; Indianapolis, Ind.: Hackett Publishing Co., 1980).

7. Ibid., vii.

8. Locke says, for instance, that children owe equal obedience to both mother and father and argued that a woman ought to retain what is hers by right or contract if a marriage is dissolved. Yet the husband as "abler and stronger" is the spokesperson and decision maker and represents publicly the needs of the entire family (Locke, *Second Treatise*, chap. 7). Thanks to Jennifer Manion.

9. Locke, *Second Treatise*, 10, 18.

10. Ibid., 22. Locke does set limits on what one is allowed to take from the pool of common resources.

11. Ibid., 13.

12. Robert Heilbroner, *Worldly Philosophers: The Lives, Times, and Ideas of the Great Economic Thinkers* (New York: Touchstone, 1999), 51.

13. Adam Smith, *An Inquiry into the Nature and Causes of the Wealth of Nations*, vol. 1 (1776; Indianapolis: Liberty Fund, 1981), 26–27. This Liberty Fund edition is an exact photographic reproduction of the Oxford University Press edition of 1976. It was published by Liberty Fund to "encourage study of the idea of a society of free and responsible individuals" (iv).

14. Heilbroner, *Worldly Philosophers*, 56: "But self-interest is only half the picture. It drives men to action. Something else must prevent the pushing of profit-hungry individuals from holding society up to exorbitant ransom: a community activated only by self-interest would be a community of ruthless profiteers. This regulator is competition, the conflict of the self-interested actors on the market-place . . . the selfish motives of men are transmuted by interaction to yield the most unexpected of results: social harmony." See the rest of Heilbroner for Smith's positive contributions.

15. Simone de Beauvoir, *The Second Sex*, trans. H. M. Parshley (New York: Vintage, 1974), 30.

16. G.W.F. Hegel, *The Phenomenology of Mind*, trans. J. B. Baillie (New York: Harper Torchbooks, 1967), 229, 231, 234.

17. See Cynthia Willett, "The Master-Slave Dialectic: Hegel vs. Douglass," in *Subjugation and Bondage: Critical Essays on Slavery and Social Philosophy*, ed. Tommy L. Lott (Lanham, Md.: Rowman and Littlefield Publishers, 1998). "While major sociological and historical studies of slavery in America refer to Hegel's analysis to explain the dynamics of master and slave,

these same studies . . . also suggest limitations in Hegel's dialectical methodology. . . . The duplicitous symmetries of Hegelian logic conceal, however, what African-American history reveals: The slave is not *in fact* the mirror reversal of the master. Therefore, the experience of the African-American slave demands a second dialectic, one that is irreducible to the Hegelian model of selfhood and freedom" (151–152).

18. Hegel, *Phenomenology*, 228, 233–238.

19. T. Walter Wallbank, Alastair M. Taylor, George Barr Carson Jr., *Civilization: Past and Present* (Chicago: Scott, Foreman, 1965), 2:27–28.

20. Freddie Hart Segrest and Phala Jordan Tatem, *The Segrest Saga* (n.p., Harline Publishing Co., 1994), 33–41.

21. Basil Davidson, *The Black Man's Burden: Africa and the Curse of the Nation-State* (New York: Three Rivers Press, 1992), 133, 138.

22. Adrienne Rich, "The Meaning of Our Love for Women Is What We Have Constantly to Expand," in *On Lies, Secrets and Silence: Selected Prose, 1966–1978* (New York: W. W. Norton & Co., 1979), 223.

23. David McLellan, introduction to *Karl Marx: Selected Writings* (Oxford, U.K.: Oxford University Press, 1988), 1. This is the Marx that Howard Zinn seeks to resuscitate in his *Marx in Soho: A Play on History* (Boston: South End Press, 1999).

24. Heilbroner, *Worldly Philosophers*, 168.

25. Douglas Kellner, "The Obsolescence of Marxism?" in *Whither Marxism? Global Crises in International Perspective*, ed. Bernd Magnus and Stephen Cullenberg (New York: Routledge, 1995), 17.

26. Marx, "Wage Labour and Capital," in McLellan, *Selected Writings*, 250. This text was first delivered as lectures to the Workingmen's Club in Brussels in 1847. These contain his first systematic exposition of his economic theories.

27. Marx, *Grundrisse*, written in 1857–58 but unpublished until 1941, a manuscript that is much more wide ranging than *Kapital*; editor David McLellan considers *Grundrisse* the "most central of Marx's works"; quoted here in *Selected Writings*, 370.

28. Marx, *Economic and Philosophical Manuscripts*, in *Selected Writings*, 79, 80.

29. Marx, *Economic and Philosophical Manuscripts of 1844*, ed. Dirk Struik, trans. Martin Milligan (New York: International Publishers, n.d.), 111, 112, 114. Thanks to Becky Thompson for pointing me toward Marx's explanation of species being—as well as sections from *Economic and Philosophical Manuscripts*.

30. Ibid., 107, 110, 111.

31. Quoted in Eagleton, *Marx*, 18, passages from *Economic and Philosophical Manuscripts*.

32. Marx, *Grundrisse*, 345–348. That capitalists regarded the individual "not as a development of history but as posited by nature," and this idea was an "aesthetic fiction" paralleled by the fiction that bourgeois relations were "immutable natural laws of society."

33. Eagleton, *Marx*, 20.

34. Ibid., 12, 18. "The ideas of the ruling class are in every epoch the ruling ideas. . . . The ruling ideas are nothing more than the ideal expression of the dominant material relationships, the dominant material relationships grasped as ideas." Thus "all forms and products of consciousness cannot be dissolved by mental criticism, by resolution into 'self-consciousness' or transformation into 'apparitions,' 'spectres,' 'fancies,' etc. but only by the practical overthrow of the actual social relations which gave rise to this idealistic humbug" (15).

35. Karl Marx, "Contribution to the Critique of Hegel's *Philosophy of Right*," in *Marx and Engels on Religion*, introduction by Reinhold Niebuhr (New York: Schocken Books, 1964), 41–42.

36. Quoted in Eagleton, *Marx*, 3.

37. Ibid., 4.

38. Alice Walker, *The Color Purple* (New York: Pocket Books, 1985), 199–201.

39. Friedrich Wilhelm Nietzsche, "The Gay Science," in *Existentialism from Dostoevsky to Sartre*, ed. Walter Kaufman (New York: World Publishing Co., 1972), 105, 106.

40. Aimé Césaire, *Discourse on Colonialism*, trans. Joan Pinkham (New York: Monthly Review Press, 1972), 15.

41. Sigmund Freud, *Civilization and Its Discontents*, trans. and ed. James Strachey (New York: Norton, 1989), 10–11.

42. Freud, *Civilization*, 60.

43. James Allen, ed., *Without Sanctuary: Lynching Photography in America* (Santa Fe, N.M.: Twin Palms Publishing, 2000).

44. Jean-Paul Sartre, *Nausea*, trans. Lloyd Alexander (*La Nausée*, 1938; New York: New Directions, 1964), 127, 131.

45. Ibid., 128, 131, 133, 134.

46. Walker, *Color Purple*, 202–203. See also *Pema Chodron and Alice Walker in Conversation on the Meaning of Suffering and the Mystery of Joy*, Sounds True Videotapes, 1999. Thanks to Becky Thompson for giving me a copy of this tape, in which these two meditating women discuss the "revolutionary power of tonglen," a Tibetan meditation practice of transforming pain into compassion.

47. Macy, *World as Lover, World as Self*, 106, 112, 113.

48. Thich Nhat Hanh, *Vietnam: Lotus in a Sea of Fire* (New York: Hill and Wang, 1967), 33–43. I found *Lotus in a Sea of Fire* in the Duke library. I had spotted the title rereading the essays of Martin Luther King, who was the monk's friend and carried *Lotus* in his briefcase. I was surprised that it was out of print, since most of Thich Nhat Hanh's other volumes do a brisk sale. Duke's card catalogue listed two copies. But I found that the one in Perkins Library had been missing for years and the one in the Divinity School library came up missing as well when I located the empty slot on the shelves. Throwing myself on the mercy of the reference librarian, I eventually ended up with the slim book in my hot hands. I found it provided a context for the Buddhist teacher so popular in the West. *Lotus in a Sea of Fire* describes a Buddhist parallel to the liberation theology that would emerge in Latin America in the next century, with Catholic priests and nuns working with the people in what Latin Americans call "base communities."

49. Ibid., 56 n.

50. Ibid., 32.

51. Simone de Beauvoir's *The Second Sex* also takes Hegel's master-slave as her point of departure for her feminist examination of the condition of women. "He is the Subject, he is the Absolute—she is the Other" (xix). Extending the master-slave analogy, she compares women's condition to that of the African Americans under Jim Crow: "For whether it is a race, a caste, a class, or a sex that is reduced to a position of inferiority, the methods of justification are the same. 'The eternal feminine' corresponds to the 'black soul' and to the 'Jewish character' " (xxvii).

52. See Joan Nestle, "Narratives of Liberation: Pluralities of Hope," *A Fragile Union: New and Selected Writings* (San Francisco: Cleis Press, 1998), 93–106.

53. Albert Memmi, *The Colonizer and the Colonized*, introduction by Jean-Paul Sartre (Boston: Beacon Press, 1967), viii–x.

54. From "Psyche: Invention of the Other," in Jacques Derrida, *Acts of Literature*, ed. Derek Attridge (New York: Routledge, 1992), 326. The editor explains: "Deconstruction's work at the limits of philosophy . . . is directed toward an undoing of closed structures in order to make possible the coming of the other; not an other which merely reinforces the same (as, notes Derrida, the other produced by racism always does), not an other which is simply outside or absolutely new, but one that displaces the very opposition of same and other, inside and outside, old and new" (311).

55. Memmi, *Colonizer*, xvii, 8.

56. Ibid., 11, 50, 69.

57. Ibid., 52, 60, 70, 74.

58. Ibid., 62–63.

59. Césaire, *Discourse*, 14.

60. Davidson, *The Black Man's Burden*, 52.

61. Memmi, *Colonizer*, 89, 117.

62. Ibid., 120, 132, 139.

63. Ibid., 140–141, 151–153.

64. Frantz Fanon, *The Wretched of the Earth*, trans. Constance Farrington and preface by Jean-Paul Sartre (New York: Grove Press, 1968), 61, 94. Gandhi and Fanon plotted two paths out of twentieth-century colonialism. In the United States Martin Luther King and Malcolm X reflect the dialectic between violence and nonviolence as liberatory strategies. King located nonviolent struggle exactly on the cusp of master-slave relations, hoping to free the psychic forces trapped in that embrace while reconfiguring structures of mastery. What is remarkable about the nonviolent movement for which King was the major spokesman was not that it failed, but that it got as far as it did in dismantling segregation and voter disenfranchisement in the South and beginning to define the larger economic structures that hold racism in its deadly place. Malcolm X and the Black Power movement, on the other hand, helped to articulate a more autonomous political and psychic position beyond, in spite of, and from which to address white failures and insidious racist systems. Leaders in various African liberation struggles, although highly influenced by Fanon, often did not see the choice between violence and nonviolence as opposites, as Bill Sutherland and Matt Meyer's interviews show in *Guns and Gandhi: Pan African Insights on Nonviolence, Armed Struggle and Liberation in Africa* (Trenton, N.J.: Africa World Press, 2000). The African National Congress, for example, was influenced by Gandhi's work in South Africa earlier in the century and shaped its first resistance to apartheid with nonviolence campaigns against the pass laws. When the Sharpeville Massacre in 1961 showed the level of violence with which the Afrikaner state would respond to this resistance, the ANC chose a policy of armed struggle that was more armed propaganda or sabotage, its main targets for decades structures, not people. By the 1980s the total strategy of President P. W. Botha resulted in a more widespread violence that brought the country to the verge of civil war. The Truth and Reconciliation Commission established by the new democratic government undertook thirty months of hearings to uncover the narratives of state violence, the interethnic violence that the Afrikaner government stirred between the ANC and the Inkatha Freedom Party, and the counterviolence of the ANC. The commission found that although the ANC was engaged in a just war and the source of South Africa's violence was the system of apartheid, some of the ANC's responsive violence had violated human rights. One of the truths the commission seemed to reveal was that although violence might be a necessary component for colonial liberation, it does not cleanse the psyche of the colonized. Quite the contrary, the nexus of violence left in the wake of war requires its own cleansing, with the TRC as an intermediate strategy, the long-term solution to which is more just structures of state and economy.

65. Sutherland and Meyer, *Guns and Gandhi*, 78, 87, 98.

66. Herbert Marcuse, *An Essay on Liberation* (Boston: Beacon, 1969), vii–x.

67. Ibid., 10–11.

68. Ibid., 10–11, 16, 17, 20, 21.

69. Terry Eagleton, *Literary Theory: An Introduction* (Minneapolis: University of Minnesota Press, 1983), 142.

70. Michel Foucault, "Two Lectures," *Power/Knowledge: Selected Interviews and Other Writings, 1972–1977*, ed. Colin Gordon (New York: Pantheon, 1980), 88–90.

71. Ibid., 93, 97.

72. Ibid., 81–83.

73. Ibid., 102.

74. Ibid., 97.

75. See Paul A. Bove, "Discourse," in *Critical Terms for Literary Study*, ed. Frank Lentricchia and Thomas McLaughlin (Chicago: University of Chicago Press, 1990). "In disciplinary societies, self-determination is nearly impossible, and political opposition must take the form of resistance to the systems of knowledge and their institutions that regulate the population into 'individualities' who, as such, make themselves available for more discipline, to be actors acted upon" (61). In such formulations exactly who or what resists remains deliberately obscure as does why the acted-upon actors might decide to behave differently within these systems of knowledge.

76. Alexander and Mohanty, *Feminist Genealogies*, xviii.

77. Foucault, "Two Lectures," 98.

78. Judith Butler articulates the poststructuralist dispersal of the self in *Bodies That Matter: On the Discursive Limits of 'Sex'* (New York: Routledge, 1993). "One might be tempted to say that identity categories are insufficient because every subject position is the site of converging relations of power that are not univocal. But such a formulation underestimates the radical challenge to the subject that such converging relations imply. For there is no self-identical subject who houses or bears these relations, no site at which such relations converge. This converging and interarticulation is the contemporary fate of the subject. In other words, the subject as a self-identical entity is no more." When Butler tries to theorize the problematic question of agency within such an understanding of "no self-identical subject," the need for some more complex understanding becomes apparent, to me at least. She wants no part of a theory that "would restore a figure of the choosing subject-humanist" (x). She argues for "the workings of an agency that is (1) not the same as voluntarism, and that (2) though implicated in the very relations of power it seeks to rival, is not, as a consequence, reducible to those dominant forms" (241). If we understand voluntarism, with Webster's help, as "any theory that regards will as the fundamental agency or principle" does this mean that *will*—"the faculty of conscious and deliberate action"—does not operate as any function of the non-self-identical subject? What part of a more complicated intersubject is "not reducible" to dominant forms of power? What makes it so? From *where* does the agency arise? What is the intersubjectivity of what Butler calls the "abject"—what Howard Thurman calls the "dispossessed"—those of us left out of dominant formations of the Subject? From soul, or spirit, I would argue, which also has its own discourse although Butler does not choose to introduce it—a tao that is always within, to be used however we like; an inner life for which Howard Thurman elicits revitalization. Without a recourse to such practices and discourses of the spirit, there is no sufficient explanation within Butler's theoretical machine for the powerful subjectivity of the abject. It is a power that those who subject them cannot fathom because it only conceives them as bodies, not as body/mind/spirits that matter. Butler, I believe, reiterates such a minimizing conception as she tries to think us beyond it.

79. Cherríe Moraga and Gloria Anzaldúa, eds., *This Bridge Called My Back: Writings by Radical Women of Color* (Watertown, Mass.: Persephone Press, 1981).

80. Ibid., 210.

81. Ibid., xiv, xvii.

82. Ibid., 205, 208.

83. Ibid., 206.

84. Ibid., xviii.

85. Shohat, *Talking Visions: Multicultural Feminism in a Transnational Age* (Cambridge: MIT Press, 2001), 10. See Becky Thompson's *A Promise and a Way of Life: White Anti-Racist Activism* (Minneapolis: University of Minnesota Press, 2001) for the emergence of multiracial feminism from liberation movements.

86. Audre Lorde, "Poetry Is Not a Luxury," in *Sister/Outsider: Essays and Speeches by Audre Lorde* (Freedom, Calif.: Crossing Press, 1994), 38.

87. Ibid.

88. Ibid.

89. Ibid.

90. Ashaka Gloria Hull, *Soul Talk: The New Spirituality of African American Women* (Rochester, Vt.: Inner Traditions, 2001), 6. "Reflecting on the rise of this new spirituality among African American women, I realize, further, that it helps to explain what appeared to be a slackening of the political energy and activity around 1980. . . . Transformative energy had not vanished, but was only quietly gathering itself before expanding to encompass an enlarged spirituality in order to effect even more positive changes, in order to 'do' politics at a higher, more spiritualized frequency."

91. M. Jacqui Alexander, *Pedagogies of Crossing* (Durham, N.C.: Duke University Press, forthcoming).

92. Audre Lorde, "The Uses of the Erotic: The Erotic as Power," in *Sister/Outsider*, 56.

93. Albert Memmi, *Dominated Man: Notes Toward a Portrait* (London: Orion Press, 1968), 88; quoted in Gandhi, *Postcolonial Theory*, 6.

94. Lorde, *Sister/Outsider*, 38.

95. Butler, *Bodies That Matter*, x.

96. "Third Worldist euphoria has given way to the collapse of communism, the indefinite postponement of 'tricontinental revolution,' the realization that the 'wretched of the earth' are not unanimously revolutionary, and the recognition that international geopolitics and the global economic system have forced even the 'Second World' to be incorporated into transnational capitalism" (Shohat, *Talking Visions*, 10).

CHAPTER 2

1. "Beijing!" *AWID News: The Newsletter of the Association of Women in Development* 9, no. 4 (August 1995): 1, 6. The genuinely international women's movement was positioned to impact the series of conferences called by the UN in the 1990s to address "problems of a global magnitude which member states recognized had grown beyond their individual ability to solve in the post–cold war era." At the UN Conference on Environment and Development in Rio de Janeiro in 1992, women's nongovernmental organizations put women's issues and concerns on the official global agenda for the first time, working closely with another social movement, environmentalism. The Rio conference led to four new international treaties (climate change, biological diversity, desertification, and high-seas fishing). The UN conference on Human Rights in Vienna in 1993 declared the link between democracy, development, and human rights. Vigorous lobbying, fueled by a tribunal of testimonies by women from twenty-three countries, brought international recognition of "women's rights as human rights." The Third Conference on Population and Development (Cairo, 1994) placed women's education and empowerment in the center of efforts to reduce population growth rates and promote sustainable development. Cairo also "built consensus for integrating family planning programmes into a new comprehensive approach to reproductive health services." The Beijing Fourth World Conference on Women would hammer out the implications of the rich global debate into a single Platform for Action for women in the twenty-first century. AWID, 1511 K Street NW, Suite 825, Washington, D.C. 20005.

2. Thanks to Melissa Schrift for helping me clarify the differences in Pinyin and Wade-Giles systems that translate the sound of Chinese words into English—or the Roman alphabet. The Chinese language does not have an alphabet, but rather ideographic characters each with a single syllable pronunciation. The People's Republic officially adopted Pinyin in 1979. The two systems account for a sometimes confusing variety of spellings: Peking to Beijing, Mao Tse-tung to Mao Zedong, Deng Xiaoping rather than Teng Hsiao-p'ing; the Yangtze to the Chang River, the Yellow River to the Huang.

3. Bruce Cummings, "Introduction," *China from Mao to Deng: The Politics and Economics of Socialist Development*, ed. Bulletin of Concerned Asian Scholars (Armonk, N.Y.: M. E. Sharpe, 1983), 7.

4. Mao quoted in Peter Carter, *Mao* (New York: New American Library, 1980), 1; *Tao Te Ching*, no. 47.

5. Quoted in Wallbank et al., *Civilization*, 1:76–77.

6. Ibid., 1:82.

7. By the time of Shang, the idea of a supreme God was already in existence. In the beginning he was called Ti, and later Shang Ti. During the transitional period from Shang to Zhou, he was then called T'ien. The Shang people believed in a supreme God who was a personality God who could issue orders and had the sense of good and evil. All the matters of weather and climate such as the wind and rain, calamities and disasters, and all the human affairs were under T'ien's control. Milton M. Chiu, *The Tao of Chinese Religion* (Lanham, Md.: University Press of America, 1984), 23–26.

8. *Tao Te Ching*, nos. 10, 12, 13, paraphrased.

9. Martin Luther King Jr., "Letter from Birmingham City Jail," in *A Testament of Hope: The Essential Writings and Speeches of Martin Luther King, Jr.*, ed. James M. Washington (San Francisco: HarperCollins, 1991), 299.

10. Howard Thurman, *Jesus and the Disinherited* (New York: Abingdon, 1949; reprint, Boston: Beacon, 1996), xiii.

11. *Tao Te Ching*, no. 6.

12. Stuart R. Schram, *The Political Thought of Mao Tse Tung* (New York: Praeger Publishers, 1969), 165; extracted from *Chung-kuo ko-ming yù Chung-kuo Kung-ch'an-tang* [The Chinese Revolution and the Chinese Communist Party] (Yenan, China: Chieh-fang She, 1940), 165.

13. Adrienne Rich, "The Meaning of Our Love for Women," 225, 227, 229.

14. Radicalesbians, "The Woman Identified Woman," in *For Lesbians Only: A Separatist Anthology* (London: Onlywomen Press, 1988), 17; first distributed as a leaflet at a New York City conference, *The Ladder* 11/12 (August/September 1970).

15. Audre Lorde, "The Transformation of Silence into Language and Action," in *Sister Outsider*, 40; paper delivered at the Modern Language Association's "Lesbian and Literature Panel," Chicago, Illinois, December 28, 1977; first published in *Sinister Wisdom* 6 (1978), which I guest edited.

16. Moraga and Anzaldúa, *This Bridge*, xiv.

17. Huorong Liu, "Service with a Smile," *Forum* 95, September 2, 1995, 16.

18. Marx, *Selected Writings*, 223.

19. Bunch, "Through Women's Eyes: Global Forces Facing Women in the Twenty-first Century," in *Look at the World through Women's Eyes: Plenary Speeches from the NGO Forum for Women, Beijing '95*, ed. Eva Friedlander, foreword by Irene M. Santiago (New York: United Nations, 1995), 24.

20. Friedlander, introduction to *Look at the World*, xxvi.

21. Santiago, "Opening Remarks," *Look at the World*, 13.

22. Gita Sen, "The Forces Shaping Women's Lives," *Look at the World*, 14.

23. Winnie Byanyima, "Global Forces and Their Impact on Women: An African Perspective," *Look at the World*, 23.

24. Sen, "The Forces Shaping Women's Lives," *Look at the World*, 15–16.

25. Bunch, "Through Women's Eyes," *Look at the World*, 24–26, 27.

26. MADRE provides monetary aid and training to women's community-based organizations in Central America, the Caribbean, and the Middle East. MADRE, 121 W. 27th Street, Room 301, New York, NY 10001; madre@igc.apc.org.

27. Marx, *Grundrisse*, 364.

28. See Laura Flanders, "Women Should Be Heard: Expertise as Well as Experiences," in *Look at the World*, 205–209; Mab Segrest, "Dangerously Rising Conservatism in the United States: Racism, Sexism and Homophobia," in *Look at the World*, 80–84. Laura's speech was

also reprinted later in her collection of essays *Real Majority, Media Minority: The Costs of Sidelining Women in Reporting* (Monroe, Maine: Common Courage Press, 1997).

29. Walt Whitman, "Crossing Brooklyn Ferry," in *Modern Poets: An Introduction to Poetry*, ed. Richard Ellmann and Robert O'Clair (New York: Norton, 1976), 4. See Mab Segrest, "What's Sex Got to Do with It, Y'all," in *Neither Separate nor Equal: Women, Race, and Class in the South*, ed. Barbara Ellen Smith (Philadelphia: Temple University Press, 1999), 245–270.

30. Ralph Ellison, *Invisible Man* (New York: Vintage, 1972), 3.

31. Ibid.

32. Marta Benavides, "The Impact of Conservatism on Women's Lives," in *Look at the World*, 77–79.

33. Rachel Rosenbloom, ed., *Unspoken Rules: Sexual Orientation and Women's Human Rights* (San Francisco: International Gay and Lesbian Human Rights Commission, 1995).

34. *Forum 95*, September 4, 1995, 11.

35. *Forum 95*, September 2, 1995, 3.

36. Maria Elana Hurtado, "Punishment for Silent Crimes Urged," *Forum 95*, September 6, 1995, 15.

37. Yevette Collymore, "Debt Scrap for Africa," *Forum 95*, September 8, 1995, 5.

38. Leah Wise, "Foreword," *We Are the Ones We Are Waiting For: Women of Color Organizing for Transformation*, written and edited by Rinku Sen (Durham, N.C.: Urban-Rural Mission [USA], 1995).

39. Hugh Pearson, *The Shadow of the Panther: Huey Newton and the Price of Black Power in America* (Reading, Mass.: Addison-Wesley, 1994), 113.

40. Schram, *Political Thought*, 254. On this continent, however, the Panthers' Huey Newton took a progressive stand on uniting with homosexuals in a revolutionary fashion: "A person should have the right to use his body in whatever way he wants to. . . . Maybe a homosexual could be the most revolutionary. . . . Homosexuals are not enemies of the people" ("A Letter from Huey to the Revolutionary Brothers and Sisters about the Women's Liberation and Gay Liberation Movements," August 21, 1970, in *The Question of Equality: Lesbian and Gay Politics in America since Stonewall*, ed. David Deitcher [New York: Scribner, 1995], 33.).

41. According to Jonathan Spence, *Mao Zedong* (New York: Viking, 1999), Schram's *The Political Thought of Mao Tse-Tung* is "the most important Western guide to the life and works of Mao" (179); Schram has edited four of the multivolume series *Mao's Road to Power: Revolutionary Writings, 1912–1949* (Armonk, N.Y.: M.E. Sharp, 1992). Spence has excellent annotated endnotes for the current state of Mao scholarship. Peter Carter, *Mao* (New York: New American Library, 1979).

42. Spence, *Mao Zedong*, 52.

43. Mao Zedong, "Toward a New Golden Age," extracted from the manifesto written by Mao for the first issue of his magazine, *Hsiang-chiang p'ing-lun*, in July 1919; quoted in Schram, *Political Thought*, 163.

44. Spence, *Mao Zedong*, 52.

45. Carter's *Mao*, chaps. 10–14, traces the military and ideological contributions of Mao during this period.

46. Schram, *Political Thought*, 272, 287.

47. Ibid., 270–271. In his biography of Mao, Carter argues that the Red Army did operate with much less corruption than Chiang's troops, which accounts for the way Mao was able to build up the strength and numbers of the Red Army. Spence's biography doesn't really ever explain Mao's remarkable success.

48. Ibid., 280.

49. Quoted in Carter, *Mao*, 74, as a brief verse Mao wrote to help his troops remember the guerilla tactics they were evolving, as part of his overall strategy to make the ideas the communists were fighting for understandable to peasants and working people.

50. *Tao Te Ching*, no. 69.

51. Carter, *Mao*, 86.

52. Mao, "Loushan Pass," in Schram, *Political Thought*, 283.

53. Carter, *Mao*, 98; Spence, *Mao Zedong*, 86.

54. Spence, *Mao Zedong*, 97–101.

55. *Tao Te Ching*, no. 3.

56. Resolution of the Central Committee, "On Certain Questions in the History of Our Party since the Founding of the People's Republic of China," June 27, 1981; *A Documentary History of Communism and the World from Revolution to Collapse*, ed. Robert V. Daniels (Hanover: University of Vermont, 1994), 281.

57. Spence, *Mao Zedong*, 130.

58. See Tsering Shakya's *The Dragon in the Land of Snows: A History of Modern Tibet since 1947* (New York: Penguin Compass, 1999) for a balanced account of the Chinese occupation of Tibet.

59. Various sinologists sort through post-Mao interpretations of Mao's rule in *China from Mao to Deng*. Editor Bruce Cummings groups the collection into three broad interpretations—Deng brought an abrupt change for the worse; an abrupt change for the better; or continuities between Mao and Deng were greater than discontinuities (3).

60. Schram, *Political Thought*, 367.

61. "In the soviet districts, marriages are now contracted on a free basis. Free choice must be the basic principle of every marriage. The whole feudal system of marriage, including the power of parents to arrange marriages for their children, to exercise compulsion, and all purchase and sale in marriage contracts shall henceforth be abolished. Although women have obtained freedom from the feudal yoke, they are still labouring under tremendous physical handicaps (for example, the binding of feet) and have not obtained complete economic independence. Therefore on questions concerning divorce, it becomes necessary to protect the interests of women and place the greater part of the obligations and responsibilities entailed by divorce upon men." Decree of the First Session of the Central Executive Committee of the Chinese Soviet Republic, December 1931, in Schram, *Political Thought*, 337.

62. Yan Jiaqi and Gao Gao, *Turbulent Decade: A History of the Cultural Revolution*, trans. and ed. D.W.Y. Kwok (originally published in Hong Kong as *Zhongguo "Wenge" shinian shi* [Hong Kong: Xianggang Ta-Kung pao she, 1986]; then as *Wenhuadageming Shinian shi* [Taipei: Yuan Liou Publishing Co, 1990]; references herein from Honolulu: University of Hawai'i Press, 1996), xiii. Yan and Gao's work establishes a history of the Cultural Revolution as part of China's de-Maoification from within China and was widely read there.

63. Yan and Gao, *Turbulent Decade*, 1–7, 529–532.

64. *Tao Te Ching*, no. 9.

65. Gethin, *The Foundations of Buddhism*, 17–27.

66. Interview by André Malraux with Mao in *Religious Policy and Practice in Communist China*, ed. Donald E. MacInnis (New York: Macmillan, 1972), 17.

67. Ibid., 5, 15.

68. Mao, "Dialectical Materialism—Notes of a Lecture," in Schram, *Political Thought*, 182.

69. Yan and Gao, *Turbulent Decade*, 248.

70. Ibid., 82.

71. Ibid., 139.

CHAPTER 3

1. Claims inside the World of Coke Museum, Atlanta.

2. Melissa Turner, "Coca-Cola Scores Big on Olympics," *Atlanta Journal-Constitution*, July 12, 1991, C-1.

3. See Pat Hussain and Jon-Ivan Weaver, *Olympics Out of Cobb Spiked!* (Atlanta: self-published, 1996), for a full account of this campaign.

4. Hussain and Weaver, *Spiked!* 87. "And the percentages were higher [than 40 percent] in some sports like swimming and gymnastics. One hundred percent in men's ice-skating."

5. For the full contents of the "Contract with America," see *http://www.newt.org/contract.htm*, June 18, 2001.

6. John Stacks, "Good Newt, Bad Newt," *www.time.com/time/special/moy/1995/goodbad2.html*, 2. Cuts of $189 billion over five years would raise to $750,000 the threshold for assets not subject to estate and gift tax (affecting fewer than 1 percent of U.S. citizens) and lower personal capital gains tax rates (benefiting 7 percent of the most wealthy households, the ones with profits from investments). A proposal to raise taxes on the working poor cut the earned income tax credit. Another cut Medicaid but left in place home mortgage deductions for mansions and second homes.

7. Jay Bookman, "Keeping Humanity in a Brave New World," *Atlanta Journal-Constitution*, July 28, 1996, R-3.

8. See *www.projectsouth.org*.

9. *Misplaced Priorities: Atlanta, the '96 Olympics, and the Politics of Urban Removal* (Atlanta: Project South, n.d.), 1.

10. Melissa Turner, "Coca-Cola Scores Big on Olympics," *Atlanta Journal-Constitution*, July 12, 1991, C-1.

11. Chris Roush, "Coca-Cola Forming Team for Ad Campaign," *Atlanta Journal-Constitution*, November 10, 1995, E-1.

12. *Misplaced Priorities*, 7.

13. "Money Worries Over, ACOG Says," *Atlanta Journal-Constitution*, October 12, 1995, C-3.

14. Douglas Blackmon, "Airport Upgrade Proposed at Cost of $170 Million," *Atlanta Journal-Constitution*, January 13, 1995, F-1. The money would pay for projects like a $170 million upgrade for Atlanta's Hartsfield International Airport to bring in new conventioneers and $157 million for the Olympic Village. Melissa Cook reported that ACOG did break even, raising and spending $1.7 billion (telephone interview, December 2001).

15. Lindsay Thomas, quoted in "Lawmakers Wary of Grand Schemes," *Atlanta Journal-Constitution*, in Project South's files, n.d., Atlanta.

16. *Misplaced Priorities*, 13.

17. "The Olympic Games and Our Struggles for Justice: A People's Story," in *As the South Goes: The Newsletter of Project South* 3, no. 2 (summer 1996).

18. *Misplaced Priorities*, 20–21, 23.

19. U.S. District Court Judge J. Owen Forrester denied a preliminary injunction against the antiloitering ordinance because he said the plaintiffs did not show that city officials knew that some police officers arrested homeless people without probable cause. But Forrester did grant partial relief against the part of the ordinance that prohibits aggressive panhandling. "It seems to the court that the city of Atlanta is largely indifferent as to how its laws are enforced upon this group of people for whom we are using the nomenclature the 'homeless.'" "Judge Rejects Plea to Block Arrests of Homeless, but Sets Some Limits," *Atlanta Journal-Constitution*, July 18, 1996.

20. Melissa Turner, Mike Fish, and Bert Roughton, "The Sweet Smell of Money Attracts a New Breed of Olympic Stewards," Special Report: "The Selling of the Olympics: How Money Has Changed the Games," *Atlanta Journal-Constitution*, July 12, 1992, G-3.

21. *Random House Webster's College Dictionary*, s.v. "private."

22. Turner et al., "Sweet Smell of Money," G-4.

23. Ibid. Corporate money would be $107 million for the 1988 winter and summer games; $167 million for the 1992 games, and an expected $333 million for 1994 winter and 1996 summer games. The *AJC* series in 1992 warned, prophetically, of the corruption that was likely to accompany such huge amounts of money by poor to nonexistent methods of accountability. "There is now so much money and so few rules that the IOC, and perhaps the

Olympic Games themselves, are ripe to fall. The temptations have become too great for even well-intentioned people, and the opportunities irresistible for those with darker motives."

24. Frederick Allen, *Secret Formula: How Brilliant Marketing and Relentless Salesmanship Made Coca-Cola the Best Known Product in the World* (New York: Harpers, 1995), 27.

25. Ibid., 20, 23. Other of Doc Pemberton's inventions included Indian Queen Hair Dye, Triplex Liver Pills, and a blood fortifier.

26. Claims in the World of Coke Museum.

27. World of Coke Museum.

28. Smith, *An Inquiry*, 1:26–27.

29. Ibid., 1:18, 73.

30. Ibid., 1:66.

31. Ibid., 1:67.

32. Ibid., 1:70.

33. W.E.B. Du Bois, *Black Reconstruction in America, 1860–1880* (New York: Atheneum, 1979), 5.

34. W.E.B. Du Bois, "The Coronation," editorial in *Crisis* 11 (1911), in *An ABC of Color* (New York: International Publishers, 1983), 42.

35. David Levering Lewis, *W.E.B. Du Bois, Biography of a Race* (New York: Henry Holt & Co., 1994), 8–9. "The message of Karl Marx delivered by Du Bois to all Africans, as to the rest of the less-developed world, was that the market economy perfected in northern Europe always made the weak weaker—and most of the strong weaker. Du Bois had shaped and launched upon the rising tide of twentieth century nationalism the idea of the solidarity of the world's darker peoples, of the glories in the forgotten African past, of the vanguard role destined to be played by Africans of the diaspora in the destruction of European imperialism, and, finally, as he grew older but more radical, of the inevitable emergence of a united and socialist Africa."

36. Smith, *Wealth*, 1:22. Emphasis mine.

37. Ibid., 1:48.

38. Du Bois, *The Souls of Black Folk* (New York: New American Library, 1982), 199.

39. Michael Eric Dyson, *I May Not Get There with You: The True Martin Luther King, Jr.* (New York: Simon and Schuster, 2000). In 1965, thirty-six people were killed in urban revolts; in 1966, eleven people; in 1967, eighty-three people were killed in seventy-five major riots (84).

40. King, "A Testament of Hope" in *A Testament of Hope*, 313.

41. *Misplaced Priorities*, 2.

42. Allen, *Secret Formula*, 285.

43. Ibid., 337–339. The duo of Woodruff and Hartsfield brought in Ivan Allen to broker a 1960 agreement between two dozen of the city's leading businesses and demonstrators from Atlanta University, joined by King. Their sit-ins at the Magnolia Room at downtown Rich's department store led to the desegregation of Rich's facilities several years before I had my vision of consumer opulence on the Rich's escalator. King called it "the first written contract we've ever had with [the white man] . . . after waiting one hundred years." While he preferred moderate politicians, Woodruff also supported Herman Talmadge, arch segregationist and race-baiter, who served as governor, then went on for four terms in the U.S. Senate, "leaving behind a state house that remained enemy ground to a million black Georgians" (316).

44. Thanks to Leah Wise for this insight.

45. "The Olympic Games and Our Struggle for Justice," 8.

46. *Misplaced Priorities*, 4.

47. Stephen Fenichell, "The Ambassador from Atlanta," *Delta Sky* (July 1996): 110.

48. Ibid., 115–117.

49. John Huey, "The Atlanta Game," *Fortune*, July 27, 1996, 44.

50. Dyson warns against a "reactionary appraisal" of Young's metamorphosis—his "[extraordinary] comfort with the system of wealth and power he so heartily castigated"—given Young's accomplishments for social change and racial good. These disclaimers notwithstanding, Dyson does call Young's present stance a "dismally low-sighted acceptance of self-interest as the substitute for racial progress and economic equality" and finds these politics a "poor substitute for what came before" (*I May Not Get There*, 91–93).

51. Du Bois, *Souls*, 111, 114.

52. Perry Anderson, *The Origins of Postmodernity* (London: Verso, 1998), 54–55.

53. Frederic Jameson, *The Cultural Turn: Selected Writings on the Postmodern, 1983–1998* (London: Verso, 1998), 23; Anderson, *Origins*, 5–6.

54. Anderson, *Origins*, 12, 46.

55. Jameson, *Cultural Turn*, 35, 3.

56. Ibid., 5–7, 10.

57. Ibid., 16.

58. Michael Eric Dyson does a remarkable job of dealing with these concerns and many others in *I May Not Get There with You*. See pages 273–275 for the Time-Warner figures.

59. James Cone, *Risks of Faith: The Emergence of a Black Theology of Liberation, 1968–1998* (Boston: Beacon Press, 1999), xvi–xvii.

60. Dyson, *I May Not Get There*, xv, 8.

61. See Kenneth L. Smith and Ira G. Zepp Jr., *Search for the Beloved Community: The Thinking of Martin Luther King, Jr.* (Valley Forge, Pa.: Judson Press, 1998).

62. Marx, "Economic and Philosophical Manuscripts," 79.

63. Thurman, *Jesus and the Disinherited*, 21, 28.

64. Ibid., 21.

65. Ibid., 22, 26, 28.

66. Ibid., 37.

67. Allen, *Without Sanctuary*, image 22.

68. Thurman, *Jesus and the Disinherited*, 50.

69. Ibid., 57.

70. Ibid., 70.

71. Ibid., 83, 108, 109.

72. Thurman, *With Head and Heart: The Autobiography of Howard Thurman* (New York: Harcourt, Brace & Co., 1979), 5. In Thurman's early manhood, the black self was also carefully tended at Atlanta's Morehouse, where both Thurman and King attended college. Here impeccably respectful treatment by elders and teachers offset the climate in a state "infamous for its racial brutality; . . . [for] lynchings, burnings, unspeakable cruelties [that] were the fundamentals of existence for black people" (36).

73. Thurman, *Jesus and the Disinherited*, 35.

74. Ibid., 101.

75. See Robin Kelley, *Hammer and Hoe: Alabama Communists during the Great Depression* (Chapel Hill: University of North Carolina Press, 1990), 48–49.

76. Dyson, *I May Not Get There*, 33–34, 36.

77. See "Mama, Granny, Carrie, Bell," in *My Mama's Dead Squirrel: Lesbian Essays on Southern Culture* (Ithaca, N.Y.: Firebrand Books, 1985); also see Lillian Smith, "Three Ghost Stories," in *Killers of the Dream* (New York: W. W. Norton, 1978).

78. Dyson, *I May Not Get There*, 108.

79. Related in Michael N. Nagler, introduction to M. K. Gandhi, *The Way to God*, ed. M. S. Desphande (Berkeley: Berkeley Hills Books, 1999), 13.

80. Martin Luther King Jr., "Pilgrimage to Nonviolence," in *Testament of Hope*, 40.

81. Ibid.

82. King's existentialism is influenced by his study of Kierkegaard, Nietzsche, Jaspers, Heidegger, and Sartre, and especially Paul Tillich. "In their revolt against Hegel's essentialism, all existentialists contend that the world is fragmented. History is a series of unreconciled conflicts and man's existence is filled with anxiety and threatened with meaninglessness. While the ultimate Christian answer is not found in any of these existential assertions, there is much here that the theologian can use to describe the true state of man's existence" (King, "Pilgrimage to Nonviolence," in *Testament of Hope*, 37).

83. King's insistence on human agency is in contrast to Frederic Jameson's in *The Cultural Turn*. With Jameson's death of the subject came a dispersal of radical agency. Jameson ascribes agency—the power to act— to "that seemingly disembodied force [of multinational capital as] an ensemble of human agents, trained in specific ways and inventing original local tactics and practices according to the creativities of human freedom" (47). Capitalists have such agency, while "labour movements and insurgencies, mass socialist parties, even socialist states themselves" seem "in full disarray when not in one way or another effectively neutralized," allowing capital to "follow its own nature and inclinations, without the traditional precautions" (48). We are, in fact, in a "trough" between stages of capital, when means of production are shifting, and a "new international proletariat (taking forms we cannot yet imagine)" has not yet "emerged from this convulsive upheaval" (48). Jameson calls for a "class consciousness of a new and hitherto undreamed of kind" (49). He suggests that we find it "easier today . . . to imagine the thoroughgoing deterioration of the earth and of nature than the breakdown of late capitalism" because of a "weakness in our imagination."

84. Du Bois, *Souls*, 225.

85. In *The Cultural Turn*, 8, 48–49, Jameson also describes how the "temporal paradox—absolute change equals stasis"—applies to the new global system in a way that eliminates any but the Western/modern. For in that older period, most Third World societies were torn by a penetration of Western modernization that generated over against itself—in all the variety of cultural forms characteristic of those very different societies—a counterposition that could generally be described as traditionalism: the affirmation of a cultural and sometimes religious originality that had the power to resist assimilation by Western modernity and was indeed preferable to it. *Such traditionalism was of course a construction in its own right, brought into being as it were by the very activities of the modernizers themselves* (in some more limited and specific sense than the one now widely accepted, that all traditions and historical pasts are themselves necessarily invented and constructed). At any rate, what one wants to affirm today is that this second reactive or antimodern term of tradition and neotraditionalism has everywhere vanished from the reality of the former Third World or colonized societies, where a neotraditionalism (as in certain Chinese revivals of Confucianism, or in religious fundamentalisms) is now rather *perceived* as a *deliberate political and collective choice*, in a situation in which *little remains of a past that must be completely reinvented*. That is to say that, on the one hand, *nothing but the modern henceforth exists in Third World societies*; but it is also to correct the statement, on the other, with the qualification that under such circumstances, where only the modern exists, 'modern' must now be rebaptized 'postmodern' (since what we call modern is the consequence of incomplete modernization and must necessarily define itself against a nonmodern residuality that *no longer obtains* in postmodernity as such–or rather, whose absence defines this last) (61; emphasis mine). Ella Shohat's description of time allows more for the regeneration that I argue is possible in a time "scrambled and palimpsestic in all the worlds, with the premodern, the modern, the postmodern and the paramodern coexisting globally" (Ella Shohat and Robert Crum, *Unthinking Eurocentrism: Multiculturalism and the Media* [New York: Routledge, 1994], 293).

86. Adam Smith, *Theory of Moral Sentiments*, II.ii.2.1. quoted in William B. Todd, "General Introduction," *Wealth*, 1:10.

CHAPTER 4

1. See William McCranor Henderson, *I, Elvis: Confessions of a Counterfeit King* (New York: Boulevard Books, 1997).

2. Peter Guralnick, *Last Train to Memphis: The Rise of Elvis Presley* (Boston: Little, Brown, 1994), 44–51.

3. Quoted in David J. Garrow, *The FBI and Martin Luther King, Jr.* (New York: Penguin Books, 1981), 120.

4. Jeff Bradley, *Tennessee Handbook* (Chico, Calif.: Moon Publications, 1997), 8, 393.

5. *Crusader for Justice: The Autobiography of Ida B. Wells,* ed. Alfreda M. Duster (Chicago: University of Chicago Press, 1991).

6. Guralnick, *Last Train,* 29.

7. Guralnick did two excellent histories before the Presley biographies: *Feels like Going Home: Portraits in Blues and Rock 'n' Roll* (New York: Harper, 1971); and *Sweet Soul Music: Rhythm and Blues and the Southern Dream of Freedom* (New York: Harper, 1994).

8. Dyson, *I May Not Get There,* 272.

9. Marx, *Grundrisse,* 436–437.

10. See *In Search of Elvis: Music, Race, Art, Religion,* ed. Vernon Chadwick (New York: HarperCollins, 1997). Chadwick is the impresario of the Memphis version of the Elvis Conference.

11. See notes 26 and 28 of chapter 1.

12. Lawrence Buser, "Nichopoulos Gives Defense for Dosage," undated clip in *An Elvis Presley Scrapbook,* comp. William F. Currotto (Memphis, Tenn.: Patchwork Books, 1996), 42.

13. Guralnick, *Last Train,* 481.

14. *Elvis Presley's Graceland: The Official Guidebook,* 2d ed. (Memphis: Elvis Presley Enterprises, 1996), 22–23, 25.

15. John Bernstein, Rod Gibson, Lee Harrison, John Hounsel, Church Michelini, Charles Parmiter, Ken Potter, and Allan Zullo, "Elvis Pressley's Roots," *National Enquirer* (September 27, 1977), in *An Elvis Presley Scrapbook,* 1–2. John Shelton Reed does his own assessment of "Elvis as Southerner" in *In Search of Elvis.*

16. Segrest and Tatum, *Segrest Saga,* 70–77.

17. David Roediger, *The Wages of Whiteness: Race and the Making of the American Working Class* (London: Verso, 1991), 95.

18. Segrest and Tatum, *Segrest Saga,* 352.

19. Du Bois, *Souls,* 67.

20. John S. Hughes, ed., *The Letters of a Victorian Madwoman* (Columbia: University of South Carolina Press, 1993), 48. This volume documents the thirty-year institutionalization of Andrew M. Sheffield, a woman committed to Bryce's in 1890 and living at Bryce's until 1919 when she died. She was accused of arson, suspected of sexual impropriety, and addicted to chloral hydrate. Thanks to Lucinda Ebersole (also an Elvis fan), who also had family in Bryce's, for sending me a copy of this book.

21. Hughes, *Victorian Madwoman,* 105.

22. Correspondence among Segrest private family papers.

23. Guralnick, *Last Train,* 273.

24. Ibid., 14.

25. Ibid., 474–475.

26. Dyson, *I May Not Get There,* 155.

27. Martin Luther King Jr., "Next Stop: The North," in *Testament of Hope,* 189.

28. Ibid., 317, 324.

29. Martin Luther King Jr., "Showdown for Nonviolence," in *Testament of Hope,* 65.

30. King, "Next Stop," 191.

31. Dyson, *I May Not Get There,* 111.

32. Dyson, *I May Not Get There*, chap. 5, "An Integrationist Embraces Enlightened Black Nationalism."

33. Quoted in James Cone, *Risks of Faith: The Emergence of a Black Theology of Liberation, 1968–1998* (Boston: Beacon Press, 1999), 65.

34. King, "I See the Promised Land," 280.

35. Martin Luther King Jr., "A Testament of Hope," in *Testament of Hope*, 315.

36. Quoted in Dyson, *I May Not Get There*, 87–88.

37. Martin Luther King Jr., "Remaining Awake through a Great Revolution," in *Testament of Hope*, 275.

38. Martin Luther King Jr., "A Time to Break Silence," in *Testament of Hope*, 238.

39. Dyson, *I May Not Get There*, 65.

40. Thich Nhat Hanh, "In Search of the Enemy of Man," Letter to Martin Luther King Jr., June 1, 1965, reprinted in *Vietnam: Lotus in a Sea of Fire* (New York: Hill and Wang, 1967), 106–107.

41. Young, quoted in Patricia Hunt-Perry and Lyn Fine, "All Buddhism Is Engaged: Thich Nhat Hanh and the Order of Interbeing," in *Engaged Buddhism in the West*, ed. Christopher S. Queen (Boston: Wisdom Publications, 2000), 43.

42. King, "A Time to Break Silence," 240–241.

43. King, "I See the Promised Land," 283.

44. Garrow, *The FBI and Martin Luther King, Jr.*, 68, 106.

45. James Cone's thesis is that King's theology fell into three periods. In the first, he emphasized justice; the second, love; the third, hope. "When it seemed that freedom was difficult to realize in this world, Martin King did not despair but moved its meaning to an eschatological realm as defined by the Black Church's claim that 'the Lord will make a way somehow'" ("Black Theology–Black Church," in Cone, *Risks of Faith*, 81).

46. King, "I See the Promised Land," 286.

47. Thich Nhat Hanh, "In Search of the Enemy of Man," 106–107.

48. Peter Guralnick, *Careless Love: The Unmaking of Elvis Presley* (Boston: Little, Brown, 1999), 195.

49. *Bhagavad Gita*, trans. Stephen Mitchell (New York: Harmony Books, 2000), 9.25, p. 118.

CHAPTER 5

1. Mary Kawena Pukui, *'Ōlelo No'eau: Hawaiian Proverbs and Poetical Sayings* (Honolulu: Bishop Museum Press, 1983), no. 1870, p. 201; no. 2453, p. 268.

2. Ibid., no. 283, p. 42.

3. Ibid., no. 1960, p. 211.

4. Quoted in Michael Dougherty, *To Steal a Kingdom: Probing Hawaiian History* (Waimanalo, Hawai'i: Island Style Press, 1992), 60.

5. Ibid., 79.

6. Ibid., 233.

7. Ibid., 62.

8. Pukui, *'Ōlelo No'eau*, no. 455, p. 55; no. 477, p. 57; no. 200, p. 24.

9. See Kyle Kajihiro, "Memo on Cultural and Political Background and Some Guidelines for Hawai'i Gathering," in *The Flower on the Lily Pad: AFSC's Lesbian, Gay, Bisexual, and Transgender Programming*, transcript of the American Friends Service Committee LGBT Staff Gathering, September 1998, Honolulu, 44.

10. There is some discussion of *'Aikapu*, the separating of men from women to prevent the "unclean" nature of women from defiling male sanctity, in Lilikala Kame'eleihiwa, *Native Land and Foreign Desires: Pehea Lā E Pono Ai?* (Honolulu: Bishop Museum Press, 1992), 35–36, in which the author discusses the possible advantages for women in this system.

11. Liliuokalani, *Hawaii's Story by Hawaii's Queen* (Honolulu: Mutual Publishing Company, 1995), 55.

12. Dougherty, *To Steal a Kingdom*, 131; Liliuokalani, *Hawaii's Story*, 77.

13. Liliuokalani, *Hawaii's Story*, 78.

14. Ibid., 206.

15. Ibid., 386.

16. Ibid., 386–388.

17. Ibid., 269.

18. Ibid., 396.

19. Interview with Kekuni Blaisdell in Robert H. Mast and Anne B. Mast, eds., *Autobiography of Protest in Hawai'i* (Honolulu: University of Hawai'i Press, 1996), 369.

20. Kame'eleihiwa, *Native Land*, 9.

21. Interview with Davianna McGregor in Mast, *Autobiography*, 400.

22. Dougherty, *To Steal a Kingdom*, 84, 131, 176.

23. Blaisdell in Mast, *Autobiography*, 367.

24. Ibid., 367–368; Mililani Trask in Mast, *Autobiography*, 393–394.

25. Ibid., 371.

26. McGregor (404) and Ku'umeaaloha Gomes (426) in Mast, *Autobiography*.

27. See Mast, *Autobiography*, 353–362; Mililani Trask for the nation-within-a-nation strategy (389–398); Blaisdell and others for independence (e.g., 371).

28. "Introduction," Staff Gathering, September 1998, Honolulu.

29. Noenoe Silva's testimony in *Flower on the Lily Pad* transcript, 36. Noenoe was a founding member of Na Mamo.

30. *Evans* vs. *Romer*, 822 P.2d 1335 (1994).

31. *Loving* vs. *Virginia*, 388 U.S. 1, 87 S.Ct. 1817, 18 L.Ed.2d 1010 (1967).

32. *http://www.wcc-coe.org/*.

33. Pukui, *'Olelo No'eau*, no. 2293, p. 250.

34. Ibid., no. 1564, p. 169; no. 1565, p. 169.

35. Dougherty, *To Steal a Kingdom*. "Free from terror, they were able to develop other traits," including a "gentleness of temperament uncommon in other Polynesian societies" (18, 20).

36. Ibid., 1–4.

37. E. S. Craighill Handy and Mary Kawena Pukui, *The Polynesian Family System in Ka'u, Hawai'i* (Honolulu: Mutual, 1998), 28.

38. Bhagman Shree Rajneesh, *The Book of Secrets* (New York: Harper and Row, 1977), 215, quoted in Bethal Phaigh, *Gestalt and the Wisdom of the Kahunas* (Marina del Rey, Calif.: DeVorss and Co., 1983), 44.

39. See Macy, *World as Lover, World as Self*.

CHAPTER 6

1. *Tao Te Ching*, no. 41.

2. Ysaye Barnwell, "Breaths," lyrics adapted from the poem by Birago Diop, music by Ysaye Barnwell.

CHAPTER 7

1. My project in *Memoir of a Race Traitor* (Boston: South End, 1994) of breaking down the boundaries between the personal and the historical was being pursued also by Anne McClintock in *Imperial Leather: Race, Gender, and Sexuality in the Colonial Contest*, published a year later (New York: Routledge, 1995). She wrote: "In the chapters that follow, I propose the development of a *situated psychoanalysis*—a culturally contextualized psychoanalysis that is simultaneously a psychoanalytically informed history. In sum, *Imperial Leather* is written with the conviction that psychoanalysis and material history are mutually necessary for a strategic engagement with unstable power" (72, 73).

2. bell hooks warns against the discussion I want to undertake about the damage of racism to white people. She is leery of whites constructing a "narrative of shared victimization" that "recenters whites" and obscures the "particular way racist domination impacts on the lives of marginalized [racial] groups." She prefers a solidarity "based on one's political and ethical understanding of racism and one's rejection of domination." But hooks allows that a white solidarity based on rejection of domination "does not have to negate collective awareness that a culture of domination does seek to fundamentally distort and pervert the psyches of all citizens or that this perversion is wounding" (153). It is this wounding psychic perversion that I am trying to address, without equating it with the effects of racist exploitation on people of color, some new strain of emotional "reverse discrimination." I can make these distinctions, I find, as a lesbian—I can see how homophobia and heterosexism distort heterosexual relationships in ways that are wounding, while also insisting that this pain not be used to recenter heterosexuality and obscure the fact that there is institutional power in heterosexism that falls violently and painfully on lesbians and gay men. The pain of dominance is always qualitatively different from the pain of subordination. But there is a pain, a psychic wound, to inhabiting and maintaining domination. Our acknowledging that emotional cost helps keep our white ethical/political solidarity from slipping over into a new form of paternalism. bell hooks, *Killing Rage/Ending Racism* (New York: Henry Holt and Co., 1995), 152–153.

3. Resisting Defamation was the name of a group protesting the conference. A flier handed out at the conference explained: "Resisting Defamation has identified the four principal negative stereotypes used to demean European Americans, the five principles that determine for European Americans whether a term is a slur, and the 156 slurs in common use in America today that are used to demean and demoralize young European Americans at school, on campuses and on the streets. Copies of 'Sensitivity Toward European Americans: Diversity Within Diversity' may be obtained by contacting [us]."

4. Du Bois, *The World and Africa: An Inquiry into the Part Which Africa Has Played in World History* (New York, 1965), 18–21, quoted in Roediger, *The Wages of Whiteness*, 6.

5. John Bradshaw, *Bradshaw On: The Family* (Deerfield Beach, Fla.: Health Communications, 1988), 6–7.

6. Houston Baker Jr., *Turning South Again: Re-Thinking Modernism: Re-Reading Booker T.* (Durham, N.C.: Duke University Press, 2001), 22. "It seems to me that Cash may have been not only prophetic in his realization of the deep-rootedness of the very worst of 'southernness' in the United States, but also, perhaps, desperately and sadly proleptic in his own despairing suicide, which occurred shortly after the release of his classic American book."

7. Frederick Douglass, *The Narrative of the Life of Frederick Douglass, an American Slave*, ed. Houston Baker Jr. (New York: Dell, 1997), 3–4.

8. Ibid., 3.

9. Ibid., 5, 6.

10. Henry Hughes, "Treatise on Sociology," in *The Ideology of Slavery: Proslavery Thought in the Antebellum South, 1830–1860*, ed. Drew Gilpin Faust (Baton Rouge: Louisiana State University Press, 1981), 256.

11. *Webster's New Collegiate Dictionary* and *American Heritage Dictionary*.

12. Thich Nhat Hanh, *The Heart of the Buddha's Teaching: Transforming Suffering into Peace, Joy and Liberation* (Berkeley, Calif.: Parallax Press, 1998), 164.

13. Ibid., 67–68.

14. Perhaps here we have the formula for fascist intelligence that justifies genocidal practices in the name of the superior intelligence of a master race, an intelligence seemingly devoid of human empathy or compassion. See *The Bell Curve* for its implications. Richard J. Hernstein and Charles Murray, *The Bell Curve: Intelligence and Class Structure* (New York: Simon and Schuster, 1996).

15. Mary Boykin Chesnut, *Diary from Dixie*, ed. Ben Ames Williams (Cambridge, Mass.: Harvard University Press, 1980), 25–26.

16. Pema Chodron, "The Awakened Heart," *Shambhala Sun* (September 2001): 32.

17. Hanh, *The Heart of Buddha's Teachings*, 169.

18. Hughes, "Treatise on Sociology," 258.

19. Ibid., 243.

20. Freud, *Civilization*, 11–12.

21. Freud published *Civilization and Its Discontents* (1930) in his last stage, when he was extending the insights of psychoanalysis developed over more than four decades into other spheres of human endeavor. He was expanding the theoretical core—on the interpretation of dreams as access to the "unconscious" in *Psychopathology of Everyday Life* (1904) and *Interpretation of Dreams* (1900); and the fuller evocation of sexuality as libido in *Three Essays on Sexuality* (1905) and *Introductory Lectures on Psychoanalysis* (1916–17). He had first begun his critique of religion in *Totem and Taboo* (1912) and would end it in *Moses and Monotheism* (1939).

22. Nandor Fodor and Frank Gaynor, eds., *Freud: Dictionary of Psychoanalysis* (Greenwich, Conn.: Fawcett Publications, 1958), 112. Herbert Marcuse, in *Eros and Civilization: A Philosophical Inquiry into Freud* (New York: Vintage Books, 1962), 3, paraphrases Freud: "Free gratification of man's instinctual needs is incompatible with civilized society: renunciation and delay in satisfaction are the prerequisites of progress. 'Happiness,' said Freud, 'is no cultural value.' Happiness must be subordinated to the discipline of work as full-time occupation, to the discipline of monogamic reproduction, to the established system of law and order. The methodical sacrifice of libido, its rigidly enforced deflection to socially useful activities and expressions, *is* culture."

23. Freud, *Civilization*, 49–50. Marianna Torgovnick in *Gone Primitive: Savage Intellects, Modern Lives* (Chicago: University of Chicago Press, 1990), and Anne McClintock, *Imperial Leather: Race, Gender, and Sexuality in the Colonial Contest* (New York: Routledge, 1995), have a similar reading of the "oceanic" passage of *Civilization and Its Discontents*. For Torgovnick, Freud's ambivalence toward his position as a Jew in Vienna as Europe edged toward fascism heightened his ambivalence toward the primitive, a characteristic attributed to Jews by Nazi anti-Semitism. But he was not able to reject his identification with power as "civilized": "Given the material he had to work with, Freud might have arrived at a radical critique of the very idea of 'hierarchy' and 'mastery' in the political contexts of the late twenties and thirties. . . . Instead, Freud continued to lay siege to the top level of power" (201). She agrees that there is much at stake in Freud's rejection of the "oceanic" but focuses her questions on a critique of gender, rather than on race and colonization, as I am suggesting: "He never fully considers the questions invited by his opening meditation on the oceanic. If there is a state of mind, and potentially a state of culture, that could be derived from the original relationship of our bodies to the bodies of our mothers, what differences in father-centered psychoanalytic theories would follow? What differences in relation of men and women to the physical world would follow? What political consequences would follow? Might these provide a form of 'civilization' with fewer 'discontents'?" (208). McClintock draws on Kristeva's explanation of abjection as a process by which "in order to become social the self has to expunge certain elements that society deems impure. . . . The abject is everything that the subjects seeks to expunge in order to become social" (71). She continues in a vein similar to mine: "Abject peoples are those whom industrial imperialism rejects but cannot do without: slaves, prostitutes, the colonized, domestic workers, the insane, the unemployed, and so on" (72).

24. Freud, *Civilization*, 27.

25. Marvin Harris, *Patterns of Race in the Americas* (New York: Norton and Co., 1974), 13.

26. "Editor Backs Off Series Linking CIA to Drug Traffickers," *Raleigh News and Observer*, May 13, 1997, A5.

27. Elaine Rapping, *The Culture of Recovery: Making Sense of the Self-Help Movement in Women's Lives* (Boston: Beacon Press, 1996), 69. Lawrence Grossberg, *We Gotta Get Out of This Place: Popular Conservatism and Postmodern Culture* (New York: Routledge, 1992), 292.

28. Psychoanalysis was Freud's brave attempt to heal the breech marked in Hegel between dominating self and dominated other. With Freud this dynamic had become in his later theory an internal drama: ego caught in the middle between dominant superego and repressed id.

29. Grossberg, *We Gotta Get Out of This Place*, 292.

30. Marcuse, *Eros*, xvii.

31. Jimmy Kruger, quoted in Meredith, *Coming to Terms*, 76.

32. Quoted in Meredith, *Coming to Terms*, 67.

33. Ibid., 48.

34. Ibid., 149.

35. Ibid., 32.

36. Ibid., 185.

37. Ibid., 289.

38. Douglass, *Narrative*, 2, 3.

39. Ibid., 12–13, 33, 39, 42, 66.

40. Ibid., 59–75.

41. Ibid., 81.

42. Marcuse, *Eros*, xxvii.

43. Freire, *Pedagogy*, 79, 81.

44. Allen, *Without Sanctuary*, frontispiece is also image 9; Laura Nelson and son, image 34; Leo Frank, image 30; Frank Embree, images 38, 39, 40; "barbecue" quotation on back of image 22; figures lynched together include images 8, 75, 148; "pitch cloud" in images 53, 54. James Allen's narrative explains, "Even dead, the victims were without sanctuary." These photographs are also at *http://www.journale.com/withoutsanctuary*.

CHAPTER 8

1. Gordon Chavunduka, "Traditional Medicine and Religion," in *Welcome to Zimbabwe* (Geneva: World Council of Churches, 1998), 17.

2. Desmond Tutu, foreword, Sutherland and Meyer, *Guns and Gandhi*, xi.

3. Tutu quoted in Martin Meredith, *Coming to Terms: South Africa's Search for Truth* (New York: Public Affairs, 1999), 4.

4. Tutu, quoted in Meredith, *Coming to Terms*, 26.

5. TRC testimony, quoted in Meredith, *Coming to Terms*, 84.

6. Chris Dunton and Mia Palmberg, *Human Rights and Homosexuality in Southern Africa*, 2d ed., *Current African Issues* (Nordiska Afrikainstitutet) 19 (1996): 34–35; various drafts and reports of the constitutional process can be found by searching the University of Capetown's Web Legal Information Services at http://www.constitution.org.za. Other controversial issues in the constitutional debates were the status of the Afrikaans language, the secular character of the state, the death penalty, abortion, and the right to self-defense and to own firearms.

7. Speech on Human Rights Day, March 21, 1995, quoted in Dunton and Palmberg, *Human Rights and Homosexuality*, 34–35.

8. "The Sign of Resurrection in El Salvador: A Testimony from Christians Who Accompany the People in Their Struggle," a statement released in 1981 by religious groups affiliated with the Popular Church in El Salvador, in *El Salvador: Central America in the New Cold War*, ed. Marvin E. Gettleman, Patrick Lacefield, Louis Menashe, David Mermelstein, Ronald Radosh (New York: Grove Press, 1981), 210.

9. Alan Riding, "The Cross and the Sword in Latin America," in *El Salvador*, 196–197. "Regrettably, it is an historical fact that many freedoms have to be won by bloodshed," Romero clarified. "Christian ethics admits of violence for a just cause. . . . On the condition that the evil of the rebellion does not become worse than the evil of the status quo." Patrick Lacefield, "Oscar Romero: Archbishop for the Poor," in *El Salvador*, 201.

10. A few years earlier, I had taken some time to track my own ancestors from Jamestown through various stages of settler colonialism. See Mab Segrest, "On Being White and Other Lies: A History of Racism in the United States," in *Memoir of a Race Traitor* (Boston: South End Press, 1994). George M. Frederickson did an early comparative study, *White Supremacy: A Comparative Study of American and South African History* (New York: Oxford University Press, 1981); recently Frederickson and Maurice Evans wrote *Black and White in the Southern States: A Study of the Race Problem in the United States from a South African Point of View* (Columbia: University of South Carolina Press, 2001).

11. Ernest Harsch, "South Africa: From Settlement to Union," in *The Anti-Apartheid Reader: South Africa and the Struggle against White Racist Rule*, ed. David Mermelstein (New York: Grove Press, 1987), 47–48.

12. Harsch, "South Africa," 55.

13. "Hind Swarj," in *Collected Works of Mahatma Gandhi* (Delhi: Ministry of Information and Broadcasting, 1963), 10:23.

14. Harsch, "South Africa," 59.

15. Robert Davies, Dan O'Meara, and Sipho Dlamini, "The Development of Racial Capitalism," in Mermelstein, *Anti-Apartheid Reader*, 105.

16. Harsch, "South Africa," 61.

17. Davies et al., "The Development of Racial Capitalism," 106–107.

18. Ibid., 108–112.

19. Chief Albert Luthuli, "Apartheid: This Terrible Dream," Nobel Prize Acceptance Speech, in Mermelstein, *Anti-Apartheid Reader*, 17, 18.

20. Munetsi Madakufamba, "Fluctuating Economic Growth," *Welcome to Zimbabwe*, 33.

21. UN AIDS Epidemic Update, December 1998, from the Joint UN Programme on HIV/AIDS and the World Health Organization; see *http://www.unaids.org/hivaidsinfo/statistics/june98/globalrep_e1.pdf*.

22. Dunton and Palmberg, *Human Rights and Homosexuality*, 42.

23. Behind the Mask: A Web Site on Gay and Lesbian Affairs in (Southern) Africa, *http://www.mask.org.za/Sections/Debate/debate1.html*.

24. Statement from National Coalition for Gay and Lesbian Equality, December 3, 1998, Johannesburg, South Africa.

25. Alan Paton, *Cry, the Beloved Country* (New York: Simon and Schuster, 1987), 83.

26. Ibid., 88.

27. Davies et al., "The Development of Racial Capitalism," 108.

28. Dennis Brutus and Ben Cashdan, "World Conference against Racism: South Africa between a Rock and a Hard Place," Z Net Commentary, *http://zmag.org/zsustainers/zdaily/2001-07/11brutus.htm*.

29. Mandela, "I Am Prepared to Die," in Mermelstein, *Anti-Apartheid Reader*, 222.

30. Nelson Mandela, *Long Walk to Freedom: The Autobiography of Nelson Mandela* (Boston: Little, Brown and Co., 1994), 137.

31. Mandela, *Long Walk*, 239–240.

32. Quoted in Alan Brooks and Jeremy Bruckhill, "The Soweto Uprising," in Mermelstein, *Anti-Apartheid Reader*, 230.

33. Anso Toms, "The Fight Goes On," Behind the Mask: A Web Site on Gay and Lesbian Affairs in (Southern) Africa, *http://www.mask.org.za/sections/Profiles/profile5.html*.

Chapter 9

1. Sebastian Bakare, *The Drumbeat of Life: Jubilee in an African Context* (Geneva: World Council of Churches, 1997), 33.

2. Deprose Muchena, "Moments in Pre-Independence History," in *Welcome to Zimbabwe*, 23–24.

3. "To the Nations of the World," speech to the Congress, quoted in David Levering Lewis, *W.E.B. Du Bois, 1868–1919: Biography of a Race* (New York: Henry Holt & Co., 1993), 251. The Second Pan-African Congress was held in Paris in 1918 concurrent with the Paris Peace Conference out of concern for the future of Africa in the new postwar scramble. In "Pan Africa," a *Crisis* editorial, Du Bois had done the math, calculating that by the time World War I broke out in 1914, the "Scramble for Africa" after the Berlin Conference in 1884 meant that "the number of souls thus under the rule of aliens, in the case of England, France, Germany and Belgium, amounted to more than 110,000,000." Germany had lost her four colonies in defeat. "It is the question of the reapportionment of this vast number of human beings which has started the Pan-African movement. Colored America is indeed involved." Du Bois, the "premier architect of the civil rights movement in the United States [and] . . . among the first to grasp the international implications of the struggle for racial justice," was on the way to becoming the "father of Pan Africanism." As ever a brilliant debunker of white hypocrisy, he observed: "What Europe, and indeed only a small group in Europe, wants in Africa is not a field for the spread of European civilization, but a field for exploitation. They covet the raw materials—ivory, diamonds, copper and rubber in which the land abounds, and even more do they covet cheap native labor to mine and produce these things. Greed, naked, pitiless lust for wealth and power, lie back of all of Europe's interest in Africa and the white world knows it and is not ashamed." See "Pan Africa" in Du Bois, *ABC of Color*, 103; originally in *Crisis* 17 (1919).

4. Sutherland and Meyer, *Guns and Gandhi*, 24, 26, 34, 63.

5. Lewis, *Du Bois*, 3.

6. Sutherland and Meyer, *Guns and Gandhi*, 34.

7. *A Call to Prophetic Action: Towards the Jubilee Year 2000* (Harare: Ecumenical Support Services, 1998), 12.

8. Ibid., 13.

9. Brian Raftopoulos, "Fighting for Control: The Indigenization Debate in Zimbabwe," *Southern Africa Report* (July 1996): 3–4.

10. *A Call to Prophetic Action*, 33.

11. Madakufamba, "Fluctuating Economic Growth," 30–31.

12. Harvey Cox, "African Indigenous Churches," in *Welcome to Zimbabwe*, 15.

13. "Heard in Harare," in McCullum, *Together on Holy Ground* (Geneva: World Council of Churches, 1999), 31.

14. Bakare, *Drumbeat*, 19.

15. "Sex—Almost a Non-Issue," in McCullum, *Together on Holy Ground*, 18.

16. Carol J. Fouke, "Women Challenge the Church," in McCullum, *Together on Holy Ground*, 20.

17. Jacqui Alexander, Lisa Albrecht, Sharon Day, and Mab Segrest, *Whose Hands Are Clean?: Feminist Writing in the Spirit of Struggle and Resistance* (San Francisco: Edgeworks, 2002).

18. "Globalization of the productive system means that the various countries now need to be classified according to the relative weight of the 'active army' and the 'reserve army' of labour within their society. . . . Using this criterion, the great bulk of labour power in the heartlands (i.e., the center) participates in the active army, because of the way in which central economies gradually took shape in favourable conditions that cannot be repeated. . . . The industrializing Third World, on the other hand, had none of these favourable conditions that might have averted the wilder forms of capitalist expansion. And in what one may call the Fourth World, excluded from industrialization at that time, the social system has thrown up extremes bordering on caricature; the reserve army here comprises the great majority of the population—the marginalized poor and the peasant masses denied the fruits of any agrarian revolution." Samir Amin, *Capitalism in the Age of Globalization* (London: ZED Books, 1997), ix–x.

19. W.E.B. Du Bois, "Message to the Accra Conference," excerpted in *National Guardian*, December 22, 1958, and reprinted in Du Bois, *ABC of Color*, 210.

20. Luke 4:18–19, King James Bible.

21. Catherine Caufield, *Masters of Illusion: The World Bank and the Poverty of Nations* (New York: Henry Holt and Co., 1996). Caufield, who worked for five years as environmental correspondent for *New Scientist*, drew on the World Bank's own internal documents, some leaked to her privately, and interviews with current and former bank employees.

22. These institutions include the International Bank for Reconstruction and Development (IBRB, 1945)—making high-risk development loans to governments; the International Monetary Fund (IMF, 1945)—harmonizing monetary policy; the International Development Association (IDA, 1960)—making higher risk development loans to governments; the International Finance Corporation (IFC, 1956)—making loans to private companies; and the World Trade Organization (WTO, 1995)—overseeing trade relations.

23. Caufield, *Masters of Illusion*, 72.

24. Ibid., 79–83.

25. See also Eboe Hutchful, *The IMF and Ghana: The Confidential Record*, referenced in *Guns and Gandhi*, 261.

26. Caufield, *Masters of Illusion*, 90, 89.

27. Ibid., 89.

28. In Woods's five-year tenure, the bank made $6 billion in loans, relative to $7 billion in its first fifteen years.

29. Caufield, *Masters of Illusion*, 93.

30. Ibid., 97–98.

31. Ibid., 132.

32. Miriam Ching Louie, "Are My Clothes Clean? Women and the Global Assembly Line," in *Women's Education in the Global Economy* (Berkeley, Calif.: Women of Color Resource Center, n.d.). This workbook can be ordered on the Web or from the Women of Color Resource Center, 2288 Fulton Street, Suite 103, Berkeley, CA 94704-1499; *chisme@igc.apc.org*.

33. Ibid., 121.

34. Ibid., 134.

35. Ibid., 144.

36. Ibid., 145.

37. Ibid., 149.

38. Sutherland and Meyer, *Guns and Gandhi*, 261.

39. Caufield, *Masters of Illusion*, 155.

40. Ibid., 162, 330–331, 333, 335.

41. Quoted in Richard Drinnon, *Facing West: The Metaphysics of Indian Hating and Empire Building* (Minneapolis: University of Minnesota Press, 1980), 42.

42. N. Barney Pitanya, "Africa: The Footprints of God," African Plenary Address, World Council of Churches Assembly, December 8, 1999, Harare, Zimbabwe.

43. Shohat, *Talking Visions*, 10.

44. *A Call to Prophetic Action*, 1, 2, 6.

45. Ibid., 6. "Lean and Mean," *Southern Africa Report* (July 1996): 2.

46. John Makumbe, "Post-Independence Politics," in *Welcome to Zimbabwe*, 28, 32.

47. *A Call to Prophetic Action*, 3–4.

48. Julian Borger, "U.S. Inquiry into Claims Black Voters Were Stripped of Rights," *London Guardian*, December 4, 2000; and Julian Borger, "How Florida Played the Race Card: 700,000 People with Criminal Past Banned from Voting in Pivotal State," *London Guardian*, December 4, 2000.

49. Nathan Newman, "The Jim Crow Five and the Coming Political War," December 13, 2000, from *BRC-news@list.ta.ca*.

50. Quoted in *Free Press*, edition 5 (1995), 14.

51. Briefing on Human Rights in Zimbabwe, issued by Gays and Lesbians of Zimbabwe, January 1, 1997, Harare, Zimbabwe.

52. "Male and Female He Created Them: Human Rights Based on God's Law," Pastoral Statement, Zimbabwe Catholic Bishops' Conference, January 1996, Harare, Zimbabwe.

53. The homophobic campaign was part of Mugabe's bid for reelection, which he won in March 1996, raising again the issues of "the cankering worm of debauchery and the affliction of homosexuality," the gay and lesbian threat to national culture and morality that was by that time substantially frayed by Mugabe's own policies. The next year, the government also sought to ban GALZ from the book fair, but GALZ got a court order to allow their participation, although threats were widespread and the stand was in fact trashed by a mob. The attacks on GALZ were accompanied by widespread human rights abuses of homosexuals in Zimbabwe (Briefing on Human Rights in Zimbabwe, issued by Gays and Lesbians of Zimbabwe January 1, 1997, Harare Zimbabwe).

54. Letter from GALZ, signed by Oliver Phillips, to the WCC and in the briefing packet for the January 1, 1997, Briefing on Human Rights by GALZ, Harare, Zimbabwe.

55. See Gerald Kraak, "Class, Race, Nationalism and the Politics of Identity: A Perspective from the South," in *The Right to Be: Sexuality and Sexual Rights in Southern Africa, Development Update*, vol. 2, no. 2, 1998. This entire issue is a fascinating exploration of issues of identity and other politics in terms of violence against women, gay life and liberation, and AIDS and human rights in southern Africa. See also Chris Dunton and Mai Palmberg, *Human Rights and Homosexuality in Southern Africa, Current African Issues* 19 (November 1996). It covers Zimbabwe, Namibia, Botswana, and South Africa.

56. See *http://www.ufenet.org/press/2000/economic_apartheid_pr.html*.

57. Hugh McCullum, "Dimensions of an African Assembly," in McCullum, *Together on Holy Ground*, 8.

58. Quoted in Meredith, *Coming to Terms*, 186.

59. Ibid., 289.

60. Ibid., 304.

61. Quoted in Meredith, *Coming to Terms*, 304.

62. World Council of Churches, *Together on the Way*, final report of the Harare assembly, "The Debt Issue: A Jubilee Call to End the Stranglehold of Debt on Impoverished Peoples, December 1998," at *http://www.wcc-coe.org/wcc/assembly/fprc2c-e.html*.

63. Ibid.

64. Pitanya, "Africa: The Footprints of God."

65. Somé, *Healing Wisdom*, 17, 15.

66. *The Bhagavad Gita*, 3.9, p. 63.

Epilogue

1. Norm Dixon, "South Africa: Grassroots Struggles Revive," *Green Left Weekly*, August 15, 2001; http://www.greenleft.org.au/back/2001/460/460p16.htm.

2. Roy, "The Algebra of Infinite Justice," *The Guardian*, Sept. 28, 2001, p1. *www.guardian.org/magazine*. Other sources say that heroin from Afganistan goes primarily to Europe. 1.

3. Sara Diamond, *Roads to Dominion: Right Wing Movements and Political Power in the United States* (New York: Guilford Press, 1995), 163.

4. Ibid., 237–238.

5. Roy, "The Algebra of Infinite Justice," 2.

6. Rosalind Petchesky, "Phantom Towers: Feminist Reflections on the Battle between Global Capitalism and Fundamentalist Terror," Presentation at Hunter College Political Science Dept Teach-In, Sept. 25, 2001.

7. Carolyn Forché, "Ourselves or Nothing," *The Country between Us* (New York: Harper & Row, 1981), 58–59.

8. Somé, *Healing Wisdom of Africa*, 50.

INDEX

About the Author

Mab Segrest is an organizer, teacher, and writer who lives in Durham, North Carolina. She has worked across genres and political movements as essayist, organizer, poet, anti-racist, and lesbian for more than twenty years. Her *Memoir of a Race Traitor* was named an Outstanding Book on Human Rights in North America and was Editor's Choice for the Lambda Literary Awards. She is Acting Director of Gender and Women's Studies at Connecticut College.